LINN COUNTY KANSAS

A HISTORY

William Ansel Mitchell

HERITAGE BOOKS
2025

HERITAGE BOOKS

AN IMPRINT OF HERITAGE BOOKS, INC.

Books, CDs, and more—Worldwide

For our listing of thousands of titles see our website
at
www.HeritageBooks.com

A Facsimile Reprint
Published 2025 by
HERITAGE BOOKS, INC.
Publishing Division
5810 Ruatan Street
Berwyn Heights, MD 20740

Original:
Linotype work done by J. W. Mitchell of the La Cygne Journal
Presswork done by Campbell-Gates of Kansas City
Bookbinding by Charno Bindery, Kansas City

International Standard Book Number
Paperbound: 978-0-7884-2678-0

LINN COUNTY

KANSAS

MOUND CITY, KANSAS

July 4, 1926.

Mr. W. A. Mitchell,
5420 Baltimore Avenue,
Kansas City, Missouri.

Dear Mr. Mitchell:

    Old citizens of this county have recently read with much pleasure a republication of the newspaper stories you wrote in your early manhood about the part our pioneer citizens had in the creation of the great state of Kansas, and the influence of their lives upon the destiny of the nation at large. They have been recognized as of great historical value by the Kansas State Historical Society, and most of them have been republished by the Society in its recent volume of Historical Collections. We want to express our gratitude that so much of our early history was saved from utter loss by your generous attention to it at the time when many of our heros were passing away.

    And we want to ask that you now take up the work of compiling this with additional material obtainable into form for permanent preservation and publication at an early date, believing that your ability and your loyalty to this community best fits you to do this work so important to us.

Ed. R Smith   Mrs O E Morse

Edward Goates   R H Marrs.

F N Devoe   A R Wayne

J. N. Marshall   H. A. Strong

L F Osborn   W L Sutton

Henry Plumb   M B Armsby

THEIR LAST APPEAL TO KANSAS

(On Sunday, June 14, 1925, about a dozen of the "old timers" of Linn County were entertained at a dinner at the Commercial Hotel in Pleasanton by John A. Hall of Pleasanton, Clarence J. Trigg, W. A. Mitchell, and J. Frank Smith, the last three now from Kansas City. On Tuesday, June 16, the following written by Fred Trigg appeared on the editorial page of the Kansas City Star:)

A dinner party, given to a group of the oldest pioneers of Linn County at Pleasanton, Kansas, Sunday, must have carried a stirring appeal to all Kansas. The old pioneers were the guests of four younger men, themselves sons of pioneers of that historic Kansas county. The purpose of the dinner was to get in concrete form, and from eyewitnesses and participants in the fight to make Kansas a free state, an accurate account for preservation of some of the Kansas history that once was familiar to the people of the entire country, but which has not been saved either to Kansas or the nation. Kansas has been negligent of its great wealth of historic interest. The state has not preserved its history even in the matter of keeping the record properly, and as to the erection of memorials and markers Kansas has been shamefully neglectful.

There is a feature of state-wide interest, therefore, in the dinner that was given to the old pioneers at Pleasanton Sunday, for they begged the people of the state to make some provision for saving the history that is passing with them. Kansas should heed the appeal. The average age of the men who were guests at the Pleasanton dinner party was 82. Some of the guests were 88 years old and one was 89. In all reason they will not for many more years live to tell the story. They are the last of the survivors of the old days in that section of the state, which, next to Lawrence, made more history of vital importance to the state than any other part of Kansas. These men were in the forefront of the great American conflict over the question of human slavery that brought the issue to its final head and ushered in the Civil War. The men at the dinner all played an important part in the Kansas struggle. Some of them were actual leaders in the movement of that day—and afterwards they took the same active part in the peaceful but none the less interesting work of building the state that is now Kansas.

What will Kansas do to preserve the heritage these men are leaving? Not a monument has been erected; not a marker placed; not a spot in the territory they offered their lives, a willing sacrifice, to make free, has been set apart as a memorial to their wonderful work. And these now are all that are left. Most of them have gone. Have they been forgotten?

At the Pleasanton dinner the pioneers appealed for some adequate and fitting memorial, not for themselves, but for their old friends and neighbors who fought, and died, in massacre, in battle and in other struggles that attended the big conflict of that day. It is the last appeal, doubtless, these men ever will make. It comes to Kansas as from the grave. What answer will Kansas make to them?

LINN COUNTY, KANSAS

A HISTORY

By

WILLIAM ANSEL MITCHELL

Written to give and preserve the more intimate knowledge
of incidents of world-wide importance and marking an
epochal period in the history of the human race.

COPYRIGHT 1928

Linotype work done by J. W. Mitchell of the La Cygne Journal
Presswork done by Campbell-Gates of Kansas City
Bookbinding by Charno Bindery, Kansas City

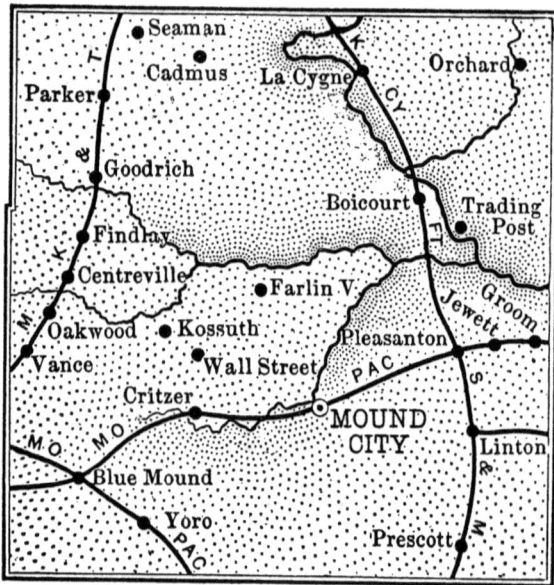

LINN COUNTY, KANSAS: A HISTORY

The manuscript for this history was finished and ready for the printer when the writer had a casual conversation with Judge Frank P. Sebree, a staid old Missourian of Saline county, intimately familiar with and proud of the best traditions of his state. Speaking of our Linn County, he made the innocent inquiry: "How are those old Redlegs, anyway?" Now to understand that term Redleg you must know that it meant Linn County men who waded knee deep in the blood of their Missouri neighbors. For more than a half century this term has been peculiarly offensive to me, so I replied to him, "Why, Judge, there never was such an animal as a Redleg. The term implies bloodshed and the closest scrutiny of history will prove that the only Missouri blood ever shed on Linn County soil was when Jennison and his men escorted four intended murderers to the Missouri line and told them to travel east and never return, 'and to make sure we will know you if you do come back we will place this mark on you', said Jennison as he leaned over in the saddle and cut off the ear of the prisoner nearest to him. Really, the free-state settlers of Linn County were the aristocrats of the world. They trace their lineage right on down from Magna Charta and they and their ancestors created everything in the world worth having. At every notable event they were not only on the right side but won out."

It is a fact that no community of equal size anywhere in the United States had so many families representative of the best Anglo-Saxon people ranging all the way from the Crusaders under Richard Coeur de Leon, at Runnymede, and down through European and English history to America with all its brilliant achievements and wonderful men. Their stories are told in this book as a truthful record of their good lives and not as an attempt at a literary exploit. Ninety percent at least of the first settlers here were religious people with a deep reverence for their Creator and a kindly feeling for their fellow men. More than half of the first comers were Quakers and the next element were Presbyterians and following them poured in the Christians of the Campbellite sect. If in the half decade immediately preceding the Civil War Linn County had failed in its duty toward Christian civilization the clock would have been turned back to the days of Nero. For good or for evil the situation was so evenly balanced that it required four years of warfare and a million lives to reach a decision which saved the American Union.

Only the romantic tales of the Scottish Border, with all the embellishments permitted by poetic license, could compare with thrilling tragedies which were every day experiences of Linn County pioneers, and which need only a bare recital of their facts to amaze the later generations who have only had their story in fragment handed down to them by that old family freemasonry from father to son. Here was staged the last defiance by the Anglo-Saxon to the age-old enemy to human liberty—the last note of defiance which could only be answered by an appeal to arms. Here appeared the last great Puritan, direct from the Mayflower, and here he wrote on the pages of History that which will live as long as men read and think. Here was created a literature that fired the imagination of all good men, that uplifted and glorified the ancient devotion to the doctrine of liberty and equality of all men before the law. Here was held aloft the Torch of Liberty and the fierce hate, malice and treason of evil men only fanned it to brighter and hotter flames. From here went the evil men—"without local habitation or name"—back to the Carolina coast to fire on Fort Sumter and start the awful carnage of the Civil War!

Few people realize as they gaze upon a beautiful bronze work of art in a great park in Kansas City that the inspiration for the beautiful Vanderslice monument to "The Pioneer Mother" came to him as he was traveling through Linn County in 1838, being his interpretation of the characters of the great pioneer women with whom he had come in contact in the wilderness, and now it is an imperishable testimonial to his own lofty ideals and his own beautiful personality, and it is a faithful portrayal of the early settlers of Linn County.

And only a few blocks away they will find another monument in the name of McGee street to perpetuate the name of the man who in 1856 went to Cassville, Georgia, and addressing a public gathering of people in the streets asked for money and men to drive the free state people from Kansas. The aged physician who presided at the meeting volunteered the services of his two sons and made a gift of one thousand dollars to the cause, and appealed to others to do likewise. And they gave and they came, their money and their men committing the Marais des Cygnes Massacre at the command of Hamelton, son of that presiding officer, an awful crime in which more lives were immolated on the altar of human freedom than were sacrificed at the great Boston Massacre in 1774! This is a truthful portrayal of the slave power.

Linn County is the culmination—the very flower and fruit —the hope and the climax—of centuries of strenuous effort by the Anglo-Saxon race toward the perfecting of the finest code of living ever developed on this earth. Linn County achieved a place in history as one of the high peaks that marks epochal periods downward from Runnymede where seven hundred years ago we met King John and forced him to give to us the great signed Bill of Rights known as "Magna

Charta."[1] This was an important step forward but when the smoke of battle was blown away it was discovered that the main beneficiaries were the Barons—the landed gentry—to whom the King parcelled out the crown lands of the kingdom. In turn the Barons set about parcelling out these lands to their own followers organizing a feudal system. It was a military scheme wherein the strong fighting men were rewarded with rich favors while the real strength of the country was ground down to a condition of serfdom not much above abject slavery. The Barons became a part of the governing power of the kingdom and assumed the balance of power as the House of Lords. But right then and there began the most beneficent thing that ever happened to the human race since Christ came upon earth. The great mass of the people had no rights enforceable in courts. They were as nearly powerless as could be imagined. When the barons began parcelling out the lands to their favorites many of the weaker serfs found themselves either dispossessed or hampered in the enjoyment of their long established privileges. In one instance a serf was shut off from a path which led to a spring. This poor miserable excuse for a man assembled all his neighbors and they appeared en masse before the legal representative of the crown known as the "magistrate." To this official they proved that for generations that family had obtained water from that spring and that the "right of way" to that water was sacred to them and must not be taken away. Stout insistence won a favorable decision from the magistrate and his decree was written into the books and this case became a "precedent" recognized in courts whenever a serf urged similar rights. And so was established the "right of commons" where a serf was interfered with in the grazing of his milch cows and horses. And so also was fixed his "right of estovers"—his ancient right to take fuel from a forest. This system grew until it covered every personal and property right of an Englishman of whatever station in life and was handed down to us in America as the English Common Law. It is still the dominant principle in the administration of justice in our courts. And the words "right of way" have been almost a household phrase in America, but "right of commons" has disappeared as the country has settled up. The Common Law came on down through English history for centuries, never taking a step backward, always some new "right" being

1. It is an interesting and significant fact that at nearly all the great historical events in the history of the people who made England there were present the ancestors of the people who made Linn County. As early as the year 1200 when Richard Coeur de Leon was the Lion-Hearted King of England, and leader of the Crusades for the recovery of the Holy Land, the ancestors of the Thorne family lived in Eastern Wales and when in 1215 King John succeeded to the throne he conferred the honor of knighthood on Sir William Thorne and this direct ancestor of Phil Thorne of Mound City was undoubtedly present and witnessed the signing of that wonderful document known as Magna Charta—more than seven hundred years ago! Linn County boys and girls interested in history should read the story of Robin Hood and Maid Marian and Friar Tuck and Sir Robert Fitzwalter, actual persons who lived in daily association with the ancestors of boys and girls who are our neighbors and friends now. And it will give you a good description of their manner of living in those old days.

secured through the action of some citizen. During the reign of Charles the First a valuable concession obtained was the Habeas Corpus Act for the enforcement of the provision of Magna Charta which says that "no freeman shall be disseized or distrained of his liberties or rights, or in any other wise damaged, nor will we send upon him or take him or his property, or outlaw or banish him from the realm, except by the lawful judgment of his peers and the law of the land."[1]   It was a common practice of the Stuart kings to throw into jail those they disliked and forget them, and this Habeas Corpus writ took them out of jail and into a court for trial   Still Charles could not stop the outcry against him and it is interesting to note that the ancestor of citizens of Linn County sat on his jury and rendered a verdict of "guilty of treason" and signed his death warrant,[2] his head being chopped off at Whitehall Palace January 30, 1649.

For ten years England was governed as a commonwealth, practically a republic, with Oliver Cromwell as its guiding genius.

In 1660 the monarchy was restored, Charles the Second[2] succeeding his father, and though a dissolute, evil man, he had the longest term of any English king, having for twenty-five years all the powers of the British throne. His reign was disturbed by much turbulence and in his term the second great Bill of Rights was presented and its concession permanently fixed the principle of representative government by strengthening the powers of the House of Commons in Parliament.

And so for three-quarters of a century there poured into the American colonies a steady flow of people who sought a home remote from England and Europe where every generation had to give its blood and treasure to the demands of some whim of religion as then represented by politicians of base, mercenary, criminal types of men. Already Plymouth Rock had become a high peak in the progress of humanity, a beacon of welcome to those seeking religious liberty. And it is proper to here note that lineal descendants of these people became the controlling forces that made this Linn County we are talking about, people who stood as courageously and as strenuously for the rights of humanity as had their ancestors at Runnymede, at Whitehall, and at the siege of London. There

1. With this phrase in Magna Charta in 1215 originated the idea from which later developed our trial by jury, though it was for four hundred years an implied right rather than an established one. The Habeas Corpus Act of 1627 brought an accused man into court for trial by a jury.
2. It was Thomas Harrison, ancestor of a Linn County family, who sat on the jury that tried King Charles and returned a verdict of treason against and assessed his penalty at death, and signed his death warrant next to the signature of Oliver Cromwell. Colonel James Finley Harrison now sleeping in Mound City Cemetery was a lineal descendant of this Thomas Harrison. Others of this family were Ben Harrison, president of the house of burgesses in Virginia in 1776, a powerful patriot in the Revolutionary struggle, and William Henry Harrison, president of the United States in 1841, and Benjamin Harrison who became president by defeating Grover Cleveland in 1888. Read the sketch of Colonel Harrison in this book. And it was an ancestor of the Croxton family at La Cygne—Bradshaw—who presided at the trial of Charles the First.

was never a people comparable with the Anglo-Saxon race in its genius for government and in the strength and sustained character of its citizens throughout a thousand years of its development, and the men and women who came into what is now Linn County lived up to the best traditions of their distinguished ancestry. And they were proud that they had a dignified history of their own starting at Plymouth Rock,[1] Boston, Concord, Faneuil Hall, Valley Forge, Independence Hall, the Cow Pens, King's Mountain, Quebec, Ticonderoga, New Orleans,—and they brought all this history as a birthright to their children.

In 1854 all the country north of Red River and west of Arkansas, Missouri, Iowa, and Minnesota to the Canadian line was "Indian country," inhabited only by savages, and the government only such as could be administered by the military. White people had no right in the country, except those few who obtained special privileges as traders with the Indians, or as missionaries. It was a marvelously big country and in its primitive condition was very rich in its natural resources. In what is now Linn County, on most of the flat lands where alluvial soil had settled, grass grew so rankly that men traveling on horseback were hidden in it while over the rolling hills the rich prairie grass was waist high to a man. All forest country along the water courses was a thicket affording protection to wild life. Every variety of animal and bird was present. The main herds of buffalo in literally millions came to the forest line of western Missouri. Deer and antelope were everywhere and wolves and bear followed and fed on them. Wild turkeys[2] were found in every tree top and prairie chickens, especially at frost time in the fall, were measured by acres in estimating the size of the flocks. Wild bees furnished honey that was gathered by the barrel.[3] Hickory nuts, walnuts, hazel nuts, and pecans furnished good food enough to subsist a considerable population of humans. Wild plums and persimmons furnished palatable and nutritious fruits. Blackberries and strawberries were abundant. Fox grapes were a delicious contribution to a rich diet. The uncontaminated waters of the streams were alive with fine food fish. Water

1. The ancestors of Dr. Henry Plumb landed at Plymouth Rock in 1635, fifteen years after the Mayflower party, Old John Brown, the Linn County hero who gave up his life at Harper's Ferry, was a descendant of Peter Brown the ship's carpenter of the Mayflower, John Phelps Kenea of the La Cygne Journal was a cousin of Old John Brown and of Dr. Plumb, the Finch family had a representative at Valley Forge, the Gowing ancestors at both the Cow Pens and King's Mountain, Wash Hinds' ancestor was at Ticonderoga and Quebec—these progenitors of the people who made Linn County were all in the Revolutionary struggle. Ancestors of the George W. Moore family were officers under General Jackson at New Orleans.
2. See Wash Hinds' statement that he killed thirty-nine turkeys one spring —so fat they would burst when they fell out the tree. And L. F. Osborn came here in 1853 and carried away wild honey by the barrel.
3. James Osborn in 1853 came to a spot three miles southwest of Mound City with barrels which he filled with honey from bee trees. He returned in 1854 and built the home in which his family has lived the past three-quarters of a century.

fowl covered the rivers and lakes with geese, ducks and brant in season. Wild rice furnished a form of grain. In the forests wild hops covered great trees fifty feet high and Indian turnips and other flowering plants gave beauty and color to a rich background. Timber of all kinds sufficient for an empire awaited the taking.

Such was the inviting picture in 1853 when the national government proposed to crowd the Indians farther west and create new states and state governments for white people. It was a rich prize which unfortunately was to be obtained only by fierce contention and the force of armed conflict. Twice before the very life of the nation had been threatened by the slavery of black people brought from Africa and compromises were solemnly entered into only to be shamefully violated and agreements broken.

History to be valuable must be so well founded in truth as to command the abiding faith of its readers, and it must be in such agreeable narrative form that it is easily assimilated by the average reader and become a part of his thinking system. The writing of the history of Linn County puts a very serious obligation upon its author and compiler. The history of Linn County is one of the high spots in the history of the Anglo-Saxon race. It stood out at a critical time as a beacon light to the best elements of humanity when the road forward was very dark. The tragedies of its first five years were not mere transient incidents in a local disturbance—they were the beginning of a new epoch in human affairs. The climax came when the eleven men were shot down at Trading Post. The appeal from the Marais des Cygnes Massacre brought instant condemnation upon this red shame—this innocent shed blood which was "a blush as of roses where rose never grew."

To write the history of Linn County one must go a good ways back to visualize the fierce contentions which were destined to come to a focus here. Two men very eminent in history quarreled over a backyard fence. George Calvert was the colonial governor of the colony of Maryland under the title of "Lord Baltimore." William Penn[1] was the colonial governor of Pennsylvania without any baronial title. Two men of such radically different types of character are rarely found. Calvert[2] was an aristocrat fresh from the English court with great experience and natural ability. He belonged

1. Thomas Elwood Smith and Newlon Smith and a host of other citizens of Linn County and their children are lineal descendants of the parents of William Penn, an influential family holding important offices in the court of Charles the First. Some of them took up lands in Pennsylvania and still have title deeds with the signature of William Penn. Mrs. Ed. R. Smith has this lineage, and Mrs. T. J. Blakey of Pleasanton, Mrs. Will Blaker, and Miss Jessie Smith.
2. Mrs. Stroup of La Cygne is a lineal descendant of the Calvert family through Cecil Calvert.

to the Catholic Church, was a slave owner, and maintained an almost exclusive elegance in social life. Contrasted with him was William Penn, not only a Quaker but the leading spirit of that religious sect both in America and the continent of Europe and in England. Penn not only did not own slaves but his co-religionists were the first in America to pass resolutions protesting against the bringing of black people from Africa into slavery. George Calvert wore the dainty court dress of England while William Penn wore the drab clothes of a Quaker without a touch of color.

After years of contention they both died and left to their descendants the quarrel over the back-yard fence. Surveyors tried for ten years to establish the right line without success, until about 1730 two very distinguished scientists noted for precision in mathematics were summoned from England to make a final survey between Pennsylvania and Maryland. These men were Charles Mason and Jeremiah Dixon and this line they established became famous later as "Mason and Dixon's Line" because the fight for the extension of slavery was forced to a compromise on agreement slavery should not go north of that line.[1]

The north was north and the south was south—but, contrary to Kipling's philosophy—it was inevitable the twain should meet. From the north there flowed westward a steady stream of emigrants[2] to people the west with the diversified genius of New England. From the south[2] there flowed westward a steady stream of emigrants bent upon the extension of slave territory, many of these being poor whites forced out of competition with the cheap black labor yet hoping to secure land and slaves and raise themselves from a condition as bad or worse than slavery.

These two streams of emigrant pioneers met when they crossed the Mississippi into what was to become Missouri. About 1818 the American Union was almost disrupted by the quarrel, but by 1820 the "Missouri Compromise" was agreed upon whereby slavery was not to be urged north of parallel 36° 30' (that being the southern boundary of Missouri) yet Missouri was admitted as a slave state extending three hundred miles north of the compromise line.

For forty years these two streams of humanity flowed into Missouri and built up a wonderful state that was an empire in itself. Even on the western state line of Missouri fences

1. The Quakers were not permitted by their church rules to resist violence with violence, hence they would not fight—and here originated the foolish idea of the southern people that one southern man was equal to a half dozen northern men—a rank psychological error forever dispelled when they met the first Bucktail regiment from Pennsylvania.
2. The New England emigrants traveled well established roads or used boats on the Ohio river to reach St. Louis, while through Kentucky and Tennessee southern emigrants followed "traces" through the wilderness, crossing the Mississippi river in boats.

were set up inclosing the farms of settlers and many were eagerly looking over into the beautiful prairies westward.

The slave labor of black human beings had made all the states of the South very wealthy. World conditions favored their peculiar industry of producing cotton for the mills of England to weave into cloth for the world. Eli Whitney invented a machine called a "gin"[1] which separated the fibre or lint from the seed and made it available at once for spinning and weaving, making competition from old countries like Egypt (where the lint was separated by hand picking) a negligible interference in the markets of the world. The cotton planters of the south were becoming so affluent as to have a powerful influence on the finances of the world and to dominate the politics of the United States. They grew to be arrogant and began a campaign of open treason against the republic their ancestors had created. They flouted the idea that slavery should not go north of Mason and Dixon's Line in violation of the agreement reached before the Revolution. They had almost disrupted the Union when Missouri was admitted as a slave state, and now violated their pledge then given that they would not ask that slavery should be instituted north of the south line of Missouri. They organized armed forces to occupy Kansas and sought by a campaign of terrorism and murder to control over all opposition.

On May 30, 1854, Congress passed the Enabling Act which permitted white men to enter this land and set up their government. Coupled with this act was a resolution offered by Stephen A. Douglas, an Illinois Congressman born in Vermont and wavering between right and wrong. This resolution conferred upon the settlers of the new state the power to determine by their own votes whether the state should be free or slave. It was an artful invention to accomplish the repeal of the "Missouri Compromise" and immediately throughout the south men armed with every weapon then available were organized into companies to march into and occupy and by a war of terrorism and murder drive out and keep out all settlers who were opposed to slavery. James Buchanan, then president of the United States, although a Pennsylvania man, was in sympathy with and loaned all the powers of his administration to the evildoers by appointing land agents and federal court officers that would do their bidding. The Federal Court and the Land Office were both at Fort Scott and they became active agencies in opposing free state settlers. The infamous Clark who headed five hundred men in a raid through the county in

---

1. This mechanical invention was so important as to revolutionize the greatest export business then developed in the United States, yet it was not more important than the creating of the wheat harvester, which was thought out and brought to perfection in a little three-man broom factory on the farm of James Wishart in Scott township, Linn County.

1856 was an officer of this court. This was the situation when a steady stream of settlers entered Linn County in 1854. They brought only the barest necessities with them. In that year less than fifty crude log cabins were built to shelter families who only sought a home in peace with all people. They were notified by a horde of marauders that they were not wanted here and would not be permitted to stay, as their assailants purposed to make this a slave country and there was no room for people who entertained different ideas. Men were shot down before their wives and children, both in daylight and darkness, and the more terrifying the scenes the more they suited their purpose in discouraging others from coming to occupy this fair land. It was the beginning of a hideous nightmare of murder and rapine that lasted five years—really the beginning of the War of the Rebellion, five years before they had the courage to fire on Fort Sumter.

Linn County was the key to their strategy and was necessary to the slavery scheme. On the north Miami county was yet occupied by Indians, and on the south Bourbon county was the seat of the Federal Court and the Land Office which with all their powers and organized functioning were promoting in every way possible the desperate adventures of the slave owners and their murderers. Linn County was the back door through which they were to sneak and possess. Even after they had lost the northern part of Kansas Territory they evolved the new scheme of acquiring possession of the southern half of Kansas and setting up slavery as an institution in a new state to be created here and to control the great Indian Territory on the south for a future similar purpose.

Naturally, the greatest strife over slavery was on the border line between the slave and the free states. Back in the interior of the slave country the black chattels were kept in fear of their lives by hideously inhuman methods. The slave owners were beginning to realize that their institution was getting top heavy, that a man owning a thousand slaves had only one vote in public affairs, whereas in the free states a similar number of people would mean a thousand and one votes with all the force and courage of a clear conscience. The Ohio river meant freedom to the slave if he could only get to the north side of it and into one of the mysterious stations of the Underground Railway. The slave was almost a free man when he reached Ohio, but when he reached the Canadian border and stepped on British soil he was free and with all the power of the then greatest nation on earth to protect him.[1]

Probably the hottest spot in all this contention was Cincin-

1. It is an interesting fact that at this very time Victor Hugo finished and issued in book form his story of "Les Miserables", in one later edition of which he commented on the horrors of the Marais des Cygnes massacre as told to him in Whittier's poem and in John Brown's "Parallels," and of slavery in Harriet Beecher Stowe's "Uncle Tom's Cabin." These two books were probably the most universally read of any ever written.

nati. It had grown to be an important commercial center. The Ohio river brought to it freight from Pittsburgh and the country eastward and from Cincinnati there was distributed by cheap water transportation[1] everything to provide for the needs of a population that had settled up nearly all the vacant land clear across Missouri to the line of Kansas Territory. Cincinnati was growing rich off the trade of both free state men and proslavers, and the merchants of that time sought to steer a midway course through the strife becoming each day more acute. Such a situation developed many strong characters in men and women who were to exert a powerful and lasting influence on Linn County. On the north side of the river was the home and the influence of Joshua R. Giddings, one of the first five anti-slavers elected to Congress, and Tom Corwin,[2] the latter governor and later United States senator. There lived Dr. Lyman Beecher at the head of Lane Seminary, where young men prepared for the ministry. It was from here that Henry Ward Beecher went out into the world with his wonderful personality. And another member of this family was Harriet Beecher Stowe who in 1853 revised and published in book form her novel "Uncle Tom's Cabin", which stirred the public conscience not only of this country but of all Europe by its expose of the infamies and cruelties of the slavery institution. Lane Seminary was a school for preachers, yet it practically resolved itself into a debating society in which young men developed their talent for oratory and logic that they might go out and fight the institution of slavery. And a number of them were from slave-owning families whose homes were on rich plantations where every indulgence in ease and idleness failed to dull their consciences to the crime of it. It is interesting that some of the best of these later came to Linn County and took part in the strenuous life of pioneer days here.[1]

On the Kentucky side of the river there was great prosperity. The Cincinnati merchants were so eager for this rich trade that they even truckled to their demands by refusing to accept into membership in the Presbyterian church by letter people who were opposed to slavery; some of the best families now living in Linn County having suffered this humiliation. A rich section of the country was the valley of the Licking River, a stream which originates up in the hill country of eastern Kentucky and flows north, emptying its waters into the Ohio almost opposite Lane Seminary. Here lived a young man who was destined to win for himself a place in history and add luster to a name already made famous at Paris in 1572

1. It was the age of the steamboat; in 1858 steamboats plied regularly on the Kaw river between Kansas City and Junction City.
2. Mrs. Alfred A. Carpenter, living on the hill east of old Brooklin, was a Corwin, her father having been a cousin of the Ohio governor and senator. She has papers showing her people to be descended from the kings of Hungary of some four hundred or five hundred years ago. Her people ranked with Kosciusko, Kossuth and Sobiesko.
1. See Index, Augustus Wattles and John Otis Wattles.

and at Quebec in 1775. He was destined to become the most distinguished man and the most trusted leader in later years in Linn County. He was a well educated school teacher and had employment in the Licking Valley tutoring the children of the rich planters and thus having an intimate knowledge of the workings of the institution of slavery. He was in 1853 in the prime of his manhood, thirty-nine years old, with two children left to him when the wife of his youth had passed away. In that year he was married again to a young woman who proved a courageous and loving mate for him and a fond mother to his two bereaved children, and an honored citizen of her new home in Linn County.

This was the beginning of James Montgomery. He was born in Ashtabula county, Ohio, the northeast corner of the state, on December 22, 1814, with a remarkable family history. They were Scotch and of such station in life that when King James the Fifth died in 1542 and left his baby daughter, Mary Stuart, to succeed to the throne of Scotland, she was sent at the age of six years to Paris to be educated in the household of Henry the Second, king of the French. Of course she was attended with all the pomp and ceremony of her station and a company of Highlanders in their quaint Scottish uniforms was a part of her queenly retinue, giving an interesting touch of color to the gay French court. Young Gabriel Montgomery,[1] ancestor of our Linn County hero, was the commander of this troop with the title of Captain of the Scottish Guard. He was a cultured and capable man and became a favorite and close associate of Henry II, whose wife was Catherine de Medici. In the meantime at the age of six years, Mary Stuart was betrothed to Francis, son of King Henry, and on April 24, 1558, they were married. On June 29, 1559, there was a brilliant social event on the commons alongside the famous prison called the Bastile. All the notables of Europe were assembled for a three days program. Tilting or jousting was the popular sport, the Knights being in full armor and riding their best horses. Armed with a lance, they approached each other at full speed and attempted to unhorse or throw out of the saddle the opponent. Young Gabriel had been made a French Knight by Henry with the title Count de Montgomery and was eligible to run in the lists, and was chosen by the King to tilt with him even against his expressed reluctance to put his liege in jeopardy. But Henry insisted and they approached each other full tilt and Henry received the shock of Montgomery's lance against his shoulder, when a horrible accident happened. The brash wood of Montgomery's lance broke and the sharp splintered end pierced the helmet worn by the King and passed through his eye into his brain. After awful suffering King Henry died eleven days later on July

1. Another noted Kansan, Governor John A. Martin, claimed this same line of descent.

10, 1559, at the age of forty years. Count de Montgomery was so saddened by the tragedy he retired to his country estate, a broken-hearted man. Mary Stuart's husband succeeded to the throne carrying her into a queen's place before she had taken her throne in Scotland. A few weeks later, in September, Francis II and Mary were solemnly crowned at Rheims, Mary Stuart thus becoming Queen of the French, Queen of Scots, and her French relatives also claimed the throne of England for her. In December, 1560, her husband the King died, and she became simply Queen of Scots. Succeeding them on the throne at Paris was Charles IX, and under the influence of his mother Catherine de Medici there was planned and carried out the most despicable crime in all history, known as the massacre of St. Bartholomews. The Religious Reformation was then at its height. The Paris Kings had been relied upon to support the Lutheran reforms, but Catherine de Medici, an Italian woman of low origin, exerted enough influence upon her young son now King to make him reluctantly consent to the murder in the night of St. Bartholomew's Day of all the Huguenots in France, and with the cry "For God and the King!" four thousand men were killed that night in Paris and throughout France the massacre counted seventy thousand victims. Count de Montgomery was a Presbyterian and was known to be in sympathy with the Huguenots. They tried to kill him but he escaped on a horse which he rode ninety miles to the coast and reached the Isle of Jersey and from there back to Scotland, where he got ships and sailed back to the French coast to aid his friends but was captured and was beheaded May 27, 1574. He was a wonderful man, one of the most interesting figures in European literature. His family two hundred years later were established at Dublin, Ireland, and from there Thomas Montgomery served as a member of the British parliament. He had three sons who were graduated from Dublin University, one of whom was the grandfather of our Linn County hero, and another who became an American patriot, one of Washington's most trusted generals—General Richard Montgomery, who is credited with having almost added a half a continent to the American Republic when he was killed while assaulting the British stronghold at Quebec on December 31, 1775. His grave is now in St. Paul's Churchyard in New York City.[1]

With all this history back of him the modest school teacher of the Licking Valley started in 1854 for the new lands of the west to escape the horrors of the slave country. His mode of traveling is still talked about by men whose parents saw it and handed the story down to their children. He had cut a big linden or basswood tree and fashioned it into a "dugout" canoe. It was not a large boat, having a very limited carrying

1. Read tribute to General Richard Montgomery on panel in court house in Mound City. Montgomery, Alabama, was so named in his honor.

capacity left after Montgomery and his wife and two small children were in it. But not much bedding or clothing was needed in those summer days. That is the way they left the Licking River, and no one knows how far they traveled in that boat, but late in the summer they had arrived at Westport Landing, and a few weeks later they were in Bates county, Missouri, where they tarried long enough for James to take a look at Linn County and before frost in 1854 they were established in a log house five miles west of "Sugar Mound" on a claim Montgomery had bought from a pro-slaver who had gotten "cold feet" and wanted to quit.

Thus James Montgomery began his career in Linn County right at the beginning. The pro-slavers were in the majority and were in control. They had moved in a few families in a colony from the south, but the most of them were single men roving in bands they called "posses" who interviewed new comers and told them free state people were not wanted and would not be permitted to make their homes here—that this was to be a slave state—and death was all that was offered those who opposed it. Montgomery was besieged at his home. In the night time bullets tore the "chinking" from between the logs, and Mr. and Mrs. Montgomery and the children slept on the floor to be below the level of their gunfire. Early in 1855 the pro-slavers surrounded the house and set fire to it, compelling the inmates to stand and witness the destruction of all they had on earth. But they did not go as they were ordered. Their horses and cows had been carried away by the marauders, but the Montgomerys were taken and secreted in the homes of those fortunate enough to have avoided thus far the wrath of these murderers. There had grown up the nucleus of what was to become a strong co-operation for mutual help among the free state settlers. Within from three to five miles distance lived James Osborn, Temple Wayne, Jasper Dingus, Zack Gower, Samuel Morrow, Sammie McGrew, Adam Poor, Abe and Tom Hargis, Paul Neiswonger, William Turner, Burgess Wright, Theodore Tedford, William Park, and a short time later Amos Durbin and Ed. R. Smith and his father. The situation was desperate and through necessity they sought council with each other. There must be understanding and concerted action in case of need. So they gathered under mutual pledges of secrecy at a house near Sugar Mound and climbing into the little attic room at the top they sat by the light of a single candle and formulated their plans for building an organization of defense. It was very simple. They pledged their lives and their fortunes to each other. Free state settlers moving in were to be met and given assurance they would have sympathy and aid if they needed it. Gradually these newcomers were initiated into full affiliation. For recognition in the dark a simple password was devised, "Up! up! up!"[1] not only an identification of the user but a warning in itself, just as the lost hunter gave three rapid shots from his rifle to call his companions. Three rifle shots meant an immediate assembly at or near Montgomery's place.

The situation grew to be more and more tense. There was scarcely a week without some ugly crime to bring distress and indignation to the families of all the free-state settlers. Montgomery was frequently shot at and his numerous escapes made him thoughtful to secure better protection for himself and family, so when his home was burned he assembled a number of friends who went into the timber and cut down good sized oak and walnut trees. From these trees logs eight feet long were cut out and the center section eight inches thick was split out with wedges. A chalk line was snapped on the edge to insure accuracy and a broad-ax made both sides as smooth as a sawed board.[2] With both sides dressed the slab was turned down and a chalk line marked the full width it would hew out. When finished a tenon six inches long was cut on each end. In the meantime the site of this new house was selected up on the side of the hill where is had a wide range of vision.[3] A stone foundation was laid and on it were logs twenty-four feet long and mortised to fit the tenons on the timbers dressed out in the woods. Each stick was measured to fit its mortise and numbered for its place. When all was in readiness the various timbers were assembled, stood on end side by side, augur holes bored through mortise and tenon and an oak pin driven through to hold it. A mortised log received the tenons at the top which were secured in like manner by pins. Thus Fort Montgomery was a log house with the logs set vertical, so cleverly and accurately put together that there was nowhere a crevice big enough for a bullet. It was larger than the average log house, being sixteen by twenty-four feet. A big fireplace was cut into the end facing the northwest and there was a door cut on the north into a "lean-to" similarly made and about ten by twelve feet in size. An outside door was set in near the southeast corner and another outside door near the northeast corner, with porches. One little window set higher than a man's head furnished the only light and ventilation on this first floor, and when the thick puncheon doors were closed and barred it was a fort indeed. In the northwest corner a slightly inclined ladder led through a hole two feet by four feet into the room upstairs which had some distinction of its own. Three logs were laid horizontally on the top mortise log with a scallop three inches deep cut out at two places in the log. Similar scallops were cut out of the top log so that when placed

1. This was a remarkable historical incident, the very beginning of what became famous as the "Jayhawkers".

2. There was a skill in the use of these tools. Examine the few specimens left, among them a log from Montgomery's Fort in the court house at Mound City, and from Old John Brown's Fort at the scene of the Marais des Cygnes Massacre now in possession of John A. Hall at Pleasanton.

3. See location on map—Fort Montgomery.

in position they made portholes six inches wide and two feet long on the north and south sides, and one in each end, affording ventilation and light and permitting free use of rifles. Rafters carried a roof of shakes rived out of clear oak and dressed with draw shaves. In the construction of this house the work was done out in the forest and like Solomon's Temple very little noise was made by hammer and saw as they put it together. There was one feature that even few of the friends knew about and that was a crude tunnel that had previously been dug and filled up during the work of building and which was secretly reopened when Montgomery moved in. This enabled him to save his life several times when "posses" came in and searched for him.

Montgomery now had eight inches of solid wood between him and the bullets of his enemies. Back of his house on the north the hill came to a point perhaps a hundred feet from the fort, and from this look-out anyone could be seen approaching and a member of the family was frequently stationed there. When Montgomery heard the crack of a rifle and the impact of a bullet near him he fell into the tall grass and was hidden, perhaps for a week, unable to get to the house. At milking time Mrs. Montgomery would saunter forth with a milk pail on her arm and go to where the cows were in the opposite side of the little valley, always conscious that murderous eyes followed her. There was a code they had agreed upon and when she called the cows he knew that at that spot she dropped a package of food for him which she had concealed under her skirts. She would even see the murderer crouching in some comfortable concealed spot waiting a chance at his victim. Once Montgomery had been kept out for a week and finally reached the house under cover of the darkness. The boy Jim was now ten years old. He volunteered to go out and watch while his father got some rest. While he crawled about on his belly, moving very stealthily, he reached out his hand and felt a man's boot. A moment later the door at the house opened and he saw the man rise to his knees with his rifle ready to shoot anyone seen inside. Once six horsemen appeared and asked for him, telling Mrs. Montgomery they meant to kill him on sight. When they failed to get him they went on ten miles to the cabin of James Arthur and enacted quite a scene which is told in the story about Mr. Arthur. Once the proslavers came in the night. A candle was burning upstairs giving enough light to give them a bead on the porthole, through which they fired, the bullet flattening against the rafter and falling on the bed beside Mrs. Montgomery. Enraged at the futility of their efforts they took Montgomery's wagon apart and carried it up on the hill and set it up and carried up and placed on it a good big load of hay. This they set fire to and shoved it backward down hill guiding it toward the house by the tongue. It would have been a serious matter had it run against the "lean-to" with its low roof, but fortunately one of the front wheels struck an obstruction and cramped it so that it veered away and stopped where Montgomery could see his wagon burned up while the fiends were skulking in the shadows out of reach of his rifle. Once that fall they had Montgomery cornered in the grass after frost time. The timber wolves had banded together and getting on his trail they surrounded him in the night and he could almost feel their teeth as they nabbed at him. He dared not use his voice so he got up and danced around and flung his arms till the wolves concluded he was a new kind of animal they wanted nothing to do with.

This went on till 1856 when George W. Clark made his raid through the county, starting from West Point, Missouri, with five hundred cutthroats. They covered a swath ten miles wide, burning every house occupied by a free state man, running off all the cattle and horses, and impressed men with wagons to haul away what they plundered from the houses. In this raid they violated women. The story of Old Wash Gowing and Joshua Sheek tells the extent of their wickedness.

But retribution was coming to them. Something "happened" over on Pottawatomie creek that excused Old John Brown from that neighborhood and he came over here. He was a friend of the Wattleses, having come from the same neighborhood in Connecticut. And Montgomery was a man to his liking. The hospitality of Fort Montgomery was always open to him, but there were soon too many of the Brown party and he took possession of an old log house a little southeast of where Switzer now stands. It was a very crude structure, but Brown had a way of building up stone outside a house as high as a man's shoulders. In this Brown, and Kagi, Realf,[1] Tidd, Hazlett and several others maintained what became known as Fort Brown. Montgomery's personal following was now upward of fifty men who gave him the utmost loyalty. And now that Old John Brown with his prestige and rugged fearlessness was with them, they felt that the tide was turned and that they were going with it rather than against it. Montgomery turned the tables by going with his good riders to offensive proslavers and told them: "The shoe is on the other foot now. This is going to be a free state and only free state men will be permitted here. In punishment of your past sins you are banished and required to travel toward Missouri as fast as your horses can carry you." Some of the mild proslavers made terms with Montgomery and were permitted to stay on probation, but it was the beginning of the end with most of them.

The first county court met August 7, 1855, at Paris. As the Bogus Laws under which they were elected were a copy of the

1. Richard Realf, the literary man of Old John Brown's party, was said to be a relative of Lord Byron.

Missouri statutes what we now call county commissioners were "judges." There were three of them—R. E. Elliott, L. M. Love, and Briscoe Davis. They divided the county into three townships—what is now the eastern tier was Richland township, the central strip being Scott township, and the western Johnson township. By authority of the Bogus Acts they appointed a full set of county officers as follows: James Fox, treasurer; Joseph D. Wilmot, clerk; James Driskill, assessor; Willam Rogers, surveyor; Elisha Tucker, coroner. S. H. Hayze and George Overstreet were given certificates as delegates to the Lecompton constitutional convention. These were all proslavers, of course. They were arrogant and confident and treated the few free state men with contempt. The proslavers acted collectively, while at this stage of the game the free state man and his wife and children could only stand and listen when a "posse" surrounded them and not only robbed them of their horses and cattle but burned their home and threatened their lives. Of course, these newcomers were shy and timid under such treatment and could only hide out in the brush. Some of them were heroic pioneers and stayed through it all, but many of them walked back into Missouri. This went on until Clark made his raid through in the late summer of 1856. In the meantime the free-state men had begun to get acquainted and to exchange views. Montgomery's new log house was up and was known far and wide as Fort Montgomery. Late that fall Old John Brown became a permanent accession to their ranks. Montgomery's men who had met in a little attic room over at Sugar Mound now numbered fifty[1] horsemen with good rifles and pistols. They resolved it was time for them to assume the offensive, and their first adventure was to go up to the ranch of Briscoe Davis, one of the county "judges." He had really good improvements on his land on the north fork of Big Sugar where Keokuk now is. They found Briscoe at home and Montgomery acted as spokesman while fifty[1] good men sat astride good horses and held fifty good Sharp's Rifles at "present." Briscoe was told plainly that the worm had turned and instead of listening to his threats and abuse they were now telling him to go at once, to pack up and get out bag and baggage. While this parley was on, Dr. Barton Robinson came along and offered Briscoe a bargain price for his improvements and a few days later when Montgomery's men checked up on the situation they found a very fine English-bred family in possession and that Briscoe had gone permanently to Missouri. Montgomery's men next went to Trading Post and cleaned out the saloons and started the drunken rounders in a bunch toward the state line minus their guns.

1. This number of fifty is definitely fixed by that number of Sharp's rifles brought down from Westport Landing by Rev. B. L. Reed and delivered to Montgomery. Somehow the Bushwhackers learned of this and it was what caused their awful treatment of Reed at the Massacre.

Not a shot was fired—not a drop of blood spilled. They were elated and encouraged. Most of the numerous newcomers now were avowed freestaters who had come across Iowa and Nebraska and south by way of Lawrence till in a very short time three hundred men—instead of fifty—would assemble at Montgomery's call.

The story of Montgomery's life gives the names of most of that "immortal fifty." No place on the national scroll of fame would be too good for them. Exposed to real dangers, they did their parts in the great and tragic drama then being acted out in a colossal way. No act of evildoing is charged against them. No human life was taken in the "clean up" they made all over Linn County. They lived, died, and are buried here, and their children are now in the third and fourth generation of good honest citizenship.

This "fifty" achieved immortality as the first and original "Jayhawkers". When they first began to assemble at his call and ride with Montgomery they were spoken of in derision by the proslavers as "Jayhawks". This term originated when Pat Devlin, a rawboned redheaded young Irishman who openly affiliated with the free-state men, returned from a prolonged absence of many days in Missouri. He staged a very dramatic return. Up at Ebenezer Barnes' store at Sugar Mound quite a crowd of settlers had assembled and anxiously awaited the arrival of a queer cavalcade coming up the hillside road. It was soon discovered to be Pat Devlin leading a horse literally loaded down with every conceivable kind of kitchen equipment —pots, pans, skillets, spiders, Dutch ovens, rolling pins, butcher knives, cake cutters, jugs with the handles tied together and thrown across to balance, some filled with rum, some with molasses, things of pewter and brass and copper. Curiously anxious to know the secret of it they questioned Pat who said that over in the "ould countree" there was a bird that "just took things" and he suspected this horse had somehow acquired the habit of the jay hawk. Pat had eaten in every home in the county and knew every utensil belonging to them and as he unloaded the loot he handed to this woman a spider stolen from her home by the raiders, and to that woman a Dutch oven, and to another a brass kettle—and a shout of joy went up as treasure after treasure was taken from the load and returned to its owner for those things were indispensable in those days when they had no stoves and open fireplaces were the only fires for cooking.[1] Pat Devlin shrewdly made the most of his opportunity and the story of the return of the Jayhawk was soon a common joke. The proslavers in derision used this term to designate Montgomery's men, who finally accepted it as a badge of honor. And it is to the high honor of Linn County that the first clutch of Jayhawks in this

1. Pat had visited the camp of outlaws at Westpoint and recognized this property, secretly getting possession of it.

western hemisphere were hatched here and have always since affectionately roosted on our standards and have given to a great state the battle cry of Jayhawk! Our students in the university should proudly maintain this as our Golden Legend. It is our birthright, our open sesame, our war cry![1]

Up to this time the free state man had been assaulted individually, overpowered, insulted and kicked and cuffed about, helpless to resist a mob of cutthroats. Now they knew their strength and faced the future with confidence. Montgomery had fifty men who would assemble within an hour after his call. Somehow every man seemed to have fallen heir to a Sharp's Rifle (or Beecher's Bible, as they were then called, and a "testament" in the shape of a cartridge box.) They made Montgomery their spokesman and he talked very plain language. Shortly after Clark's raid Montgomery assembled his men and they rode over to Trading Post, which was the headquarters of all the deviltry on the Kansas side. They found a crowd of drunken ruffians who looked with astonishment at the fifty men on strong, well-fed horses, all carrying nifty repeating rifles and plenty of ammunition. Montgomery made his persuasive talk to them, compelling them to put their cheap old guns and pistols in a pile, and then dismounting he entered the saloon and with a number of willing helpers rolled out several fifty-gallon barrels of whisky. Montgomery took an ax and smashed in the heads of the barrels and allowed the liquor to flow a hundred yards down toward the river. And mind you, this was the only instance or record where "destruction of private property" could be proven against Montgomery or his men. He allowed them to take food for themselves and their horses, but never tolerated pilfering in any form, nor vile language nor unbecoming conduct. His men were above that, anyway.

Rumors came to them of another threatened invasion. The information seemed to require action, so Montgomery called together three hundred men and told them what seemed threatening, so they resolved to go over in a body and size up their enemies. They approached old Balltown in Vernon county and in passing old Leconte's farm there was some activity at the rear of the house that needed explaining. A lane led down a quarter of a mile to the big house. Montgomery designated ten men, including Ed R. Smith, to go in and look the place over. As they neared the house some fifteen or twenty men ran through the brush into a ravine where their horses had been tied and rushed away. The ten men rode on around the house when a door flew open and a man fired two barrels of a shotgun at Ed R. Smith.

1. Richardson in his book "Beyond the Mississippi" says that on June 13, 1858, when he visited Kansas he "found all the settlers justifying the Jayhawkers, a name universally applied to Montgomery's men, from the celerity of their movements and their habits of suddenly pouncing on an enemy."

One charge of the buckshot struck Ed's horse in the head and neck and the next found a permanent resting place in the flesh of Ed's legs and thighs where he carried them till his death. They sat Ed down by a tree and his affectionate horse came up bleeding and weak and rubbed his nose against Ed's face till Ed broke down and cried. In mercy the animal was killed. Old man Leconte came out and blustered around that he only acted in self defense and was sorry, and that he would take Ed into his own rooms and nurse him till his recovery. Ed knew what those murderers would do if they returned and found him there so he emphatically declined, and suffered a painful ride home. A wide reconnaissance failed to locate the threatened trouble. Their trip strengthened the confidence of the Kansas men to take care of themselves. This was their only "invasion" of Missouri.

For the next five years Montgomery was the recognized, acknowledged leader in Linn County, with a following of men who almost idolized him. In this book will be found many references to him, every one a tribute. They were long, lean, weary years. Somehow, Montgomery managed to always have a "Sunday suit." From the first he had always maintained family prayers and always appeared each Sunday neatly dressed to preach to some gathering of his neighbors. His spare time was spent reading his Bible, even to the last day of his life. When the Civil War came on he was called to Leavenworth and was offered the colonelcy of the Third Kansas Regiment. Men who had known him in Ohio raised and financed a whole company to help make up his regiment. These men started for Kansas and at Lathrop, Missouri, the cutthroat banditti had burned a bridge till it was so weakened it let the whole train into a wreck that killed forty men and discouraged the others so they returned home. Political intrigues and manipulation by those seeking commissions nearly ruined this regiment, but Montgomery finally brought them down to guard the border, spending several months at Camp Defiance in what is now Potosi township just west of where Mine Creek crosses the state line. Subsequently, President Lincoln selected Montgomery to go into South Carolina and round up the refugee negroes after the emancipation, and he had a thousand mounted black men—Second South Carolina Colored Regiment—whom he led through Georgia and the Carolinas striking wherever they could deal the heaviest blow. At the battle of Olustee, Florida, February 20, 1864, his regiment is credited with saving the entire Union army from capture.

The noble woman whom Montgomery married in 1853 was Miss Clarinda Evans of the Licking Valley, a younger sister of the mother of our present John Ellington. The story of the family life and numerous children is given elsewhere.

Among many interesting characters of 1854 and 1855 was Zack Gower, a Campbellite preacher who came here from Texas; he was an outspoken free state man; he made his home a mile south of the court house; he died and is buried over at Mapleton. Another good reliable man was Paul Neiswonger who lived on what is now the Gates place. William Turner lived just north of Alf Wayne's home in the village; his wife was such a good housekeeper that their hired man complained she required him to "shave the splinters off the stove wood." Burgess Wright was a brother-in-law of Temple Wayne, having married Mr. Wayne's sister; the Wrights were from Ohio. Samuel A. Morrow whose wife was a sister to Jasper Dingus came here from Hickory county, Missouri; a son Henry Morrow now lives at Blue Mound. Abe and Tom Hargiss were young Kentuckians who lived on the place where Amos Durbin afterward made his home. Blunt Perry, James Ferris, and Theodore Tedford, and the Dement Brothers, nephews of Ebenezer Barnes, were among the early day heroes of Linn County who rode with Montgomery and carried Sharp's rifles. John Marr who married Miss Laird, a sister of Mrs. John Ellington, lived on a farm now occupied by John and his wife. Barney Richardson, a Mr. Wolf, were of this group.

Just around the hill to the southeast of Old John Brown's Fort and a mile from the home of James Montgomery and about three miles due west of Mound City was the cabin of Hiram Jasper Dingus who was of German descent and born January 9, 1830, at Estesville, Scott county, Virginia. In 1854 he was a government freighter hauling army supplies between Fort Leavenworth and Fort Scott. Resigning from the government service he married Elizabeth Angeline Wayne, a sister of Alf Wayne, and settled down to pioneer life on his claim and was a close neighbor and intimate associate of Montgomery and also of Brown when he appeared on the scene. On May 19, 1858, he by accident started up the "west trail"[1] to Westport Landing. Had he gone by the "east trail" he would have arrived at Trading Post just about the time the victims were assembled for the massacre by Hamelton's men. As he was an outspoken free state man, well known and cordially hated by the Bushwhackers, he no doubt narrowly escaped these murderers. The Dingus children were Henry Winfield who married Lorinda Giles, Martha Elizabeth who married John Daniel Bower, now in abstract business at Mound City, Hiram Winford who married Ethel I. Wilson, Louis Clareton who married Opal M. Rownd, Mary Ellen who is unmarried, and John Orum who married Cora M. Rownd. They were close friends of the Montgomery family and Mrs. Bowers tells many stories she had heard her mother relate. At one time Mrs. Dingus was at the Montgomery home when she saw her

<hr/>

1. This went straight north and intercepted the Santa Fe trail in Johnson County, thence straight into Westport Landing.

hostess go out on the porch and eagerly scan the surrounding country as she shaded her eyes with her hand. Apparently satisfied, she came back into the house and lifted up a section of the puncheon floor whereupon a big wooly black head bobbed up and a runaway slave took from her hand a plate filled with food and retreated to a mere hole under the floor. He was traveling by the "underground railway" and this was a typical passenger station. Mrs. Bower says Montgomery was a poor financier and relied greatly on his wife's management of the family affairs. He was a well read man and was a fluent, even eloquent, speaker before any audience and made an impressive appearance by the neatness of his clothing.

Mr. and Mrs. John D. Bower had two sons who served their country in the World War. Burnette Orum Bower was a student at Kansas University and within three months from leaving school, including only two months in a training camp, he was a first lieutenant of aviation in the battle of St. Mihiel. He was twenty-five months in the air service and on his discharge from the service he was married to Dorothy Bigelow of New York. The younger boy was Cecil Lloyd Bowers who served twenty-seven months in the heavy artillery. He had graduated from Manhattan Agricultural College and after discharge married Bess H. Hansen.

Lewis Franklin Osborn with his father James Osborn came up the Marais des Cygnes valley, from Bates county, Missouri, in the fall of 1853 with barrels in which to carry home wild honey. At a point three miles southwest of where Mound City now is he was so entranced by the beauty of the country that he vowed a certain spot of ground was to be his when the country was thrown open to settlement, and on March 20, 1854, he arrived at that spot and settled. He was accompanied by Adam Poor and Mike Canovan and the latter's two boys Mike and Ed and with their help he built a log house 20x20 with clapboard roof, not a nail used in its construction. It was for many years the biggest house in that part of the country and all local affairs centered there. Old Mike Canovan stayed and settled on a claim southwest of what is now Blue Mound and the little stream on which he located is still called Irish Branch in honor of old Mike's nationality. There were Indian scares and once the Indians came and took all their cattle. All the men were typical frontiersmen with full beards and sometimes looked very fierce. In the fall they would go a day's travel westward and find the main herd of buffalo, sometimes closer home, and bring back the winter's meat and robes for bedding and coats. The Osborn home was a hospitable place where Montgomery was frequently an honored guest as their most intimate friend. Lewis now religiously puts a boquet of flowers on Montgomery's grave each Memorial Day. They had a subscription school and paid $1 for each pupil three months.

Lewis Franklin Osborn was born in Bates county, Missouri, January 16, 1849, being the son of James Osborn from North Carolina, who was a strong Lincoln man and strongly anti-slavery. Lewis F. Osborn was married to Mary Wright who was born in Ohio. Their surviving children are Lewis F. who married Emma Garver; Byron who married Olive Beardsley; and Martha who married Wiley J. Cox, all of Mound City. The children of Lewis F. are Mrs. Morna Lemon, Mrs. Hazel Priest, and Mrs. Nella Lamereau.

William Park was born May 19, 1810, in Madison county, Kentucky, being the oldest son of Richard Park and one of nine children, four boys and five girls. William spent much of his time in his boyhood days with his grandfather on his mother's side, Wm. Kindred, who came from England prior to the Revolution and who during that great struggle took an active part on the side of the Whigs. After the war Mr. Kindred settled in North Carolina and at an early day in Kentucky history removed to that territory and reared a large family. The educational advantages of Kentucky a half century since were not much better than of the present day and William Park was not favored with much learning of the book kind; though under many difficulties he did manage to acquire a fair common school education. February 9, 1830, being then twenty years of age, he married Elizabeth McAnally who was born May 3, 1807, in Sullivan county, Tennessee. The McAnallys were Virginia people of Scotch-Irish descent who removed from Tennessee to Madison county, Kentucky, when Elizabeth was but six years of age. After their marriage the Parks "set up" for themselves on rented land working constantly for a living, a bare sufficiency, for some seven years. During this time there were born to them three children, D. F., Martha and Susan. In 1837 with their little household goods stowed in a wagon of Kentucky make, wonderful and fearful in shape, hauled by one yoke of steers with one horse in the lead, and with fifty dollars in the purse, a march was made for the New West. After thirty days in the wilderness they stopped on Sweet Spring creek, Randolph county, Missouri, two miles from Huntsville, and there purchased the first bit of mother earth owned by them, being forty acres of land upon which with characteristic energy they proceeded to build up a comfortable home, and where was added to their family six more children: Nancy, Louisa, Lucinda, John, Henry and Sarah. In the spring of 1854 with a small party of his neighbors he visited parts of Iowa with a view of locating but it was too far north and too cold. Returning from Iowa, he visited Linn County in the fall of 1854. He returned to Missouri, sold out, and in the fall of the same year removed to Kansas with all his family except Martha and Susan, the first of whom married Thomas Walden who some years afterward died leaving Martha a widow with four children. She sold out her farm in Missouri and in 1864 removed to this county. Susan married Theodore Tedford and with him came here in 1854.

After the organization of Linn County in 1856 Mr. Park was elected one of the first justices of the peace in the new county. Mr. and Mrs. Park for more than half a century were members of the Baptist Church. Of their nine children D. F. Park married Sarah Barnes, the eldest sister of Frank and Charles Barnes; Martha and Susan we have already mentioned. Nancy married John Wayne, Louisa became the wife of Samuel Baldwin. Lucinda married Rev. John R. Baldwin.

Mrs. Anna Sumner Corbin had four sons to care for when her husband Nathan died at Woodstock, Connecticut, in February, 1843—Myron M., Jesse Sumner, Byron B., and Nathan Albert. Early in 1857 she arrived in Linn County with her four boys and they were at once a part of the community, doing heroic work in the border warfare. These people were all of Puritan blood and in Connecticut had become familiar with the course events were then taking and enthusiastically aligned themselves with their free state neighbors here. Anna Sumner Corbin was a first cousin of Senator Charles Sumner of Massachusetts, a distinguished leader in the United States Senate. Connecticut was the birthplace of Old John Brown and it was perfectly natural this new home should be an attractive place for him, so he became an intimate friend of these four boys and their mother. The three older boys did a full part in protecting the neighbors from the raiders, but the youngest boy was yet of too tender an age to leave home. Young Nathan went in the spring of 1861 to Galesburg, Illinois, to enter college there, but when President Lincoln asked for volunteers to suppress the attack upon Fort Sumter he at the age of nineteen years enlisted in Company K of the Forty-fifth Illinois Infantry and served under Grant and Logan in their memorable campaigns till the close of the war, when he returned here. He married Mary E. Robinson on July 18, 1877, and they created a beautiful home at Blue Mound where she died in 1887. In 1890 he married Ida Robinson, a sister of his first wife, and they had a daughter Nathana. They were conspicuously honored citizens and at his death on January 23, 1914, the county lamented the loss of a good man. See the story of family of Myron M. Corbin in story of David Linton family.

John Ellington is probably the only man living in 1928 who from the age of ten years was in every day association with "Uncle Jim" Montgomery. His mother's sister, Clarinda Evans, was married to James in 1853. By a former marriage he had two children—James and Nancy—then probably six or seven years old. These children are remembered as clever, Nancy being an unusually pretty girl. The mother of these two children is now nameless, there being no record of her family. James the boy went west with a load of apples about the time of the Bender crimes and as he was never heard of afterward there has always been a suspicion that he was one of their victims. Nancy married a man named Judson Veach and that is all that is preserved of her history—gracious little lady descended from many heroic sires—gone into oblivion. Clarinda gave eight children to James, six of whom lived to maturity, and true to their pioneer tradition they long ago left here for the new lands. Evan was the first, then Jane, John, Hugh, and Lewis, all of whom went to Seattle, Washington, where Lewis is reputed to have made a million dollars on lumber contracts in 1905 to 1910 and lost most of it in speculation and lost his health and was sent to a sanitarium and has since been lost to his relatives here. The other children are also gone into the unknown. The last born child was Nellie who is also gone, no one knows where. In 1910 Lewis was here from Seattle on a visit and is seen in the picture of Fort Montgomery standing between his cousins Frank Ellington and Miller Ellington, the latter standing next to the house. John Ellington remembers much about Montgomery after he returned from the Civil War, his last service having been in the Carolinas, Georgia and Florida. John remembers the home life in the good stout Fort Montgomery, the hollyhocks that grew all about the place, and rosebushes and other flowers, and the neatness and comfort of that home under the management of Mrs. Montgomery. James had come home from the war pretty much of an invalid and gave the greater part of his time to reading and preaching. He had at that time six hundred forty acres of land. A number of families of colored people followed him all the way from South Carolina and he located them in shanties all over his place. He was not a good manager, they said. Anyway, the farms produced more than there was a market for and nobody got rich. He was easily irritated by wrongdoing and quick to punish it. Some of Montgomery's cattle disappeared and he suspected a family named Mullins. Montgomery went to their house and found the family seated at dinner. He walked right in to where they had their rifles on racks at the ceiling, took each of the guns, went outside and deliberately broke them over the logs at the corner of the house and then notified the family they must move out of the country within twenty-four hours. They went. On another occasion a breachy mule belonging to Montgomery went to a neighbor's place, leaned against the fence till it gave way and went into the field to feed on green corn. Of course it made trouble, and Montgomery sent his boy John to bring home the mule. The neighbor was still angry and slapped the child in the face and sent him home crying. Montgomery went insane with rage and started with a revolver to settle with his neighbor—no man could slap his child! Ellington saw Mrs. Montgomery throw her arms about his neck and pleaded with him not to commit some awful thing he would always regret. Many incidents of this kind showed the high tension at which he was then living. Every morning he would step out on the porch with his rifle and sighting at a rock four hundred yards across the valley would test the accuracy of his aim, always knocking a little cloud of dust from the target he aimed at. He was reputed to be wonderfully clever with a gun. He had a high tenor voice of great purity of tone and led in the singing at all services, using a "tuning fork" to get the pitch. His strength gradually diminished and on January 1, 1871, then only fifty-seven years old, this exemplary character passed away in Fort Montgomery and he was buried in that soil he loved so well, but was later moved to the National Cemetery at Mound City—a national cemetery that not many know exists. He sleeps alongside another hero—James Finley Harrison,—Cavalier with generations of historic sires, who rode as a conqueror through the City of Mexico alongside Lieut. U. S. Grant.

John Ellington, a Scotch Irish pioneer, raised a family in the Licking Valley where the river of that name empties into the Ohio at Louisville. He had a son named Isaac Ellington who married Sarah Evans, of a very good family of that vicinity. They moved to Cooper county, Missouri, near Boonville, arriving there April 20, 1855, and eight days later our John Ellington was born on April 28. They lived there till March, 1864, when they all came to Linn County to join James Montgomery and family, Mrs. Montgomery being a sister to Mrs. Ellington. They traveled the entire distance in wagons drawn by oxen. They were too late to get in on the border troubles, but for the remaining seven years were close and intimate associates of Colonel Montgomery, who died in 1871. The numerous Ellington children all remained here. John the first born married Lida Laird; Mary Jane married Douglas Walker; Frank married Emma Cassidy and had two children Warren and Fern; Isaac Miller married Fannie Applegate and had three children, Carl, Gladys and Hollis; Alice married Charles Stansbury and had two children Opal and Cleo; Ella married Guy Adams, their children being Verne and Lester; Charlie went to Texas where he married; Clara married Moses Applegate, their children being Blanche, Hazel and Ralph; Alonzo married Stella Teeters.

John Ellington who married Lida Laird, has three children living—Floyd who married Elva Teeters; Clyde married Louisa Melsee; and Vera who married J. O. Bruce and now lives in Kansas City. The parents live at the old homestead near old Fort Montgomery, on one of the prettiest homesites in Kansas.

Isaac Harrison Marrs was born near Fayetteville, Washington county, Arkansas, where he says some good people come from. In October, 1855, he moved to Kansas with his father, James Harrison Marrs (born in Kentucky in 1821) and family of six children (the wife and mother was Martha Landers whom he married in Kentucky). They came here in an old-fashioned Tennessee wagon drawn by three yoke of oxen. The first stop was made at the home of Uncle Davie Reece (an uncle to Mrs. Marrs who had come here from Washington county, Arkansas), where Capt. O. E. Morse lived at the time of his death, east of Mound City. "We then moved south across the prairie through the tall grass. This trip I shall never forget as we met a fire coming from the south. The flames were tremendous and seemed to threaten everything before it, but we back fired and drove in where it was burned. When the fire was over we traveled on until we came to Lost Creek and there we settled. The farm now belongs to A. H. Ball, near Mantey." Hard times and privation befell them at this time. There were four families in the crowd and the first thing they did was to build a house. They soon had a log cabin 14x16 with wooden chimney for the fire place and dirt floors. Thus they lived all that winter.

"The slave trouble commenced at this time and of course we were in favor of a free state, as nearly all newcomers were and we worked and fought to that end. I think it was in August, 1856, that runners came from Fort Scott headquarters notifying all those in favor of a free state to leave the country within three days. We left, but returned in October prepared to stay. And stay we did. We found all the improvements and crops destroyed. However we had quite a little crop of sod corn, pumpkins and melons and the like, but we had another hard winter with very little to live on. We killed wild game for meat and went to Missouri to get our bread. There was a small camp of Indians at the mouth of Elk Creek and they had some squaw corn to sell. The squaws made split baskets and sold them to the white people. Sycamore tea was mostly our drink and parched corn coffee.

"In 1857 we began to raise some crops and prospects were brighter, but the troubles were still growing worse. The men had to hide out nights for their lives as the bushwhackers were out most every night; one party one night, the next night or two another party.

"Well I remember the night the shooting occurred at the W. H. Wasson farm at the mouth of Elk Creek, where three men were shot down and one wounded, and one night there were several others killed. I also remember when Guthrey was hanged on the mound south of Mapleton, known as Guthrey's Mound. Talk about scary times, we sure had some those days! No schools or churches, no government of any kind. One other exciting time occurred—in 1858, I think—when there came through our neighborhood a small herd of buffaloes and of course everybody was after them to get some buffalo meat. They got one and it was divided up so we all had some of the meat. That was one time they all forgot politics and had a good sociable time.

"Curious to say, I well remember the faces of Jim Lane, James Montgomery, Dr. Jennison, John Brown, and others who put up at father's home, and mother was glad to provide something to satisfy their hunger. Some of these men were not perfect saints by any means, but tit for tat was all the go those days. For instance, soon after the shooting of three free state men at the side of the road, at old Sugar Mound store, which is the haunted house now owned by Col. J. D. Snoddy, a squad of men were caught near Trading Post by Dr. Jennison's men and paroled, one being marked by Jennison by cutting off one of his ears so he might know him thereafter whenever he saw him.

"Soon after this came the Hamelton Massacre at Trading Post, which every one is familiar with. The admission of the State of Kansas as a free state was the strife at that time, but glory and right settled that question.

"The year of drought came in the fall of 1860.[1] It tried the merry hearts of the men who were working hard to regain a start after the loss of time and lives and privations during the three preceding years. During this year men solicitors were sent abroad to solicit aid for the suffering and those who were poor and unable to help themselves. Aid stations were selected and men were appointed to distribute the provisions among the people, according to their needs and wants. But not strange to say there were some pets so-called because they received more help than others. Nevertheless, it was a great help. Our agency was at Daton, three miles south of Mapleton, on the ridge. Stockmire was the agent. I remember well having to ride a poor horse, without a saddle or blanket, every Saturday, and get father's rations. Oh, how tired and sore I was, but would forget it all when mother prepared the corn meal, bacon and beans, which cheered up all the family for the following week.

"In 1861 the agitation of the Civil War began, and closed in 1865, gaining the victory of freedom over slavery, in which the writer served for three years in the glorious cause of our country."

Isaac Harrison Marrs of Mound City is one of the few survivors of the old Indian wars in the state. Marrs was just a "kid" when he entered the service in the early '60s, and was stationed at Fort Larned, which at that time was a formidable army camp. Mr. Marrs not only has the distinction of having served in the Indian campaign but he also has the distinction

1. The relief fund to aid settlers in Kansas during the drouth of 1860 was the result of a startling letter dated Mound City, Kansas, written by Thaddeus Hyatt of New York. Hyatt was imprisoned for failing to give information asked of him about the John Brown raid. The letter about the starving drouth victims brought a generous response from all over the country.

of having been the cause of a near Indian outbreak in the war and was the subject of long and somewhat exciting negotiations between the United States government and the Indian war councils. Marrs once killed an Indian. He was not more than sixteen years old when he was placed on sentinel duty one night. The army was on its nerves at the time because it was in the midst of a host of savages. In a communication written by Capt. A. W. Burton (our Capt. Burton) of the Twelfth Kansas, stationed at Fort Larned at the time, it is stated that from twenty thousand to thirty thousand Indians were camped within a few miles of the Fort. In the night Marrs heard a horse coming toward the fort. He had been instructed to keep diligent watch against any approach of the enemy. In a loud voice Marrs challenged the horseman, who came galloping on without response. Again Marrs challenged without receiving a response. "Halt!" challenged Marrs the third time, and when the wild rider gave no answer and did not stop Marrs raised his rifle and shot. The horseman rolled from his mount, shot through the head. Marrs called the officer of the day, Lieutenant Pellet, and told him that he had "shot some fellow out there." Investigation proved that it was a Cheyenne Indian. Col. Henry Leavenworth, in command of the fort, exonerated Marrs and called the chiefs and mighty men of all the tribes together and explained the matter to them. But they were not satisfied. The parley was continued for several days, the Indians threatened to take to the warpath in revenge. The garrison numbered only a small band of soldiers, and the Indians felt that they had all the advantage. They would accept neither explanation or apology. Finally they agreed to peace on one condition, Marrs was to be turned over to the Cheyennes for punishment.

In his report on the incident Captain Burton of Company H of the Twelfth Kansas Cavalry says: "Since writing the foregoing page I have been out to the council of the delegation of Cheyennes and officers of the garrison. The Cheyennes agree to settle the difficulty if Marrs is given up to them. I do wish we had a few more troops, so that we would not need to listen to the 'mumsters.' As it is, if I were in command, I would let them know that we ask no favors from them. But let it come to what it will, not one hair of Marr's head shall be touched until they have killed every man in the garrison."

Marrs was not delivered to the Indians but it was a period of anxiety for him, knowing that there were about twenty thousand Indians just outside the fort waiting to welcome him to their arms for the purpose of showing him what they could do to a white man that had killed one of their tribe. The Indians were deterred from making war and reconciled to denying themselves the pleasure of handling Marrs upon the representation that the government was sending a big army to the relief of the fort.

Mr. Marrs enlisted from Bourbon county, but for many years he has lived at Mound City. He was seventy-eight years old in 1926. He entered the army at the age of fifteen. Even at his present age he is very much of a lively citizen, taking an interest in the life of his home town. He has for years been the "backbone" of the Methodist church in Mound City; a quiet, unassuming, peaceful, and much loved by his fellow citizens—about the last man, indeed, that would be picked out as one who once came within a hair's breadth of having caused a war between Uncle Sam and the Indian tribes of the West. He has been justice of the peace, police judge, and custodian of court house for twenty-five years.

In 1854 a boy seventeen years old came to Twin Springs in what became Scott township and lived with his sister, Mrs. Adaline Westfall, wife of Abraham Westfall who lived on what is now known as the Frank Shinkle farm. This boy was Isaac Newton Croxton, born in 1837 in Carlton, Carrol county, Ohio. This family is one of the most ancient of England and was honored in all branches of military and civil life. The family originated in Cheshire about the time of Edward the Confessor and were so prominent in church matters there are now at least six "livings" or curacies bearing the Croxton name.[1] The Croxtons had good excuse for a hasty exit from England as they were a part of the revolutionists who brought Charles I to grief and this Croxton family was intermarried with the Bradshaws one of whom presided at the trial of Charles I, and when Charles II came to the throne at the Restoration the first thing he did was to dig up the rotten corpse of Oliver Cromwell from its grave in Westminster Abbey and hang it in chains at Tyburn Gate, so the Croxtons came to America as fast as they could get here. They espoused the Quaker faith, but it is claimed another branch came on the Mayflower. Their family history reads like a "story book." Isaac Newton Croxton later married Matilda Hewitt, a relative of the famous Ball family of New York. They came out to Kansas, first stopping at Paola where the Peoria Indians had a reservation, later locating on a claim near Fontana, then going over to Rockville where he had a general store, and later enlisted in Company D, Fifteenth Kansas Cavalry and served to the end of the war. When the Gulf railroad came through and the town of La Cygne was started Croxton opened a hardware store there in partnership with Mr. Lobdell whose son then a small boy is now Hon. Charles Lobdell of the Federal Farm Loan Board with offices in New York City. Ike got out of the hardware business by being elected sheriff of Linn County in

---

1.   Croxton Vicarage in Norfolk, Croxton Rectory in Cambridgeshire, Croxton Vicarage at Thetford in Norfolk, Croxton Curacy in Staffordshire, Croxton Menial in Lincolnshire and Croxton Curacy in South Leicestershire. The family name originated from the river Croc, and a village grew up they called Crocston —hence Croxton.

1872. His children have all done very well. William L. became
a railroad man now stationed at Des Moines, Iowa. In the
World War he was sent to Russia with the rank of captain.
While in Manchuria Will was married to Zena Parominsky,
daughter of Admiral Parominsky of the Czar's navy and she
gave him a daughter, the first female born in the Croxton
family in fifty years. The second son was Edward L. a remarkably bright, popular fellow who was employed in banks
in La Cygne and Pleasanton and who disappeared about 1890
and never since heard of. George W. the third boy married
Lillie Black of the family of James Glasgow Black of La Cygne
(who trace back maternally to the DuPonts of powder fame
and to their own family ancestors at Glasgow, Scotland). The
oldest son of George and Lillie is Dillard who served in the
U. S. Marines during the World War and was physical in-
structor at Paris Island, South Carolina, later served on the
warship Arizona and saw service in the campaign against the
Turks. Dillard married Bernice, daughter of Andrew and
Ella McMichael of the Cadmus neighborhood. Another boy is
George Junior now in the U. S. Navy at San Diego and who has
achieved distinction in athletics, being champion runner of
the fleet. Lovett Ben is the third boy and is followed by Dan
the youngest.

Dr. James Riley Wasson came to Kansas in 1855, first
locating at what is now Fulton but later came over into Linn
County onto the present Wasson farm on section 20 in Stanton
township. In 1858 a band of Bushwhackers came over from
Missouri and proceeded to carry away all his possessions, including a valuable pair of mules. Dr. Wasson and a friend
named Conrad Travers fortified themselves as best they could
in the cabin, where Travers was killed by a volley fired through
its thin walls and Dr. Wasson was wounded very badly in the
arm and side. His brother took him to Dade county, Missouri,
where he recovered after three months careful treatment. He
was married to Miss Hardwick K. Riley and in 1867 they came
back to their farm, where eight children were born to them.
William, the eldest, was principal of the Mound City schools
in 1875 and later was county superintendent, and James O.
became a school teacher and married a daughter of Enos Mills.
Dr. James Riley Wasson was born in McMinn county, Tennessee, in 1829, and studied medicine under Dr. John Jones
of Missouri, returning to Tennessee, and from there to Kansas
in 1855. He died shortly after his wife's death in 1881.

"This truly historic character, early settler, widely known,
revered, honored, beloved and distinguished citizen of whom
we are met on this occasion to pay to his memory a deserved
tribute of reverential respect, was born in McLean county,
Illinois, February 19, 1832, and departed this life at his last

home adjoining Mound City, March 12, 1924, at the remarkable age of ninety-two years and twenty-two days." Thus
spoke Ed. R. Smith at the funeral of his old time friend,
Captain Charles Barnes. In McLean county, Illinois, April 7,
1853, Charles Barnes and Miss Mary A. Johnson, formerly of
Ohio, were united in the bonds of happy wedlock. To this
marriage was given in the course of passing years, five children, being Sarah B., wife of our esteemed citizen B. C.
Garrison; John B., now a resident of the state of Washington;
Daisy B., wife of Larry J. Higgins; James Eldon, and little
baby Henry, who died in his infancy.

Charles Barnes and his heroic young wife, she with her babe
yet in arms, and his parents, Ebenezer Barnes and wife, after
weary and long weeks of travel overland through a sparsely
settled country, largely roadless and bridgeless, arrived in this
county before it was organized, October 17, 1855. Ebenezer
Barnes established himself at what was then widely known in
the sparse settlement and still is as Sugar Mound. He succeeded to the "betterments" of one Stockton and to the first
postoffice established in this county, and maintained therein
a small stock of groceries. In the meantime Charles Barnes
established his home in a beautiful grove of fine timber adjoining what is now Mound City. Both Charles Barnes and brave
old father were conservative in character though strongly in
support of free state principles, in consequence of which during
the summer of 1856 G. W. Clarke, custodian of the United
States Land office at Fort Scott took command of a mob
already organized for the purpose and raided this county with
the declared object of driving out all settlers not in accord with
and in support of proslavery principles. In the course of the
march of this bushwhacking band of assassins they burned the
unoffending cabins found on their way, and arriving at the
store and postoffice and gathering place of the few settlers,
the cabin home of Ebenezer Barnes, who defied Clarke to do
his worst, they robbed him and destroyed every movable thing
about the place including the little postoffice. Fortunately at
this particular time, Charles Barnes was away on a trip to
his former home in McLean county and thus saved his only
span of horses and a wagon. Following this in the spring of
1857 the settlers, for their better protection, organized a
military company of which command Charles Barnes was its
first lieutenant, and ever on the alert with but a moment's
notice gathered his neighbors and marched with all speed to
the Trading Post following the receipt of the news of the
unforgettable, ever memorable Marais des Cygnes Massacre
of May 19, 1858.

It was late in the fall of 1855 that Charles Barnes in
company with his father and David W. Cannon laid claim for
townsite purposes to the present townsite of their town and

in the spring of 1857 founded the present city, with Charles
Barnes as the first president of the town company, which
important office he held until the present city was organized
December 27, 1870, with T. Elwood Smith, Elim W. Bartleson,
W. R. Biddle and S. L. Ives as its first village officials. In the
fall of 1857 the Smith-Trego-and-Smith saw-mill having gotten
into operation Charles built the first frame house erected on
the townsite and established the first general mercantile store
here and to it brought and became the first postmaster in
Mound City. Indoor work did not agree with Mr. Barnes and
soon afterwards he sold out his business and was succeeded
by J. H. Trego and the brothers Thompson and Simpson Atkinson, recently of Bucks county, Pennsylvania. Captain Barnes
was a county commissioner two years beginning in 1858.

In the year 1837 a band of about one hundred and fifty
Pottawatomie Indians came from their old home in Indiana
to Linn County. At first they set up their wigwams on
Pottawatomie creek in Miami county. Their chief was
Nespwawke. He had been baptized in the Catholic faith and
he sent an invitation to Reverend Felix L. Verreydt and
Reverend Christian Hoecken, two Jesuit priests then living
among the Kickapoos near Fort Leavenworth, to come and
teach them. They arrived in January, 1838. The Indians had
not definitely decided on a location but soon chose a site at
the headwaters of Big Sugar Creek about four miles northwest
of where Centerville now stands and built a church where
regular services were held until 1840 when a larger church
became necessary by reason of additional migration of Pottawatomies from Indiana. A school was opened in 1839 and a
separate school for girls was opened July 15, 1841. The
settlement was called St. Mary's Mission, and notable among
the priests connected with it were Reverend P. J. Verhaegen,
S. J., Superior of the Jesuits in Missouri, and Father H. Aelen
and Brothers A. Mazella and George Miles. On June 17, 1846,
this reservation of land was sold to the government and a new
reservation was given the Pottawatomies on the Kaw river
where the present prosperous city of St. Mary's now stands
with its St. Mary's College, which really started at Centerville
in Linn County in 1838. What was a lively Indian village of
several hundred people with substantial buildings for church
and schools and teepees and wigwams for the natives utterly
disappeared when the tribe started for their new home on the
Kaw river twenty-eight miles west of Topeka. Possibly the
buildings were destroyed by fire, as no legend has been handed
down as to their fate. Now on the same ground is the white
man's town of Centerville with the Missouri, Kansas and Texas
railroad running through it, a substantial, up-to-date village
modern in every particular.

Five miles south of La Cygne[1] a bald promontory grows out of the western prairies and juts boldly out into the valley landscape. On the north side it drops abruptly from its crest near three hundred feet to the waters of the Marais des Cygnes, which runs along its base. The Gulf road diverges slightly from its five-mile air line course from the northwest and passes under its brow, and a few rods beyond there is a station for the thriving little village of Boicourt. Unlike the bold north front of the hill, on the south there are smooth slopes and a cozy site for perhaps a hundred cottages.

In one of the cottages not far from the station there lives a man of slight build, yet full rounded frame of only medium height, with kindly gray eyes set in a face of rather unusual intelligence, and a personality that is marked by a courtliness which charms his visitor at once. He is one of the men of Linn County who may be taken as a fair type of the heroic settlers of the decade of 1855-'66. Back of a modesty which hides too much of valuable unwritten history is to be learned a career of remarkable interest.

A few days since the writer had occasion to call on him for some information, and having obtained it, was for awhile the guest of this man—widely known David Sibbett. Seated in his home I was charmed with the expanse of beautiful scenery stretching out in all directions, a panorama of undulating prairie and forest, marked off into farms and so dotted with peaceful homes that one can hardly realize at first that within the range of vision were the scenes of remarkable events— events marking epochs in the history of our country and affecting the destiny of nations. Its early history was not stained with the tragedy of later years, yet rich in interesting events. The first white man to enter from the east the region now known as Kansas was a Frenchman, M. Du Tissenet, who in October, 1719, visited the native Osage Indians in their village very close to where Pleasanton now stands, and with about the population of the present white village. He reported them to Louis XV of France as a handsome people living in the affluence of vast herds of cattle and with abundance of grain, fruit and game. Many years later, in 1764, the intrepid Choteaus visited the region, but up to 1834 it is not known that any white man had here taken up his abode. In 1806 Zebulon M. Pike passed through the valley on the expedition which resulted in the finding of Pike's Peak. He visited the Osage Indians, and reported to the authorities at Washington that "the country around the Osage village is one of the most beautiful the eye ever beheld," and mentioned a venerable warrior, White Hair, as the principal chief. And then looking off at the range of hills toward the southeast one thinks of the Ozark mountains and remembers the pretty story of Evangeline Bellefontaine—Longfellow's "Evangeline"—who in

1. This was written in February, 1895.

about 1768 came up from the Acadian settlements in Louisiana
looking among the French trappers and Indians for Gabriel
Lajeunesse, her lover, who had been so ruthlessly torn from
her as related by Longfellow; and as Evangeline crossed the
Ozark mountains and visited the Indian villages she must have
met the Osages here, and thus was the first white woman to
set foot upon what is now Kansas, and no doubt heard the
pretty Indian legend and gave to the river the pretty French
name, "Le Marais des Cygnes."[1]

But from the time Pike visited the region in 1806 there was
a long and uneventful period. In 1834 Jean Baptiste began to
do business at what is now Trading Post, about two miles
southeast in the heavy forest. There was a military road
running from St. Joseph by way of Fort Leavenworth straight
south through Trading Post which in 1842 had a log fort to
accommodate a company of men (see sketch by Amos Tubbs).
This road went on south crossing Mine Creek where in 1864
the battle was fought, to an Indian agency where Fort Scott
now is. Vanderslice was in charge of this agency. He was
an influential man and in 1842 he convinced General Winfield
Scott that it was the logical place to locate a United States
fort, and in this way Trading Post lost its opportunity to
become a great city. The military road went on from Fort
Scott to Fort Smith in Arkansas and to Fort Gibson in Indian
Territory. In 1838 a Catholic mission was established where
Centerville now is. This later was moved to what is now St.
Mary's on the Kaw river west of Topeka and is sketched elsewhere in this book. There seems to have been nothing worth
recording from then till 1854, when the opening of the Kansas
Territory was the very incipiency of activities in the "irrepressible conflict." From then on there is no lack of dates
and events. Off to the northeast six miles, in plain view, is
the scene of the Hamelton massacre in 1858; above it on the
hill is the little fort built by Old John Brown; off to the west
is Mound City, Paris, Brooklin, Mansfield, Moneka, and between, countless farms on which were seen the fires of the
burning homes of lovers of liberty in the border war; scenes
of martyrdom everywhere; places where pages of history were
made by men who became famous or infamous by the making.
The whole sweep of the horizon to the east marks the route
of Price's panic-stricken horde flying before the federal troops
in October, 1864, and at Mine creek, eight miles south, is the
scene of their last stand, where was fought a bloody battle,
with 25,000 men involved, with all the atrocities of civil war—
where several hundred rebels were killed and one hundred fifty
Union soldiers "bivouacked on Fame's eternal camping
ground."

Fit place indeed for a heroic soul to calmly sit in contem-
plation of life's merciful and sometimes merciless mutations.

1. Read "Naming of the River," an Indian legend in this book.

Yet here is a man who for forty years has from this hill seen all of life pass in review before him. While it was not my original purpose, I can not refrain from recording the remarkable story I have heard from Mr. Sibbet.

In 1855, Mr. Sibbet, then about twenty-eight years of age, had been visiting in Petersburg, Virginia, and there formed the resolve to come west. He paid a brief visit to his home and birthplace in Cumberland county, Pennsylvania, and after the manner of traveling at that time, by a series of steamboat and ox-team journeys arrived at Independence, Missouri, on the 30th day of March, 1855. Here a most curious and lasting impression was made upon him by the people he met, as the men were invariably aged and decrepit, while the women and children were in the usual proportion of a town population. He was so impressed by the entire absence of vigorous men, that he commented on it to some of the people, and was told that "all the men who were able had gone over into Kansas to vote!" Subsequent events proved that on that very day they had voted in sufficient numbers to elect the bogus legislature hereinafter commented upon. Sibbet continued from Independence to Westport, now a part of Kansas City, where he stayed till May, 1855, when the cholera broke out, and he and his younger brother Samuel fell in with William Chouteau and rode with him to Trading Post. Another incentive than escape from cholera prompted him to leave Westport, as the place was crowded with blustering, murderous proslavery men, and at the hotel all the men slept in one big room, and the principal conversation was in scheming to make Kansas a slave state and in cursing "abolitionists". Once he was awakened and questioned as to where he came from, to which he replied "Petersburg, Virginia," which seemed to satisfy his questioner that he was in favor of slavery.

Arriving at Trading Post he heard of a thriving settlement five miles west and went there, bought a claim, broke ten acres, farmed a little and taught school. There were more people in the neighborhood then than now. He taught in a log house with a hole covered with muslin to admit light and as he was appointed postmaster in 1856 (and served continuously till 1893—thirty-seven years) he became intimate with the people, a majority of whom were proslavery in their views. Thus he and his free-state friends were isolated, and the news they got from the outside world was all colored to suit the other people. Although he was postmaster, during the days the bogus legislature held power they did not even permit newspapers or writing of any kind defending free-state ideas to enter the Territory, making it a felony and an "incendiary" act to do so, and frequently some settler was burned out because it was learned he was a subscriber for the New York Tribune.

There was enough excitment to keep off ennui in the little settlement. The free-state people were in the minority and intent upon making homes had scattered out over the prairies, while the proslavery people were there for a political purpose—to acquire dominion—and clannishly held together in the town. Importations from Georgia, Alabama and other southern communities supplied in sufficient numbers the kind of men to carry on a guerilla war of intimidation. They were undoubtedly not of the best southern people. Still there were men of intelligence, refinement and influence among them. Among Mr. Sibbet's acquaintances was a Mr. E. O. Brooks, who kept a general store, and as the place was growing into a town Mr. Sibbet suggested that it be called Brooklin—a combination of Brook and Linn, the name of the county—which was adopted. There was a sort of militia organized, with proslavery men in control of it. A big stock of whisky in Brooks' store supplied the rather dissipated frequenters of the place.

Brooks got into some trouble and left without disposing of his stock of goods, and a short time after Mr. Sibbet met him at West Point, Missouri, and purchased the store and took into partnership with him Zebediah William Leasure, who had moved into the community from Richland county, Ohio, with a wife and two children, Marion Franklin the La Cygne lawyer being the oldest. They continued in partnership a few months when William M. Cannon, a Pennsylvanian, bought out Mr. Leasure, and the firm was then Sibbet & Cannon till the spring of 1860, when they traded the store for a farm at Brooklin and some cattle. Visions of wealth appeared to them in the shape of farm products and live stock, and they bought hogs and cattle extensively which were put in the pastures of the river bottom lands. But 1860 was the year of famine. Not a single roasting ear grew on their corn. For thirteen months not a drop of rain fell. The cattle and hogs drifted away and were never seen and Mr. Sibbet was left penniless.

But the years between 1855 and 1860 were not uneventful. The proslavery people were asserting themselves continually. The bogus statutes made it a felony punishable by death to be a subscriber to a free-state newspaper, and the penalty was frequently inflicted. There were times when burning homes could be seen at every point of the compass, where death and the torch were being carried by self-appointed raiders. Samuel Nickles, who until a few years ago lived about ten miles southeast of La Cygne, was burned out and ordered to leave because of a New York Tribune being found in his house by some of the marauders.[1]

In May 1858 Mr. Sibbet saw a man named Evans ride excitedly into Brooklin, who stated there was a mob of outlaws murdering the settlers around Trading Post. The necessities of the time were apparent to Mr. Sibbet, and securing a rifle

1. Under section 3 of chapter 151, "An act to punish offenses against slave property, Laws of 1855," much suffering and tribulation and many indignities were meted out to free-state families.

and a bag of buckshot with which to arm free-state settlers, he mounted a horse and rode about forty miles over the prairies to the west, asking the settlers for aid for the Trading Post people. The next morning the trackless prairies were covered with horsemen all converging at Brooklin. Two companies were hastily organized, the first electing Gideon Potts captain the second John Gates of Brooklin. They hastened in military order to Trading Post only to find that Hamelton's horde of assassins had selected their victims and taken them north to kill them. Following, they found where eleven men had been shot down in cold blood by a mob under Charles Hamelton of Missouri; but the "wolves of the border had crept from the dead," Hamelton saying, "We must get out of this. Who knows but what Jim Lane is in the brush there with a thousand abolitionists!" That day and event was the beginning of a new epoch in American history. The story of the atrocious crime was telegraphed throughout the North and Whittier immortalized it in his poem "Le Marais du Cygne."

The great hero of the time was not far away. Old John Brown was in Linn County, and with Montgomery and his men visited the scene of the massacre. George W. Creager was there, and talked with Brown, whom he says was a quiet observer of all that was said and done, without seeking to influence them. It was two years after the trouble at Osawatomie, in which Fred Brown had been murdered in a cowardly manner by a mob under Rev. Martin White. Fred Brown had been surrounded and ordered to surrender. He showed the most heroic courage, and as Martin White pointed his huge pistol at him calmly walked up to the murderous old man who claimed to be one of God's vicars. When Fred stood in front of Old White, the latter deliberately shot him through the heart, and the cursing outlaws loudly applauded the act. Old John then came down into Linn County and established a fort with Montgomery and some of his neighbors on Montgomery's farm, five miles west of Mound City.

Thorton Creager and Mr. Sibbet went out there to visit the fort and see the famous Brown. They found Montgomery's farm all right, but were mistaken by Mrs. Montgomery for enemies, and received a defiant reply to their inquiries for the men, she saying they would receive company at the fort, showing them the way. The found the fort in a small cornfield, in the center of which was a high knoll on which the log fort was built, the whole being surrounded by an enormous rail fence. They halloed, and several men appeared with rifles ready for service to receive them. They were allowed to come in, Sibbet being mistaken to be Robert B. Mitchell, who was becoming known as a leader in sentiment of his community, and had some views of his own somewhat antagonistic to Brown's methods, though thoroughly in sympathy with the cause. Sibbet soon set them right as to his identity, but as he was an intimate friend of Mitchell's he defended his views in a conversation which followed with Montgomery. They were inside the fort, a log house with portholes, and half the space given to one big bed in which all the men slept together. In the midst of the conversation Mr. Sibbet was startled to see a gaunt, haggard old man rise up in bed, his venerable white beard sweeping the coarse, dirty blanket, and with loud voice and vehement gestures he denounced Sibbet's views as visionary and impractical, saying the saber and the rifle were the only remedy for the great wrongs perpetrated by the proslavery people. This was Sibbet's introduction to Old John Brown. The discussion grew warm. Sibbet took the stand that Brown's ideas were too radical, and sought to argue by saying that the great wrong done to Brown by the murder of his son had made him unconsciously and naturally revengeful. But Brown warmly disclaimed the motive of revenge, and avowed that all his actions were done in the name of God and liberty!

Thornton Creager became very sick, and was taken care of in the fort that night, and Sibbet spent the night at Montgomery's house. Mr. Creager says that there was earnest discussion among the men, but as he was very sick he did not hear much of it. Once, when he used some western vernacular rather expressive and a little profane, Brown corrected him, saying there was no excuse for such language. But he was very kind to him, and at night they slept side by side on the bed on the floor. No watch was set, but a fierce dog was chained at the door to announce visitors.

This visit to John Brown was intensely interesting to them, both because of the people and the most eloquent discussions with such dramatic surroundings. Kagi, who was one of Brown's most noted followers, Montgomery, and the celebrated poet and orator, Richard Realf, of Indiana, were present at the fort. They now realize that Brown was right in his treatment of the situation, and believe but that for his heroic leadership the cause of human freedom might have been defeated in the border war. It was the last of Brown in Kansas, for in that little fort the details of the Virginia raid were being formulated.

After going from the fort to Montgomery's house, after the interview with Old John Brown, Mr. Sibbet spent a pleasant evening with the family. The house had but one room below, and was very tidy, with a nice bed in it. Montgomery told Sibbet he was to sleep there, but Sibbet insisted he did not want to discommode the family, and that he would climb up into the little garret and let Montgomery and his wife and children sleep below. Montgomery said no, that they never slept there, and showed Sibbet that the wall had been perforated with bullets which had also gone through the bed in search of Montgomery. Sibbet stayed in the bed that night without trouble, but says he has since felt how thoughtful it was of his host to tell him of the pleasant practices of his neighbors.

At the election held March 30, 1855, there were enough illegal votes to render the election void, but the proslavery candidates met and organized that which has since been known as the Bogus legislature. What is now called the senate was then the council. Henry Younger, the father of the famous Younger outlaws, was the member of the house of representatives from the district of Linn, Miami, Franklin, and Anderson counties.[1] His fellow representatives were W. A. Heiskell, Allen Wilkinson and Samuel Scott. This Bogus legislature met at Pawnee, on the Kansas river, in accordance with a proclamation of the governor, and after having organized by electing their officers, they passed a law to remove the seat of government temporarily to the Shawnee Manual Labor School (now known as Rosedale), where they again convened on the 22nd day of July, 1855. Mr. Younger had never lived an hour in the territory, but his proslavery views qualified him with the people who elected him. Mr. Sibbet afterward met him and remembers him as a bright, pleasant gentleman.

Naturally trouble resulted from the attempt to enforce their so-called enactments, and in 1857 an election was held in which every voter went to the polls looking like a walking arsenal, and the free-state men not only voted but saw that the ballots were counted. The result was a big free-state victory. Robert B. Mitchell and Addison Danford were elected representatives and Hiram B. Standiford elected member of the council; but the latter died shortly after election, and a special election was held at which Sibbet was elected and took part in the proceedings of the first legal legislature of Kansas. They met at Lecompton, but the members were compelled to live at Lawrence because of the lack of accomodations. It was then the acts of the Bogus legislature were declared illegal and were expunged, and the statutes, which had been printed and distributed to the members, were condemned and ordered to be destroyed by fire. Of course it was impossible to destroy them all, scattered as they were, but a bonfire was started in front of the Eldridge House in Lawrence and George W. Dietzler, speaker of the house of representatives, marched out in a dramatic manner, holding a copy of the unholy edicts aloft, and as a symbol of their complete effacement cast the book into the flames with the Shakespearean quotation, "Out, damned spot!"

Mr. Sibbet had been given a copy as a member of the council, but, unlike many of the members, did not have it with him to

1. Henry Younger was a representative from the seventh district, not a councilman. His fellow representatives were W. A. Heiskell, Allen Wilkinson and Samuel Scott. The councilmen were A. M. Coffey and David Lykins.
1. Hiram B. Standiford. For sketch see Kansas Historical Collections, vol. 10, p. 207.

cast into the fire, and it now reposes in an obscure corner of his library. Getting it he pointed out its peculiarities.

The book itself is an interesting study as an illustration of the subtle methods employed to overturn law and precedent and to obtain dominion over and make subservient to sordid, mercenary interests the vast extent of country then unpeopled. The volume is like an ordinary octavo statute, in sheep binding, and has nearly eleven hundred pages. The title page reads:

"The Statutes of the Territory of Kansas; passed at the first session of the legislative assembly, one thousand eight hundred and fifty-five; To which are affixed the Declaration of Independence and the Constitution of the U. States, and the act of Congress organizing said Territory, and other acts of Congress having immediate relation thereto. Printed in pursuance of the statute in such case made and provided. Shawnee M. L. School. John T. Brady, Public Printer, 1855."

The preface was written by "Samuel A. Lowe, superintendent," his title no doubt meaning that he superintended the compilation and publishing of the bogus enactments. His remarks cover five pages, and give a resume of the proprietorship of the territory from its occupation by the French by right of discovery till 1762, when it was ceded to Spain, and its retrocession October 1, 1800, to France, and from France to the United States April 30, 1803.

The body of the Bogus laws was copied almost verbatim from the Missouri laws, which had been the English common law since 1816, when it superseded the civil law of France and Spain.

In the main body of the laws was the act defining and naming the counties, beginning with Johnson county, which was described as it now exists; then Lykins (since changed to Miami) and then Linn, with practically the same boundaries it now has. There were a great many names given to counties which did not stick, as Crawford was called McGee; Montgomery was called Dorn; and among other names which failed to preserve a place on the map were Weller, Richardson, Breckenridge, Madison, Godfrey, Hunter, and Calhoun. It was provided by the act that the county seat of Linn should be located within three miles of the geographical center of the county by commissioners to be elected in October, 1855.

There were one hundred and forty-seven special acts relating to the incorporation of towns and companies and to ferries and roads. Quite a number spoke of Linn county places still familiar. Martin Taylor and John Ballard were given the monopoly of a ferry and ford where the old mill stands which was built at considerable expense by R. A. Denton in 1870, on the Mundell farm, and Taylor lived on the farm now held by William Griffin. The ferry was operated opposite where Thornton Creager now lives. Many roads were provided for which crossed the river at Graham's ford, where La Cygne now stands, one from Westport, Missouri, to Fort Scott, and one from West Point, Missouri, to Cofachiqui, the county seat of Allen county. There was provision for a road from Niswanger's ford on Little Sugar, past Sugar Mound (now known as Mound City) to Giareau's old trading post on the Marais des Cygnes.

But the one act in which all the designs of the proslavery people were centered was "An act to punish offences against slave property." This was the title of the act intended to establish and perpetuate the institution of slavery in Kansas Territory, and a more rigorous measure was never proclaimed by a legislature nor decreed by a monarch. It absolutely forbade the expression of sentiment against slavery in any form—by speech, writing, printing, or permitting such things to be done. The act had thirteen sections, the first six of which had the uniform prescription of "death" as the penalty of violating it, while the following six were cunningly worded to describe the same offenses, and declared them a felony punishable by imprisonment—yet by fiendish design every victim would have been liable to the death penalty if the court was in the mood to so construe the law. The thirteenth section made any person conscientiously opposed to slavery disqualified to sit as a juror.

Mr. Sibbet had an interesting military career. The feeling of the people was such that when President Lincoln called for 75,000 men there was a meeting hurriedly called to meet at Robert B. Mitchell's place, called Mansfield at that time, and a company was organized with Mitchell captain, Byron Ayres lieutenant, and Ezekiel Bunn second lieutenant. They went to Lawrence, intent upon making Mitchell colonel of the regiment to be organized, but were defeated in this because their company was not full. Sibbet hurried back to Linn county and got enough to fill it and Mitchell then got the coveted colonelcy.[1] It was not long till they were on the first great battlefield of the West at Wilson Creek, and their bravery there is recorded with that of the Union army. At Wilson Creek Sibbet was an ensign, Mitchell insisting that his friend should have an office, and this was the only one left.

This Second regiment was enlisted for three months, and when mustered out Sibbet was penniless, and after a visit to Brooklin he walked to Leavenworth, where he served in the state militia, but during the entire time, present or absent, he was postmaster at Brooklin till 1870, when the office was removed three miles east to the railroad at Barnard (now Boicourt), and Mr. Sibbet went with it, and continued as postmaster till removed by Grover Cleveland in 1893—thirty-seven years of continuous service as postmaster.

Mr. Sibbet came west without any intention of taking part

1.   Second Kansas Volunteer infantry, organized at Lawrence, June 11, 1861; mustered into service June 20.

in political affairs, and it was by accident that he located among and lived with the proslavery people. It is very creditable to him that he maintained his own ideas on popular questions against their persuasions. Once he was visited at Mooney's boarding house in Brooklin by the noted James P. Fox, and told that while in good conscience he was right, that he ought to profit by the opportunity by adopting the proslavery ideas, as the free-state people would not be in control of affairs for twenty-five years to come. A few days later Fox was in such desperate straits that he stopped a friend in the road, robbed him of his horse, and escaped into Missouri, and afterwards became the leader of a "posse" of marauders that murdered and pillaged in Linn County.

John Green, born in Lowell, Massachusetts, and given a college education, came west in a very early day and established a home on the Missouri side of the line and married Jane Delaney, who was born in Ohio, and they had a son Theodore born in that pioneer home at the northeast corner of Linn County in the year 1831. John Green was the earliest settler of record in that part of the country and was mentally and physically very active. He brought in high class breeding stock of both horses and cattle, and sowed the first blue grass ever seen in this country, and established the first grist mill. There were many Indians here then, mostly Osages and Pottawatomies and Miamis who were moved west after their defeat at Tippecanoe in Indiana. The Greens got along very well with the Osages, but the Miamis and Pottawatomies still remembered their wars and defeats and were vicious, stealing, and suspected of murders. At one time in 1848 Mrs. Green had a pot of beans suspended over the fire in the big fireplace and an Indian boy entered the house while she was out. Mr. Green went in and saw the young Indian deliberately polluting that preparation of food. In anger he threw the young buck out and as he showed fight Green picked up a stout green hickory "poker" used at the fireplace and struck him on the head, killing him. As Mr. Green was acting in self-defense he did not feel badly about the result, but he was not able to explain to others of the Indians who at a distance saw the affray. They were very angry and made evident their intention to retaliate. Sarah, Mr. Green's third child, now Mrs. Elias Jarred, ran out and bridled Black Bird and brought him to her father, who mounted him, and surrounded by an angry mob of Indians he was started for their camp near what is now Trading Post. On the way they abused him and threatened to burn him at the stake. He talked the Indian languages fluently and understood their intentions and was getting into a very uncomfortable state of mind. It was now in the night, quite dark, and at one place the horses stopped at some difficult place and he slipped off onto the ground and was feeling around over the surface when the Indians yelled and asked him what he was doing. At that moment his hand closed on a good sized club of wood and springing on the back of Black Bird he struck the Indian horses right and left across the snout and his horse bounded away towards home, where he arrived safely. For a long time he was in danger from the Indians, but he treated them all good naturedly and finally furnished them fat beeves for a big pow-wow and was reinstated in their favor. At the time General Ewing's Order No. 11 was being enforced in 1863 John Green realized his entire family was in danger and he was afraid to take them into the concentration camp at Butler. He sought safety in the big bend of the Marais des Cygnes river northwest of where La Cygne now is. It was even then known as "Hell's Bend," and was a refuge for many people at that time, there being a narrow bottle neck entrance on the east and the balance protected by the impassable big river. During this time Mr. Green became very ill and died before capable medical aid could be brought to him and was buried at Fontana. Six children came to them. Theodore the first born married a Miss Scott, daughter of Sam Scott of Scott township, Linn County, and thereby incurred the anger of his father who never permitted him to come home. Commodore, the second child, grew to manhood and disappeared at time of Price's Raid, presumably murdered. The next Green child was Lucy, who married Rev. W. W. Gwynne, a Baptist preacher. The other Green children were Artie and John, of whom we have no record. And to this day, in the third and fourth generation following him, the exploits of this grand old John Green of 1831 are talked on the roadside by boys who have adopted him as their hero. Sarah, the girl who rode Black Bird into a gang of snarling, angry Indians and gave him to her father and no doubt thus saved his life, was a frontier heroine. At five years of age she would ride all day long with her father on his cattle range, and as she grew to womanhood she was a prized member of such society as was then developed in a community where the seething hate of the slave-holders made scant room for such staunch New Englanders as John Green's family. She saw the Price Raiders burn the home of a settler on Walley Mound and heard them laugh as three children were burned to death. She married Robert Kyle, a young man from Cynthiana county, Kentucky,—the only one of a large family who defended the Union. They had three children, Harry G. Kyle who married Bertha Bowen of Centralia, Kansas; Lilly who married George Worlein of Linn County; and John Lark Kyle who married a Bates county, Missouri girl. Along about the Centennial year Robert Kyle, the husband and father, began to fail in health and it was finally decided to move the family to Oregon. Two wagons were elaborately fitted up with a bed cross-wise at the rear for the invalid, who however made the trip with few breakdowns and drove one team over the rough roads while Sarah drove the other, Lilly and John Lark, then mere children, dividing their time with father and mother, while Harry G. then barely eight years old, rode a spirited horse from the old John Green stock. This was in 1879 and for three months they were on the old Oregon trail by way of Salt Lake City to Baker, Oregon. Every mile of that distance Harry rode horseback and he had the serious duty out on the plains of riding on a distance ahead and gathering up a pile of buffalo chips and store them in the feed boxes with which to make fire to cook the family food for the next meal. The arrival at Baker City was an epoch in Harry's life for there his parents bought for him the first "store clothes" he ever had. Previously his mother had made all his clothing. They went on up into the mountains and built a home in the Willough Valley and that home is still there carrying the name of Kyle's Gulch. Robert Kyle died there and Sarah and her children came back to the old home and after years of toil taking care of her children she married again to Elias Jarred, a Union soldier who had settled in Lincoln township east of La Cygne, and they had four chil- dren: Jesse who married Lelia Bennett, daughter of John Bennett of Bates county, Missouri; Myrtle who married Jesse Echord of La Cygne and has had three children; and Forest and Dorothy who are unmarried. Harry Kyle was a "sooner" in the rush into Oklahoma, but later settled down and went to Kansas University, from which he graduated from the collegiate and law courses and of course found Bertha Bowen, who became his wife. Harry established his office in Kansas City where he has been for many years a leading citizen, a very successful and prosperous lawyer, and frequently men- tioned for mayor and other large honors.

Captain Herbert Robinson and his three brothers, James P., Lander, and Fremont, were well and favorably known in the Territorial days, and Herbert was a popular officer in the Civil War. Their father was Dr. Barton Robinson who was born in England, and who had some wealth when he arrived here. About that time Montgomery and his men, equalling about fifty horsemen, had gone up to the place of Briscoe Davis on Big Sugar Creek near what became known as the village of Keokuk. It was a finely improved place. Briscoe Davis was one of the first county officers appointed in 1855 and had been a very active proslavery man and had served on many "posses" that notified free state families to move out and stay out, and upon a second visitation had burned their primitive little homes. So that Montgomery's visit to notify Davis to take notice and get out was while Dr. Robinson was in the neighborhood looking for a place, so it was easy for him to conclude a purchase of a fine farm. Dr. Barton Robinson was the first "gold digger" in Linn County. He discovered a vein of quartz on his land which carried a trace of gold and there was quite an excitement for awhile. The Robinson boys were all quick of intellect and of rare courage. In 1862 Herbert sat down to a game of poker and got $900 ahead of the game with Lander trying to have him quit and cash in, but he wanted to "break the bank" and played till the house got it all back. Herbert married a daughter of Henry Blackburn, another English born man, and left several sons and a very pretty daughter named Josephine who became the wife of Jacob Minor.

Another English born man of the group was Thomas Slater of Scott township, who got to be wealthy and quite influential. When the author of this book was having quite a struggle to get bread and butter, Uncle Tommy would come to town with half a load of apples, some potatoes, cabbages, and other eatables, and backing up to our fence would shovel them out and try to sneak away, when mother would call to him that there was some mistake. "Well, you see, Mrs. Mitchell, prices are so low I'd rather give them to Billy than take them home!" He brought them intentionally for me, bless his soul!

Timothy Shaffer came from Ohio to Linn County in 1868. His wife was Catherine Shank. His son Perry married Susan Guynn from Iowa. They were living on the old Blacks farm when the Price raid went through. Samuel Perry Guynn and his brother-in-law, W. K. Evarts of Company E Sixth Kansas Cavalry, were on a visit at the Shaffer home and in uniform. They started about 9 a. m. and at the Fisher farm northwest of Pleasanton met twenty rebels who shot and killed Samuel and stripped his uniform from him and wounded Evarts in his arm, but he escaped. Perry Shaffer's son, Leroy married Lovena Akers and the daughter Pearl married Harley Johnson.

The ancestors of the Holmes family of Potosi township were from Dublin, Ireland. Two brothers graduated from Dublin University in 1757[1] and immediately set out for America where they became instructors in the Colonial schools and both became patriots of their adopted country. They made their home in Virginia and served in the revolutionary war from that colony. One of these brothers was John Holmes the grandfather of James Charles Holmes who came to Linn County in 1859 and purchased a farm three and a half miles southeast of what is now Pleasanton. He was born in Virginia, June 28, 1813, and married Virginia Miller, born April 11, 1824, who gave him four children: Kern Holmes Brunner,

1. It was at this time that General Richard Montgomery and his two brothers graduated from Dublin University. They were very likely classmates. Another family from Dublin at that period is that of——?

Alice Holmes Steers, Wallace Holmes, and Martha Holmes Spencer, these children all born in Indiana. By a second marriage to Margaret Brunner of Washington, Indiana, six additional children came to him, they being Nancy Holmes Lamb, Mary Holmes, James, Bolivar Adams Holmes, James Davis Holmes, Virginia Holmes, James Coutts Holmes and John Holmes. They all came to Linn County except Alice who stayed in Indiana. The father was a progressive successful man, handling large herds of cattle. He was a charter member of the first Masonic Lodge in Mound City. Wallace and Bolivar served in the militia, the former being killed by an Indian in one of the border troubles. James was a little boy of twelve when the Price Raid came through and his mother told him to go into the woods and hide. The Confederates captured him and thought he was carrying messages and would have killed him had not his mother arrived and explained his predicament.

Bolivar Adams Holmes married Louisa Lamb, a daughter of Reuben Lamb, and of their ten children all grew to maturity except Edward who died in infancy, and are well remembered as James Reuben, Mary Lillian Stark, Alice Emily Bradley, Margaret Nancy Saunders, Martha Virginia Craig (wife of Clint Craig, editor Pleasanton Observer), Adeline May Kennedy, Edna Elizabeth Hiatt, Jessie Orsa Wright, and Richard Wendell Holmes. Bolivar Holmes was postmaster at Pleasanton at the time of his death. When Louisa Lamb (the mother of this household) was sixteen years old, the Price Raid came through. She had an adventure that would stagger a modern flapper of that age. A neighbor woman whose husband was away in the Union army wanted to go to her parents sixty miles away and Louisa volunteered to take her, walking alongside a yoke of oxen with a bull whip, her pony tied to the rear of the wagon. The first night they spent in an abandoned jail and in about a week they got through and Louisa mounted her pony and started home. On her way back she had to pass through the battle field at Mine Creek and her pony became very nervous and unmanageable at the sight of the dead men scattered all about on the prairie.

Zebediah William Leasure[1] did a good deal for Linn County in the early days by giving to it his numerous offspring and by defending it from the enemy. Both he and his wife are of German descent, though the Leasures came to this country from England with William Penn. Mr. and Mrs. Leasure (who was Louisa Catherine Creager) left Richland county, Ohio, in the fall of 1854, with their first born, Marion Franklin, and settled in Montezuma, Poweshiek county, Iowa, where he engaged in the mercantile business, but the severe winter discouraged him and the next spring—1855—he came on to

1. This was written by Mr. Mitchell in 1895.

Linn County, having at Montezuma had a daughter (now Frances Leasure Stevenson) added to his family. He took up a homestead at Brooklin and has lived there ever since. There have been born to them here Loretta Elizabeth, Emmet, Lincoln, Augustus William, Emery Ellsworth, Emma Josephine Lehr, and K. Carson Leasure.

Shortly after their arrival here there were stories of great gold discoveries at Pike's Peak, and in company with Thornton Creager, George Weldon, Nathaniel McCarty and a man named Conrad, he started for the Peak. They had spent all their available wealth for their outfit. When they got out on the plains a war party of Comanches surrounded their camp, stampeded all their horses, and left them on the prairies with their loaded wagons, which was something of a predicament at that time. Many days were spent in wondering how they would get out of it, but finally a Santa Fe freighter traded them a yoke of small Mexican cattle and they slowly worked their way back, and have not gone on gold hunting expeditions since. After that there was too much trouble at home for foreign expeditions.

Captain Leasure was a trusted friend of Montgomery and of John Brown, and with his friends generally joined the organized companies of the western part of the county. For a while they suffered raids from a band of proslavery men who infested Rockville, up in Miami county, and they went up to send them back to Missouri and succeeded. After a fight with the bushwhackers, they drove them into a frame church, and there seemed to be no results from rifle shots put into it. George Creager had borrowed a big shotgun of enormous bore from Hugh Huston, and had it loaded with slugs. He was the object of considerable derision and was called the artillery of the expedition, but when the bushwhackers took refuge in the church he was asked to try his gun on them. The first discharge sounded so like a cannon and the slugs ripped off so much of the siding that the occupants jumped out and ran for the timber and for Missouri.

These expeditions became necessary frequently and at the most inopportune times. Once they stopped their threshing machine and left at a moment's notice and were gone a week.

After the Marais des Cygnes massacre in 1858, the proslavery people did all their work through a secret organization, and the free-state men found it necessary to resort to similar methods to keep themselves informed of the doings of the enemy. This was a rather embarrassing situation, as some of the proslavery people were their everyday associates, some of whom were companionable people when not influenced by political matters. Marion Leasure remembers that on one occasion a room was set apart in their house in which his father was to entertain some company, and he, childlike, was curious to know why the family were not invited, and listened to the proceedings. After a few had gathered the door was closed and a man put in charge of it. Newcomers announced themselves by giving three raps on the door. If he was a member the following was the formula for his reception; "Who is there?" "Star." "What Star?" "John Star." "Come in." Settlers, thus assembled from many miles around, would then compare notes and devise ways and means to protect their lives and property.

The proslavery people had had their lodge organization from the beginning. Secret Indian treaties made at Washington were made known to them, by which lands then held by the tribes would be relinquished and thrown open to settlement. As this information was valuable, it was only intrusted to those who would strengthen their side and keep the secret. For a long time they were not detected, but after the free-state people got the ascendancy it was no longer safe for them to gather in such numbers in the settlements, and they of necessity met in the forests of the river bottoms, and many a coon hunt and wolf drive wound up in the meeting of a "Blue Lodge," "Social Band," or gathering of the "Sons of the South," as their different organizations were respectively called. The last place where they are known to have met was on a spot where the Marais des Cygnes river strikes Hensley Point, three miles southwest of La Cygne. Some free-state man invaded their stronghold rather by accident, where he saw a lodge of Knights of the Golden Circle in session, and what he learned and exposed scared the proslavery people into an abandonment of further work in that line, and many were soon in the guerilla camps on the Missouri line.

Captain Leasure stayed at Brooklin till 1862, when he enlisted in Company I, Second Kansas Cavalry, and as about that time soldiers were needed, he did not wait till uniforms could be furnished, but went forth as a cavalryman clad in his wedding suit, and took part in the lively battles at Newtonia, Cane Hill, Prairie Grove, Van Buren, and Fayetteville. At Newtonia his regiment was ordered to take a rebel battery, and they took it, but in the melee Leasure's horse was shot all to pieces, just as he handed the rein to the "fourth trooper," and he went into the action on foot and completely riddled that wedding suit, of which he frequently hears since. While in Arkansas his horse fell upon him, seriously injuring him, and on January 24, 1863, he was discharged because of his disability. In August, 1864, Governor Carney sent him a commission as captain of Company K, Sixth Kansas militia, with rank dating from September 26, 1863. Each county was given a regiment, and the companies were raised by townships. At that time the Miami Indians occupied nearly all of what is now Lincoln township, so it contributed its men to Captain Leasure's company K in Scott township. A very strict military discipline was enforced. The headquarters of the regiment

were at Mound City, with James D. Snoddy as colonel and
Ed R. Smith as lieutenant colonel. Each company was assembled every Saturday afternoon at some central spot and
given a half day of steady, hard work at drilling. Regularly
every Saturday morning an orderly was sent from each company to headquarters at Mound City, and the orders issued by
the colonel were read to the various companies during the day.

At the time of Price's raid this regiment had a campaign of
hard marching and severe fighting, and had the funny experience of bringing the enemy home with them and licking them
in sight of their families. They were in the battles of Big
Blue and Hickman's Mills, and then were cutting souvenirs
off the coat tails of the rebels until they got to Trading Post,
where the two armies encamped on the night of October 23,
1864. From the homes of company K the camp fires of the
armies were plainly visible, and at dawn their breakfast dishes
were shaken by the concussions of the cannonading, and by
ten o'clock the big fight at Mine Creek was in full blast. The
following is the roster of the company October 9 to October
26, 1864:

Officers—Z. W. Leasure, captain; Elias Snook, first lieutenant; Thornton Creager, second lieutenant; Richard Hill, first
sergeant; J. H. Milton, second sergeant; John C. Milton, third
sergeant; Henry Lansdon, fourth sergeant; S. E. Ewing, first
corporal; Ezra Moore, second corporal; James L. McCarty,
third corporal.

Privates—Sylvester Armstrong, Henry Auchey, Frank
Augur, A. D. Colson, Daniel Chase, John Copenhaver,
William Dillon, Henry Dalmier, David Davenport, Julius
Davenport, John W. Ewing, Anthony Frietche, William J.
Frey, John Freer, Robert Foster, George W. Fulkerson, Wash-
ington Gowing, Drury Gowing, William S. Gray, Levi A. Hod-
son, Daniel J. Hodson, Oliver D. Harmon, George Hart, Harvey
Hart, Wilson Hensley, E. Hill, Joel Hester, George Humiston,
Ira Lawrence, Henry Long, William Long, Andrew J. Loomis,
Alexander Lemon, John Lemon, Ford E. Lamb, John Moore,
Joseph Moore, J. McGinnis, Edward J. Merrill, Jesse Milton,
George S. Mooney, Samuel Miner, William Padley, Joseph W.
Payne, Alpha Payton, Asa Palmer, Sanford Riley, Marion
Riley, Amos Robinson, James C. Stewart, James Smith, Daniel
Smith, Joshua W. Sheek, William Summers, Green W. Shrake,
Samuel Scott, William A. Stites, Rufus Stites, P. T. Sapping-
ton, Middleton Story, William Snook, Thomas Toal, Henry
Trustey, William Trustey, Granville Tippey, Ezra Tippey,
William R. Thomas, George Walters, Andrew J. Walters,
James P. Wishart, Stephen Wood, Smith Williams, John Wil-
liams, John Whisner, Samuel Whisner, Robert Whisner.

Among the many notable characters thrown together by
the fortunes of war was George Meyers, so long a well-known

citizen after the war. He was with Leasure in the Second Kansas cavalry. He had had an exciting career previous to coming here. Born in Baden, Germany, he had gone to Switzerland to escape military service. From there he went to Paris and went into the French army for the campaign in Algiers. But he did not like French campaigning, and escaped to the United States, and from New Orleans went to Cincinnati, Ohio, and from there here. He was a brave, popular soldier, and now gets his mail at his birthplace in the Fatherland, his address being 121 Brennenstrasse, Bondorf, Baden, Germany.

Elizabeth Creager, whose maiden name was Elizabeth Mills, was born in Hesse Castle, Germany, on the first day of December, 1804. At the age of thirteen she came to America and settled near Frederickstown, Maryland. Near this place on the first day of November, 1829, she was married to William Creager. With her husband and three children she traveled from the state of Maryland to Ohio by wagon where in the midst of the forest of that new country they made for themselves a home. To this couple eight children were born, two of whom died in infancy. At an early age she was left a widow and in the fall of 1854 with her remaining six children she moved to Montezuma, Iowa. In the spring of 1855 she removed to Brooklin, Linn County, Kansas Territory being just opened for settlement. The next six years of her life were spent amidst the turbulent scenes of border warfare which preceded the great War of the Rebellion in 1861 and when war came in earnest she sent four sons to defend the flag. Three sons—George W. Creager, F. A. Creager, and John W. Creager became members of the Seventh Kansas Cavalry and T. C. Creager a member of Company K Sixth Kansas State Militia. One son, John W., lost his life in that deadly conflict, and the other three lived to a good age here. Two other children survived her, Mrs. Z. W. Leasure of this county, and Curtis Creager of Fulton, Indiana. See frequent references to the Creagers in the index.

"Uncle" David Reece and his good wife Mary deserve a place in the affections of Linn County but you can not fully appreciate them until you know the story of Pleasant Venable, an Ohio man who had gone down near Galveston, Texas, where it was hoped the mild climate would benefit his wife's health. But she sickened and died in 1839, leaving him with two girl babies, the oldest only thirteen months old and the youngest only nine days old. Mr. Venable placed his two babies with families who cared for them till Sarah Ann was four years old and Mary Ann three years old, when he started back with his children to go to his people in Ohio. They were on horseback, one faithful horse carrying all three of this pathetic little pilgrimage. When they got as far as Fayetteville in Washington county, Arkansas, he ran out of money and stopped to seek work and was offered employment by George Webber who was running a tannery there. Venable worked one day and became sick and lapsed into unconsciousness from which he never recovered. He left no information whatever about himself and children except that his name was Pleasant Venable on his way to Ohio. The court appointed George Webber to be guardian to the children and after a month he got a farmer blacksmith named David Reece and his wife Mary Reece to take them by "bounding them," a form of adoption by which children were bound to serve their foster parents. This was in about 1844. They lived at Fayetteville till 1855 when the two Venable girls were about sixteen years old. In the meantime these two good Reeces had adopted six other orphan children, so that they had nine when they arrived at Sugar Mound in 1855 and set up their home on the north end of the Mound where "Uncle Dave" was a blacksmith and good citizen till his death. All the children were educated and sent out into the world to be good citizens. It should be stated Mrs. Reece's maiden name was Randleman and she was of German stock. It was at this Sugar Mound home that Sarah Ann Venable was married to Frank Gray in 1862. Her sister Mary Ann Venable was married shortly after arriving here to Rev. Thomas Jordan, a Methodist preacher at Lawrence. She died about ten months later leaving a baby girl who was cared for by Frank Gray and his wife. John Smith, an orphan boy only twelve years old had been forced by his uncle with whom he lived to sleep with a negro slave. The boy and negro were good friends but the boy was too spirited to sleep with a slave so when he learned the Reeces and their children were going away John hid in the brush along the trail in Benton county, Arkansas, and gave "Uncle Dave" another son. Mrs. Gray here began to mother other people's children by taking into her home Susie Maupin, a three-year old child whom she raised and sent to Kansas University, where she married Guy Drummond and now lives at Springfield, Missouri, and has five children of her own. Mr. Drummond is an electrician. All this time Mrs. Gray belonged to the Methodist Church and did her full part. On January 2, 1898, Oliver Marcellus Gray was married to Cora M. Henderson, daughter of Robert L. Henderson, who had made her home with her aunt Elizabeth Wheeler two miles west of Pleasanton. The children of O. M. Gray are Frank who married Leona Park at Pleasanton and now lives on the old homestead, and a pair of twin girls named Rella and Della still in their "early teens." Oliver M. Gray is now serving his second term as county clerk. But to get back to "Uncle David" Reece. When the Clark raid came through in 1856 they captured him and took him to Westport, Missouri. At some opportunity he gave a Masonic sign and some one aided him and he was soon on his way back to Sugar Mound. Then he and his wife made a trip to Fayetteville, Arkansas, where they collected nine hundred dollars due them and Mrs. Reece carried that weight in silver and gold in a belt at her waist and almost loathed metal money by the time they arrived back at Sugar Mound. "Uncle Dave" died during the Civil War, mourned by all who knew him.

Franklin Gray was born in Madison county, Indiana, November 18, 1837. His parents, Enoc and Mary Gray, were Quakers. He remained at home and assisted his father and brothers on the farm, attending school during the winter months, until 1859, when he and his brother Dennis Gray came to Linn County, travelling in a prairie schooner. He took a claim on one hundred and sixty acres of land about five miles southeast of Sugar Mound. Shortly after his marriage to Sarah Ann Venable July 7, 1862, as stated above, he enlisted in Compank K, Twelfth Kansas Volunteers, at Mound City serving as corporal of the company until the end of the war. He was mustered out with the regiment at Little Rock, Arkansas, April 1865, but received his discharge at Leavenworth a short time after. During the time of the army service he was in the battle of Jenkins Ferry, Arkansas. His wife lived at the home of David and Mary Reece and during the battle of Mine Creek she was at the home of her foster brother John Smith a few miles southeast of Mound City on the west line of the retreating rebel army, where she got many a thrill out of the event. At the close of the Civil War Frank Gray returned to Mound City, he and his wife and Mary Reece, now a widow, settled on his claim in the northwest corner of Sheridan township. Mary Reece passing to the beyond in a year or two. On this farm which is the Gray homestead their children were born. Mary died in infancy, Ercenis C. died at the age of eight years, and Oliver Marcellus was born August 1, 1869. Frank Gray was elected sheriff of Linn county serving from January 1888 to January 1890. The farm was their home with the above exception until his death November 28, 1921. He was a member of the Methodist Church for over sixty years and a member of the I. O. O. F. lodge for thirty-seven years.

Charles William Kingsbury came to Linn County with his mother and brother David Oaerin, with Amos Durbin, his mother's father, who was from Maryland to Kentucky, Illinois, Indiana, to Linn County, Kansas. Mr. Durbin was of English and Scotch parentage; his first wife was Nancy Forsythe and the second Margaret Featheringill. The daughter Casandra Durbin married Edwin Kingsbury who went to California and died there. The boy David Oaerin went to his father in California and remained there. Charles W. married Delia Walden; Mattie J. married L. W. Wickham; Margaret married Theodore T. Shannon; Waste C. married Olive Wiggins. The Amos Durbin home was on what is now called the Ellington road. The J. B. Broadhead farm on the road just west of Mound City has a substantial brick house said to have been built prior to 1861 on his arrival here from Busti, New York.

A well known family was that of Thornton Fisher who came here from Lebanon county, Pennsylvania, in 1857 and bought a claim and lived with his sister, Mrs. Samuel Gore. He served out an enlistment in a Kansas regiment and went back to Pennsylvania and reenlisted in a regiment from that state. In 1867 having married Jane Elizabeth Brownfield of Uniontown, Pennsylvania, he brought his family here and occupied his land which is still known as the Fisher farm out southwest of Mound City. The children were William B. Fisher who married Jessie McIlvaine and still live in Pleasanton; Sarah Jane married O. E. Herman and now lives in Prescott; Isaac T. married Ada Perry, now of Harrisburg, Arkansas.

E. M. Gentle and wife came to Mound City in 1870 from Hancock county, Illinois. Their children were Charles now in Oklahoma; J. Adolphus now in Pleasanton; Alberta now in Oklahoma; E. George now on a farm near Prescott; Harry in San Francisco; Lana Avada now Mrs. H. M. Savage in Kansas City.

Among the observing and influential people of the early period were the family of Joshua Wilson Sheek and his wife Lucinda Gross Sheek.[1] They had a large family of children— Catherine, James Benjamin, Martha, Christian Riley, Malinda, Mary Ann, Jesse Lee, and Lloyd—who by force of character and by marriage among the neighboring families became quite conspicuous in the settlements. The parents were from North Carolina, where nearly all the children were born. James Benjamin Sheek is now living near where the family located forty years ago. He was born near Doylstown, North Carolina, February 28, 1836, and accompanied the family in their migration west in 1850, stopping in Iowa till November, 1855, when they came to Brooklin, Linn County. He probably saw as much of the inner life of the proslavery people as any of his time having free-state principles. He was only twenty years of age, and after the manner of the times worked at whatever offered, which happened to be general farm work for James and David Fleming, brothers of Skillman Fleming, the leader of the proslavery element and the commander of the proslavery militia. (And parenthetically it should be ex-

1. This story of the Sheek family was written by Mr. Mitchell in 1895.

plained that among the proslavery people the militia and every mob and gathering of the proslavery forces was designated a "posse.") Living among them as Sheek did, eating and sleeping with them, he became familiar with their character and learned many of their secrets. In 1856 the Sheeks were notified by a member of one of the worst bands of marauders in the country that they were in danger. They believed their informant, one Bill Royal, as they had formerly known him in North Carolina; and the Sheeks, Leasures, Creagers, and Sibbets went over into Missouri and for nine weeks camped on Mormon Fork, nine miles northeast of West Point. It turned out they were correctly informed, as the notorious Clarke came down through Linn County from the northeast with 400 raiders that were ruffians in the worst sense of the word, and from Trading Post to Mound City killed and destroyed people and property. The horrible outrages committed by these licentious freebooters were so terrible that old men who knew of them will now only talk of them in a confidential way—too villainous and obscene to be even recorded in history. It was during this raid that Samuel Nichols was burned out, and from Brooklin Hill men counted a half dozen houses burning at one time in as many different directions. At Brooklin two women stayed and braved the threatened danger—heroic Mrs. Creager and Mrs. James Mooney.

One of the interesting incidents of the Clarke raid was the capture of Wash Gowing, Sr., father of Wash Gowing, of La Cygne. The posse compelled him to hitch up his team and accompany them to haul their plunder. Houses were plundered of everything portable, which was put into Gowing's wagon, and then the house was burned. He obeyed at the muzzle of a rifle till the posse reached Linnville, where the frenzied mob surrounded the house of a free-state man and committed outrages that were worse than any ever recorded against savage Indians. There was a young man in the house sick, with his father, mother and sister attending him. Entering the house they emptied the different bottles of medicine into one mass and forced it down the sick man's throat, and as the father protested beat him into insensibility with a rifle barrel. The crimes that followed are too foul for record. Old man Gowing witnessed them, and climbing into his wagon he threw all the plunder out on the ground, and with a hatchet to defend himself, denounced the fiends and told them he would die before he would obey their orders further, and drove away unmolested. On his way home he met Sheek and told him the details of the affair.

Mr. Sheek was a close friend of Pat Devlin, the originator of the famous "Jayhawker" patronymic, and had several adventures with him. At the time the posse were raiding through the north part of the county, which resulted in the battle of Middle Creek in Liberty township, Mr. Sheek, Pat

Devlin and William Trovinger were visiting at the house of an acquaintance on the creek. The family and visitors were having a pleasant social evening, when they were suddenly surprised at finding the place surrounded by about 200 boisterous, cursing horsemen. Sheek and Devlin were persuaded to climb quickly up into a little space between the ceiling and the roof and Trovinger and the other men disappeared somewhere. When the posse asked for the men the ladies told them they had had warning and had gone for help. It was not far from John Brown's headquarters, and evidently the raiders thought it best not to molest the women, and they passed on west, meeting a body of free-state men, who gave battle to them, and they were soon scampering back to Missouri, telling exaggerated stories of meeting thousands of abolitionists with cannon, etc. After the war one of this posse told Sheek that had he and Devlin been found they would have been killed.

Every little settlement had its posse, and one method of intimidation was to enforce free-state men to do service in them. The Paris posse was particularly active in insisting that free-state men should take up arms against their own neighbors in what was supposed to be a time of peace. Sheek was for awhile staying at Mrs. Mooney's boarding house in Brooklin, waiting upon a sick man. He was repeatedly notified that he was expected to do service in the Paris posse, and at one time they came and served notice on him that trouble would result if he were not there at the next meeting time. Through Mrs. Mooney's intercession he was allowed to stay with the sick man, and not doubt escaped violence.

In May 1858 Mr. Sheek was sent by his employers to accompany Ford Lamb in driving the cattle of Skillman Fleming to Pleasant Hill, Missouri, as the free-state people were getting numerous enough to make him uncomfortable. They stopped May 18 at West Point, Missouri, then quite a good-sized town, and through curiosity visited the camp of the "posse" of several hundred self-appointed guardians of slavery, and ate dinner with some proslavery men who had formerly lived at Brooklin but had now joined the guerillas. At a little past midday their leader, Charles A. Hamelton, addressed the mob, saying there was "an expedition going south in the valley and that he wanted no man to go with it who would not obey orders—that there were some devils down there that must be attended to." The next morning, May 19, the "posse" had disappeared, and Sheek went on to Pleasant Hill, and Hamelton and his ruffians had "attended to" eleven men at Trading Post by committing the Marais des Cygnes massacre. A few days afterward "Uncle Billy" Long, of Brooklin, went to Pleasant Hill and told his relatives, who were proslavery people, of the horrible massacre, saying he had seen the victims and knew all the circumstances yet Mr.

Sheek says the Missouri people were incredulous, and would not believe that such a terrible state of affairs existed in Kansas.

In 1859 Mr. Sheek returned to Brooklin, and for a while followed carpentering. James Parent, a man named Boyd, and Sheek built that summer the big square house still standing on R. B. Mitchell's farm at Mansfield. Mr. Sheek remembers that it was necessary for them to carry a rifle on their way to and from work. He remembers that James Parent, who was thought to be a mild proslavery man, but not offensively so, had to assert his independence, and he did it in no uncertain way as he trudged along with a rifle attending to his own business.

Sheek belonged to the organization of "minute men" that were called upon at all times to repel invaders. In 1862 he enlisted in Company I, Second Kansas cavalry, and served three years, being with the regiment in all its engagements. At Dardanelles, Arkansas, he was shot through the left thigh and laid up four months. He had quite a number of rough experiences, one ball nearly scalping him, and at Prairie Grove his horse fell on him and crushed his chest badly, but he kept right along with the army till mustered out at the close of the war.

Mr. Sheek remembers that Sam Gwynne, living at Linnville, heard the firing between Price and Pleasanton at Trading Post, and started to the front, he having been a soldier in the Sixth Kansas. The rebels killed him and stripped him of his clothing on the ridge northwest of Pleasanton.

In collecting memoranda for these articles there has been found a very high regard for the Gowing family, who came here in 1855. The head of the family was George Washington Gowing, who had been born and raised in Kentucky, and not opposed to slavery, though he took no part in helping to establish it in Kansas. The family consisted of himself and wife and five sons—George W., Jr., Pleasant, Lafayette, Drury, and Thomas. Lafayette became a soldier in Company L, Sixth Kansas cavalry, and was killed in action April 5, 1864, at Stone's Farm, Arkansas. Wash, the younger, still lives in La Cygne, and Thomas recently moved to Missouri.

On coming west the family lived for a while in Cass county, Missouri, and then decided to come to Kansas, and as they were traveling in wagons, Wash, the son, came on in advance to find some old neighbors who had settled here, among them Skillman Fleming.

October 5, 1855,[1] Wash crossed at the ford where the fair grounds at La Cygne are now located, and continued west till he found Brooklin, when he returned to pilot his people. At that time all that is now Lincoln township, and to a line

1. This was the very day that Old John Brown arrived at the home of his boys on the Pottawatomie where the village of Lane now stands.

north and south along the John Calvin farm three miles west in Scott township, was an Indian reservation held by the Miamis and Pottawatomies.[2]   The Miamis were wearing citizens clothing, but the Pottawatomies were still in blankets. Wash says that none of them were troublesome. The Miamis nearly all lived in houses of some kind, but the Pottawatomies traveled around in bands.   A favorite place for making a temporary village was in the draw northwest of the present Russum farm in Scott township. Under this condition of things very few white men settled in what is now Lincoln township.   Quite a number of squatters and men who had married Indian women were, however, scattered about. Where La Cygne now stands was wild land.

When the Gowings located at Brooklin they were among old acquaintances and as the family had originally come from the slave state of Kentucky they were received as an accession to the proslavery forces.   In the condition of society then, they did not find it convenient to assert that they had come to make homes and wanted no politics, so they went along their way and trusted to luck to avoid trouble.   Young Wash was not regarded with favor by old Skillman, and was frequently asked to declare himself, but he would only say that he had come to get a home and wanted no part in politics. This made it peculiarly uncongenial for him, and, after he had taken his wife and located a farm on the ridge north of Brooklin, he would sleep out in some friendly straw stack or fence corner. Neutrality then seemed impossible.   He was distrusted among his father's friends and unknown to the other side, and he felt uncomfortable, but as all he had was there he stayed.

One night he ventured to stay within his house, and had a peaceful night till daybreak, when the sound of horsemen was heard. He was called and ordered to come out, with which he complied, expecting trouble. There were fifteen mounted men at his door, whom he recognized at once as free-state men, who had evidently been out all night. They asked for feed for themselves and horses. He replied that he did not want to give it to them, as it would give him the reputation of harboring them and get him into trouble. He was assured that his principles were well known to them, and that they would see no trouble came to him and then dismounted. Mrs. Gowing got breakfast for them with much misgiving as to what the result would be when the proslavery people heard of it. But beyond severe criticism they were never disturbed, as by that time the free-state men were beginning to get control and they did not forget to protect Wash.

2.   The Pottawatomies relinquished their lands in what is now Linn County in 1846, and in 1848 moved to their reservation on the Kansas river. The bands mentioned were probably visiting Pottawatomies. Indians have a custom of visiting their old homes, going back in large numbers and taking with them all their belongings, and their visits may be of some duration.

Once in 1856 when there were rumors of an invasion by marauders, they all went over into Missouri to camp until the trouble should blow over. At West Point, Missouri, they saw a big camp of men living in a half-military style but without any authority other than assumed. Old man Clarke was in command of it. Clarke tried to take a team from the elder Gowing and the old man said they could not have it, that he would not part with it. They then took possession of horses and man, and the next morning the four hundred ruffians of Clarke started to raid through Linn County, and took Gowing with them to haul their plunder.

There was also a young man named Smith, a son of Elisha Smith, of Twin Springs, impressed into their service, and when at Linnville Mr. Gowing took a hatchet and defied the mob, he also released young Smith from their bondage.

Young Wash came back to look after his property here, and on returning to the camp in Missouri was intercepted by Clarke's sentinels and arrested. They endeavored to take his horse, but he stood them off, and all through the night held his horse's rein while he palavered with the guard, and at daylight some of his old acquaintances got him out of the scrape.

At the time of the Price raid Wash was serving in Captain Leasure's company in the Sixth Kansas militia, and was with it at the battles of Big Blue and Hickman's Mills. When the federal army followed the rebels into Kansas near West Point it was about dark. All the soldiers were tired out. During a halt by the roadside General Pleasanton drove up in a wagon drawn by four gray mules, and there was soon an orderly inquiring for a man who knew the Trading Post country. Some one spoke of Wash Gowing, and he was ordered to report to General Pleasanton, which he did. The general questioned him as to his knowledge of the country, and then called his staff around him and told Wash to go back to his company, where he stretched out on the ground and was soon fast asleep. Very soon four officers from Pleasanton's staff, among them Gen. Charles W. Blair, of Leavenworth, came and called for him, and they started for a scout along the enemy's front.

All night they rode over the prairie looking for the rebel outposts. They found that they began at the mound at the Post and extended east. Just at daylight they found themselves right among a party of rebels, and were ordered to surrender, but instead all scampered away, the officers leaving Wash alone on the prairie, which was beginning to be covered with moving troops. He was separated from his command. For two days and nights he had been going all the time. The cannonading had begun at daylight and the rebels were scattered every way. As he was exhausted and separated from his company, he went to his home five miles west for food and rest, and was asleep from complete exhaustion when the battle of Mine Creek was on.

His father-in-law, H. R. Webb, a strong Union man, started at daylight from Brooklin for Trading Post, but before he got there both armies had passed, and in the camps of the rebels most of the food prepared for breakfast had been left untouched. The mill had been run all night grinding corn, and several wagons loaded with meal had been upset and abandoned.

Subsequently, the Gowings all took up lands where La Cygne now stands, and may truly be regarded as among the first families. At the time the town was located Wash, Jr., owned the quarter cornering where the public well on Market street now stands, and his father owned the farm on the east, now the property of David H. Jones.

In 1856 General Clark of Georgia fame marched his army of border ruffians through Linn County.[1] There was but little here for them to destroy at that time but that little they effectually disposed of. Such free state men as they were able to capture they took with them and sent under guard to Westport, Missouri. Many of them never returned. Murder and disease relieved both captured and captor. The more fortunate anti-slavery settler upon the approach of the invading army escaped through the brush, leaving his family to the tender mercy of men whose mission it was to drive away all opposition to making of Kansas Territory a slave state. General Clark assured all that he came in contact with "that there was room in the territory for but one party, and that was the pro-slavery party and all not in sympathy with making of Kansas territory a slave state had to get out, and that within an hour." James Montgomery was one of those who escaped, though vigorously pursued. In the spring of 1857 northern men and women fairly swarmed into the eastern counties of the Territory. In the fall of that year the border ruffians again took the field, for one more effort to intimidate the peaceful settlers and make them subservient to the pro-slavery desire. Among other atrocities committed at that time "old man" Denton, a prominent free state settler on the Osage river in Bourbon county, was called to his cabin door in the night time and without a word his frail old body was riddled with buckshot. This band of murderers came from Fort Scott under command of one afterwards known along the border as "Fort Scott Brockett." The only object of his murder was to strike terror into the hearts of the many free state settlers along the Osage river; and throughout the northern part of Bourbon county and the southern part of Linn. If such was the purpose it certainly failed of its accomplishment, for on the other

The story of the "Clark Raid" in 1856 was thus told by Ed. R. Smith in a letter to the Mail and Breeze of May 21, 1897.

hand it aroused the entire eastern part of the Territory to immediate and vigorous action.

General Lane at once assembled an army of between three hundred and four hundred men and marched into this county, establishing his headquarters in the timber some two miles west of Mound City, and there awaited developments. This display of free state force was sufficient to quell further murdering forays for that immediate time, but as soon as the force under Lane disbanded and marched away "troubles", as they then were termed, broke out afresh. Then it was that the afterward noted "Jayhawker Chief," James Montgomery, took the field in defense of the lives and homes of himself and neighboring settlers. He readily gathered to his standard from fifteen to fifty fearless characters, as the emergency might require, and proceeded to reenact the tactics of proslavery leaders that had operated in Kansas. He called upon every pronounced leader of proslavery ideas in this county and along the Osage river in Bourbon county and politely informed them "there was not sufficient room in the Territory for two parties, and inasmuch as the precedent had been established by their proslavery friends when in the majority, that the majority should rule, conditions now being changed and the shoe being on the other foot, he felt himself called upon and justified in calling upon them, and all who sympathized with them, regarding the future state of the Territory, to forthwith gather their traps and effects and at once emigrate to more congenial environments." Captain Montgomery had an exceedingly persuasive way and seldom had any difficulty in persuading his victims of his entire sincerity and terrible earnestness, and consequently at the several places of his calling there was weeping and wailing, but a continual hustle was on to promptly obey the dreaded Jayhawker's summons. They all went.

At and around the Trading Post on the Marais des Cygnes river in this county were settled a number of bitter proslavery, abolition hating fire eaters, chief of which was one Charles A. Hamelton, who had and occupied a "claim" just across the line in Kansas. In the spring of 1858 there was in successful operation at the Post a regular old fashioned "doggery". This place became a rendezvous for a gang of desperate characters both in the Territory and across the line, only some four miles away. This man Hamelton was the acknowledged leader of the Trading Post contingent of the proslavery element in Linn County. Hamelton had often declared his intentions toward Montgomery and his offending band of Jayhawkers, of which Captain Montgomery was fully advised.

One fine day at this time Montgomery at the head of a small squad of men quietly rode into the midst of the dozen houses or more that then constituted the Trading Post and without ceremony proceeded to clean out the proslavery headquarters by emptying the contents of the several barrels of sod-corn whisky then on hand into the highway, at the same time leaving a general notice to proslavery people to quit the Territory. This last act of alleged vandalism on the part of the Jayhawkers "broke the camel's back" and Hamelton and some of his neighbors repaired at once to the friendly hospitality of congenial Missouri.

Montgomery's work was done, and well done. Not a drop of human blood had been shed, not a dollar's worth of personal property had been taken from the evicted proslavery people. They were bid to go in peace—but to go. No burned cabins and houseless women and children with murdered or captured husbands and fathers were in his rear, as were they in the rear of the proslavery army under Clark and others. The peace and quiet of the Territory demanded heroic treatment. For the first time the free state settler felt himself secure. For the first time for months did men feel themselves safe without being heavily armed. How little they dreamed of the bloody day so soon to dawn.

Very few in this generation are students of the slave situation in the earlier stages of its development and its final explosion into one of the greatest tragedies in the history of the world. It made its first appearance in America in the year 1621. A group of black people were brought from the jungles of Africa, carried across the Atlantic in the slow sailing ships of that day, requiring three months or more to make the trip, during which time these poor wretches were confined in cages or locked up in the dark holds of the small ship without light and with not enough air and wholesome water in the hot climate of the equator. These poor things suffered indescribable anguish in their ignorance and savage superstition. They must have lost what little reasoning power they had and became raving maniacs on those seemingly endless days of sailing on and on. In times of storm they became maniacal in their mental stress. Only twenty of their number survived when the Dutch ship arrived at Jamestown, Virginia, in 1621. The black people were offered for sale just as so many swine were sold. There were two distinct classes among the white people of that time—the Cavaliers or overlords, who had powers conferred on them by the crown and who lived in comparative luxury and wore dainty rich clothing. The other class was the uneducated pioneer men and women who were out endeavoring to subdue the wilderness and make homes for themselves and drifting farther and farther away from the advantages and refinement of such educational schooling as were possible where settlements had been firmly established. It was this rich class of people who could see the possible advantages of "owning" the black people whom they could use as servants. It took a whole generation of time to develop and train these poor dumb creatures so that they became faithful and subservient. From Jamestown the practice of slavery spread through all the American colonies. Even New England became an open market for shipments of young black people from Africa. But the institution did not thrive in the cold New England climate. There were no large plantations on which they could be used to advantage in farm labor and the free white mechanics refused to teach them to be blacksmiths, wagon makers, carpenters, ship builders, weavers and such trades as would bring them into immediate competition with themselves. In the southern colonies the natural trend of events provided a strong foothold for the institution of slavery. A world-wide commerce was built up on cotton and sugar and the mild climate made it possible to use the black people profitably and to feed and maintain them cheaply in comparative comfort.

In utter subjection, the blacks became reconciled to their fate and were as docile and faithful as dumb brutes. With the markets of the world open to and anxious for the products of their labor, the system of black slavery fastened its clutches on American civilization. Eager to build up their estates rich planters kept the price so high there was no chance for the middle class to obtain slaves and get into competition with them. We had an American feudalism equal to the palmy days of King John. The riches thus produced brought on clashes with the mother country which wanted to get a part of that wealth through a system of taxes on their commerce. When the Revolution came on slavery was a bone of contention too dangerous for the colonists to talk about. The statesmen of the period could see that to succeed in their efforts to establish a new and "free" government on earth there must be no internal dissensions. Even when they had arrived at the crucial moment of declaring to the world their independence as a nation there were many men who could plainly see the inconsistency of the wording of that marvelous document we revere as the Declaration of Independence with the situation as it then existed. John Rutledge of South Carolina hesitated to sign, urging that some provision be made for the gradual elimination of the slavery institution before it should become a source of national trouble. But eager to accomplish the main purpose of national independence the negro question was put aside, the United States of America became a great separate nation and started on its way down the thorn-strewn path of history. The rich people of the south were like spoiled children and were getting entirely out of the control of the moral code. The more slaves they had the more wealth they had in such form as to put on the block and sell for big and quick money. The breeding and increase of slaves was scientifically studied and practiced. Lust became a method and many black women were mistresses to their masters and

the children that resulted took the status of the mother and
were slaves. It is to the credit of the white women of the
south that in no instance were they accused of bringing yellow
babies into the world, yet it is a fact that they knew they
were sharing their beloved husbands with a bond black woman
whose children came into her household as servants to their
half-brothers and half-sisters. They represented so much
property, so much money—and money measured manhood
very much as it does in the later years. Yet many of these
high-bred southern women sustained this situation and in the
awful struggle of the Civil War they were veritable hell cats
in its defense. Only one out of five white men in the south
were slave owners yet they attained to an amazing domina-
tion over the other four-fifths of the white men whom they
coerced and led into rebellion against their government.
Really, by a free, fair vote of the southern people uninfluenced
by the slave owning class there would have been no civil war.
But it all came to a climax and for five weary years it seemed
that the pivot on which they were to turn or overturn world
affairs was in Linn County, Kansas.

On October 5, 1855, John Brown and his young son Oliver
(then eighteen years old) and Henry Thompson (his son-in-
law) arrived at a point two miles west of where the town of
Lane now stands. At this place five of the sons of John
Brown (John, Jr., Jason, Owen, Salmon, and Frederick) had
established themselves early in 1855 on the public land with
the intention of making their homes there and developing
farm properties. They came here directly from Ohio but
most of their previous lives had been spent at North Elba
in the Adirondack mountains in Essex county, New York,
where with scant soil and the place so isolated from markets
not much progress could be made in accumulating property.
They had left their father and mother and younger brothers
and sisters in charge of a charitable enterprise whose mission
was to receive and educate black men and women who had
been given their freedom by their masters in the south who
intended to do them a kindness but put upon them terrible
handicaps. Under the black laws "freedmen" were not permitted to live in a slave country and if so found they were
put on the block and sold back into bondage to the highest
bidder. Young black men and women were taught to read and
write and qualified to become house servants and laborers and
sent back into the world to take care of themselves. Thus
John Brown was doing missionary work as much as if he were
in the jungles of Africa but there was not enough opportunity
for his numerous sons and they planned to set up for themselves in the new country in Kansas. John Brown, jr., was
married, his four brothers single. An uncle, Rev. Thomas
Adair, had already gone on and they visited at his home and

went on some eight miles and started their settlement. It was an attractive spot. Soon they began plowing and decomposition of the rank vegetation turned under by the plow produced malaria and they were soon all down with "fever and ague", a very debilitating sickness. While in this discouraging state they were called upon by self-appointed authorities and told that they were regarded as free-state men, opposed to making Kansas a slave state, that they were not welcome in the neighborhood and were notified to leave. Among these unfriendly visitors were the Shermans and the Doyles. It was a peculiarity of these proslavers that they always located at fords on the creeks where they had opportunities to observe newcomers and use their intimidating methods on such as proved to be free state people. In the case of the Brown boys they repeated their threats frequently, stole and ran off high bred Devon cattle and horses they had brought from the east, and had gotten down to such dirty tricks as burning their hay stacks and finally were "zipping" rifle bullets so near to them as to suggest their lives were in danger. These young Browns had only shotguns for securing prairie chickens and turkeys and ducks and geese to supplement their food supply. They had no knowledge of the use of rifles and were above any thought of taking human life. They wrote and told their father that if they stayed in Kansas it would be necessary for them to have equipment with which to protect themselves. The father started at once for their relief, going to Chicago where he bought a one-horse wagon and an animal to haul it. That wagon was described as heavily loaded and beside it strode the father and the two boys. They left Chicago in August and arrived October 5, making the whole distance of about six hundred miles in about six or seven weeks.

The new arrivals set vigorously to work to make the place comfortable for the winter. Contact with the proslavers was inevitable and they were soon notified, true to form. But the older man simply listened and talked little. There were a few with whom he could talk unreservedly, among them James Hanway, subsequently well known as Judge Hanway. Violence became more frequent. Atchison, president of the senate of the United States, was riding the prairies at the head of a thousand cutthroats—robbing, murdering, burning. Brown and his neighbors were called to Lawrence to defend that city against this invasion from Missouri. The necessity for organization became so apparent that all the men were assembled and organized into a company of riflemen called the Pottawatomie Rifles. There were fourteen settlers and four of John Brown's sons in this organization and they elected the senior Brown to be captain, his first military title. In this company was a boy eighteen years old named Allen Jaqua, a cousin of the author of this book, and from whom much of this information was obtained, a statement from whom is given elsewhere.

In May of 1856 they were again summoned to the defense of Lawrence but were intercepted about half way with the news that Lawrence had been sacked and burned. Soon messengers came from their home neighborhood saying their women had been threatened by the most vicious of the proslavery men. "We are expecting every free-state settler in our region to be butchered", one man told John Brown. A beautiful young woman named Mary Grant only a few days before had told Brown this story: "Dutch Bill arrived at our home horribly drunk, with a whisky bottle with a corn-cob stopper and an immense butcher knife in his belt. Mr. Grant, my father was sick in bed but when they told him that Bill Sherman was coming he had a shotgun put by his side. 'Old woman', said the ruffian to my mother, 'you and I are pretty good friends, but damn your daughter—I'll drink her heart's blood.' My little brother Charley succeeded in cajoling the drunken man away."

The proslavers hanged a settler named Manace with his two little boys begging and pleading for him, and finally turned him loose in the brush where he wandered around and finally died from injury and fright. This was in May, 1856, and the balance of this story is so well told by the late Samuel J. Shively of Paola in an address before the Kansas State Historical Society at a meeting December 1, 1903, I am including it all here, adding at the end another version of the story I heard from Allan Jaqua. The following is Shively's story:

"The occurrence of the night of May 24, 1856, near Dutch Henry Crossing on Pottawatomie creek in Franklin county, at which time five men were killed, would only have been such a sensation as ordinary murders create had it been in any ordinary time; but it was in the midst of a civil war, in a new territory, over a great moral issue, and so it became one of the incidents of that war, and the bearing it produced on the result of the issue to be settled decides its importance. I will call it a massacre for convenience, and for the benefit of the sensitive. This affair was the most important in the slave troubles of Kansas. If right, it was important, as it changed the attitude of the free-state party toward their assailants, and had much to do in the overthrow of the slave power; if wrong, it was important as being the cause of the riot and bloodshed that followed.

"Five sons of John Brown of North Elba, New York, John, jr., Jason, Owen, Salmon, and Frederick, came to Kansas, and settled on the north side of the Pottawatomie, about two miles southwest of where the town of Lane now is. Three of the boys took claims. They unloaded their goods on their

claims February 12, 1855. A man by the name of Winans
kept a store then on what is now the B. Needham farm. He
generally hauled out household goods for the settlers there
from Westport Landing. He hauled out some goods for the
Brown boys. The proslavery settlers soon learned that the
Brown boys were abolitionists, and John, jr., was especially
hated as he was more outspoken and rather the leader of the
family. At that time it made anti-slavery men about as mad
to be called abolitionists as it did proslavery men. The Brown
boys never denied being abolitionists, but took pride in the
term. Allen Wilkinson came from Tennessee and first located
at Osawatomie in the fall of 1854. The next March, 1855,
he took a claim between the Pottawatomie and Mosquito
creeks, near the mouth of the Mosquito, in the east edge of
Franklin county.

"James P. Doyle took a claim north of Wilkinson and a
little west, on the north side of the Mosquito, about a mile
from Wilkinson's. Henry Sherman with his brother William,
two German bachelors, settled on an old abandoned Indian
farm, partially improved, known as the John Jones place.
The Wilkinson place is now known as the John Powell place.
The Sherman place is now known as the James Walter place.
The Sherman place was on the south side of the Pottawatomie
and now adjoins on the east the Lane town site. Henry
Sherman was called "Dutch Henry" and the ford across the
Pottawatomie on his place went by the name of Dutch Henry
Crossing. Sherman and Doyle came out in the fall of 1854.

"The election in 1855 was held March 30 and that election
district had been designated by Governor Reeder as the fifth
and the voting-place was at Henry Sherman's, as he had the
best house in the country. The election district extended from
the Missouri line to the Neosho east and west, and north and
south from the Big Osage to the Little Osage. The Big Osage
was the Marais des Cygnes. Wilkinson kept the post-office
and was not a violent, but a smooth, clever leader. Sherman
was not very outspoken, but was sly and unreliable. Doyle
was an ignorant fellow and quite radical. None of these men
owned slaves. The poor whites who upheld slavery were more
unreasonable and intolerant than the slave-owners. Wilkinson
at first claimed he was not for making Kansas a slave state,
but they nominated him for the legislature in order to "fetch
him over." He became a very subservient tool of Atchison
and Stringfellow. Wilkinson, Samuel Scott, Henry Younger
and W. A. Heiskell were the proslavery candidates for the
legislature in that district. Had there been an honest election
they would all have been defeated.

"A noisy drunken mob came from Missouri on horseback
and offered to vote. William Chestnut, one of the judges of
the election, challenged them on the ground of non-residence.
The mob began to threaten violence, when Colonel Coffey got

up and made a speech in which he said he did not favor violence but if officers did not do their duty it would lead to violence. What he meant by duty was for Mr. Chestnut to cease his challenges. Wilkinson applauded the speech and illegal voting went on. After this Wilkinson lost the respect of all the free-state men. Mr. Chestnut had in many ways befriended him but Wilkinson was accused of selling out to the slave power after that election. After Coffey's speech the free-state men left the polls. Several young men had been posted at Mosquito creek to turn back the free-state men. Among the number were the Doyle boys who turned back Uncle Sam Houser who had walked all the way from Stanton to vote.

"Wilkinson and Sherman entertained and fed the men and the horses of the men who had come from Missouri to vote at Sherman's. Mr. Chestnut refused to certify to the returns but the proslavery candidates took their places in the legislature notwithstanding they had not a sign of a certificate or line of written authority. Mr. Wilkinson's associates in that body all but one met violent deaths in after years. Scott was killed. Younger was killed during the war. Henry Younger never did reside in Kansas but was a resident of Cass county, Missouri. He was the father of the noted Younger outlaws. Younger was a bosom friend of Wilkinson while at Shawnee Mission.

"Between the Pottawatomie and Mosquito creeks was a proslavery settlement. Just north of this, between the Mosquito and the Marais des Cygnes, was a free-state settlement, and just south of the Pottawatomie was a mixed complexion of politics. The Browns lived right in the hotbed of the proslavery nest. Some free-state men have thought that Wilkinson, Sherman and Doyle were unoffending, peaceable and harmless men. Wilkinson, elected by fraud and violence, seated by force and usurpation in a legislature the most infamous ever known, and who in that legislature voted for the black code, could hardly be regarded as unoffending. Sherman, who fed and entertained gangs of drunken, lawless invaders, could hardly be said to be peaceable. Doyle, whose boys drove back old men, actual citizens, from the polls, could hardly be said to be harmless.

"Civil war had been declared by the proslave papers of Missouri and Kansas, and the right kind of characters were picked out to be sent to carry out their declarations. A great many of the free-state settlers on the Pottawatomie were from Missouri and other slave states, and well knew the men and methods they had to deal with. The free-state men there, too, were Westerners, and had that Western disposition not to take any more than they had to. After the election of 1855 things were comparatively quiet on the Pottawatomie, except free-state and proslave men would hardly speak to each other as they would pass.

"John Brown, the father of the boys on the Pottawatomie, came out in October, 1855, and spent most of his time with Rev. S. L. Adair, one mile west of Osawatomie, until the first attack on Lawrence in December. During the summer and fall of 1855 Wilkinson, who kept the postoffice, would often misplace the mail and destroy the newspapers belonging to free-state men. His post-office called Shermanville was the concentrating point where proslave men would meet and curse and abuse abolitionists, and the ruffian conduct was sanctioned by the postmaster. After the first attack on Lawrence matters on the Pottawatomie grew more exciting. Both sides went to the relief of Lawrence, and when they returned they were more suspicious of each other. One day in 1855 Poindexter Manace, after leaving the post-office, was seen with a copy of the New York Tribune. He was told to throw away the damned incendiary sheet; he replied that it was the best paper published and the crowd jumped on him and nearly beat him to death. To avenge the outrage on Manace John Brown, jr., organized his Pottawatomie Rifles. Judge Lecompte opened court about this time in Shermanville and Wilkinson, Doyle, Sherman and George Wilson had presented about every free-state man's name to the jury to be indicted for treason. At that time in Kansas treason did not bear its United States constitution definition, but it meant a refusal to obey writs of bogus officers and refusal to pay taxes levied by the bogus legislature. John Brown jr. soon after court began summoned the "rifles" to meet on the parade-ground and the court, grand jury and all the legal functionaries of organized slavery fled to Lecompton. The Pottawatomie settlers escaped imprisonment for treason. It was only when a settler from there was somewhere else, like Partridge and Kilbourn, that he got arrested for treason. The bogus officers never broke into their settlement and took one of them.

"Early in the spring of 1856 the proslavery men on the Pottawatomie organized to drive out free-state men, and they invited Buford's men, fresh from the South, then stopping at Fort Scott, to come up and help them break up the free-state settlements.

"Early in April, 1856, Joshua Baker, who had made some improvements on his claim on the Pottawatomie, went to Missouri for his family, who were there temporarily from Indiana, and while in Missouri he was arrested and detained for a long time. About the same time, while Mr. Day, from over on the Marais des Cygnes, was at Winan's store, a man rode up and handed him this note: 'This is to notify you that all free-state men now living on the Marais des Cygnes and Pottawatomie must leave the Territory within thirty days or their throats will be cut.—LAW AND ORDER.'

"As this man was a stranger in the neighborhood he was supposed to be an advance man of Buford's Fort Scott men.

Soon after this one of Pate's men drew a revolver on Mr. Day and swore that Kansas would be a slave state, and then some others burned a cabin near his place. After the first Lawrence campaign in December, 1855, John Brown sr. spent most of his time assisting Day to improve his claim when not on the war-path. James Hanway, who lived in the settlement at the time, said of the massacre afterwards: 'I am satisfied it saved the lives of many free-state men. We looked up to it as a sort of deliverance. Prior to this happening a base conspiracy had been formed to drive out, to burn, to kill—in a word, the Pottawatomie creek from its fountainhead was to be cleared of free-state men.'

"Free-state men about Stanton, Mount Vernon and Osawatomie were being held up on the highway, many of them having to hide away in the brush at night, when news reached Osawatomie, May 21, 1856, and Winans's store about the same time, that Lawrence was being attacked. The Pottawatomie Rifles by this time were reorganized so they now had 130 men, but few of them had arms; many of them had only pistols. John Brown jr. got his company together about four o'clock p. m. and marched toward Lawrence. They made a forced march as they desired to return as soon as possible, for their own settlement was threatened with Buford's company. They stopped a couple of hours at Mount Vernon until the moon arose, when Captain Dayton's company from Osawatomie joined them. Then they proceeded on their march and stopped for breakfast at Ottawa Jones's. They there heard that Lawrence had been captured. They then went to Captain Shore's, near Palmyra, and remained the balance of the day, discussing what was best to do. They stayed all night at Shore's. The next morning George Grant came to camp with a letter from John T. Grant stating that they were likely to be attacked any night on the Pottawatomie. John Brown sr. was detailed to go down on the Pottawatomie. John Brown sr. was called Old John Brown to distinguish him from young John. John Brown, Watson, Frederick, Owen and Oliver, and Henry Thompson, Theodore Weiner, and James Townsley, constituting the famous party of eight, left Shore's about ten o'clock p. m., May 23d. Weiner rode a pony; the rest rode in Townsley's wagon.

"They camped that night one mile west of the Dutch Henry Crossing. They remained in camp the next day and started out on their mission that night. They had to operate after dark as their force was small and the proslavery settlers were likely to receive reenforcements at any time from Buford's men on their way from Fort Scott. It was a bold and daring undertaking for a handful of men to attack the proslavery headquarters in that settlement. On that same night three fre-state men living about a mile north of Doyle's had been visited and were in hiding in a ravine behind the Henry Shively

bluff. The Brown party crossed the creek, and then went
north and crossed the Mosquito and knocked at the door of
the free-state man to inquire the way to Doyle's. He was
not at home, as he, too, was in hiding from proslavery men.
They then went east, and the next house was Doyle's. Fred,
Mr. Weiner and Mr. Townsley stood guard at the road, while
the rest went to the house. They brought out Mr. Doyle and
his two sons, William and Drury. They went south and
crossed the Mosquito, when old man Doyle made a turn to
the right, in an effort to escape. Old John Brown shot him
in the head with a pistol. The two Doyle boys attempted to
get away, when the two youngest Brown boys hacked them
with short swords, and they were left dead. They went a little
further south, and got to Wilkinson's house. The same orders
were carried out as before. After Wilkinson had gone with
them a short distance, his attention was called to what he had
threatened about John, jr. Wilkinson reiterated what he said;
so the youngest boy killed him with a short sword. They
then crossed at the Dutch Henry ford, went east, and called
at Sherman's. Henry Sherman was not at home and Mrs.
Harris was present, having gone there to cook breakfast for
Buford's men, who were expected that night. She at first
treated the callers nicely, as she mistook them for Buford's
men. When she found out her mistake, she went to her house
and alarmed Henry Sherman and George Wilson. After she
left William Sherman was taken to the river; the youngest
boys killed him and threw him in the river. He, too, was
killed with short swords. At Sherman's the orders were
changed some. No one saw Sherman killed but the two boys.
Brown's original intention when he started out that night
was to capture these men and hold a trial. After Doyle's
effort to escape the plan was changed.

"The next morning there was a general supposition that all
the rifle company had returned, on account of what had been
done; so the bands on their way to the settlement came no
farther, and all was quiet on the Pottawatomie ever after
that. The proslavery power was broken and that was the
end of proslave rule on the Pottawatomie. This was the first
free-state victory. It was turning the other cheek. It protected the home and families and saved the lives of many
free-state men. From this time John Brown became known
to every one—admired by friends and feared by enemies.
James Townsley said at first he thought the killings were
horrible, but afterwards he thought it the best things that
could have happened. Soon after this affair a little meeting
was held near Greeley which only a few settlers attended,
that passed resolutions deploring the matter. Within a month
after that meeting not a single free-state settler would have
attended any such meeting. H. H. Williams who was present
said many times in his hardware store at Osawatomie that

the more he thought about it the more it looked to him to be the necessary thing.   Hendric Kinkaid who was living near there at the time said that if Brown had not struck when he did, and the way he did, the free-state people from Stanton to Garnett would have had to leave or else some one else would have had to do what Brown did.

"John Brown jr. was the most popular man in Franklin county up to this time, but he was now in prison, and soon after lost his mind.   John Brown or Old John Brown was in demand everywhere.   The free-state men knew that he was a leader they could trust.   Not a single free-state man living who lived in or near the Pottawatomie in 1856 but who says it was an act of justification and necessity to do something by somebody in that part of the country.   H. H. Day of Rantoul, John T. Baker of Lane, J. C. Chestnut of Osawatomie, and S. C. Wollard of Olathe, all approved of Brown's action at that time.   All the obnoxious proslavery men left the country immediately after these killings and no armed ruffians from the South ever came to that settlement again.

"This affair headed off the conspiracy Judge Hanway spoke of.   It broke up the nests and rendezvous of the proslavery forces in that part of the country.   After that the Missourians had no place to roost.   Other settlements were not so fortunate; they prolonged retaliation until proslave men got the upper hand and committed many depredations on free-state men, burned many homes, and took a great deal of property.   The free-state men could get no protection from federal authority.   They had asked the War Department for troops in memorials and public appeals, but the administration thought the outrages on free-state men were insignificant affairs and not worth national attention; but when the Pottawatomie plan was adopted and free-state men defended their homes in their own way then outrages on proslavery men were of momentous consideration.   Governors, judges, United States marshals, sheriffs and prosecuting attorneys called on national authority for troops, and response was speedy.   The peace policy had been tried and failed at Lawrence.   The treaty of December had been broken, and in the second attack the proslave men were successful.   The Pottawatomie settlers had twice been to Lawrence, leaving their own homes exposed, to relieve their friends at Lawrence, and had seen their friends there submit to treaties and peace compacts.   The Pottawatomie men did not believe in the treaty business; they were not diplomats.

"John Brown was thought by some to be insane, by many to be reckless, and by all to be misguided in judgment, and yet events proved his judgment better in some things than the leaders of the free-state party.   He predicted that the peace treaty with Lawrence would fail and that unless aggressive measures were adopted Lawrence would be destroyed.

He told the men at Osawatomie unless aggressive measures were adopted their town would be taken.

"The men who counseled peace fell victims to the policy and were imprisoned at Lecompton. It might have been better if the Pottawatomie men had acted only on the defensive; but free-state men had been on the defensive for two years and that seemed long enough. When should the defensive end and the aggressive begin? We have a recent illustration. When the Filipinos attacked Manila the Americans acted only on the defensive the first day, but the next day they carried the war into the jungles. Day after day the American forces pursued an aggressive campaign until their armed foe laid down his arms. The defensive plan might have been better, but the aggressive policy prevented the necessity of having to fight any more defensive battles.

"Governor Robinson says in the preface of his Kansas Conflict 'the actors in any struggle are unfitted to be the historians of that struggle.' I then tell this story, as 'twas told to me. The Brown boys and Weiner related the facts of this affair in early days to Hanway, Houser, Kinkaid, and Partridge, and these men have told it to the succeeding generation. James Townsley relates some of the details in an affidavit made long after the event, but he has not told all in that affidavit that he has frequently told to his neighbors in various conversations.

"There was no intention to harm the peaceable proslavery men on the Pottawatomie, only the obnoxious ones—the ones that gave aid and comfort to the Missouri invaders, the Buford cut-throats, and Pate's gang. The Pottawatomie policy enabled the free-state men to stay, and by staying saved Kansas to freedom. It gave notice to Missourians that no more ballot-box stuffing would be tolerated. Had the Pottawatomie policy been adopted sooner at Leavenworth perhaps the shocking cruelties inflicted on R. P. Brown and William Phillips might have been avoided. In the latter part of May, 1856, the free-state men of Kansas saw their leaders in prison, their newspapers thrown into the river, a reign of terror in Atchison, blood running down the streets of Leavenworth; Lawrence, their principal town, destroyed; armed hordes from every Southern state marching to Kansas; free-state families in Linn and Bourbon counties leaving by the hundred for their far Eastern homes; men all over the Territory going to prison for speaking their sentiments; their champion at the national capital, Charles Sumner, weltering in blood from slavery's blows for even speaking out against these crimes in Kansas. Another successful stroke and the triumph of slavery would have been complete in Kansas. This was the situation when Brown and his seven bold men appeared in the proslavery stronghold with only one pistol and a few short swords. The reason these men used ground knives was because arms were scarce—the Sharp's rifles at that time had all been sent to the relief of Lawrence. The whole national administration was using its mighty arm to crush the poor men in the prairie homes of Kansas; all the wealth and power in the south was being used against them. The pulpit thundered against them and the press abused them. Against all these odds the free-state men of Kansas exhibited the most remarkable courage recorded in the annals of the world.

"Fidelity to the cause of freedom and pluck to stay by it were essentials the people of Kansas in those early days were looking for. None doubted John Brown's faith, sincerity, or courage. That is why neighbors of my boyhood days spent so many hours and nights counseling with, associating with and fighting with old John Brown. War was declared by the proslave hosts in the fall of 1854. The proslave papers announced the policy of exterminating abolitionists. It might have been a good thing to have adopted the Pottawatomie policy in 1854, for it might have prevented the bogus election of March 30, 1855. It might have saved young Barber's life. Certainly it was none too soon, after the destruction of Lawrence and the arrival of Buford's company and the G. W. Clarke raid in the southeast.

No participant of the free-state cause in Kansas should be robbed of his glory. It required the work of all, for which each was peculiarly fitted—Robinson the statesman, Lane the orator, and Brown the hero, and all other men who leaned upon these giants of freedom. None obstructed the way but all contributed. Lane by his eloquence aroused the Kansas freemen as Patrick Henry brought to the surface the undercurrent of Virginia in 1775. Robinson was the balance-wheel of the whole movement here, and Brown drove back the lion of slavery to his southern lair. Let not a single name be erased from the honor roll of fame. John Brown became more famous than all the rest on account of his work at Harper's Ferry.

"Some Kansas historians are not kind to our own heroes, but historians elsewhere, not partizans but standard authors, put Brown in a proper place. Schouler in Volume 5 of his splendid United States History says: "Although Brown was hung for treason, he was not a felon but an enthusiast. Like a gallant man he met death, believing his cause to be right; he became a martyr, and consequently a figure in history." Professor Andrews in Volume 4 of his excellent work on United States History says: "John Brown was an enthusiast; a misguided hero, whose sufferings in Kansas had frenzied his opposition to slavery."

"I was raised among friends, comrades and relatives of the old crusader, and they were all the best of citizens. I have roamed fields in childhood where this old hero held councils to plan the blotting out of slavery from this nation. In my youth

I walked down a lane to school the famed martyr had often traveled. Hero worship is not a virtue to be taught. It is not a vice to be condemned. It is a natural impulse of the human heart. The more the sacrifice, the more the sympathy. Martyrdom for a cause attracts attention and enlists recruits for that cause. Many men of the free North had not yet conceived the enormity of the sin of slavery until men began to die for the freedom of the slaves. After Brown's execution slavery's foes united.

"John Brown was not a statesman, not a philosopher, not even a leader. He was truly a hero. He belongs to that class of heroes whose mistakes of judgment are excused for their virtues to be extolled. He belongs to that class of heroes whose daring and examples of self-sacrifice in the establishment of a principle receives the plaudits of mankind. John Brown was one of those heroes whom opponents of the cause he espoused attempt to consume his memory with flames of wrath, and whose friends of his cause smother and perish the flames by heaping thereon verdant wreaths of glory. John Brown is a contrast and yet a parallel to Charlotte Corday; one a beautiful French maiden, the other a stern man of sixty. One struck a dagger into the heart of a tyrant; though a murderess, she did her part to liberate France. The other, though an offender in the eyes of the law, did his part to free mankind. One perished at the guillotine, the other expired on the scaffold. Each takes equal hold upon posterity's imagination and sublime conscience. After John Brown's death the champions of slavery had to fight for their idol."

Shively's story is ably written, and no doubt accurate as to detail, but there are many writers on this incident who are reluctant to believe that the young Brown boys were a part of this removal committee in association with their father. It is stated in many books that they expressed horror and asked their father before others if he had been involved in the killings on the Pottawatomie, to which he replied that he had "sanctioned them." Sam Shively lived in the immediate neighborhood with his parents, grew up there, and absorbed all the information obtainable. Yet until his very interesting paper was read before the State Historical Society almost a half century later the killing of the proslavers was an unsolved mystery. It was my good fortune to have a relative associated with the Browns at that time and I feel justified in telling his story of the incident. This man was Allen Jaqua of an unusually good family at Union City, Indiana. In 1856 he, then a boy eighteen years old, was with the Browns as a special friend of John Brown, Jr. He accompanied the Pottawatomie Rifles on their trip to help defend Lawrence. They had been joined by a company from Osawatomie and other communities till their party numbered

one hundred and thirty men. Enroute they were intercepted
by a messenger who told them Lawrence had fallen, the town
burned and the proslavers were in control, so it was no use
for them to go on. Other messengers arriving from the south
told them trouble had broken out and the families were in
constant fear of violence. The effect of this news on Old John
Brown was very evident, and he took several of the older men
aside and talked with them. They were then in camp on the
roadside. In the morning the different companies were drawn
up for inspection by Captain Brown. He walked up and down
the line critically observing each of the men. He went back to
his place and asked the men to kneel in prayer. His supplica-
tion was to Jehovah, the Lord God of Moses the Liberator,
of Gideon the Liberator, and of Joshua the Liberator, thank-
ing the Supreme Commander for the favor he had shown to
oppressed peoples and now asking that He use this assembled
company to accomplish a great need among His people. He
prayed long and loud, his voice trembling with fervour, re-
minding the Lord that He had favored Joshua by stopping
the sun in its course through the heavens, that He had separated the waters of the sea for Moses and the Israelites, that
He had aided Gideon to destroy the altar of Baal—so now they
pleaded that He would use them to administer and establish
here His mighty system of justice. Still longer he prayed and
pictured the grievous woes that had come among His people
on earth that He alone could alleviate. With muscles aching
the men arose to their feet and the old hero addressed them
saying he had long promised them a chance to strike a blow
in defense of human liberty—a promise long deferred but now
coming to them as though by Divine command. Those wanting to take part in the great enterprise—who would go with
him unquestioningly, pledging themselves to do his bidding
unhesitatingly and without reservation—would take two steps
forward and remain. Jaqua said nothing ever so strongly
appealed to him, and he wanted to go, but felt obligated to
remain with his friend John Brown, Jr. Ten men stepped to
the front, the order was given to about face and march, and
the company started north, and Jaqua glanced backward to
see the ten men get into two wagons and drive off toward the
south. A few days later when they returned he saw these
same men and they talked with him about what had happened
almost as related by Sam Shively—"but perhaps I should not
tell their names." This was told at a family dinner thirty-
four years after the incident, there being present not only his
wife and two daughters, but also Ambassador Gray (ex-governor Isaac Pusey Gray, then serving as Ambassador to Mexico)
and myself. Jaqua was a man of unusual integrity and high
character, then a chief of division in the pension office. As
he spoke of those ten volunteers, and of his subsequent meet-

ing with them, one could not believe they were the young fellows known as the Brown boys.

This incident has an important bearing on history as it fixes approximately the date on which Old John Brown came into Linn County and begun to plan the great tragedy that was to end his life. After May 24, 1856, the proslavers on Pottawatomie creek were very mild-mannered cutthroats—in fact, many of them hastily moved away in silence. The free-state settlement at Osawatomie was scared, fearing retaliation, and wrote denunciatory resolutions that were to be read at a called meeting. Old John Brown visited Ben Simpson and asked that the resolution be not adopted—that the results would justify the means used. Ben Simpson read the resolutions to the meeting and stated the view entertained by Old John Brown. The result was the resolutions were abandoned and Pottawatomie creek settled down to peace, quiet and safety.

Among the very first settlers in this county was one Joseph Barlow,[1] by birth, education and prejudice a thorough Kentuckian. With other "goods and chattels" he brought with him to the Territory a number of slaves. At the organization of this county he became prominent and was made its first judge of probate and register of deeds. He was by profession a lawyer, a smooth and persuasive talker, kind-hearted and hospitable. Judge Barlow at once became leader of the more conservative proslavery element in Linn County. Strange as it may see, upon acquaintance a warm and lasting personal friendship sprang up between this man and Captain Montgomery, which on more than one occasion saved the life of Barlow, who while always an advocate of the divine right, endowed with the courage of his birth and conviction, was nevertheless conservative in his views and was never an advocate of violence and murder as a means to the end of bringing the Territory into the Union as a slave state. Montgomery had faith in the honor of Barlow and was not slow to advise him of his purpose and reason for expelling the objectionable proslavery element from the county—assuring him that there could be no lasting peace between such warring elements as freedom and slavery—that to have peace it must be all free, or all slave. Judge Barlow argued in vain against what he termed Montgomery's unlawful course, assuring him that the precedent set by proslavery leaders in wrong doing did not justify him in similar wrongdoing, and would not in the long run help the free-state cause, and if persisted in would surely bring retaliation in form and time that could not be protected against.

When Hamelton late in April of 1858 left the Territory for

1. This story of Judge Barlow was written many years ago by Ed. R. Smith for a local newspaper.

fear of a visit from Montgomery, he soon afterwards sent
word back to his friend Barlow to "come out of the Territory
at once, as we are coming up there to kill snakes, and will
treat all we find there as snakes." Barlow, upon the receipt
of this message at once left his home and family and joined
Hamelton in Missouri, where he found the evicted refugees
waiting his coming. Shortly after his arrival in Missouri a
mass meeting was called at the old town of Papinsville. The
object of this meeting was to incite an invasion of the Territory in such force as would sweep all resistance before it.
At this meeting Barlow was constituted a member of the committee on resolutions and opposed to the returning to the
meeting of such resolutions as should endorse immediate invasion. He was overruled, and such action was endorsed and
returned to the assembled mob, where they were received with
boisterous applause. Barlow, confident that such a course if
attempted would only result in disastrous failure, vigorously
opposed the adoption of such a policy. To use his language
as he gave it years afterwards it relating the proslavery side
of the events preceding the Marais des Cygnes Massacre,
assured his friends that "We are not prepared for an immediate
invasion of the Territory. We have no arms but our shotguns
and our squirrel rifles and the Jayhawkers with their Sharps
rifles would kill the half of us before we got within gunshot
of them; besides we have no food to support any number of
us when away from our homes, and there is none in the Territory. We must submit our case to the courts, which are in
our control and are in full sympathy with our purpose to maintain slavery in the Territory as a permanent institution at all
hazards. The courts if resisted will be backed by the military
power of the government, which is now Democratic and in full
accord with our purpose."

Hamelton and others addressed the meeting in fiery terms.
Barlow was brushed aside, and with an unanimous vote it was
resolved to invade Kansas instanter. That night and the next
day there assembled an army of near five hundred men fully
bent on the extermination of free state sentiment in Linn
County, and took up its line of march for Kansas. Upon arriving at the line between Missouri and Kansas a halt was called
for rest and final arrangement for descent upon the unsuspecting scattered settlers in the beautiful valley surrounding the
ancient and historic Trading Post. Here Barlow again availed
himself of an opportunity to address this mob and to better
effect. They were tired, sober and silent; they had ridden
many miles and were without food or blankets, and besides
were at the threshold of hated but dreaded Kansas. Every
man of them knew that Montgomery could not be far away.
Barlow assured them that the crack of Sharp's rifles might
now be expected at any instant. The hour was propitious; it
was midnight, and the stars above them shone down upon

this hungry, fear-stricken mob with cold and cheerless light. The sharp, rapid barking of a pair of marauding coyotes from a not far distant mound, sent an alarm through the ranks. Some declared it was the signal of the Jayhawkers; a panic was imminent. The more resolute cursed and swore at the timid. Captain Hamelton, disgusted with the evident cowardice of his drawling associates, in a rage mounted his horse, rode out of the mob about him, calling on "The Bloody Reds", his faithful personal following to "Ride to the front and follow me!" At this summons thirty-two as blood-thirsty wretches as ever "cut a throat or scuttled a ship" mounted and rode out and away over the border after their hot blooded commander. The remainder of this collection of border ruffianism, like the wolves of the border that they were, before daybreak on that eventful May morning, disappeared and were heard of no more. See story of Marais des Cygnes Massacre listed in the index.

Ed. R. Smith was an anomaly among men. As simply "Ed. R." he was known in all the remote parts of Linn County and to all the people thereof as the intimate friend of each, the first to offer a solace to every wounded heart, who carried into every communion with the afflicted a gentle philosophy that dried their tears and stopped their fears. It was "Ed. R." who gave cordial congratulations upon good fortune and who said the last kind words when the grave closed over some departed comrade, for as a comrade he regarded each. It seemed that when the Supreme Artist was weaving the destiny of Linn County he put "Ed. R." in the shuttle to reappear as a golden thread throughout the warp and woof of our community life and for almost a century he has worn well and never lost his golden colors. But "Ed. R. Smith" was slightly different, as it implied his presence in the public forum where he met the conflict of ideas, the contentions of selfish interests, the glories of exalted patriotism, the ambitions of other men —it was here he was recognized as worthy of any man's steel if forced to become a foe. But when he was listed as "Colonel Ed. R. Smith" it was certain he appeared as a power in a congressional or state convention where the dignity of his full title was generously accorded him.

Very few people would have recognized him by his full baptismal name of Edwin Ruthven Smith, for that is the way he started out at his birth at Akron, Erie county, New York, Sept. 4, 1838. His father was Ezra Hanchet Smith, several of whose ancestors had attained to some eminence as professional architects. His mother was Mahetabel Draper Smith, daughter of David Draper of Livingston county, New York. Her maternal grandmother was a Scott of the family of General Winfield Scott of the United States Army. Ed's father held to the architectural tradition of the family and was a skilled carpenter and builder. In 1857 when Ed. R. was not yet eighteen years old, it was resolved they would move to Kansas Territory and the father and Ed. R. started as the advance guard April 15. By way of railroad and steamboat they got to what is now Kansas City, and from there—fully seventy-five miles—the father and son and a new found friend named James Mooney, walked to the spot where Ed. R. lived till his death about two and a half miles west of the present Mound City. The father located a claim and started the log house which was to shelter them and the mother and other five children. The house wasn't very large and it had few windows but it did have a stout door thick enough to stop bullets and a huge timber braced across it made it secure from forcible intrusion, and a big fire place generously supplied with fuel from the timber along the creek.

Many years ago, Col. Ed. R Smith wrote a long letter to his niece, Miss May Capper, a sister of our United States Senator Arthur Capper. This letter was in answer to questions concerning himself and contains so much of the history of pioneer times we copy it in part, as follows:

"At the first call to 'the colors', I entered into the service with a good horse, a Sharp's rifle and began a postgraduate course in the saddle with but little intermission until war was officially declared between the States.

"In early May, with a company, we marched to Lawrence to join the Second Kansas 90-day service. We failed to get in that service as the regiment was fully organized with Col. R. B. Mitchell of this county in command. We returned here after drilling with the Second at both Lawrence and at Wyandotte in June, 1861. Everyone suspected of loyalty to the Union in the counties in Missouri along our border was hunted out and driven away from home and family by a blood-thirsty mob under the guise of secession. Mound City was the Mecca of the hunted Union refugee. Daily our border was crossed by men on the search of Montgomery and his well-known and justly feared 'Jayhawkers.'

"Under Montgomery, Jennison and Blunt, some three hundred loyal men, both Kansas and Missouri men, we met a little army of secessionists near Balltown and in the skirmish that ensued I had a good horse shot to death under me and received some half dozen buckshot in various parts of my body at close range. I was brought home and was laid up all the summer until the battle fought at Drywood south of Fort Scott in October, 1861. On this occasion I went to the fight with a crutch with a load of men who went from here upon hearing of Price marching on Fort Scott. All that winter I was a cripple.

"When Jennison organized the Seventh Cavalry he arranged for my joining his staff as first lieutenant and adjutant, but I was too lame and John T. Snoddy was made adjutant.

"Before I was able, I joined early in 1862 Captain Thornton's Company of the Seventh and waited in camp at Mound City for a mustering officer. While waiting, Captain H. A. Smith was commissioned and assigned to duty as Acting Commissary Sergeant under Brigadier General Mitchell, who had my name erased from the muster roll of Company G of the Seventh and I was ordered to report to Captain Smith at Leavenworth and went on duty as chief clerk in the brigade commissary and went with Mitchell's command at the time following the battle of Shiloh. At Columbus, Kentucky, Captain Smith was post commissary for a time, thence went south to Corinth, Iuka, and in September was relieved from duty at Tuscumbia, Alabama, and ordered to St. Louis and then to Macon City, Missouri, where he was post commissary until his death at that place late in December of that year. I returned home. While at St. Louis in September I took the opportunity afforded and went up the river and found my way out to where your parents and the whole family were then on a visit to your Aunt Lizzie in Iowa, where your Aunt Jennie[1] and I were married. Finishing their visit in Iowa, your father and family, with my beloved new wife, returned · to their old home in Kansas. In my absence with the army in the south my father had died and when I got home there was much to do in helping the doing of a good many things. All the money that I had saved I had sent home to my parents. Your Aunt Jennie and I set up our tabernacle in the little old log cabin with mighty little to begin with. The blessed little brave woman made no complaint. She was not the kind that halted or failed in the hour of need.

"Early in the spring of 1863 all was in direst confusion all along the border. The volunteer soldiers were on the firing line; the most of Kansas troops were in the south. All Kansas was under arms. The border of this county was almost constantly under threat of hostile invasion. Governor Carney organized the militia of the border counties of Johnson, Miami, Linn and parts of Bourbon with headquarters at Mound City, under command of Colonel John T. Snoddy, who had resigned as major of the Seventh Cavalry on account of ill health. At this time I was urged by every interest in town and otherwise to accept a commission as first lieutenant and adjutant of the militia then under arms in every county along the threatened border. John T. Snoddy died in April, 1863. Jim Snoddy succeeded him. I continued on duty as adjutant. Mind you, this was service performed without pay. How we lived through it is now a troubled dream to me. However, the days, weeks and months of the summer passed by and all survived, and during all the months we had under arms in camp one

1. Jennie McGrew, daughter of Samuel McGrew, who located on a "claim" in Mound City township where he lived until his death.

or more companies of militia on guard of volunteer army supplies, post and garrison guard and patrol of the border duty.

The awful massacre of men, women and children at Lawrence in 1863 was but a part and parcel of bloody tragedies of almost daily occurrence somewhere along the line for more than five years. The volunteer army in camp and field were armed, equipped, fed and paid. Not so the militia. Every man, wife, boy and dog was a 'minute man' and seldom if ever beyond the reach of a trusty rifle or revolver. (That stalwart grand old grandfather[1] of yours was a man whose presence in camp, in the field or wherever danger threatened—always prompt and a never-failing source of sound judgment. Boy! You came of mighty good stock).[1]

"During the summer of 1864 it was a source of constant rumor that an army of rebels was in formation in the south for an invasion of Missouri and Kansas. Its realization came in October. General Curtis commanding this Department declared the state under martial law. Governor Carney mobilized the militia. Every regimental command was called into service. And these Kansas men were not unskilled and ignorant of the use of powder and lead. Up to this time everybody of required age that was now out of the service and at home had, with hardly an exception, served an enlistment and was a trained soldier. So that the militia was a dependable organization. The Sixth Regiment of State troops, of which I had been adjutant, nearly eight hundred good men, left their camp on the 11th of October, and under orders entered Missouri and encamped in pens and about hay-stacks at Hickman's Mills on the 13th with James D. Snoddy in command. General Blunt with Colonel S. J. Crawford and Colonel J. T. Burris, volunteer members of his staff, were in camp at the Mills upon our arrival there. Moonlight with parts of the Eleventh and Jennison with the Fifteenth Kansas Cavalry, with other volunteer troops, were massed at this point. Blunt had ordered the militia of Johnson, Miami and Linn and some others mobilized at this place, waiting for information of the whereabouts of General Sterling Price, anticipating the raid of Price's army upon Kansas City and Fort Leavenworth. While in suspense, Governor Carney had ordered Major General Deitzler to assemble the militia at Shawneetown in Kansas and had ordered General Fishback, then at Hickman's Mills, to move the Kansas militia to return to Shawneetown, which General Blunt refused the militia to do.

"General Lane was a candidate for the senate, as also was Governor Carney. Colonel Crawford was the Republican candidate for governor. There was much quiet music in the political atmosphere. At Colonel Colton's headquarters of the Fifth Militia, with Colonel Jennison present, also Fishback,

1.   This was interlined for the benefit of his son, to whom this copy of the original letter was given.

Pennock and Snoddy, it was resolved to call Blunt's hand and go back to Kansas. It was arranged that Snoddy was to head the movement and move his command the next morning. Snoddy and I had made our camp while at Hickman's Mills in a very decent hog-pen—it had been the abode of former swine at any rate. It was shelter, and much better than the boys who were without tents had and who bivouaked about hay-stacks and rail pens.

"Snoddy had failed to inform me of his intentions until after breakfast in the morning, when he directed that I have the command mounted and ready for a movement. Snoddy took the head of the column and started for Kansas. We had scarcely gotten to the top of the hill west of Hickman's Mills when out came General Blunt with part of his staff with a section of a battery of 12-pound guns and tore down the narrow gulch of the crooked road along the meanderings of a tributary of Little Blue. Blunt with his guns and their support ran through and over the militia, who scattered to nearby hillsides out of the way. Blunt passed across Little Blue and wheeled about with artillery in position at a bend in the road just beyond the west bank of the stream. At the approach of our command Blunt called a halt and ordered a staff officer to 'disarm that person', indicating Snoddy. It was done without comment on Snoddy's part. I knew Blunt personally as some three years before he had assisted in removing several buckshot from my body, and he says: 'Who is in command here.' I replied that Col. Snoddy was in command. 'What are you.' Answering I said, 'I'm Adjutant.' 'Who is next in command.' 'Captain Barnes of "A" Company.' Blunt then directed Captain Barnes to return to the camping place we had just left and then directed me to march our command, without arms, in front of his headquarters as he 'had a talk to make to you Linn County men.' As adjutant, he directed me to call the company officers of the regiment to meet at some proper place that night and there elect a class of field officers for the command 'and report your action to me in the morning.' With his staff about him on the porch, in front of some six hundred loyal sons of old Linn, he gave us the first information that we had had—that Price with an army of 20,000 men was in central Missouri and headed this way. "I know that every Linn County man will do his whole duty when the time comes—and, men, it's coming!" He threatened Snoddy with dire punishment and dismissed us.

"That night the company officers assembled in a room in the mill and I was elected colonel. As such officer I rendered service during the remaindr of that momentous campaign, the success of which was the greatest moment to the safety of Kansas City and Leavenworth. The next day I was called to the headquarters of Col. C. W. Blair and made 'officer of the day' for the day's movement, and that night made a camping place on the road between Independence and Kansas City. After dark that night we went out to the bluffs and threw up some breastworks and lay down on our arms and in the morning the rebels passed to the south of us some two miles and fought Jennison and the Shawnee county militia.

"We were ordered to Kansas City and took quarters in the weeds and fence corners where the stockyards are now. Early the next morning, Sunday, October 22, I moved the command at the order of General Blunt to Westport and took up a position in the main street there, where the camp fires of the rebel army were in plain sight on the hills beyond Brush Creek. Filing to the right and crossing Brush Creek we went into action in the edge of a wood with the Fifteenth Kansas under Colonel Hoyt on our right and passed the 'compliments of the occasion' briefly.

"In the meantime Price had got his baggage and army impedimenta on the way south and with a stubborn rear guard sullenly followed after with a victorious but exhausted army in pursuit. Without food of any sort since Saturday morning, my command without our horses (as they had been left and held), we marched until midnight of Sunday and laid down in the fence corners till break of day on Monday and resumed the march after "refreshment" upon the carcass of a steer that had escaped other dangers, and without salt or coffee. Our horses had come up with the command during the night. Following our "repast" with troops to the right of us and troops to the left of us, we hurried on the trail of the fleeing rebels. At West Point on the Kansas line Generals Curtis, Pleasanton, A. J. Smith and Blunt held a conference. During the day Blunt's army had been in the advance. While at rest in the fence corners, General Blair hunted me out and asked if I did not have men in my command that were familiar with the crossings of the Marais des Cygnes river in Kansas, not far away. Assuring him that I had, he had me gather several that intimately knew of every hog path. With them we hustled back to the conference and made favorable report of safe crossing of that river at what was known as the Island Ford some several miles above the Trading Post, where it was known that Price was encamped. Curtis and Pleasanton were favorable for Blunt to take his army and move to the river and cross and take a good road to Mound City that night, with Pleasanton holding Price at the Post. Blunt was full of fight. He was in sight of good fighting waiting for him and "He'd be damned if he was going to dodge a good fighting chance." These old warriors were very emphatic and equally earnest in their opinions, the upshot being that Blunt and his staff mounted and rushed away bound for the fight at the Post in the morning or as soon thereafter as they could overtake a fight.

"Following this little side play during the night, I moved

my command to the plain prairie in sight of the Trading
Post and laid on our arms in a drizzling rain until daylight,
when Price's rear-guard was in line of battle stretched along
the high bluff to the east of the Post."

The story of Ed. R. Smith is the story of each and every
one of the pioneers. There was nothing selfish or vainglorious
in his makeup. He wanted each of those comrades who had
come down that long path of life with him to have a happy
place in the memory of men yet unborn. Had strength remained to him in his later years he would have "embalmed
in story and in song" every beautiful spot and every noble
life lived in those pioneer days. His had been a busy life
and his personality was such as to give him recognition
among the leading men of his time. He served as private
secretary to Dudley C. Haskell when as our congressman he
was a man of power in the national legislature. This position
gave Ed. prominence and influence that he used to serve many
home folks, and associations with great men who appreciated
him. When Haskell suddenly died, Ed. returned and was for
years postmaster at his home town. He had previously held
various county offices with conspicuous ability. In the course
of the years he retired to the home he had built with his
own hands and there awaited the final call which came to him
Sunday morning, November 13, 1927, full of years and honors.

The Kansas City Star, the great newspaper of the West,
gave this editorial tribute to him on November 15, 1927:
The death of Col. Edwin R. Smith at Mound City, Kas.,
removes another member of that small remaining group of
pioneers who laid the foundations upon which Kansas was
built. One of the best known of all that historic band was
Col. "Ed. R." Smith, as he was familiarly known.
Mr. Smith went to Mound City immediately following the
opening of the Kansas Territory for settlement. With his
father, he walked from Westport Landing to Mound City.
They were seeking a home for the young man, and they walked
on through Mound City to a point two miles southwest of that
town, where they took up a claim of 160 acres. There Mr.
Smith erected a house out of the timbers cut from the new
claim, and there he lived in the same house until the hour of
his passing Sunday morning—seventy-two years.
There were troublesome times in Kansas for five years
immediately following the advent of Mr. Smith in Kansas.
The desperate fight that led to the Civil War began with the
opening of Kansas to settlement; the fight to make it a free
state on one side, and to extend slavery into the Northwest
on the other. Mr. Smith took a prominent part in that great
struggle.
At that time there was a leader of the free state group,

Col. James Montgomery, whose name is written on almost every page of Kansas history during its territorial days. Montgomery was in command of a small army of volunteers who were guarding the Kansas line in the section between Fort Scott and what is now Paola. In that army Ed. R. Smith played a leading role.

At one time Montgomery conceived the idea of capturing a command of the federal army, and of bringing on the crisis that came on four years later and actually placed his men in a position in the hills surrounding Mound City to accomplish that purpose. Protesting that the movement would be unwise, but bowing to the decision of his superior officers, Mr. Smith was in command of one division of the Montgomery band that occupied a stragetic position for the attack. But Colonel Montgomery gave up the daring idea at the urgent request of free state leaders from Lawrence.

With the breaking out of the Civil War Colonel Smith entered the conflict and saw the fall of the old slavery dynasty. In those trying days of early citizenship, which required great courage, his was one of the keen minds that planned the 5-year contest. He was an associate of Charles Robinson, Jim Lane, Sam Wood and the host of men who piloted the cause of the free state party.

What history was in the life of Col. Ed. R. Smith! When he went to Kansas there was not a railroad in the state. There was no Lawrence, no Topeka, no civilization. When he walked from Westport Landing to Mound City he did not pass through Olathe or Paola—there was nothing but prairie and wild open country where these two now old towns stand. Kansas stretched westward to include Pike's Peak and a part of the Rocky Mountains. He saw Kansas admitted to the Union, attended the inauguration of the first governor of the state, the first legislative session; saw the state university established—saw, and helped to bring about, the development of the Kansas of today.

Others whose hands helped to lay the foundation stones of Kansas lived only to see the building of that state partly completed. To Col. Ed R. Smith it was given to see the full realization of the dream of those first pioneers who planned for the state that should grow upon that foundation.

Col. Ed R Smith was married three times, first to Miss Jennie McGrew, daughter of Samuel McGrew and sister to the mother of Senator Arthur Capper; his second wife was Miss Quinn, daughter of Probate Judge Quinn; and his third wife Miss Helen Smith, daughter of Newlon Smith, who trace back to the William Penn family. A son, Frank, by this marriage, survives with his mother.

Columbus Williams arrived in Linn County in June 1857

with his parents and four brothers and two sisters. They were from Fulton county, Illinois. They got right into the "border war." Of one incident Mr. Williams says: "About forty Bushwhackers came into Linn County by way of Barnesville where they got a warm reception at a rude breastworks with portholes through which the defenders gave them such a dose of cold lead that they gave it up as a bad job and passed on to my father's farm two miles west of where Prescott now is. We had heard the gunfire at Barnesville and father and brother Mike and I were prepared for them. When they came galloping up we opened on them with Sharp's rifles and we soon had them on the run. We had no desire for sleep that night and when morning came we found seven horses with saddles and bridles and holster pistols. Several of the horses were dead and the others so badly shot up we killed them to end their suffering. We heard afterward the mob carried way three of their number dead, and they sent word to us they were coming back to be avenged. There were at that time some U. S. soldiers at Potosi and we sent a messenger there to ask protection against this threatened return attack. The soldiers came but the Bushwhackers failed to show up. When the war came on I joined the Fifteenth Kansas Cavalry under Captain O. A. Curtis. Most of our time was spent in the west and southwest against the Indians. Later Joe Ury and I were made dispatch carriers between Fort Scott and Fort Smith, our route taking us over the Boston Mountains where rebels and rebel sympathizers were very numerous. We experienced many amusing and some very serious incidents. The Fifteenth Kansas met Price's Army at Lexington and for seven days fought them all the way to Westport. From there we chased them right down the line and licked them badly right in sight of the old home farm on the Military Road. General Blunt commanded our army and had about ten thousand men against twenty-five thousand under Price. I was mustered out of the service at Leavenworth November 1, 1865." When the township was organized in 1867 Mr. Williams was given the honor of naming it and he promptly announced it should be called Sheridan after General Phil Sheridan.

William Laughlin Sutton was born in Osage county, Missouri, May 23, 1851, being the son of Willis Mitchell Sutton, to Kentucky from Tennessee. (Willis Mitchell was a relative who became the son-in-law of General Nathaniel Greene.) His grandfather was Thomas Sutton who was captain of some two thousand Tennessee troops which held back the British regulars at New Orleans and greatly aided General Jackson. Our William Laughlin Sutton was married in 1873 to Anna Elizabeth Murray who was the daughter of Daniel Murray and niece of William Henry Murray who had come from Illinois to Polk county, Missouri. Their children are Lena who married Luther Jackson; Wilbur Wallrau, who married Zelma Daugherty at Pleasanton, and Claude at home unmarried. He was here at the organization of the county and knew Fox who laid out the town of Paris, and Robert Paris who married the daughter of Joseph H. Barlow. A brother to Mrs. Sutton died at Camp Sherman, Mississippi, while a soldier in the Third Missouri United States Volunteers. He had laid in the "sand pits" in front of Vicksburg and was found unconscious from sunstroke. Soon after their arrival here R. B. Mitchell and his brother Barney opened a law office and later Barney Mitchell became the first county clerk.

The Miltons of Scott township were from Ohio, the wife and mother being Esther Holloway who had been born in Baltimore, Maryland. They came here from Schuyler county, Illinois, in 1857. Their first child was Martha, who never married and was affectionately remembered as "Aunt Mattie." She was a remarkable woman rejoicing in outdoors life and could do a day's work equal to any man, though a gentle and refined woman. Jesse served in Capt. Leasure's company of the Sixth Kansas Militia and married a Miss Vandervere, Mary Ann married William M. Stark, John married Kate Early, Elisha married Eva Clearwater, George married Anna Redding.

"Tandy" Witcher was from Kentucky, where he had married a Tennessee woman. They lived always near Boicourt. Their children were John who married Addie Gates, William who married Minnie Baugh, Joseph married Hattie Steel, Minerva married Joe Carpenter, Fannie married Sam Jenkins, and Lona married Charley Mays.

William Goss[1] was born at Gosport, Indiana, March 20, 1832, where he lived till he was married in 1853 to Miss Martha Ann Hendricks of the distinguished family of which Vice President Hendricks was a member. Five children from this marriage are still living—Florence (now Mrs. Doctor Splawn of Kincaid), Alice (now Mrs. Doctor Sellers of Prescott), Joseph Thomas, James Grant, and Laura Vienna (now Mrs. J. A. Broyles of Spring Hill).

Mr. Goss came to Kansas in the fall of 1856 by way of West Point, Missouri, where he was intercepted by the noted Clarke and asked for his "pass," and much surprise was expressed that he had none. Clarke was trying to keep out New England free-state people and generally had them reveal their identity by a discussion of cows. Goss passed their examination all right. Had Mr. Goss said "keow" he would

1. This article was written by Mr. Mitchell in 1895.

never have entered here or elsewhere. Clarke had been a purser in the navy and had for some reason forsaken the sea for the plains. He was the man who led the Clarke raid through Linn County that fall.

Goss visited the country around Trading Post and was so pleased that he paid $300 in gold to a man named Jackson for a quarter section on the state line due east of Trading Post. That was one of the things he would not do now under similar circumstances as he could have had equally as good for the taking. For the first time in his life Goss was in a slave country, for less than a mile away was the establishment of Charles A. Hamelton, who had sixteen negroes and lived in a pretentious manner. He had a race track and entertained the neighboring gentry with racing. There were quite a number of proslavery families there then, among them Nathan M. Hawk and a Mr. Swingley; both stayed through all the trouble and were highly respected citizens.

Goss was right on the state line and could see a great deal of the strife. He soon learned that the best thing for a man with his free-state ideas and combative temperament was to avoid collision with the Missourians, so that when he saw squads of horsemen riding over the prairie he would lie flat on the ground, and if he happened to be plowing with his oxen he would turn them loose and lie in the furrow till they disappeared.

An incident of the beginning of the troubles was the proposed joint effort of the people on both sides of the line to establish order. A United States marshal got the Kansas people together after the passage of the amnesty act in February 1859 and proposed that they act under his authority and cultivate a friendship with the Missouri neighbors, promising to arm them with government guns. This sounded so fair that a great number gathered on the appointed day and marched over to the Dryden brothers' farm about seven miles east of Trading Post in Missouri, where they were to powwow with the Missourians and establish peace relations. Captain Weaver, an army officer, arrived at the rendezvous at the same time they did with a big prairie schooner filled with muskets from the government arsenal at Jefferson City, which were simply piled in like cordwood. There was a canvas cover on the wagon, and just as the team stopped there was a sad tragedy. Captain Weaver saw a prairie chicken and remarked that he would shoot it, and reached through the loop in the canvas at the rear of the wagon and was drawing one of the muskets out when it exploded, sending the bullet through his brain. Instead of this quieting the people and making it easier for them to negotiate, there was soon another event almost as exciting. A moment after Captain Weaver's death a Missourian pointed out old "Sammy" Nickel, who was peculiarly offensive to the proslavery people, and tried to shoot him. Someone prevented him executing his threat and a moment later there was a clear line of demarcation between the Kansas men and their neighbors. The most of them were without arms but they retreated in good order and brought old Sammy home uninjured. Peace negotiations were declared off. Nickel was a harmless old man with a large family, and his only offense was in detesting slavery and subscribing for the New York Tribune.

William Goss had with him a younger brother Thomas and as they were not so rich then as now they were under the necessity of seeking employment a part of the time in Missouri to keep themselves supplied with necessities. Two years after William's coming he was joined by his father Joseph and brother David and families, and the entire family have since lived here and have been held in high esteem, holding various military and civil offices.

William Goss has a high admiration for all the men of that time who did so much and in such a courageous way for the cause of liberty. Many of them differed radically as to methods, but all were sincere in their friendships and did much to protect the defenseless families out on the prairies. He remembers Montgomery's first military organization, a heterogeneous collection of infantry, cavalry and artillery, all in one command. His most vivid recollection of Montgomery is of seeing him in his ragged and grotesque looking officer's "uniform" after his company had come to Trading Post to protect some settlers from a raid. He had been out on a long tiresome chase and looked weary and exhausted, but a young negro was being instructed by him in the mysteries of the alphabet. Montgomery never countenanced plundering, though much of it was done by his men, and he realized that to restrain them would lose to him their services. But he did think it perfectly legitimate to live off the enemy when their depredations made it necessary to oust them.

Gradually as the irrepressible conflict began to develop Montgomery was succeeded in the active command of those expeditions by Charles R. Jennison, who had recently made his home at Mound City. Jennison was a very young man then, small in stature, and nervous in temperament. Whenever he laid his hand on the enemy the blow was not soon forgotten. He was not out for amusement. There were about four hundred men who answered his call and fearlessly rode into Missouri with no other authority than his commands. Petty invasions by the plundering Missourians were promptly punished.

After the war had begun Jennison was in command in Mound City with the Seventh Kansas regiment. He knew all the settlers so well that he at once proceeded to determine who were going to fail the Union cause in its hour of need.

He rode out along the Missouri line and called on the various proslavery men to take the oath of allegiance. Goss was present when he came to Hawk's place, where he also found Mr. Swingley. They demurred a little at the manner of presenting the matter to them, but took the oath as requested. While the interview was going on the party saw one of Swingley's sons riding away toward Missouri, and he was next heard of as a colonel in the Confederate army. Subsequently there was quite an interesting incident in his career. When the Union army was cannonading Charleston with the big gun, "Swamp Angel," the rebels in the city took Union prisoners and placed them where they would be exposed to the fire of this famous cannon. This young Colonel Swingley had fallen a prisoner of the Union army, and he was among the rebels taken out and placed opposite the rebel batteries. This had the desired effect, and prisoners on both sides were soon removed from such brutal exposure.

Company B of Jennison's Seventh regiment were stationed at Trading Post for the protection of the citizens, but they plundered so much that the citizens held an indignation meeting and sent William Goss to Mound City to complain to Jennison. The colonel was very indignant at their conduct and ordered their transfer to Mound City, which was accomplished before Mr. Goss had time to return to his home.

They frequently had high old times over politics as late as 1860. There was a meeting of some kind held at Paris, and Goss and one Jack White, of Trading Post, went over with some neighbors. White was an enthusiastic fellow, strongly free state and yet having a very great friendship for Judge J. H. Barlow, who was the proslavery candidate for probate judge. When the party was ready to return home there was considerably more "inspiration" aboard than when they came. As they drove out in a wagon White stood up waving his hat and hurrahed for "Lincoln and Barlow." This was more than the proslavery people could stand, to have their candidate's name mentioned in the same breath with "Abolitionist Lincoln," and they mobbed the party in the wagon at once. After considerable rough usage White was made to see the error of his ways, and the party ordered to move on.

In 1860 after Lincoln's election to the Presidency the Missourians called out their militia and put a cordon of soldiers along the Kansas line, determined to keep Kansas men in the place they had been so anxious to keep them out of. Goss had only a mule and Nathan M. Hawk one horse, so they doubled up to make a team to go to Balltown in Missouri to mill. As soon as they crossed the line they were arrested by the militia and taken into Colonel Bowen's tent, who kept them all day and night, trying to learn something about Kansas affairs. Finally he treated them to a very nice whisky toddy and turned them loose. This Colonel Bowen was the man who carried the dispatches between Grant and Pemberton at Vicksburg, resulting in the surrender of Pemberton's army.

When the Sixth Kansas militia was with Pleasanton's army chasing Price up at Hickman's Mills, Goss was first lieutenant of Company N of Valley township. This regiment had a remarkable experience on this campaign, which cannot be told here for want of space, but which we hope to give after treating the companies separately. At the request of Montgomery, then a colonel of the volunteers, Goss and M. W. Gouin, lieutenant of Company M, were sent on a secret expedition to Trading Post to remove arms secreted there in the mill. They went around by Twin Springs and came across where Boicourt now is. Morgan Fickes fell in with them.

They went on to the Post and accomplished their mission, and Goss went on to old Sammy Nickel's place and was standing talking with the old man when they saw the lead of the rebel column coming through the narrow valley north of the Post. The moment they crossed the line into Kansas the whole army spread out like a fan and parties of pilfering sneaks were seen at all the farm houses. They realized that it would not do for them to stay there long, and started to give the alarm to the settlers at the Post. Nickel was riding a spirited horse which refused to go in any direction but towards home and Goss had to help the old man away.

By this time the country was swarming with rebels. William Priestly fell in with Goss and they retreated slowly so as to study the movements of the rebels. After they crossed the river they were reasonably safe and from their hiding place saw one of the first to enter the village. He evidently wanted to make good use of his opportunity as he went from house to house plundering and insulting women. He was quite conspicuous, as he wore a brilliant red flannel shirt. Priestly was very indignant at the fellow's actions and asked Goss's permission to shoot him. Goss was at the time lieutenant of Company N, and Priestly deferred to him even under these circumstances. Finally the fellow committed an atrocious act in plain view and Goss told Priestly he had no objections to him indulging his own wishes and Priestly promptly put a rifle ball through the fellow. On returning to Trading Post next day they found the red-shirted rebel still alive, which he owed to the women, as some of the Seventh Kansas recognized him as a thief and would have hanged him had not the women objected to killing a wounded enemy, however detestable a record he had.

Mr. Goss was nominated in the military camp at Mound City in October, 1864, and elected to the legislature, and was a member during the famous senatorial election resulting in sending Gen. James H. Lane to the United States Senate, against whom Mr. Goss voted under instructions from his constituents. The same legislature ratified President Lincoln's emancipation proclamation, Mr. Goss signing the joint resolution.

David Goss became captain of Company D, Sixth Kansas volunteer cavalry, his brother James being first sergeant, and Thomas, another brother, corporal. The father is still living at Trading Post at the advanced age of ninety-one, and four generations recently gathered at his home to the number of seventy to celebrate the old gentleman's birthday anniversary.

James Goss was born April 3, 1841, at Gosport, Indiana, a little town named in honor of his grandfather; died August 10, 1926, at his home in Pleasanton, Kansas; age eighty-five years four months and seven days. In 1858 at the age of seventeen years he came with his father, Joseph Goss, from Indiana to Kansas, locating near Trading Post in Valley township. During the border struggles leading up to the Civil War Mr. Goss saw much of it. At the second call of President Lincoln for volunteers to assist put down the rebellion he joined Company D, Sixth Kansas Cavalry Volunteers, and faithfully served his country until the Union soldiers were victors, being discharged at Leavenworth in 1865. He came back to the Linn County farm and took up his work where he laid it to one side a few years earlier to do his part to uphold his country and the Star and Stripes. October 22, 1866, he was united in marriage to Miss Mary Ellen Merritt, a young lady of eastern Miami county, who survives him. To this union eight children were born, Stella A. passing over when a little child. The survivors are Mrs. Lewis Weeks of Frewater, Oregon; J. E. Goss of Watonga, Oklahoma; Edgar M. Goss of Pleasanton; Mrs. Fred Arnold of Globe, Arizona; Mrs. C. J. James of Parsons; Mrs. F. J. Carson of Butte Falls, Oregon, and Mrs. Ina Beatty of Pleasanton. He is also survived by eleven grandchildren, two great grandchildren and one sister, Mrs. Mary Rowley, south of Mound City. In 1867 he and the wife moved from Valley township to a farm two miles north of where now stands Pleasanton and here they raised their family of useful citizens.

In 1754 Major Frederick Goss of the King's Army became the head of a family that has had 2250 descendants in 1890 a large number being citizens of Linn County, among them being William, Thomas, David and James Goss, all born at Gosport, Indiana. James, born April 3, 1841 married Mary Ellen Merritt (born in Jackson county, Tennessee, June 21, 1846). She was the youngest of eleven children born to Fleming Merritt and Ann Magann, from North Carolina through Tennessee on their way to California. When they got into Bates county, Missouri, Ewing's famous Order No.

ll hurried them on to Rockville, Kansas, where they became acquainted with young Isaac Croxton who was running a store there, Shoemaker the postmaster, the Binkleys, the Shannons, and the Douds, and of course James Goss whom Mary Ellen married there October 22, 1866. They came to the farm known as the David Goss farm two miles north of Pleasanton. Of their surviving children Emma Belinda married Lewis Weeks; Ernest James married Minnie Moore; Edgar Merritt married Carrie Tucker; and Mary Ellen married Fred Arnold.

In considering the first decade of Linn County it is interesting to study the antecedents of men who became prominent in the struggle and learn the motives which prompted them to brave dangers and suffer great hardship.[1] The reviews of the lives of John Brown and James Montgomery show them to have been zealots in the crusade against slavery. The conditions in 1855 and early 1856 were such that every man was a law unto himself. Without even the shadow of authority life was taken and property confiscated by the antagonistic elements. The social and political system was unique and peculiar to the country. It had but two phases at that time. If a man was opposed to making Kansas a slave state he was a free-state man, and if he did not contribute himself body and soul to that cause he was a Bushwhacker with the capital B. There was no neutral ground.

However justifiable the practice of retaliation and reprisal may have been at first, it could not go on forever. Yet right here a new difficulty was discovered. The system was so convenient to many who had been fighting in the name of liberty that they were loathe to discontinue the practice of getting a horse or other necessity from some enemy whom they conceived had no right to it anyway. And when the free-state men were in the ascendancy in 1856 there were many who espoused their cause for the exercise of the imagined license to plunder and rob, and they were soon indifferent as to whom they took from. With them the horse of a free-state man was frequently deemed more convenient than a proslaver's.

At this juncture there came into the country a man who was without doubt actuated by motives entirely different from those of most of the early settlers. He was in the prime of life, a veteran of the Mexican war, and highly gifted in the legal profession, whose entire experience and teaching made the turbulence and disorder very distasteful to him. He had been an influential Democrat, and felt it a duty to aid his party friends at Washington in maintaining order. He quietly established himself in a little log house on the lonely prairies northwest of where Mound City is located, and brought there

1. This article was written by Mr. Mitchell in 1895.

a young wife who had been reared among the refinements of life at the national capital, and to the astonishment of many of the impoverished settlers, there were in that little log house a piano and a goodly library. He pursued the even tenor of his way without aligning himself with either faction, claiming to be a Democrat and in favor of law and order, and soon found himself distrusted and marked for destruction by both parties. Yet he was elected to the legislature in 1857 as a free-state man and became a prominent figure in terri- torial affairs, and was afterward a brigadier general of volun- teers in the Union army. His intimate connection with the history of the county makes it desirable to give his life in detail.

Robert Byington Mitchell was born in Mansfield, Ohio, of Scotch-Irish parents, April 4, 1823, and after a preparatory course in the public schools became a graduate of Kenyon college, where he showed a decided inclination for a military life, organizing and drilling his classmates in the tactics then in vogue. After college he began the study of law with Hon. John K. Miller, of Mount Vernon, Ohio (who had been minister to the court of St. James), where he was fitted for the bar. There was an interruption to these studies, however, when the Mexican war broke out, as Governor Babb gave him a commission as second lieutenant in what was known as Morgan's Company, and he served gallantly in this first and last war of conquest. He was severely wounded at the storm- ing of Chapultepec and reported dead, but finally came out of it with astonishing vitality. At the close of the war he returned to Ohio and took up his practice, and in 1855 was mayor of the city of Mount Gilead; and in January of that year was married to the woman who came with him to Linn County, and who has since been one of the most historic and influential of Kansas women—Miss Jennie St. John, daughter of Hon. Henry St. John, who was then member of congress for the Mansfield, Ohio, district.

During that year he visited Kansas Territory on legal business, and thinking it a good field for professional advance- ment made arrangements to return, and on October 8, 1856, he arrived at Paris, Linn County, with his wife and a young child. Within two weeks their lonely surroundings were made more dismal by the death of their first born. But they bravely rallied from their affliction, and moved into the log house that had been built on their "claim." It was as crude as the average settler's cabin, but strong. A huge rail fence almost hid it from sight. One of the last presents received by Mrs. Mitchell on leaving her eastern home was a large quantity of "morning glory" and old-fashioned hollyhock seed from a motherly old neighbor, and the morning glory vines soon climbed over all that fence. The stick chimney and the cabin were nearly hidden by these graceful vines, many of which found their way between the clapboards on the roof, and there were everywhere great stalks of hollyhocks standing like sentinels about their new home. Mitchell was a vigorous man, and soon had several men at work "opening" that land. A young law student from Ohio, Byron P. Ayres, soon joined them, and the two legal luminaries, for lack of professional practice, joined the men in plowing and fencing, and other hard work incidental to homesteading. At that time there was no domestic help to be had at any price. Black people were such a source of contention they were not allowed to stay and white servants were very scarce. Thus all the hard work of preparing food for five ravenously hungry men devolved upon Mrs. Mitchell, who, though belonging to a practical family, had never had such work to do. But she bravely did as best she could, and they had many diversions to cause them to forget their hard work. Music and hunting were both to their taste. But when it rained they had a doleful time dodging the water that fell through the clapboard roof.

They had many of the mishaps which befall people new to the peculiarities of a country, and one of them was quite expensive to Mitchell and to Ayres, and of insufferable annoyance to everyone else. Around the walls of the cabin was a shelf upon which was spread the law library. It happened on one of their holidays, when Ayres and Mitchell were "dressed up," that they espied upon the bookshelf what they took to be a pretty chipmunk and resolved to present Mrs. Mitchell with a pet. They effected its capture, but instead of a chipmunk it turned out to be what scientists call a Mephitis mephitica, and as a result of their contact with it their clothing was worn out on the fence a distance from the house, where they hung it in the hope that an offensive odor it had acquired would leave it.

A fairly good idea of the times may be gained from the statement that divine services were not allowed to go unmolested. There were times when itinerant preachers would announce meetings, and some settler's house served as a church and a dry-goods box as a pulpit, on which reposed the Bible flanked by ponderous revolvers. Some of the substantial yeomanry invariably stood guard over such meetings, and there are many noble Christians still living who were taught divine truths under such difficult circumstances.

Just over a hill from Mitchell's cabin, about four miles away, was Montgomery's house, where John Brown was stopping, and near it the fort to which they resorted when danger was imminent. There was no intimacy between Mitchell and Brown and Montgomery. He was as much opposed to slavery as they in principle, but did not agree with them as to how the question should be treated, and as a matter of fact Montgomery and his men were very distrustful of Mitchell. **Brown** kept aloof from him, but was almost daily seen by them when he was in the community. Brown was eccentric in everything. He was out riding over the prairies on a spirited horse almost daily, usually wearing a military overcoat with a cape lined with red, and with a slouch hat and his flowing beard he was a sight never to be forgotten as he swept along like a sprite with the speed of the wind.

The first time Mitchell appeared in public was at a free-state convention held at Paris. Montgomery was there and made a speech advising free-state men to hold their ground and fight for the advantage they had thus far gained. Mitchell followed him, appealing for law and order, assuring the people the courts would protect them in their rights, and that he had no doubt of the triumph of the free-state principles without resort to violence. Montgomery replied to this in a fiery speech in which he disclaimed any faith in the courts or in the administration at Washington. It is to be remembered there were many things at that time well calculated to excite the most intense partisan spirit. James Buchanan had just been inaugurated President, and the long-deferred decision in the Dred Scott case had been handed down by Chief Justice Taney. That famous decision was naturally regarded as a prostitution of the judiciary of the country to the uses of the slavery powers, as it was extra judicial and not called for by the case before the court. President Buchanan hastened to give the decision his unqualified approval, and the effect here where the slave question was at white heat was to intensify both parties. This was the condition of things under which Mitchell sought to defend national Democracy and to establish law and order where murder and rapine were bringing their natural sequence of retaliation and reprisal.

But it was at this meeting Mitchell laid the foundation of lasting friendships. Thomas H. Preston, who had never seen him before, went over and sat down beside him and commended his speech in favor of law and order, and many others recognized his ability and believed in his integrity. The result of this acquaintance was that Mitchell received the nomination of the free-state party for member of the Territorial legislature which met December 7, 1857. He was elected over Charles A. Hamelton, of West Point, Missouri, who had previously lived just east of Trading Post, where he had a number of slaves and kept up quite an establishment. Hamelton evidently was grieved over his defeat, as he came back the next May and murdered several of his former neighbors, with whom he had not the slightest personal or political trouble.

Mitchell worked indefatigably to establish legal order, and through his efforts a grand jury was established, with Henry M. Dobyns as foreman, but he was shortly afterward succeeded by Thomas H. Preston. They found twenty-nine indictments at their first session for various crimes, and it created a great furore. Many of the free-state men feared it was a scheme of their enemies to make them answer for their acts in defense of their homes, while numerous law breakers saw in it a menace to their profitable practices. The result was that Mitchell again became the object of dislike. Several times parties called at his house with a rope and made their gruesome purpose plainly evident to Mrs. Mitchell, who bravely met them, and when requested escorted them through the house to prove his absence. Once when returning after night from a visit to Moneka they were stopped by three armed men, who no doubt intended to kill him, but after a few minutes' parley they drove on unmolested.

In 1858 Mitchell was one of the Linn County delegation of four to the Leavenworth constitutional convention, the other three being Dr. Addison Danford, Robert Ewing, and Thomas H. Butler. This convention proved futile, like the first two at Lecompton and Topeka, and their constitution failed of adoption. Mitchell then became Territorial treasurer by appointment, which he held till relieved by the state treasurer elected in 1860. It should be remarked here that Mitchell's integrity received a thorough test, as he was holding office without bond, and received from his predecessor vast sums of money which were nowhere charged to him or to any account. When the state treasurer relieved him he turned over four thousand dollars in gold that had been found by him unaccounted for.

An effort was made by the legislature in 1859 to conciliate the troublesome factions, and on February 11 it passed the "amnesty act," which pardoned all offenses growing out of political differences. It was not successful in restoring peace, however.

After Abe Lincoln became President in 1861, it was soon proved that Mitchell was a patriot above party jealousy, for at the first call for troops there was a meeting held on the public square at Mansfield, May 14, and a company of the brave men of the county organized, who made him their captain. The regiment not yet being organized, the company marched away to Lawrence with the name of the Mansfield Blues. Mitchell was a born commander, and had considerable acquaintance among military men of the state, having been twice commissioned inspector-general of the territorial militia by Governor Medary and reappointed by Governor Robinson when the state was admitted. The Mansfield Blues became company F of the Second Kansas infantry volunteers, organized at Lawrence June 11, 1861.

The company succeeded in having Captain Mitchell elected colonel of the Second regiment, and he received his commission as such from Gov. Charles Robinson June 3, 1861. Byron P.

Ayres became captain of the company. The following is the roster as it was mustered:

Officers.—Byron P. Ayres, captain; Ezekiel Bunn, first lieutenant; Barnett B. Mitchell, second lieutenant; David R. Coleman, third lieutenant; Wilson Betts and Franklin Newell, first sergeants; Thomas W. Greenly, Walter W. Godley, William C. Gibbons and David Sibbet, sergeants; Hiram Lathrop, Francis M. Tolivar, Edwin C. Caldwell, Thomas H. Copp, and Henry C. Adams, corporals; Jacob R. Lundy and Francis M. Frazell, musicians.

Privates.—James Armstrong, Warren Armstrong, Charles S. Atkins, Jonathan C. Broadhead, Henry L. Barber, James H. Belcher, Hanley P. Bailey, William Braunch, Ira D. Bronson, Francis A. Creager, Mathew Dowling, Edward D. Furge, James A. D. Frazell, Lawrence W. Fear, John Gilden, John H. Gould, John Herman, John Hines, George Huff, John C. Isbell, Elhenan Johnson, Charles Lyman, John Lyons, David A. Meeker, James McNickle, Benjamin B. Miller, James Miller, Peter J. Miserez, Aquila B. Massey, Thomas O'Riley, Morris Pitman, John Preston, Hiram Reynolds, Lester Ray, Isaac Rutlege, William T. Sudberry, George Spain, John S. Snook, William T. Swaney, William Snook, Michael Tooney, Caius M. Tompkins, James Thacker, John F. Wright, Davidson R. Way, James K. Williams.

Colonel Mitchell then took the Second regiment to the defense of Kansas City, and some few weeks later joined the army of General Lyon at Springfield, where they took part in the second great battle of the Rebellion, at Wilson creek. They gave battle to an enemy almost three times as strong numerically and won a practical victory till the two great leaders fell. Mitchell was riding at the head of his regiment into the thickest of the fight when he was shot and fell. General Lyon, a beloved patriot, saw the colonel fall, and shouted to the regiment that he would command them, and with a major general for their leader the regiment kept on, but brave General Lyon had gone but a few paces when he received his death wound, and fell expiring into the arms of a soldier. General Sturgis succeeded him in command of the army, but the controlling spirit was missing, and the great victory about to be achieved was abandoned and the army retreated to Springfield. The Second Kansas regiment were for the first time under fire, and only a few days after the great Bull Run disaster to the Union army in the East, and their heroism at Wilson creek is a bright page in the history of the Federal army.

Mitchell's wound was such that he was for a long time confined to the hospital. Then he served on court-martial duty at Washington till the next spring, when he returned to Kansas and gathered his old command together, they having been disbanded by expiration of their term of enlistment.

He reorganized them as the Second Kansas Cavalry, and was stationed at Fort Riley, when on April 8, 1862, he received a commission as a brigadier general from President Lincoln, and was ordered at once with his command of 2,000 men to Pittsburg Landing, where they arrived after the battle, and then did service throughout the South, and made a notable record.

General Mitchell's qualities as a military leader were of a high order, and but for having incurred the bitter political enmity of Gen. James H. Lane would have attained the rank of a major general, to which he was brevetted.

At the close of the war he was commissioned governor of New Mexico Territory by President Johnson and served four years, his wife and child, Henry St. John Mitchell, now division superintendent of the Memphis road, with residence at Fort Scott, and who was born at Mansfield, Linn County, accompanying him. Subsequent to 1870 he lived for many years in Washington, where he died January 23, 1882, and was buried in the famous Congressional cemetery.

Mrs. Mitchell has always retained her citizenship in Kansas and has taken an active interest in its welfare. June 30, 1882, congress voted her a pension of $50 a month, but she has not been content to live idly as a pensioner. In 1889 she learned that by taking a homestead, the four years' military service of her husband would be deducted from the five years required upon it, so she went with some acquaintances to Kearny county and took a homestead fourteen miles from Lakin, the county seat, a station on the Santa Fe railroad, where she again spent a year in pioneer life, receiving a patent for the land in her own name.

When the board of lady managers of the World's Fair at Chicago was being organized, Governor Humphrey had the selection of two ladies to represent Kansas upon it, and named Mrs. Mitchell as one of them, and she received a commission as such from President Palmer of the World's Fair Commission. Subsequently there was an organization of the ladies of Kansas, in which Mrs. Mitchell did a most creditable part in traveling over the state and forming county societies which were to gather the material for a state exhibit. It will always be a matter of regret that Governor Lewelling, when he succeeded Humphrey, removed Mrs. Mitchell and her associate, Mrs. Lew Hanback, from the state association, for political reasons, which did much injury to the work then in progress. It was the more deplorable because of the making the exhibit a political matter, whereas Mrs. Mitchell had been appointed as a Democrat by a Republican governor in order to avoid partisan criticism. Her commission as a member of the national board, however, enabled her to carry out enough of her projects to give the state a creditable showing.

The name of the general has been perpetuated in Linn

County by giving it to Robert B. Mitchell Post No. 170, G. A. R., and his widow, who did so much for the community in the early days, was initiated into full membership and given all the secret work of the patriotic order—a compliment never before paid to woman. The post recently removed the remains of their first born from the grave out on the prairies to Oak Lawn cemetery, La Cygne.

One of the most vigorous personalities of territorial times was Thomas Hess Preston[1] of Scott township, a man who has always been characterized by remarkably strong convictions and with indomitable courage to do what he conceived to be right. He has fought his own way in the world from childhood and acquired all his education and knowledge in the hard school of experience, and it is very greatly to his credit that he has achieved so much.

Mr. Preston was born September 28, 1819, in Trenton, N. J., his father being of English descent, his paternal grandfather a sergeant in the British army, and his maternal grandfather being John Hess, gamekeeper to Lord Maxwell of County Armagh, Ireland. His father died when he was an infant and Tom became the mainstay of the family. His talents soon took him to sea, and he obtained employment with the coast service in various ways as seaman and cook generally. In this way he visited nearly all the seaport towns on the Atlantic, and remembers the big event of the first steamboat in New York Harbor. It was during this time that he acquired the hatred of intoxicating liquors that has characterized him ever since.

Subsequently he became an apprentice in a woolen mill in Philadelphia, but later quit that and learned stonemasonry. In Chester county, Pennsylvania, November 23, 1840, he was married to his present wife, then Margaret Jane Robison, and to them have been born seven children, Martha (now Mrs. O. D. Harmon), John Hess, Elizabeth Emma (now Mrs. Aaron Lanning) born in Pennsylvania, Thomas Jefferson and Mary Frances born in Iowa, and Alice and Sigel who were born here.

In 1851 Preston removed with his family to Van Buren county, Iowa, and in 1857 came to Linn County, accompanied by the families of John Robison, William Robison and William Snook. Preston bought a half section where Augustus Leasure now lives, while Snook and the Robisons located near Twin Springs, where their famlies still live. They all took half sections as it was a provision of the Bogus statutes to enable proslavery people to spread over as much land as possible, but of course they were subsequently restricted to a quarter section.

While pioneering in Iowa Preston had acquired the trade of blacksmithing, which he here found invaluable, and he soon

1. This story of the Preston family was written by Mr. Mitchell in 1895.

had a forge fired up on his farm, the old bellows of which is now rotting in his orchard.   He drove an ox team to what was called Tate's bank, east of Trading Post, where every man mined his own coal as well as paid for it.

Among Preston's earliest acquaintances was Robert B. Mitchell for whom he had a great admiration and lifelong friendship, though they parted company politically when the Republican party was organized.   For a time after their arrival there was little excitement and no trouble, but soon it all broke out again.   When the guerillas over on the state line became quiet for awhile, there was thieving by men who strongly protested their free-state principles, yet took horses and other loose property from any citizen convenient.   It got to be intolerable.

There then existed the Paris posse under command of Russell, who claimed to be a United States marshal from Arkansas.   He had about two hundred men in his posse and gave them arms brought here by Captain Weaver from some government depot in Missouri.   Their headquarters were at Paris.   Singularly enough only proslavery men were enlisted under Russell, and it soon became evident the posse was to be used to sustain their political friends, so it was in great disfavor among free-state men.

A noted character of those days was Hugh Huston, an Irishman, who lived where Joseph Teagarden now lives.   Old "Hughey" as he was familiarly called was all Irish and of full width in his brogue, a United Brethren preacher, and accustomed to meeting most of the people and taking part in public assemblages.   He was thoroughly honest and hated the evil doings then prevalent.   He was an ardent free-state man and when necessary shouldered a gun to protect settlers' homes from murderous invaders.   Yet he was always preaching honesty to the free-state fellows who were suspected of a lapse from rectitude.

At the time Russell's posse captured Elihu Fairbanks and held him under arrest at Paris, Montgomery's men retaliated by taking prisoner George W. Moore, who then lived on the present George Cassidy farm, and took him to Montgomery's fort.   There was great excitement.   Fairbanks was only a boy of nineteen, and the complaint against him was purely political.   Moore was a neighbor of Preston's and there was a pleasant acquaintance between the families, so soon Mrs. Moore, who was an invalid, sent for Preston and begged him to use his influence with Montgomery to save Moore from further trouble and effect his release.   Preston was here placed in a predicament, as he was a known friend of Mitchell's and Montgomery would not favor his requests.   Knowing Huston to be friendly with Montgomery, he persuaded "Hughey" to go to the fort and try to effect an exchange of Moore for Fairbanks.   Late in the night Huston returned, saying Montgomery consented to the exchange, and they went to Paris to see the posse, who rejected the proposition to exchange prisoners, saying the Jayhawkers would have to wade in blood before they got Fairbanks. After much parley the posse marched away with their prisoner for Lawrence, where Jim Lane received them courteously at a public house and in relieving them of their guns dropped them all through the floor into the cellar, and then the populace set upon Russell and his men and drove them out of town with stones and clubs and gave Fairbanks his liberty. Fairbanks is now living at Farlinville and Russell has never been heard of since the Lawrence incident.

Preston and Huston were then puzzled to know how to effect Moore's release. They finally thought of an eccentric old man named Addis, living up on Turkey creek, who was an influential friend of Montgomery's, and they started to ask his aid. On the way they had to pass through a town that has long since disappeared from the map and from the memory of most men—Douglas—which was in the creek bottom about two miles east of where Farlinville now is. There was a general merchandise store and several houses. As they neared the little town in the brush a shot was heard and they saw Moses W. Beaver riding toward them with a part of the pro-slavers after him. There had been a battle at Douglas and Beaver had captured a red blanket by one corner, but was so closely chased he had no time to get a better grip on it. His pursuers stopped, but Old Hughey wanted an explanation and started to chase after him, when Beaver brought his rifle to bear on him, but on recognizing Huston, met and talked with them. Soon four others with red blankets came hurrying along, among them Pat Devlin, who wanted to shoot Preston under the impression he was one of their enemies. Beaver and Huston interfered or Preston would not have survived the meeting long. Huston did not like Devlin, and there was a sermon preached to him right there. Finally through the intercession of Addis Montgomery prayed for Moore and after having him eat as his guest sent him home.

Huston then related that on his first visit to ask for Moore's release Old John Brown, who was at the fort, mistook Huston to be one Charles Clark, and drew a pistol so large that even brave Hughey trembled before it.

Thomas H. Preston visited Montgomery at one time and learned the cause of his being so relentless in his retaliation against the Missourians. His family had been turned out on the prairie and their home burned. Afterward he prepared to defend his family, and had loaded himself with pistols and other weapons and surrounded himself with a band of brave and determined men. Of course there was complaint that his actions were lawless. Through Mitchell's influence Preston had been appointed deputy sheriff with full powers, and when ordered to take a force and arrest Montgomery and his men he was somewhat embarrassed, but called out two hundred men, who met at Paris and marched to Montgomery's fort. By the time they got near there a blizzard very happily dispersed them and drove them home, and next day Preston resigned as deputy sheriff. It was a scheme to break up Montgomery's force with which he did not sympathize.

At the time of the Marais des Cygnes massacre in 1858 there was a very general response to the cry from the Trading Post people for help. Mitchell and Montgomery were together for once. As they approached West Point, Mitchell feared vengeance might be visited upon the innocent and counseled sending a committee to ask for the murderers, while Montgomery was for dashing in and taking the whole town prisoners. While parleying, men were seen leaving the town on the opposite side, and Montgomery and his men gave chase to them, but they got away. None of them were captured at this time, and only one paid the penalty by hanging at Mound City in 1863, an incident that will be given elsewhere.

Shortly after the murder, Z. W. Leasure told Preston that Yealock, one of the assassins, had returned and was at his cabin just above the Island ford on the east side, and with great secrecy suggested they get together and capture him at night. Accordingly Preston got Arvoy Thomas, and they stopped to get Peter Border, but Peter had no gun. Thomas gave him a gun, when Border discovered he had no horse. Preston got him a horse, and then Border said his wife was not at home and it would not do for him to leave. They then went to Leasure's, where a dozen had assembled and chosen John Y. Gates to lead the expedition. As the man they wanted was a desperate character, everybody in the crowd was slightly nervous as they rode through the forest. They finally dismounted and crept near the cabin, and when within about a hundred yards Gates saw a shadow of something, and shouted "Look out! Take trees!" which quite a number hastened to obey, but Preston had gotten so near the cabin that he walked into the open door and found it had been long deserted.

The Arvoy Thomas mentioned was a noted character, always in trouble because of his free-state principles. He was not a bad man, but uncouth and miserably poor. He had a wife and children, and a yoke of oxen was his principal worldly possession. He was good hearted, and always did his neighbors a good turn when opportunity offered. At the time of the Hamelton massacre he walked barefooted with the relief party, without enough clothing for comfort even in summer. He was a monstrous eater and every man who went out that day will remember how Thomas ate at Sammy Nickel's. The pro-slavery people tried every way to scare him out of the country, bringing charges against him before one Hayes, who claimed to be a justice of the peace. Hayes was a bad man and a great bully. Hayes had no legal right to prosecute Thomas, and he ignored the summons. Hayes gave judgment against him, and assessed the costs at forty dollars, and told the "witnesses" they would have to collect enough to pay their fees. This was an excuse for Skillman Fleming and his posse to persecute poor Thomas, so they set out in force to visit him. Of course he was powerless to resist, and suffered great indignity. Finally they tired of worrying him and turned to take his yoke of cattle which had been tied to a tree. Just at this juncture Mrs. Arvoy Thomas appeared with a kettle of boiling water and a dipper and a liberal application of it soon sent the posse away without the cattle. Thomas stayed awhile longer, but finally Preston learned of another scheme to have him before "Justice" Hayes, and suggested that he do something to avoid trouble. Thomas said he would go down and settle the costs assessed against him by Hayes. The latter was celebrated for his profanity and his assaults on people with a big bowie knife. As Thomas approached him at Brooklin to settle his account, Hayes began abusing him, and finally said he would "cut the heart out of the abolitionist," and pulled his famous bowie knife from his breast and stood with the point resting on a table between them. Poor quiet Thomas here rose equal to the occasion, and closely imitating the manner of the old bully he drew a great knife from his breast and told Hayes he was ready for a settlement on those terms. Hayes showed abject cowardice, and after making a laughing stock of him, Thomas told him he would give him two dollars instead of forty dollars if he would promise to keep his posse away and leave him in peace, to which Hayes agreed. They failed to keep faith with him, though, for a short time after Preston learned of trouble in store for him, and Thomas and family left in the night and were never again heard of.

Mr. Preston was the first master of the first lodge of Masonry here, which was established at Twin Springs in 1866, and subsequently moved to La Cygne. He also served as foreman of the first grand jury, which met at Paris in 1858 and found twenty-nine indictments at its first sitting, among them some against Charles A. Hamelton and several of his men implicated in the Marais des Cygnes massacre. One of them was arrested in 1863 and tried at Mound City, where he was convicted and hanged, one of the survivors of the tragedy acting as his executioner. (See story of hanging of Griffith.)

Josiah Lamb, who served as a delegate from Linn County to the Wyandotte convention which framed the constitution of the state of Kansas in 1859, was one of those forceful but unpretentious and modest characters who deserve a much better tribute than they will ever get because of the passing away of nearly all who knew about him. The Lamb family is of the oldest colonial stock and helped to make several states in the American Union. Josiah's parents settled in an early day near Richmond, Indiana, right on the Ohio line east of Indianapolis. That was at one time one of the biggest Quaker settlements in the west. From there a large party went into Iowa and in 1857 a party of about forty Lambs came into Linn County from Iowa. As will be seen in the sketch following, Josiah was a son of Restore Lamb and his wife who was Millicent Winslow. Josiah married his cousin Ruth, who was a Quaker preacher.[1] He was an expert millwright. A distant relative is Giles H. Lamb, a lawyer by profession at Yates Center and a member of the Kansas Senate from that county who sends the following family sketch: "My uncle Basil Lamb who died a few years ago told me that Josiah Lamb was his cousin. Basil was about ninety-three years of age when he died and I got the history of the family quite largely from him. His father's name was Barnabas. They came from North Carolina to eastern Indiana in the early settlement of that country and took land near what is now the city of Richmond. I do not know just who the parents of Josiah Lamb were. They were old-fashioned Quakers as were all the early members of that branch of the Lamb family, but I am inclined to think as I remember it now that Uncle Basil told be that Josiah was a son of Restore Lamb." An interesting old letter sent to Senator Lamb is authentic and gives all the information known of the family.

"Oregon, Holt county, Missouri, 4th Mo. 2nd Day, 1878.— Dear Friend and Nephew: Finding a letter directed to Willis Lamb and there being no person in this country by that name, having a brother of that name, though he lives in eastern North Carolina, I took the privilege to open the letter. My name is Isaac Lamb, a brother to Barnabas Lamb, thy grandfather. Now, to answer thy request, I will begin as far back as I can ascertain through tradition or otherwise. Henry Lamb, one of the early settlers in America came from England in the sixteenth century, settled in Eastern North Carolina; some years later, removed to the western part of the state. His son Isaac Lamb married Elizabeth Nixon and remained in the same settlement, raised a family viz: (also whom they married) Phineas, Dorothy White; Restore, Millicent Winslow; Zacariah, Miriam Griffith, Armager, Sarah Munden; Elizabeth, Thomas Stover; John, Sarah Smith; Joseph, Lovey Smith. John Lamb and Sarah Lamb, formerly Smith, remain in the same settlement, raised a family, viz: (and whom they married) Hosea, Mary ———; Barnabas, Ruth Bently; Achsah, Exum Elliott; Ery, Rebecca Pearson; Miles, Nancy Modlin; Rachel, Charles Harred; Jemima, Joshua Trombled; Willis, Mary Newby; Phineas, Hulda Bundy; Isaac, Catharine White; Lydia, Daniel Gwinn. The foregoing is as near correct as I

1. Their children were all influential people. Ann married Enos Mills; Miles married Nancy Helmers; Jonathan married Anna Collins; Joseph married Jane Winters; Lydia married David Lindsay; Susanna married John Collins; Erma married Henry C. Smith; and Calvin married Ella Daly.

am able to give. Hosea Lamb's wife's family name I cannot
give at this time and the name of Hosea's wife. If thee should
find any not correct, please correct them and excuse the writer
of this. Perhaps some of thy father's people can give thee
the family name of Hosea's wife. Thy Uncle Jacob perhaps
can give thee the name required. This is principally given
from memory as thee has no intention to publish this, I will
not hesitate to let thee have it as it is. With resepct, thy
friend and uncle, Isaac Lamb."

James M. Arthur who served in the legislature and in 1859
was a member of the Wyandotte convention which framed
our constitution was a Kentuckian by birth and of very meager
schooling but of rare good judgment and strength of character.
He was a "Free Stater" of enough note to be sought for killing.
His wife was of the Day family and a relative of the Cottles
who were also from Kentucky and by preference would have
aligned with the proslavers. At the time the "posse" went
to the home of James Montgomery to kill him they were so
incensed at failing to find him they went on to the home of
Arthur near Centerville and required Mrs. Arthur to get up
an elaborate dinner for six men, and showed their appreciation
after eating by placing six revolvers at her head and threatened to "blow her damned head off" unless she told the hiding
place of her husband. He at the time was lying full length
under a bench on which was set several stands of bees, a
growth of weeds aiding in his concealment. He heard every
word of abuse the brutal Bushwhackers heaped upon his wife
but had to bide his time for visiting his wrath upon them.
The shock she suffered caused her to become a physical and
almost a mental wreck. They have a son, A. B., yet living in
Centerville township, who is probably the oldest native born
in the county. The family home was a mile and a half north
of Keokuk when he arrived in the troublous pioneer days.

It is a curious historical fact that every southern sympa-
thizer in that Wyandotte constitutional convention refused to
sign the document after it had been adopted by a vote of
more than two to one. Of the fifty-two delegates in the convention 14 were from Ohio, 6 from Indiana, 5 from Kentucky,
2 from Massachusetts, 6 from Pennsylvania, 3 from New
Hampshire, 4 from Vermont, 2 from Maine, 5 from New York,
1 from Virginia, 1 from England, 1 from Scotland, 1 from
Germany, 1 from Ireland.

Enos Mills became a prominent farmer in Sheridan township and married Ann Lamb, a sister to Miles. Their children
were Oma; Sarah married Charles T. Winslow; Ellen married
a Mr. Bruen; Belle married a Mr. Wasson; Enos became
famous and influential in creating the Rocky Mountain

National Parks and had a beautiful home at the foot of Long's Peak. Horace and Enoch live in Estes Park in Colorado.

Thomas Elwood Smith, son of John and Jane (Buckman) Smith, was born in Bucks county, Pennsylvania, January 5, 1827. His parents were members of the Society of Friends. The father was one of the most active and independent of the early anti-slavery men, and was one of seven in a county containing 50,000 inhabitants who voted in 1840 for James G. Birney for president of the United States. The mother was in Pennsylvania Hall when it was fired by a proslavery mob, and escaped from the burning building. They were both unostentatious but earnest self-sacrificing laborers in the cause of universal freedom. Mr. Smith's ancestors were cousins of William Penn, who immigrated to America with him, and actively cooperated with that distinguished philanthropist in the settlement of his colony. The house in which Thomas E. Smith was born, built in 1738 and still standing in good repair, is a substantial stone building erected on land the title to which bears the signature of William Penn, and was the farm on which the seedling of "Smith's cider apple" originated. Thomas was the second of three children. The elder sister was the wife of Dr. Howard A. Trego of Newton, Bucks county, Pennsylvania; the younger, Hannah E., resides with her parents at Mound City. He was first sent to the common schools of his native state, which among the Friends were of a high standard; then to Kennett Square boarding school for boys, and from there to Benjamin Hallowell's high school at Alexandria, Virginia, a noted school among the Friends, and in charge of a very distinguished member of that society. Among his associate pupils were General Custis Lee, later to be of the Confederate Army; two sons of General Winder of the United States Army; a son of General Jessup; two Carrolls, direct descendants of the signer of the Declaration of Independence, and many of the sons of the most distinguished American statesmen. Upon leaving school, having acquired a solid English education, he settled down to a farmer's life on the old homestead, where he remained until his removal to Mound City, Kansas, in 1857.

He was an active participant in the presidential campaign of 1856, working and voting for John C. Fremont, became deeply interested in the settlement of the free-state question in Kansas, and although enjoying plenty and prosperity in his native state, found the spirit of his ancestors too strong upon him to enable him to remain in quietness at home while such a struggle as that along the border was in progress, and accordingly, came to the disputed territory, to bear his part in rolling back the tide of slavery and constituting the coming state a free commonwealth. Although there had been some outrages perpetrated the previous year, the free-state troubles really began in 1857, and with the troubles there **Mr.** Smith was intimately identified, sparing neither time nor labor to aid the cause. He barely escaped the Marais des Cygnes massacre and led a life full of perilous incidents, and there were but few nights during long periods of time on which he was not called out for the defense of his persecuted neighbors or the protection of his own home.

Upon his arrival in Kansas Mr. Smith with his cousins, Edwin Smith[1] and Dr. J. H. Trego, erected a saw and grist mill on Little Sugar Creek to which grists were sometimes brought a distance of one hundred miles. In connection with this they engaged in cabinet making and the manufacture of shingles, and in company with some others organized the Mound City Town Company, laid out the site and commenced building the town. The original mill company continued business until 1859 when the entire establishment was burned. After this misfortune Mr. Smith rebuilt the mill which he operated until 1865, when he sold out and engaged in the hardware trade in the city, but in 1871 he bought back his mill property. He was frequently called into service with the militia during the war—once to the defense of Fort Scott—and generously contributed to the support of the state troops so frequently on duty along the border.

Mr. Smith belonged to both the Masonic and Odd Fellow societies. Brought up in the Society of Friends, with a birthright in that society, he was liberal in his religious views. February 7, 1853, Thomas Elwood Smith was married to Rebecca Savery Betts, daughter of Thomas Betts, a prominent Pennsylvania farmer. They had seven children: Elliott, of San Juan county, Colorado; Jessie B., Howard, Mary, Susie, Walter and Maggie.

Bucks county, Pennsylvania, contributed more than any other one community in the United States to the citizenship of Linn County and they had contributed just as generously to the cause of liberty in the colonial struggle, though as Quakers they had to do it very diplomatically, as in the case of John Head, ancestor of Mrs. Thomas John Blakey. Mr. Head told Robert Morris, the financier of the Revolution, that the laws of his church forbade him to contribute to a war fund, but added, "Here are the keys to my chest—take what thee needs!" Robert Morris got $60,000 in gold from that chest that helped to tide over a critical situation in Colonial affairs. Among the Bucks county people who are still citizens here are Alfred Blaker Poole, now manager of the Lumber yard at Pleasanton, a son of George C. Poole, now deceased; John Higgins, who had two sons, Larry and Peter, and Hannah who married M. White; Thomas J. Smith; James Rickard; Cary Smith, who lived near Wall Street;

1. Well known as "Little Ed." He left a large family of children.

Henry Walmsley Blaker; George Wyncoop; Herman Smith, who married Mamie Davis, daughter of Frank H. Davis of La Cygne; and William Smith, brother of Herman; and John Wildman Blakey, now at Blue Mound.

Thomas John Blakey of Pleasanton is one of these Bucks county people who has made good in Linn County. His earliest American ancestor was Jeremy Langhorne, who came on the companion ship to the "Welcome" on which William Penn came in 1682, and he built the first stone house in what is now Bucks county, the finish wood for which was brought from England. This was a notable house with walls three feet thick and was surrounded by thousands of acres owned by Langhorne outside of Penn's grant. It was in this house that our Thomas John Blakey was born. He was one of the younger generation to come to Linn County and on April 22, 1886, he was married to Mary Betts Smith, daughter of Thomas Elwood Smith of Mound City, and to them were born Eleanor Blakey, now the wife of Charles M. Blackmar, the lawyer of Kansas City; Letitia, the wife of Dr. Ivan R. Burkit of Ashland, Kansas; Jessie Elizabeth, the wife of John C. Madden of Forest Hills, New York; and Margaret of New York City, who is unmarried.

David W. Cannon came to Linn County in 1854 and settled on a farm adjoining the southeast side of Mound City. He took a leading part in all community affairs and is affectionately mentioned by many of the pioneers quoted in this book. He was a free state man, notwithstanding the fact that his father was a wealthy Kentuckian who owned many slaves. He represented Linn County in the First Territorial Legislature which met at Lecompton and which elected Jim Lane speaker of the house. In 1857 he became probate judge of Linn County and was an active member of the Mound City town company. Judge Cannon was born April 3, 1815, at Glasgow, Barren county, Kentucky, his parents being both from well-to-do Irish families. He was married in 1849 to Miss N. H. Walthall who was born February 16, 1816, in North Carolina. In 1850 they moved to St. Charles county, Missouri, in 1854 coming from there to the farm on the slope of Sugar Mound adjoining Mound City, where he lived till his death in 1892, full of years and honors.

John Calhoun Cannon, son of David W., was born August 3, 1850, at St. Charles, Missouri, coming with his parents in childhood to Linn County, where he was always affectionately known as "Johnnie" Cannon. He graduated from Kansas University and was associated with Col. James D. Snoddy in law practice. For a time he lived at Sedan, Chautauqua county, and was probate judge of that county. In 1882 he was a candidate for congress against Tom Ryan of Topeka. In 1884 he returned to Linn County and in 1890 was elected county attorney and later was elected judge of the sixth judicial district, consisting of Linn and Bourbon counties. He was married at Mound City September 8, 1886, to Miss Dickie Van Buskirk and to them two children were born, Zella, now Mrs. John Austin Hall, and John Marshall, who served in the United States Navy during the World War and is now in the ordnance department of the Navy at San Diego, California.   In 1908 because of declining health Judge Cannon took his family to California, where they lived until 1918 when they returned to Fort Scott, where he died February 28, 1925.

The Tubbs family were an intimate part of the history of Trading Post and vicinity. They were of very respectable origin, the paternal grandfather having been Thomas Tubbs of Amsterdam, Holland, where he belonged to one of William Penn's Quaker churches. His wife was a London woman. They came to America. His son Thomas Jefferson Tubbs was born in Lucerne, Pennsylvania, and was married to Matilda C. Long, (whose father Elias Long was a refugee from Germany after preaching the theory that the occupant and user of land had rights paramount to that of the owner. He was told that if caught in Germany after a certain date his head would be chopped off.)   There were eight children from this marriage who came to Linn County from Morris, Grundy county, Illinois, with the mother in 1857—L. G., J. M., E. L., Ada, Amos C., Mary who married Mr. King R. Powell, and Sarah who married Mr. Eastman.   Thomas Jefferson Tubbs had died at Monroeville, Ohio. Mrs. Tubbs was a resourceful woman and not only managed her boys and girls successfully but made good friends of everyone. When they arrived at the Post in 1857 the "Military Road" was actively used through to Fort Scott about thirty-five miles further south and on to Fort Smith in Arkansas. The fort at Trading Post had been abandoned and was turned over to civilian uses and Mrs. Tubbs and her family occupied the officers' quarters, two room at the northwest corner which were the most carefully constructed. They were made of carefully hewed logs, the spaces between chinked and plastered with lime, while the balance was built of round unhewn logs. Amos C. Tubbs, who now (1926) still lives at Trading Post, was then a boy about twelve years old and of a precocious nature. He had a liking for music and was regularly tutored on the violin by Matt Ellis, a cultured young man of the neighborhood who in 1863 was shot dead by a soldier at one of the neighborhood dances, remembered as one of the early tragedies. Amos became so proficient on the fiddle that when in January, 1859, Old John Brown was making a farewell call on the Tubbs family he asked Amos to play one of his favorite hymn tunes and gave

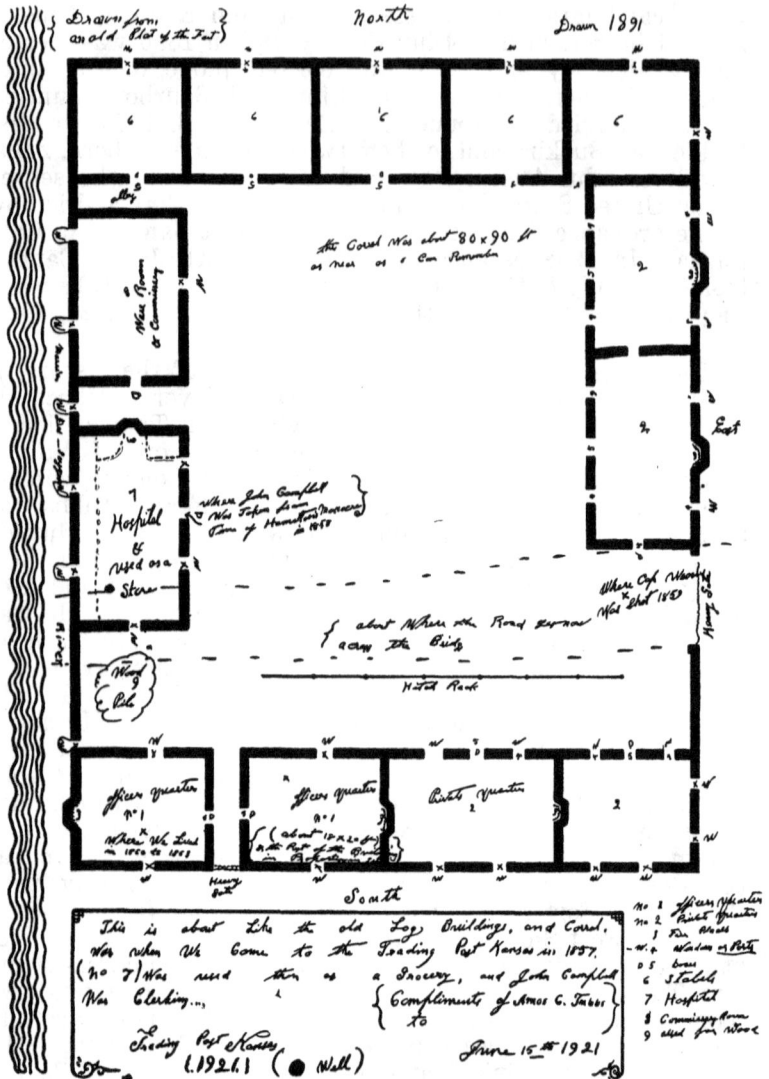

In 1838 General Winfield Scott of the United States Army was in this Western Department and passed through Linn County on his way from Fort Leavenworth to Fort Smith in Arkansas. He was quite impressed by the military importance of the country about Michael Giareau's trading post on the Marais des Cygnes river, and in 1842 returned and built a fort of logs big enough to house a company of dragoons and their horses. Each of the houses for the men had fireplaces. A hospital and store houses were provided. Later, under the influence of Vanderslice who had an Indian agency on the Marmaton river thirty miles south, he was convinced that point was a more suitable site as to distance and he abandoned this Trading Post fort and established Fort Scott. You will notice in the sketch that the present Short Line highway goes right through the center of this old fort right at the east end of the bridge which was built in 1870. The houses for the officers' quarters were of hewed logs and very nicely made. In 1870 they were occupied by Mrs. Tubbs' family and by Dr. Massey and family. It is a curious fact that the maternal grandmother of Ed. R. Smith was a cousin to General Scott.

to Amos a personal gift to remember him by.[1] Old John Brown
was then known to every man, woman and child both in Kansas
and western Missouri, revered as a saint by the Kansans and
feared as a veritable devil by the Missourians. The Tubbs
home was a favorite stopping place to Brown. Amos appeared
one morning with a book from the family library and proceeded to draw on the front fly-leaf a map of that now long
forgotten fort and for fifty years that old book was thumbed
by curious visitors, till in 1921 to save the map, Amos copied
it into the form shown in this book.

Elias, older brother to Amos, went in March, 1858, with
an "overland ox train" contracted by Chouteau and Avery
to carry government supplies to Salt Lake, Utah, and this
boy at nineteen years of age was "second wagon boss", his
duties beginning at sundown and continuing till sunup, watching through the night against surprise attacks by Indians
and rounding up the oxen to prevent straying, getting his
only rest in one of the big wagons as the train of some
twenty-five wagons, drawn by six to seven yoke of oxen each,
some 350 head of cattle, each wagon carrying 6000 to 7000
pounds, pulled westward in the early spring and summer of
1858, across the plains in every day association with roving
Indians, yet never disturbed. Cattle were preferable to horses
as they could subsist on grass and no feed had to be carried.
At Salt Lake City he bought a pony and with his wages ($240
in gold) in his pocket came back to his home by the same route
—and only a boy of nineteen! He still lives at Trading Post
(1926) and is a fine, dignified old man.

In 1857 a regular stage line was maintained between Fort
Leavenworth, Fort Scott and Fort Smith in Arkansas. The
arrival of the stage was a great event. Two fully armed
soldiers sat on the box with the driver and the passengers
were generally army officers or government officials of importance, so that the Tubbs home was always in touch with
the outside world.

There were many Osage Indians here at this time. They
were good natured and friendly and never made any trouble
for the whites. They were very fond of maple syrup and
each spring would tap the maples about the Post and boil
down the sap. They completely spoiled Amos's appetite for
the syrup by their practice of taking a dirty blanket off a
bed and straining their maple syrup through it.

Dr. Aquilla B. Massey was quite a character at the Post.
He had come here from Pennsylvania where he had traded
some worthless stocks in a coal company for seven hundred
acres of land adjoining the Post, but as land titles here were
not well protected, he finally abandoned his hopes of develop-

1. This was a snuff box now in the possession of author of this book as a
gift from Amos. It had been carried for many years by Old John Brown.

ing a fortune here. They were cultured people, Mrs. Massey and Anna and Jack, their children, helping in such social life as the people had. Dr. Massey was a close confidant of Old John Brown and was probably the last to talk with him when he left Trading Post. Dr. Massey practiced medicine here and became very familiar with all the people.

Amos Tubbs was a wonderful boy for detail. In an old book he has written down the names of heads of families who in 1858 lived in "the valley" adjacent to Trading Post as follows: Sam Polk, Sammy Nichols, William Hutchens, Oliver Westover, Ace Rogers, John Mayham, Bill McGuire, Tilman Clark, Uncle Jacky Williams (a preacher), Riley Williams, Mid Story, William Hensley (old squealin' Bill), William Hairgroves, Mark Robinson, Bill Circle, Nathan M. Hawk, George Charney, J. McMine, Matt Ellis the musician, Bill Nichols, Ben Westover, Bill Westover and Wash Jackson. The McMines were from New York and had brought with them some fine pieces of cherry furniture. When they became discouraged and started back to New York they gave several fine pieces to Amos which he still has. At the time of this writing (1926), Amos lives alone in the old home, which is a veritable museum of interesting things. In the grounds surrounding the house he has every variety of fruit tree and over fifty varieties of flowers and sixty stands of thrifty bees from which he sells tons of honey. He keeps a milch cow and maintains quite an establishment for a bachelor eighty years young. His museum attracted the attention of the Smithsonian Institution at Washington.

Amos C. Tubbs of Trading Post tells the following story of the experiences of his family at the time of the Price Raid:

"In October, 1864, we were living in Green Valley, about two miles southwest of Trading Post on Big Sugar Creek on what is since known as the Tom Goss farm. In the evening of October 23 my sister Ada was to go to Trading Post to stay as a companion to Mrs. Edmiston, whose husband was a soldier then in service at Fort Scott. Mother directed me to saddle the pony and accompany her. When we were about a mile from home, just west of Horseshoe Lake, close to the mouth of Big Sugar, a hundred men rode out of the timber toward us. We stopped, astonished. One man advanced and asked if we had a gun, and was I a soldier? The others came closer and laughed in ridicule at the idea I might be a soldier, but I replied proudly that I was a drummer in the militia. In a soldierly manner I asked him what command he belonged to, and at this reply, "General Price's Advance Guard", I at once took on a very serious view of the situation, and in my fright those rebel soldiers looked to be at least ten feet tall. The officer was talking to sister Ada and upon learning we were going to the Post he said we could not possibly get through, as fifty thousand men were to camp right there in the woods. He detailed four men to escort us back to our home.

"When we arrived home there were about a hundred men about the house, helping themselves to anything that took their fancy. I was surprised to have one of the rebels put his hand on my shoulder and say, "Hello, Amos, how are you, old pardner?" I told him I could not remember him and asked his name, to which he replied: 'Names are out of fashion now-a-days.' He gave the same reply to mother's question and added: 'Mrs. Tubbs, if I could help it, not one thing should be taken, but the boys are nearly starved.' One man was eating pork right out of the brine, and another raw pumpkin. When they took a lot of carpet rags from a barrel outside the house I protested and an officer told them to gather them and replace them in the barrel, which they did. A big platter of chicken and dumplings my mother had prepared for her family disappeared almost instantly.

"About that time two men who apparently did not belong to this outfit came up and asked me for a new pair of boots I was wearing. They started to take me behind a haystack to shoot me, using much ugly language, saying they would kill me because "nits grow into lice."

"At this one of the first party of rebels ran to the door and yelled: 'Phoebe, come here quick, they are going to kill this boy.' The leader (who was a mystery to us) came running and released me and directed his men to shoot the offenders if they came back after being run off the place. This incident disclosed to us that this commander who called us by name was Major Phoebe, who had lived with us several weeks and who had owned a store on the west side of the river at Trading Post. A few minutes later a man rode up to the fence and talked with Phoebe a few minutes and rode away. I asked a soldier if he knew who that soldier was and he replied: 'Sure—that was Major Hanley.' It was Absalom Hanley who had boarded with us over a year.

"About sundown twenty men rode up to where I was sitting on the fence and asked if that was where the Widow Tubbs lived, and one spoke up and said, 'Yes, you can tell by the carpet rags scattered about.' Mother came out and they told her not to be out of the house after dark, and if anything went wrong to come to the door and shout for help and they would be there.

"One man asked for 'a little wood', another asked for water but our water supply was short and not good. He asked where we got water and I told him he had better not go there, and he said he knew why. (They had polluted the water supply even to their own disadvantage). We locked the doors and went to bed and slept as though there was not a rebel within a thousand miles of us.

"Mother had just gotten in our winter supplies. The wheat was ground and about four hundred pounds of flour was stored in the house, as was also the pork for winter. They had taken nearly all of it, when one ruffian spread his blanket and up-ended the flour barrel to get what little was left when Major Phoebe made him put it back, saying: 'These people must have something to eat till they can get help.' They added about five pounds of pork to our relief and a pound of butter. One man had taken a tray of six pounds of butter in cake form and Ada told him he must not take it. The other rebels spoke up and said, 'Give her a cake of it,' so we thus got our pound of butter. Just before dawn they rode up to the house and asked how we fared. Mother thanked them for their kind-ness. They all shouted 'Goodbye' as they rode away.

"I climbed to the top of the house and was looking east when just at break of day a big thing came flying over the tree tops, spitting fire and squealing and whining like some animal in a rage. Then so many more followed it that the expression 'hell broke loose' only modestly described it. From my place on the roof I yelled to mother and sister: 'The color is changing—it is blue now', as crowd after crowd of Union soldiers came hurrying by. The shells were from a battery on Prairie Mound.

"At the mouth of Big Sugar our boys captured a rebel battery. As the big army moved through the woods in ir-regular order, owing to the swampy nature of the ground, the rumble and noise and the continual firing of guns of all sizes from rifles and pistols to big cannon—in all this roar and tumult it seemed that all the world had gone crazy but us. In our house dishes and window sash and stove pipe were rattling from the vibrations of the concussions. Gradually the tumult grew away from us off to the south.

"The next day my sister's husband, King Powell, came up from Fort Scott and we went over the battlefield and were amazed at the wreckage of war material of all kinds, horses cut in two by solid cannon shot, everywhere terrifying evi-dence of 'man's inhumanity to man.' The rebels had run the mill at night and started wagons south as fast as loaded, but many were wrecked and abandoned.

A few days later a man drove up to where I was fixing a fence and inquired: 'Is this where Mrs. Tubbs lives?' I recognized him as Uncle Ben Bradley of near Mound City. When they heard of our being robbed his father had said, 'Ben, hitch up and take them something to eat.' While he got the team his father and mother and wife Nellie were busy carrying out all sorts of provisions for our relief, and directed him to go by the store and purchase groceries, which he did. This generous act was indicative of the character of the pioneer people of this county."

The Tubbs family had another thrilling experience in Kansas history. In 1872 they went to Labette county to take up homesteads. In paying some money due to a neighbor Amos Tubbs exposed a roll of $85. 'That old man's face looked like a rattlesnake about to strike when he saw that roll,' remarked his brother. It made them cautious about further intimacy. The old man was John Bender and the discovery that his door-yard was a private graveyard for his victims occurred only a few weeks later.

In the ninth volume of The Kansas Historical Collections the story of Company A of the Eleventh Kansas Regiment is told in a very interesting way by Henry E. Palmer, who served as a second lieutenant. This relates to the Price raid and the following tells what happened in Kansas:

"Price was forced to make a sudden change in his plans. Instead of pushing Blunt and Curtis he suddenly started on a trot, which soon increased to a run, down the line between Kansas and Missouri, for the Arkansas River. We followed in hot pursuit. Colonel Moonlight with his brigade, in which were all the men of my regiment save the twenty men with me, pushed out on our right flank to head off any rebel movement into Kansas. I was ordered by General Pleasanton to keep with his command.

"That night late, about 11 o'clock, we reached a point near Trading Post on the Kansas side and I was ordered to let the main column of our cavalry pass. For hours until daylight an unbroken line of cavalry in column of fours closed up, was passing without a halt. It was raining from 11 P. M. until nearly daylight; a cold, nasty rain. We could not unsaddle and rest our horses or ourselves, but had to sit down on the roadside in the mud, keep awake, and take our medicine. It was an awful night; wet to the skin, teeth chattering horribly.

"October 24 we passed Trading Post, following the enemy in Kansas, and found they had burned every house and barn in reach of their command after robbing and plundering the same, taking clothing from the women, even to the dresses they had on, and wraps from the helpless infants, and that they had shot old men and boys. The Apaches or any band of western Indians could not have made any plainer trail of desolation and murder than this retreating rebel army made while they were marching only a few miles in Kansas. They made us understand by the wrecks and ruins left behind what they had intended to do if they had got as far north as Leavenworth and could have swept down through Kansas as they had planned. But they found to their sorrow that the old war phrase that they had learned from Kansas men at Springfield and at Prairie Grove, 'Kansas is pizen to the hull on 'em,' was no joke. We bivouacked another night on their trail.

"Next day, October 25, about noon, we overtook a large force of rebels trying to cross Mine creek. They were in

Kansas, some three or four miles west of the line. Our advance saw the situation at a glance and charged, every man following. About 3000 men made a wild run for the rebels. It was a grand, inspiring sight. I shall never forget it. We captured over a thousand men, nine pieces of artillery, and many officers, among them General Cabell and General Marmaduke. I saw General Maramduke get off his horse, for he was surrounded, and give up his sword. One of my men said, 'General, are you hungry? If so, I have some hardtack.' The general accepted the proffered food and ate heartily.

"After this disaster General Price burned most of his wagons and fled as fast as he could for the Arkansas border, finally crossing the Arkansas river with about 25,000 men.

"October 25 was my fifteenth day of activity, fighting every day, and actually having no sleep for five days of this time."

The capture of General Marmaduke at the battle of Mine Creek has had a persistent romantic interest because of the fact that a sixteen-year-old boy named James Dunlavey compelled the rebel general to acknowledge surrender by handing over to the boy his revolver with shooting end reversed. The circumstances were particularly interesting, much complimentary recognition being given to the boy, who was placed in the hospital at Fort Scott, where his superior officers gave him much praise and the ladies of Fort Scott gave him testimonials of their esteem. Four days after the battle James wrote the following letter to his father, H. Dunlavey, at Bloomfield, Iowa, which is a very valuable bit of the literature of Linn County:

"Fort Scott, Kansas, General Hospital, October 29, 1864.— Dear Father: It is with pleasure that I once more try to address you a few lines. I received a letter from you at Sedalia on the Pacific Railroad and now by way of answering it I will tell you something of our pursuit of Price and the fighting we have done.

"I was in the fight at Independence on the 22d and at Big Blue on the 23d. At Independence we captured two pieces of artillery and at Kansas City there was three pieces captured by General Blunt. On the 24th we marched fifty-five miles and came up within two miles of Price's rear, where we camped for the night. The next morning as soon as it was light our batteries opened fire on the enemy and soon after a charge was made in which one cannon and thirty wagons were captured. General Pleasanton's command—to which the 3d Iowa Cavalry belonged—was then ordered to the front. Our regiment (the 3d Cavalry) occupied a position on the big prairie about two miles from where the wagons were captured. The rebels made a stand when General Pleasanton ordered us 'Left Front, in line, and charge!' which was magnificently done. The General never halted but charged their

line and drove them before him, and the only sound that could
be heard save the thunder of the cannon and the roar of small
arms was the clarion voice of the gallant general shouting
amid the din 'Come on, my brave boys.' The first shell that
reached the 3d exploded right in front of me, throwing the
pieces all around me and filling my eyes with dust and dirt.
One piece struck me in the right wrist and another struck
my horse on the knee, cutting it badly. As soon as I got the
dirt out of my eyes and the sick spell which the shock occas-
sioned passed off, I put spurs to catch up with the command,
but could not find Company D, but fell in with Company C,
and thinking I could fight as well there as any place, I stayed
with it. I had fired five shots, when to my right I saw rebels
dressed in the Federal uniform, and mistaking them for Union
soldiers started toward them. They were at this time running.
When I got within a short distance of them General Marmaduke saw me shooting at the 'Butternuts' and he mistook me
for a rebel (as he had so many dressed in our uniform) and
started toward me, cursing me for shooting at him. I saw
he was mistaken, and that I had all the advantage of him,
so I let him come up within about thirty steps of me when
I leveled my carbine upon his breast and ordered him to surrender. He was riding rapidly and before he could rein up
was close by my side. He had no arms except a revolver;
this he turned in his hand and presenting the breech to me
said, 'I surrender myself a prisoner of war,' at the same time
telling me he was General Marmaduke[1] and requesting me to
take him to General Pleasanton. I did not know where Pleasanton was and therefore took my prisoner to General Curtis.
The general thanked me and told me to keep the revolver until
further orders but the officers say that I will get to keep it.
The officers have nearly all extended to me their congratulations and say they are satisfied with me as a soldier. One of
General Pleasanton's staff officers called on me this morning,
took my name, company and regiment. In Company D there
was two killed, R. A. Buzzard and John Christy; wounded,
William Reeder in the head (I am afraid dangerously), E. Ball

    1. John Sappington Marmaduke, the rebel major-general captured at the
Battle of Mine Creek, was born on a farm in Saline county, Missouri, March
14, 1833. The family was of English descent from Westmoreland county, England, to Westmoreland county, Virginia. His father, Miles Meredith Marmaduke,
was an early settler in Missouri, and served as the eighth governor of the state.
The son John S. was graduated from the West Point Military Institute in 1857
and served in the cavalry under Albert Sidney Johnson. When the war clouds
gathered his family belonged to the Thomas Benton Hart faction in politics,
in favor of slavery but opposed to dismemberment of the Union. At a family
gathering he discussed secession and asked advice and a senior member of the
family said to him, "John, there can be but one result. Slavery will be abolished.
But you must decide for yourself, following your own convictions." He turned
traitor to the government that had educated him and went south. While in
the Confederate service under General Walker he quarreled with that officer and
in a duel that followed killed Walker. Marmaduke never married. He became
the twenty-fifth governor of Missouri, January 2, 1885. He was thirty-one
years old when captured at Mine Creek.
    Edward Carrington Cabell, who surrendered at Mine Creek, was from a
Virginia family; graduate of Washington College and University of Virginia;
was Congressman from Florida; removed to St. Louis in 1860; served on staffs
of Generals Price and Kirby Smith in Civil War.

in the leg slight; J. Koons in the leg slight, and myself in the right wrist slight. I remain your affectionate son, James Dunlavey."

Much maudlin sentiment has been wasted on the "gallantry" of such characters as Marmaduke and Cabell, proof of which is here given with this renegade riding in a crowd of rebels dressed in the blue uniforms of the Union army and shooting down such soldiers as were deceived by them. Only a half hour before they had murdered Sam Gwynn under such deceptive circumstances and one of these hell hounds was no doubt wearing the bloody clothing they had stripped from his dead body. This was a common practice of the rebels. They killed one hundred and twenty-five men at Baxter Springs by the same ruse. Yet here was a mature man, thirty-one years old, a graduate of West Point at the expense of his government, where he was taught the honorable side of the military profession, riding intimately among a crowd of murderous rough necks, dressed in false colors. "Gallant" Marmaduke! As well say "Gallant" Quantrill.

Writing on "The Black Flag Character of the War on the Border", Capt. H. E. Palmer of the Eleventh Kansas Cavalry makes these comments on Linn County men and events: "The battle at Drywood, Missouri, east of Fort Scott, September 2, 1861, was a dash by Colonel Montgomery with about twelve hundred men and our mountain howitzer then known as 'Moonlight Battery,' against over five thousand rebels with six Parrott guns, the famous Bledsoe battery, the Confederates commanded by Gen. James S. Raines. So bold and determined was our assault that Raines was content after he had shaken us off to move on south without trying to capture Fort Scott as he had intended to do. Thus from early spring until October, 1861, Lane's brigade fought under the black flag—the rebels opposed to us, Upton Hays, General Rains, Davidson, Standwaitie and his Choctaw and Chickasaw Indians, Coon Thornton (the worst daredevil of them all), Quantrill, Thrailkill, Bill Anderson, Arch Clements, Jesse James (who made Missouri notorious after the war), his brother Frank, Cole Younger, Si Porter, Cy Gordon, Bill Todd, Dick Yeager—all officers under Quantrill, commanding guerrilla bands—started in under the war cry 'No surrender except in death!' The Kansans under Lane, Montgomery, Blunt, Jennison, Anthony, Hoyt and others, accepted this challenge, and until General Fremont in October, 1861, issued his order against this retaliatory work and forced a reorganization of Lane's Brigade, and sent Lane out of the army and back to the Senate, there was no pretension to the amenities of civilized war. When General Marmaduke, General Cabell, and seven Confederate colonels, surrendered with over a thousand men at Mine Creek, in October, 1864, some of their captors were

Kansas men of my company and regiment who were prompt in according them fair treatment, manifesting no spirit of revenge. Our men divided the contents of their haversacks with the hungry rebels. Don't forget that our enemy was as often clad in the Union blue as in the butternut or rebel gray."

In a diary kept by John Howard Kitts of the Twelfth Kansas Regiment under date of October 9, 1862, there is this comment on Linn County: "Camped on Sugar Creek. Next morning passed through Paris, Linn County, about 7:30 o'clock. Passed through Mound City at noon, stopped in town about an hour while it was raining. We were called into line again and the rain was pouring down in torrents. A train of twenty wagons met us here that had been sent up from Fort Scott. We were ordered to stack arms and marched on leaving a few men to attend to having the arms put into the wagons. It rained nearly all of the afternoon. We at last arrived at Fort Lincoln, where we camped for the night. Fort Lincoln is constructed of logs, hewn out and put up, and is a pretty strong structure. It is used for the purpose of confining prisoners. It was guarded by several companies of negroes that had been raised for the Twelfth Regiment but the government would not accept them as soldiers. (Fort Lincoln was located on the north side of the Osage River, a few miles north and west of where the town of Fulton now is, and almost due south of Mound City.)

Jared Fairbanks brought his wife and four girls and three boys here from Jefferson county, New York, arriving in the fall of 1857 and settling on a claim three miles southwest of Farlinville. The family were originally from Massachusetts, where the wife and mother was born as Roena Vibber. This family became quite prominent in the border war. Elihu the oldest son in company with Captain Alec Seaman took four slaves belonging to Judge Barlow of Paris and routed them through the Underground Railroad to liberty. A great hubub arose over this and Elihu was arrested by a "posse" and roughly handled as they took him to Lawrence for trial and punishment. Considerable resentment was shown by the free state men and a crowd of horsemen followed to Lawrence and released Elihu. In the meantime the neighbors seized George W. Moore over near Brooklin and held him at the Fairbanks home as a hostage for the safe return of Elihu. Among the free state guards was a man named Beeson who asked Moore to take a walk with him in the timber, at which Moore suspected a scheme to kill him, but old Jared told him he was as safe in his home as if guarded by the whole Federal Army. Old John Brown was very friendly with the Fairbanks family and was frequently at their home. Lew Wesley was the second son and the youngest was Silas Sidney, who has been known as the most cheerful cripple. In early boyhood some fearful malady had twisted his left leg till the hip joint was forced out, yet he has gone through life more cheerful than most men and has always made a full hand in harvest or on a foray into Missouri, as when he went with sixty men to Pleasant Gap in Bates county to punish the murderers of Manning and Upton. Harriet Sylvana became the wife of Captain Alec Seaman.

Rev. William Long came to Kansas from North Carolina in 1859 with a half dozen boys, all born in the "old north state" except the youngest, Lloyd, who was born near Lone Jack, Missouri. The other boys were Enos, John and James who served in the Sixth Kansas Cavalry; Will who drove a team in the militia; and Bloom who "went south" and lost his life in the Indian Territory. Lloyd is still living at Chetopa. James Long married Mary Elizabeth Chamberlain in North Carolina and their son Wiley living north of Pleasanton has two children, Arthur and Beatrice. Rev. William Long was under suspicion of being too friendly with certain proslavery people and narrowly escaped vengeance through the friendship of David Sibbett of Brooklin, who vouched for his good character and loyalty.

Samuel Lee Hamilton of Liberty township was one of the most noted of the early settlers. He came from his birthplace at Carrolton, Illinois, in 1860, with his young wife Mary Ann Enos who was born in New York, her father being a Methodist preacher. "Sam" as he was known everywhere, served in a Kansas regiment under Captain John Alexander. The author of this book remembers the appearance of Sam Hamilton at a county convention at La Cygne in the fall of 1871. All this western country was at that time sore over the way Wall Street manipulated the finances of the country and the favorite indoor sport of Sam was in "twisting the tail of the octopus." There were only about fifty men present and four or five women who came in from a dressmaker's in an adjoining building. Sam sat in gloomy silence modestly at the back, and only responded after repeated calls. He walked up to where the presiding officer sat, turned round and glared at the crowd. He had a big head, large features, eyes shaded by shaggy brows, and a mouth that looked cavernous when he talked loud and fast. But he just glared at the assembly—then took off his coat and threw it aside. He glared some more— then took off his vest and threw it after the coat. This left him standing in a bright red flannel shirt that seemed to stimulate the fury that was burning within him. He glared some more—then began to unbutton that shirt, and the women got so scared they rushed for the door and left. But Sam only loosened it to his waist and threw it open and broke out into a regular conflagration of hot words that held the crowd spellbound. His words fairly burned as he pictured the women of the rich in silks and the pioneer women in ten-cent calico —a favorite and particularly racy story he was fond of telling. He poured out his wrath like a vomit, his features contorted and working like a storm. From that day to his death he was expected at every annual meeting, and even after he begged off and delivered his farewell address, that speech was asked for ten years longer. He was much honored for his rugged character and fine integrity. They had one son, Alfred Perry, who is now an influential Methodist preacher. Their daughter Elizabeth married a young Englishman, now Uncle James Tyson of Goodrich. Lydia married John Warnock and long since passed on. The youngest, Emma, married Will Brownrigg and now lives on the old homestead. Rev. Alfred loves to talk about those early days—of the blue stem grass that would hide a mounted horseman, of loping his pony across the prairies knee deep in flowers, of the wild cucumber and wild hop vines, wild peas, of deer, turkeys, and prairie chickens. In 1860 a band of Indians camped at their spring and the chief of the Osages offered to trade three of his pappooses for Alfred Perry.

James Tyson was born in Westmorland county, England, in 1843, came to America in 1855, and to Linn County in 1865. He married Elizabeth Hamilton November 20, 1870. Their children are Anna who married Nelson Hawkins, Robert who married Blanch Harrison, and Iva who married Leonard Finch.

Thomas Speaks and wife came here from near Indianapolis, Indiana, in 1857. They had four boys, William, Joe, Hiram and Henry. On September 21, 1860, Hiram was married to Lucette DeFreese, whose father had come from Tennessee with two boys and six girls, of whom only Lucette and her brother John, who lives in Vernon county, Missouri, are the survivors. They were neighbors to the Mannings when he and Upton were killed, Mrs. Manning (who was Lizzie Stewart) having lived at the DeFreese home before her marriage. Her father, William Stewart, was from Pettis county, Missouri. They were near at the time of the murder of old Mr. Seright. In fact, Hiram slept out in the fields most of the time while she cultivated the ground and took care of the horses and cattle. Four men came one night and asked for Hiram and to lessen their disappointment they carried away everything loose and went on to the home of Elisha Webb and William Speaks and robbed them of practically everything, showing a special fondness for the men's clothing. Among their neighbors were Samuel Shoemaker, Adam Smith and Fred Smith from Ohio and John Garrett from New York. Mrs. Lucette Speaks still maintains her home in Pleasanton.

Jeff Fleming was a Kentuckian born of Scotch parents in Bath county, that state, October 8, 1820. The family lived for a while in Shelbyville, Indiana, and later in Savannah, Missouri. In the fall of 1858 they came to Linn County where he was an influential citizen. He was a member of the legislature in 1864, served as county commissioner and was sergeant-at-arms of the Kansas Senate in 1877. The children surviving are Robert, born in Shelbyville, Indiana, in 1851; Mary who is druggist at the Osawatomie Institute for Insane; George a cattle man in Texas; and Inda, who married Dr. Stanley H. Brooks and now owns the Brooks Hotel in Mound City. Madison Fleming was a brother to Jeff. His son William was a soldier in the battle of Mine Creek.

Reverend James M. Iliff, a pioneer of Kansas, was born in 1834 in Champaign county, Illinois, married Casandra S. Dennis in 1853 in Allamakee county, Iowa, came to Kansas in 1858 and settled on a claim he had taken in 1857 four miles southeast of what is now Mound City (then Sugar Mound) on upper Mine Creek in Linn County. With his young wife and babies in this virgin country with neighbors two miles away they established a home for the family for sixty years, living first in a tent, then a log house, soon a box house and later a home of more pretentions which he built from native material, he being a carpenter. His wife Casandra S. Dennis Iliff was born in Vermillion county, Ohio, in 1833, of English and German parentage. Her grandfather Andrew Dennis is said to have been with Washington at Valley Forge during the Revolutionary War. Her father was Daniel Dennis and mother Cassandra Stump of Virginia. Cassandra S. Iliff died at Mound City in 1909 and James Massa Iliff in 1915.

James Massa Iliff was a descendant of Richard Iliff the Quaker of England who prior to the Revolution came to New Jersey and later to Bucks county, Pennsylvania, where he died in 1783, leaving three sons—John, James and Joseph. John, the great grandfather of James Massa died in 1806, leaving five boys—Benjamin, John, James, Samuel and Joseph. Benjamin, the grandfather of James Massa died in New Jersey in 1805, leaving four sons and two daughters—Valentine, John, Mary Ann, Elijah, Benjamin and Susan—the father of James Massa being Valentine, who was born in Bucks county, Pennsylvania, in 1797 and died in Eldorado, Iowa, in 1852. Valentine married Esther Moore, of Scotch-Irish lineage, in Pennsylvania in 1818. Leaving this state with their belongings in a one-horse wagon they crossed the mountains westward to Ohio, then to Illinois, and on to Wisconsin, where the wife died in 1850. Valentine then went to Iowa to live with his

children. Like many of the kindred, Valentine was devoutly
religious and the possession by James M. of his father's license
—issued by Peter Cartright, authorizing to preach in the
Methodist church—is highly prized.

Eight boys constituted the family of James Massa Iliff,
of whom four died in childhood and youth. Those who reached
adult life with their families are Daniel A. Iliff of Pittsburg,
Kansas, born in Iowa in 1855, married Ida R. Buck (also a
Kansas pioneer, whose father settled in Bourbon county in
1860; the daughter, Ida R., was born in Illinois and died at
Pittsburg in 1926). Their children are Winfred H. Iliff of
Baxter Springs, M. Floyd Iliff of Oklahoma City, Ethel Mae
Iliff Nicholl of Muskogee, Oklahoma; Theo. L. Iliff of Topeka.

Ezra Milton Iliff married Edith Galloway (they have two
boys, Roy M. Iliff of Los Angeles, Lloyd G. Iliff of Kansas
City.)

James N. Iliff married Kate Jessup; their children are Ira
I. Iliff of Pittsburg, Cassandra Iliff King of Muskogee, Paul
J. Iliff of Muskogee.

Benjamin G. Iliff of Los Angeles married Julia Gilbert, who
died in 1907. Later he married Ora Lewis. By the first
marriage the children are Robert Iliff of Nevada and Frae
Iliff Sullivan of Montana and Benjamin, jr., of Los Angeles.

Upon locating in Linn County James M. Iliff at once became
identified with the activities of this part of the state, always
interested in its welfare and development. He continued
active in the affairs of county and state until his death in
1915. He stood for equal rights to all men and bowed the
knee only to his Heavenly Father. During the Kansas-
Missouri troubles over "states rights" like other newcomers
he was forced to defend his home from marauders who sought
not only plunder but murder. It was not safe to have lights
in the home after dusk. It was considered proper to carry
arms to church and on business. Strife became so intense
that the neighbors fought for the principles they cherished.
On a hill a mile east of the Iliff home a neighbor was called
at night to his door and shot. A short time later a call came
to the Iliff home for him "to come to the door on business."
He was in Iowa settling some business matters when the first
call for troops came. At the next call for volunteers he
enlisted at Mound City in 1862 in Company K, Twelfth Kansas
Infantry. While stationed at Westport he was commissioned
first lieutenant and transferred to the Division of the Mississippi with headquarters at Covington, where he remained
until the close of the war. It was while here that General
Price raided Kansas and the family lost all their belongings,
being left on the battlefield without food for two days.

Word came that Price was at the Trading Post on the
Marais des Cygnes and was coming to sack Mound City. Every
man not fit for military duty and boys in their teens were

drafted for guard duty, none left to aid women and children. Mrs. Iliff with her children and aged and invalid mother went to the home of her sister, Mrs. Almira May, near present Antioch school house, whose husband had with James M. Iliff enlisted in Company K. United States troops were rushed to Mound City and flanked Price's army driving them south. These two families thus fell into the line of retreat, just south of Mine Creek where the Battle of Mine Creek was fought, on the 24th of October, 1864. The night before rumblings could be heard over north. These two families were about to have breakfast when the confederates swooped down on them, cleaning up everything eatable, taking clothing and stock and destroying much property. Price made a stand about a mile south. The United States artillery were rushed to battle line just a little distance west of the May home. All was noise and confusion, none knowing when battle would begin and what the fate of these women and children would be. As soon as Price got his train over the McCauly hill his army moved on without a shot.

After the Union army had passed two boys from these two families (Dan Iliff then about ten years old, and his cousin Erastus H. Jones, some older) like all curious lads "went out to see what they could see", and since there seemed to be plenty to see they kept on seeing, going back over the battle-field across Mine Creek. Horrifying sights never to be effaced from memory. Men dead, others wounded, moaning, crying for help, bleeding, dying, horses fallen, wagons and cannon wrecked, destruction everywhere. Later to the improvised hospital in the Mound City school house where the wounded were being cared for, and over on Sugar Creek to where the Confederate soldiers were being buried, went these curious boys. In the diary of James M. Iliff is found: "Oct. 28, received word that Price is retreating south of my place. How glad and yet how anxious about my family!" Each day following had notations with "no word from home." "Are all my friends forsaking me." On November 8, "Thanks to Kind Providence, my loved family is safe but property all taken by the rebels. How this letter relieves me!"

Ida R. Buck's father and mother (parents of Mrs. D. A. Iliff) living thirteen miles west of Fort Scott, were in town just after Price went east of Scott, trying to get food supplies for their family. Here he with his team was commandeered to follow with provisions for the Union Army and she was set afoot for this long walk to carry such supplies as she might be able to secure to her little children at home, her son in his teens in the home guards, an older son in the Regular Army, her husband (who in the defense of home a few years prior had been shot by a horse thief) incapacitated for active service. There was no assurance that any would be returned to her.

Is it any wonder that this noble state has been referred to as "Bleeding Kansas"?

The drouth of 1860, the grasshopper scourge of 1875, the Texas fever which destroyed the cattle, prairie fires uncontrolled, small market for what could be produced, but little money in the country, made living a problem. Provisions had to be freighted from Missouri river points by teams which took two weeks or more for a trip. Cotton grown or wool produced was picked, carded, spun, and woven into clothes, and shoes were made at home. The Iliffs were somewhat fortunately situated as they lived on the main road from Kansas City to Fort Scott and often sold prairie hay to campers on Mine Creek.

Until suitable houses could be provided the Iliff home was the meeting place for religious worship. James M. Iliff was a factor in building up the church of his choice. Soon after the Civil War he entered the Methodist ministry, served as secretary of his conference for thirteen years until compelled to retire on account of infirmities. Much credit is due him for the preservation of the early day church history and the maintenance of its institutions. Among his papers are found names of men prominent in the early church struggles and their connection with Kansas activities of the times. He was a charter member of Lodge No. 24, A. F. and A. M. and first junior warden at Mound City. He interested himself in the political affairs of county and state, held positions of trust, the last being that of probate judge. His grave is in Battle Field Cemetery, southeast of Mound City, where are also his wife and children.

Mrs. Casandra Dennis came to Linn County in 1857 from Washington county, Ohio, and brought several children who have been noted for good citizenship, among them Mrs. J. M. Iliff, wife of Rev. Iliff, and Mrs. Almira May, and a son, Daniel P. Dennis, who had been born May 3, 1829, in Washington county, Ohio, and who was married at Ty Branch, Iowa, on November 7, 1857, to Susan R. Fewel. To them came three daughters, Margaret born in Iowa, Winnie and Stella born in Missouri, and Bruce born near the Battle Field school house south of Pleasanton. The girls became noted in their work in the public schools and Bruce learned the trade of a printer and later owned the La Cygne Journal in 1898. He married Florence Atkinson of La Cygne July 12, 1903. He afterward moved to La Grande, Oregon, where he owned the Evening Observer and now owns the Klamath Falls Observer. He is credited with being a strong force for better things in his newspaper and has won recognition throughout his state. Of the girls Stella Dennis married G. M. Shattuck of Valley township, where they lived till 1901, when they moved to Lead, South Dakota, where she died in 1922. Winnie Dennis is now teaching at Portland, Oregon. Margaret Dennis was married to John W. Swesey of Blue Mound on April 28, 1888, and later moved to Cowley county, when Mr. Swesy died in 1895. In 1900 Mrs. Swesy was married to Dr. H. L. Clarke of La Cygne, her venerable uncle Rev. J. M. Iliff performing the marriage rites at Pleasanton. Their two children are Mrs. Charles Love of Lawrence and Lucile, a senior student at Kansas University in 1927. The father Daniel P. Dennis was a soldier from 1861 to 1864 in Company L, Fourth Iowa Cavalry. He died at the Leavenworth Soldiers Home in 1904, and Mrs. Susan R. Dennis died at La Cygne in 1909.

Elim W. Bartleson was born in Philadelphia January 9, 1837. His mother, a Whittaker, died when he was ten years old and the father, who was a contractor, took the children to a village called Falling Waters near Martinsburg in what is now West Virginia. He was fifteen years old when he went to Wapello, Iowa, in 1852, where he worked on a railroad survey and later joined his sister at Marion, Iowa. He worked in a saw-mill and grocery and carried mail from Center Point to Waterloo, and when the war came on enlisted at Center Point in Company B. Twentieth Iowa Volunteer Infantry and served in Missouri and Arkansas until 1865 when he was discharged at Mobile, Alabama. He had been married in 1860 to Marian Alice Brice and she had come on to Linn County with her father, Dr. S. M. Brice. Thomas Shaw, who had married Dr. Brice's sister, was a pro-slaver and as he and his four sons had to leave Dr. Brice took over his claim and thus became a neighbor to Ed. R. Smith. He knew and expressed a high regard for Mrs. Ezra Hanchet Smith and also Nettie Smith who married Jack Ranney of Miami county. From an unsatisfactory farm experience he went to Bob Kincaid's store and later had a store at Farlinville where he was postmaster. In 1868 he went to Mound City and had a feed store and in 1869 bought McReynold's drug stock at Pleasanton and moved it to Mound City, but in 1889 moved back to Pleasanton to stay.

At the time of the Price Raid Jim Scott was county treasurer and feared for the county property. He brought the books and money to Bartleson's house and Mrs. Jim Scott and Mrs. Bartleson found a hole in a bank dug out by some animal and converted it into a temporary county treasury by storing their junk in it. The next day Mrs. Bartleson and Mrs. Jabez Broadhead rode over the battlefield and saw both the dead and the wounded lying untouched. Mrs. Fletcher Broadhead, who had joined them, was wearing a white skirt which she took off and tore into bandages for the wounded. The Fletcher

Broadheads were from Bucks county, Pennsylvania, and were Quakers. He was a brother to Jabez, who was from Busti, New York. Dr. Samuel McMillan Brice helped to organize the Republican party in Iowa. His wife was Esther Tolman who was from Augusta, Maine. Dr. Brice achieved fame as the originator of Brice's Early June peach.

John Palmer from Ohio and Rebecca Hart Palmer had a home close to the crossing of the Military Road at Mine Creek. Their daughter Barbara Jane had married Melville Cox Dolson in Scotland county, Missouri, in 1859, and their surviving child of this marriage is now Mrs. Albert H. Mantey at Mound City, where Mrs. Dolson maintains a home adjoining them. The women folks were witnesses of the most severe fighting of the Battle of Mine Creek and a clever account of it by Mrs. Dolson is given in this book.

George W. Jones, one of the most genial souls that ever lived anywhere, was long an honored citizen of Linn County. In 1871 he located at Fort Scott. In 1875 he was made principal of the public schools at Mound City where he served till 1879, when he became county superintendent of schools, and then became assistant state superintendent of education. Mr. Jones was born in Madison county, Indiana, September 6, 1849, where he was educated and was employed as a teacher.

Several old families of some note in Scott township were William Huggins and wife Margarite (they had a son named Seneca and daughter Olive who attended the Wattles college at Moneka), they lived near old Hughey Huston who gave the land out of his farm for Prairie Home cemetery; the Huggins were from Illinois. Another neighbor was James Snyder whose daughter Melissa married the son of Nathaniel McCarty; another was William Stites who was a soldier in Captain Leasure's company of state troops. He was something of a rhymster and possibly surviving members of his company will remember his "poems".

Alfred Wayne married Mrs. Rettie Ann Jones Roberts, daughter of Louis Bruce Jones of Indiana and his wife Elizabeth C. Roberts whose parents were from North Carolina. These Matthews, her parents, settled in Lawrence, Kansas, when there were only three houses and later came to Linn County in 1894. Alfred and Rettie had one daughter Anna Alfred who married Ernest R. Perry, (now of Osawatomie). By a previous marriage Rettie had two sons— Ervin Melvin Roberts in railroad work at Bellingham, Washington, and William Boyd Roberts of Mound City. Alfred is a son of Temple Wayne, one of Montgomery's men in 1854. He remembers that when they entered Kansas Territory in

1854 they did not see a house west of the Missouri line till they arrived at Sugar Mound, quite a stretch of wild country. In 1901 Alf cut a cottonwood tree on the David Cannon farm and got a thousand feet of good lumber from it. He remembered when the place where the tree grew was a field with not a tree in it, showing what forestry would do for us if properly practiced.

Abraham Frisbie of a Connecticut family married Mary A. McClure in McDonough county, Illinois, December 19, 1851, and they lived there till his death in 1882. He was a veteran of the Mexican War from Wheeling, West Virginia, and was in the Seventy-eighth Illinois in the Civil War. In 1886 Mrs. Frisbie came to Linn County with her son James Philemon who has served as county clerk and was on the selective draft board during the World War. He married Jessie Shattuck, daughter of Captain William H. and Mary A. Shattuck. Their children are Glenn Harlan who enlisted in the World War and served in France and later married Ada Tyler; James Wilbur who enlisted at eighteen and served in France and came home and married Mary Mendenhall; Arthur Elliott who is a teacher in Montana; and Howard who is a student in Emporia College.

Jackson Calvin and his wife Almira Taylor came to Linn County from Indiana in 1885 and located in the valley south of Boicourt. Their children are Elmer who married Nettie Shattuck; Otis married Maggie Church; Ed married Effie Williams; Alonzo married Nora Shattuck; Dillard married Ina Shattuck (and they have four children—Maurice, Mildred, Dale, and Marjorie); William lives in Oregon; Alice married James Miller; Delia married Nile Carpenter; and Lily married Walter Hyatt.

Hopkins Carpenter was born on a ship in Long Island Sound and had six children by a first wife whose name we can not give. These children were brought to Linn County. Hettie married Hank Dunlap; Hopkins married Olive Sparkman; Melissa married John T. Kennedy; Charles married Minnie Sheets and later Lena Gates; Harry married June Beach; and Curry became general passenger agent of the Milwaukee and St. Paul Railway and died at his home in Minneapolis. Hopkins Carpenter the father was married again to Eric Boling of Zanesville, Ohio, who was a near relative of Mary Todd who was President Lincoln's wife. Their children were Albert A. who married Annabel Corwin; William W. married Victoria McCleary; Walter S. married Nellie McCoach; Franklin Pierce married Elizabeth Miller; and Thomas married Julia Porter. Hopkins Carpenter sr. was one of three men riding with Sam Gwynn, a soldier, when he was killed northwest of Pleasanton and stripped of his clothing by Price Raiders in

Ohio, that Emma Wattles, third child of Augustus, was born on July 15, 1842. Because of failing health Augustus retired to farm life till in 1855 he started with his family for Kansas, accompanied by John Otis Wattles and his family. They first settled on a farm in Douglas county but in 1857 they felt the urge to be a part of the struggle to make Kansas a free state, so they moved to Linn County and settled on the prairie north of Sugar Mound. The great increase of settlers made it desirable to have the convenience of a town with a post-office, school, stores, churches, etc., so they set about incorporating a town, taking ten acres at each of the four corners at the intersection of sections 36 and 31, 1 and 6, townships 21 and 22, ranges 23 and 24. Augustus had previously made a trip from Lawrence to Fort Riley and one night he was given shelter and food at the home of an Indian near Silver Lake. There were two little girls in the family about the age of his Emma at home and he became quite interested in their beauty, intelligence and gentleness. One was named Mo-ne-ka, which the parents told him meant "Morning Star." Upon his return home he mentioned the little girl so admiringly that the town makers gave her the compliment of calling their town Moneka. The men forming the town company were Erastus Heath, J. N. O. P. Wood, Augustus Wattles, J. O. Wattles, Julius Kuler, Andrew Stark, and W. F. Marney. John O. Wattles built a frame house of native lumber in the summer of 1857, and Augustus Wattles built a stone house with floors of native oak and finishing and doors of native walnut in 1858 and 1859. The Town Company erected a two-story frame building for a hotel, and with the help of the neighborhood in general built a school house of two stories, the frame of native timber and the floors and siding of pine from Arkansas, two members of the town-company going all the way to Arkansas and hauling lumber to finish the school house, traveling all that dreary way with ox teams. This school house was finished and school opened January 1, 1858, with Mrs. Hulda Goodwin as teacher with Miss McGrath as assistant. Mrs. Goodwin had previously conducted a young ladies' boarding school at West Point, Indiana, about ten miles north of La Fayette, and she was an experienced and valuable person to the community. It is an interesting fact that from this first school in Linn County several children went out into the world and attained to international fame. This was the first effort for higher education in Linn County, the course above the grade approximating our present "Junior High". The settlers were highly appreciative of this opportunity for schooling their children and there were notable examples of students traveling many miles each day to get the benefits of their teaching. One girl pupil was Olive Huggins, daughter of William and Margarite Huggins whose home was in the center of Scott township near the present

Prairie Home cemetery. They were from Illinois. "Ollie" Huggins rode horseback each day to and from Moneka, a distance of twenty miles for the round trip, to prepare herself to teach school. Think of that, you who now yell "Jayhawk!" The town company soon had the nucleus of a frontier town, with postoffice, blacksmith shop, grocery and dry-goods stores, and families preparing to make homes. In the summer and fall of 1857 and in 1858 the following families settled in the town site or vicinity, and remained until after the war: Erastus Stark and family, O. P. Watson and wife, W. H. Wheeler and family, F. C. Bacon and family, Cyrus Goodwin and wife, Lyman Strong and family, George Dennison, Mr. Andrews and family, Hamilton Schooley and family, John A. Lefker, Augustus Wattles and family, J. O. Wattles and family. All these families were living in or near Moneka at the time of Marais des Cygnes Massacre and only one, Mr. Andrews, left at that time. As he was taken prisoner with those who were shot but liberated, his neighbors felt that he was excusable for wanting to leave the county. Of the young men who came to the Moneka settlement in 1857 and '58 and stayed until '61, most of them enlisted. They were H. P. Danforth, William Holbrook, Alf Tanner, A. D. Perrin, Charles Perrin, Orlando Morse, Orlin E. Morse, L. Crawford, L. Garrett, A. Stark, T. W. Wattles, Owen Botkin, Murray Botkin, J. H. Stearns, David A. Crocker.

The land upon which Moneka was located was a part of the Miami Indian Reservation and on account of some irregularities it was taken out of the market and the town company could not give title to lots. This stopped the growth of the town.

At the beginning of the town of Moneka there came two boys aged twenty-two and twenty respectively who were to live to years and honors in Linn County. Their parents were John Eaton Morse, who was a native of Vermont and Nancy Tillson Morse, a native of Canada.[1] The parents had gone from Vermont to New York and then to Huron county, Ohio, where Orlin Eaton Morse was born at Peru, March 27, 1837, and when he was twenty years old he and his brother, Orland Stuart Morse, two years his senior, started for Kansas where they joined their former neighbors, the Danforths, who were also from Peru, Ohio. The two boys started a store at the Wattles crossroads. Nobody had any money in those days and in a little while the Morse boys had "trusted" out their entire stock of goods and were unable to replenish their stock. They did not give way to discouragement but started a furni-

1. John Morse of Vermont married Esther Eaton, moved to New York state, and from there, with their two sons, Daniel Morse and John Eaton Morse to Huron county, Ohio. John Eaton Morse married Nancy Tillson of Peru, Ohio. Their two sons Orlando Stuart Morse and Orlin Eaton Morse were among the first settlers in the town of Moneka, coming there in the spring of 1857.

ture factory, using the abundant walnut timber. In this work they excelled and scattered over Linn County now are many pieces of their handiwork that are worthy of preservation as real objects of art. Mrs. O. E. Morse has a dining-table and two bedsteads that are of beautiful lines and finish, the table legs having flutings that show exquisite good taste in design and would now rank high in comparison with early Duncan Phyfe or other famous New England designs. In 1861 Col. James Montgomery organized the Third Regiment of mixed infantry and cavalry but afterward all the cavalry with that of the Fourth Regiment was put into what became the really famous Fifth Kansas Cavalry and the enlistments from Linn County were in "D" Company, where Orlin E. Morse at twenty-four years of age found himself a second lieutenant. Henry Seaman was captain, Dr. J. H. Trego first lieutenant, O. E. Morse second lieutenant, Miles Lamb and Eugene Baird sergeants, William Baird corporal. O. E. Morse was captain when the regiment was mustered out. All of the infantry enlistments were put into the Tenth Kansas Cavalry under Colonel Tom Moonlight.

When O. E.. Morse was only twenty-one years old he was of the party who planned an expedition into Virginia to effect the release of Old John Brown, confined in the jail at Charles-town under sentence of death for his attack upon Harper's Ferry, the charge being "treason to the State of Virginia." Captain Morse wrote the story of this remarkable incident for the State Historical Society and it is incorporated in this book.

O. E. Morse was married to Emma Wattles in October 1864, just after he was mustered out of the service. They had six children: W. L. Morse, a builder at Mancos, Colorado; John O. Morse, lawyer at Mound City; T. W. Morse, editor at Topeka; Stuart T. Morse, farmer, Greenville, Florida; O. R. Morse civil engineer at Ft. Worth, Texas; Eleanor Eaton Morse died in 1910. John O. Morse married Sara W. Trego, daughter of Dr. J. H. Trego, one of the original members of the Mound City Town Company.

Augustus Wattles died in 1874, being only sixty-nine years old. His wife was Susan E. Lowe, a sister of David P. Lowe who was at one time judge of this judicial district, and who survived him. He left four children who showed themselves worthy of their heroic sire. Sarah Grimke[1] Wattles after the Civil War married Dr. Lunday Hiatt and lived in Denton,

1. Sarah Grimke was a remarkable woman in a noted family. In 1825 her father was a judge in the higher courts of South Carolina and owned a thousand slaves. Slavery was so repugnant to the two daughters that they devoted their lives to the abolition of it. Sarah Grimke never married but her sister Angelina Grimke married Theodore Weld, who was one of the debaters at Lane Seminary and became a co-worker with William Lloyd Garrison and Gerrit Smith. The first born child of Augustus Wattles was named after Sarah Grimke.

Texas. Theodore Weld Wattles served as sergeant in Company D in the Fifth Kansas Cavalry and re-enlisted in Hancock's Veterans and afterwards lived in Colorado where he died in 1907; Emma Wattles married Orlin Eaton Morse whom she survives and maintains her own home in Mound City. Mary Ann Wattles had a remarkable career. After graduating from Oberlin College she was sent as a post-graduate to Munich, Vienna and Paris to complete her studies in medicine and surgery and became a member of the faculty of the Woman's Medical College in New York City, the first great woman's medical school. She married Carrol Founce and made her home in Creed, Colorado, where they now live.

John Otis Wattles was a graduate of Yale and was a noted lecturer prior to the Civil War. He was intimately associated with William Lloyd Garrison and Gerrit Smith, two wealthy men who led the fight against slavery. Mr. Wattles helped in various large enterprises to help the black race, in establishing the schools in Mercer county, Ohio, and as a lecturer throughout the north. His wife was Esther Whinnery who was from Columbia county, Ohio. He died at Moneka in 1859. They had three girls whom the mother kept in the little school in Moneka till the close of the Civil War, when she took them back to Oberlin College to complete their education. Of these children, Celestia graduated with honors and was sent to Leipzig for post-graduate work and was made professor of music at Oberlin College on her return, making many trips to Europe to further equip herself during her forty years service. Harmonica Wattles married Marshall Woodford and made her home at Warren, Ohio. Theano Wattles taught several years and married Frank Case and lived at Canton, Ohio.

The work in Mercer county, Ohio, by the Wattles family was in caring for negroes whose masters had emancipated them from bondage and made free men of them. It is a fine page in history which records that there were many slaveholders throughout the South who voluntarily not only gave their black people liberty but furnished money by which they secured land in their own names. Mrs. O. E. Morse gives the following clear explanation of this situation: "By the laws of Kentucky, slaves could not be liberated and allowed to remain in the state. By the laws of Ohio, negroes could not be brought into the state unless provided with means of support to prevent their becoming a public charge. Therefore the master furnished the money and Augustus Wattles entered the land at the Land Office in Dayton, Ohio. In the name of heads of families, they receiving the deeds and were settled on their own land. These slaves were liberated and moved to Ohio from 1835 to 1838 and had built cabins and cleared fields and had their children in school by 1839 and 1840, more than

twenty years before the Civil War. Their freedom was a free
gift from their masters and during this work of establishing
this colony the schools in Cincinnati were kept up, pupils by
this time paying for tuition.

Orland Stuart Morse, brother of O. E., married Prudence
Swingley of a large family who came from Maryland to Ohio
and to Illinois and to Linn County, making their home near
Mansfield. Their children were Mattie M. now in Chicago;
Orlin B. Morse; and Eldon S. Morse, an official in the state
printing plant at Topeka. Another of the Swingley girls
married Andrew Stark of Mansfield who served a term in
the legislature.

Abraham Johnson Jackson was born in Hancock county,
Indiana, December 11, 1836. He was a son of Andrew Jackson
born May 24, 1805, and Elizabeth Jackson born April 20,
1802; they were married January 16, 1827. Abraham was
married to Nancy Helen Oldham born in Hancock county December 22, 1838. The family came to Linn County September
18, 1879, from Henry county, Indiana. Their surviving children are Ida May who married G. W. Gifford of Prescott, Jessie
E. who married Harry Baker of Pleasanton, Ernest who
married Nanie Cockrell of Hume, and William Herman who
married Tillie Taylor of Pleasanton. About 1890 Ernest
Jackson came to Washington, D. C., with a letter from Senator
Perkins addressed to the sergeant-at-arms of the United States
senate who was to give him a job as a messenger. He reported
to me first and next morning I took him up to the capitol
and introduced him. He had only been in town overnight and
didn't know one street from another. The office of sergeant-
at-arms is a big place and he was a bit impressed. They gave
him a fine horse beautifully equipped, and a few minutes later
handed him a big envelope addressed to "The President of
the United States, White House," and told him to deliver it.
Before I got home in the evening I read the story of his adventure. He started out in the general direction of the White
House but got lost. As a joke he was sent in the wrong direction and wandered around till a reporter for the Star found
him and set him right. He entered the White House where
the doorkeeper politely offered to take the letter, but Erny
insisted he was to deliver it to Ben Harrison. The President's
doorkeeper wanted to receipt for the papers and take them in,
but Erny still insisted he was to deliver them to the President,
and Ben Harrison left his chair and shook hands with the
boy and took the papers. It made a good story that gave all
Washington a laugh. Erny put in his time on short hand
writing and qualified himself to become court reporter when
he resigned his job and came home.

Among those who came in 1858 were Franklin Newell and his wife Elizabeth Martin Newell. He was born in Indiana and she near Wheeling, West Virginia. They settled on a farm five miles northwest of Mound City near Mansfield. He was in a Kansas regiment at Wilson's Creek and was taken prisoner and after being exchanged he enlisted again in the Twelfth Kansas Infantry and served till the end of war. During the drouth of 1860 he had taken his family to Iowa where Lina Effie was born. She became the wife of Isaac A. Davis who had been a soldier in the Fifteenth Kansas Cavalry and was probate judge in 1907. The other Newell children were Minnie who married William Ayres of Centerville, Annie married William Robertson of Indiana, Louisa married John Chambers of Centerville, Elva married James Rowland of Hillsdale, and Belle married Russell Schultz of Severy.

The responsibilities of local self-government and the rival interests involved therein has always been a fruitful source of trouble to pioneer communities. In Linn County there was not much contention as yet over politics as it was either to be "free state" or "pro-slaver." But the question of the location of the county seat was a ghost that was always walking. In the beginning Paris had the county officers and had grown to be a village of some 200 population in 1859. At that time Elwood Smith, Edwin Smith, the Barneses, and others, had obtained a regular charter for Mound City and had a saw-mill and gristmill running, and were asking people to "watch our smoke." When the vote was taken on the proposition to relocate the county seat 978 votes were cast in the county, of which Mound City received 507 and Paris 471. The county commissioners directed the sheriff to bring the various county offices to the newly chosen capitol. When the sheriff attempted this he found the building at Paris called the "court house" deserted and empty and he so reported to the county commissioners. Mound City became excited and it was proposed to go over with enough men to forcibly take possession of the county property and move it. At this time Dr. Charles R. Jennison approached the sheriff and suggested that he be deputized to accomplish the removal and promised immediate results. But the sheriff was terror stricken when the crowd dragged out "Brass Betsy", a 3-inch-bore brass cannon about three feet long and mounted in a clumsy way on a home-made carriage with about two hundred feet of rope attached with which to pull it by hand. Jennison assured the sheriff it would not be necessary to fire a shot and after much excited discussion Jennison was equipped with the legal authority to do the work and a hundred hands grasped the rope and pulled old "Betsy" to Paris. Pat Devlin, the original and noted "Jayhawker," was in immediate charge of the cannon. The county officers were found in their several homes but pretended ignorance as to what had become of the books and equipment of the different offices. "Why, your fellows came and raided the court house and we don't know what they did with the books!" Marching to the log house in which the probate judge lived they got the same reply when Jennison gave some stentorian orders to Pat Devlin. "Depress that gun! Depress that gun! Aim to take about three feet off the corner of this house!" Taking out his watch he stepped opposite Hairgrove and said, "I'll give you just five minutes to produce those books or down goes the house." Hairgrove turned white and howled that his family were in the house. "That's your business—two minutes of time gone!" "Three minutes." At this Hairgrove wilted and said he would perform if the cannon was trained in some other direction. This was done, but Devlin still stood with the lanyard ready to pull should order be given. Jennison went inside with Hairgrove and pried up pieces of the puncheon floor and found the probate records in an excavation that had been made for them. In like manner each of the county officers surrendered as gracefully as they could. The Mound City crowd "took home the bacon" with so much hilarity it excited inquiry, when it was found that the entire party—even "Old Betsy"[1]— was without a grain of powder!

The story of the origin of the town of Pleasanton is a romance of the business history of the county. There were many rumors then of new railroads to be built. Already the Kansas City, Fort Scott and Gulf was coming south and in 1869 was running trains through to La Cygne. Something seemed to puzzle the engineers and there was much uncertainty as to where the tracks would go. Trading Post confidently expected they would not only be a station on this road but also on the road to come through from St. Louis on an east and west course. Six hundred acres were platted out into what would have been a magnificent townsite with beautiful natural surroundings. Over west of the Boicourt lakes Colonel James Finley Harrison had a large tract of land ready to welcome the builders of a metropolis. On beyond was Mound City quite eager to be absorbed into the new order of things. But the north and south line seemed to hesitate at La Cygne. Several new men appeared upon the scene. Dr. Nehemiah Nickerson from Meriden, Connecticut, and a Mr. Allen from the same town, associated themselves with Dr. Henry Plumb from Wolcott in their state, after they had all attained to military honors in the Civil War and were seeking business and professional locations in the new western

1. This "Old Betsy" was a real cannon cast at Geneva, Illinois. It was sent out without mounting to escape detection by the Missourians, who robbed emigrants of dangerous looking armaments.

country under the firm name of Nickerson, Allen and Company, Dr. Plumb being the company. They conducted a hardware store for a few months at Harrisonville, Missouri, but it did not measure up to their expectations and they were arranging to go to Texas when a pedlar with a small stock of goods in a wagon told them about Trading Post and immediately they started for that rather famous place at that time, June, 1867. They found engineers running lines everywhere about the town and they were so assured of its future that they brought a stock of hardware there and opened a store. After only a few weeks the stakes were set for what is now the Frisco railway, leaving them off the direct line to wealth. Then Tuck Williamson arrived from Greenville, Indiana, and he and Dr. Plumb thought the Dave Goss farm two miles north of where Pleasanton now is was an ideal site for a town. Uncle Johnnie Baugh and Bartlett Baugh, two high class Kentucky men, also owned land there and joined their forces to those of Plumb, Williamson and Goss, but this scheme hardly got started. Later Dr. Plumb and Tuck Williamson bought a quarter section from Ira D. Bronson at the northeast corner of what was to become Pleasanton and later added to it a quarter section which they bought from Sanford Hough. They had old Judge Barlow draw up the papers, including application to the county commissioners for authority to plat and develop a new city in Linn County, which was granted. A special commission of citizens was named to see it was all done decently. In the meantime a rival company was laying out a town west of the railroad right of way which was now plainly marked out. Tuck and the doctor went to Kansas City to see Octave Chanute, chief engineer of the railroad, and got a cordial reception. Dave Goss and they offered the railroad half of their enterprise to locate the town there. Judge Linton spoke for Linn County at large and made a notable speech. Colonel Kersey Coates was present as the representative of the railroad company. Somehow they did not get any definite committal to their project from Engineer Chanute. There was town talk in the air everywhere. Deland had a mill at Mound City, and when the railroad was assured moved it to the place it would cross Mine Creek and announced to the world the town of El Mino he was going to build there and Hank McGlothlin hauled lumber there from Trading Post to start the town. In the meantime Morgan Fickes owned the northeast quarter of section thirty-six and he resolved to build opposite that started by Dr. Plumb and Tuck Williamson. He went to Kansas City and he talked to Octave Chanute as a separate and sole entity, not complicating his proposition by even so much as mentioning the railroad company. He offered Chanute every other lot if he would locate the station on Fickes' land. Chanute accepted and soon two rival towns were growing side by side both honoring the name of the general who had brought his army there in pursuit of the rebels—Pleasanton. Hank McGlothlin hauled his lumber back from El Mino and that town died aborning. The lumber went into the first houses built in the new town. The Kincaids built a store on east sixth street as did also Charlie Wheaton and Fairfield from Olathe. The first store completed and opened was that of Nickerson, Allen and Plumb, the first building of any kind in the town. Talbot came over from Trading Post and built a store at Broad street between Main and the railroad and had a stock of groceries, but his health failed and he went to Albuquerque where he died soon after. Van Zandts came in with a stock of farm implements. Two rival business sections were running and nobody getting anywhere. Finally Dr. Plumb saw the futility of the rivalry and persuaded Kincaids to come over on the west side where the opera house now is, this building being built later by Kincaid and D. A. Crocker. Charlie Wheaton was the first postmaster in his store on the east side. Grandpa Whitman came from Trading Post to the new town. This complete consolidation brought about friendly feeling to all and the town started a real growth. The first bank was on east side of Main street south of Broad. Koch owned he bank. The Methodists built the first church at northeast corner of Seventh and Main streets, Old Man Hammond who owned a mill in north part of town being a leading spirit in it. He was from Ottumwa, Iowa. The first school was held in the Presbyterian church where it now is. Dick Blue was one of its first teachers. Miss Hargroves had a private school where Lieutenant Governor Dan. Chase now lives. The first blacksmith shop was on the east side. The first gristmill was owned by William A. Hammond at the northwest corner of the townsite. King Powell who married Miss Tubbs afterwards had this mill. The first hotel was at northeast corner of Main and Broad streets, first owned by a Mr. Butler and afterward by Squire Newell from Centerville township, whose grandson Frank A. Davis now represents the Rosedale district in the Kansas legislature. The second hotel was a pretentious affair that gave the town fame all over eastern Kansas, the Gulf House, built by Morgan Fickes, where the home of W. C. Travis was built after the destruction of this hotel by fire. The Masons had the first lodge organized with Dr. Plumb first master, followed by Van Zandt. The Odd Fellows were next. The first permanent school was on the hill-top in its present location. The first lawyer was Winfrey, who went back to Kentucky where he became a judge. Dr. Plumb was the first doctor, followed by Dr. R. J. Peare. The first depot was on the west side of the tracks at Sixth street. Josiah Sykes' hotel was at northeast corner of Sixth street and right-of-way. Thus the town of Pleasanton blossomed out into its present thrifty community of homes, destined for a permanent prosperity.

Dr. Henry Plumb has arrived at ninety-one years of age with the love and respect of the entire people of Linn County. He comes from a notable ancestry and was carefully schooled in his early manhood. His first American ancestor was John Plumb who landed at Boston in 1635, and his maternal grandfather was John Jordan Kenea of Wolcott, Connecticut, grandfather also of John Phelps Kenea of La Cygne, and who served eight years as a captain in the Revolutionary War. His paternal grandfather Solomon Plumb served in the war of 1812. Dr. Plumb had the honor of being valedictorian of the class of 1861 at Yale and immediately enlisted in the service of his country in the Civil War, accepting a commission as surgeon of the Nineteenth Connecticut Infantry which later became the Second Connecticut Heavy Artillery with fourteen companies. He was later detached and sent to be chief of a division hospital in the Army of the Potomac. Dr. Plumb was born in Wolcott, New Haven county, Connecticut, May 29, 1836. He had many relatives of the name there, so many that the street on which they built their homes lost its original name because everybody called it Plumb street. He married Sarah E. Tolles of Plymouth, Massachusetts, daughter of Captain Zenus Tolles of the State Militia. Their children are Charles Waldo Plumb born at New Milford, Connecticut, April 12, 1862, and Harry Averill Plumb born in 1867 in Waterbury, Connecticut. Mrs. Plumb and her two boys joined the doctor here in 1867. Senator Preston B. Plumb of Kansas was of this family; he was born October 12, 1837, son of Ichabod, a wagon maker. The Plumbs are Norman by descent going back to 1188 in Normandy and to 1272 in England.

Abram Weeks came here in 1856 from Orange county, New York, and married Eliza Virginia, daughter of Bartlett Baugh. They made their home a mile north of Pleasanton. They were Quakers. Their children are Joseph Bartlett Weeks who married Malinda Ann Rice, daughter of John Rice who came here from Winterset, Iowa. Charles Emmert was next. Della Emma married Robert McIntyre, Sybil married Vernon Tolliver, Harry is single, Lester married Virginia Madison, Sadie married Roy Mortimer, Teddie and Edward Lee are single.

Telling the story of the murder of her father, Joseph Seright, by a band of Bushwhackers in the night of December 11, 1861, Mrs. S. E. Lerow of Stillwater, Oklahoma, writes: "It was a bright moonlight night, almost like daylight. After retiring my mother heard shooting, which afterward proved to be the Bushwhackers shooting at Mr. Hill who ran a store at old Potosi, one and one-half miles southeast of where Pleasanton now is, who escaped from them but they robbed his store. When she heard this shooting she tried to induce my father to leave the house and go to where my brother

Isaac Seright and his brother-in-law Tom Ford were hiding, but he was not well physically, having chills and fever, and after arising and dressing remarked he was feeling so badly he did not care to lay out in cold and damp and perhaps they would not come, as often was the case. So he lay down on the bed fully dressed. The next thing we knew they were pounding on the door for admittance. As soon as mother opened the door they rushed in and filled the room, middle aged men and a lot of boys not over twelve or fourteen years of age. Mother asked, "Who are you?" They replied: "We are Texas Rangers." My father in meantime had stepped into a side kitchen. There seemed to be two leaders in the gang—one stood at the bedside of my sister-in-law, Isaac Seright's wife, who was recovering from a serious siege of pneumonia, and prevented others from stealing bed-covers from her bed. All other blankets, quilts, coverlids, etc., were taken by them. A part of the crowd going into the kitchen discovered my father, bringing him back into the room, thence out into yard. As they brought him through the room my mother said: "Surely you would not hurt him." The other leader answering: "Not one hair of his head shall be injured." That part of the crowd were acquainted with my brother who was in hiding is attested to by the fact that the leader who stationed himself by the bedside of my sister-in-law asked: "Where is Isaac?" By this time they had taken all they wanted from the house and now departed, all mounting, riding off, except one; my father yet standing in the yard, my younger brother and sister standing in the door. What happened from now on I was not an eye witness to myself, but the brother and sister before mentioned were. They said the man left behind threw his gun over his saddle as if in act of mounting, pointed toward our father, shooting him, killing him almost instantly. After he did this he mounted and as he was riding away a man came rushing back, asking angrily, "Why in h---l did you do that?—didn't I order you not to shoot?" Later some soldiers were stationed at what was then known as Military or Rocky Ford on Mine creek. They captured a man whom they thought perhaps might have been in this raid, sending for my mother to try and identify him, she taking me along thinking I might perhaps be able to recognize him also, I being at that time twelve years of age. But although the man when brought to confront us for identification showed much concern and distress, great drops of sweat standing on his forehead and veins of temple and forehead standing out like cords, we were not able to positively identify him as being one of the marauders. I can yet recall, after all these years, the relieved look on his features at our verdict."

Jacob Bechner and his wife Elizabeth Day Bechner were

from Botetourt county, Virginia, and from there to Wisconsin, where their children were born, and came to Linn County in 1857, settling on eighty acres that subsequently became the south end of the Pleasanton town site. They found pioneer experiences pretty tough, at first had to get mail at Westport and later at Sugar Mound when old Ebenezer Barnes became postmaster. They were intimately acquainted with James Montgomery who is remembered as a small man of about 120 pounds weight with brown hair and whose speech and manners indicated he was a well educated man. They were great admirers of the courage of Mrs. Montgomery and quote her as saying at one time: "Well, I hope Jim will come home. If they take all his legs and arms off I want them to send his body home and I will take care of him." One of the men remembers that when Montgomery was commissioned to raise a regiment in South Carolina during the war the negroes were having religious services outdoors with a barrel for a pulpit and at Montgomery's effort to enlist them they were very suspicious and evasive. The negroes were armed with clubs and looked bad. Finally Montgomery said: "Let us pray," and in fervid eloquence Montgomery prayed with his eyes closed and when he opened them all suspicions and all clubs were gone and the negroes rushed to enlist. They also knew Jennison, "a little man of sandy complexion, quick as a mink." Jennison offered the Senior Bechner $200 for a horse the latter owned, saying that "if I rode that horse I would not be afraid of the Devil." But the horse was not for sale. Among their neighbors were Bartlett Baugh, John Baugh, Joe Babb, Hank McGlothlin, the Tubbs and Serights. They were all forced to be constantly on the alert and for many months the elder Bechner slept out in a corn shock or in the brush. They were suspicious of every one they did not know. At one time a crowd was going over towards Trading Post on Muddy Creek to vote, near Old Johnny Baugh's place. As they approached they saw old Johnny bringing his horses in from the prairie, and when he spied these voters he took them to be horse thieves and made strenuous efforts to escape with his horses—putting a permanent joke on Uncle Johnny Baugh still told after three quarters of a century. In this family group were Joe Day and Nelson Day (both born in Genessee county, New York) brothers of Mrs. Bechner, and Chester Cowell who married Lydia Day, her sister. Of the Bechner children, Ellen married George Harris of Bourbon county; William Wallace married Lottie Vanarsdale Jamison, and Abraham Lincoln (who was called a pet name till after Lincoln's death in 1865) now lives in California. By a previous marriage by Mrs. Bechner there were two sons, Ambrose Craft and John Craft, who served in the Fifteenth Kansas Cavalry in Company M, under Captain Mentzer.

George Roach Saunders and his wife Emily Burland were both from Bristol, England. They were prominent in business and social life. In 1880 Josiah Sylvanus Palling and Harry Gloster came over from Bristol and joined their uncle at the time when George R. was running the bank at La Cygne. Harry Gloster was cashier. He became homesick and wanted to sell his stock to Saunders and being refused he took the book value in money and left his stock in place of it and next showed up in Bristol, England, and it is said he actually served in the World War, at an advanced age. Jo. Palling has been for many years the popular landlord of the Palling House, the big hotel of the town.

Jack Mays was born in Warrensburg, Missouri, but came to Kansas in time to enlist under Captain David Goss in Company E, Sixth Kansas Cavalry. In 1865 he married Ellen Huff, whose family were from Illinois, and they made their home on a farm three miles south of Cadmus in Scott township, where ten children were born to them, seven boys and three girls. Of these John lives at Greeley, Charlie in Kansas City, Oscar in Pleasanton, Zoie now Mrs. Louis Johnson at Kossuth, Frank at La Cygne, Hattie now Mrs. Sank Little at Elsinore, Claude in Kansas City, Marsene at Topeka, Ed at Fort Scott, Bessie now Mrs. George McBride at Pleasanton. Frank's boy enlisted in the World War from La Cygne, and was placed in charge of a convoy for delivery of supplies to various American corps.

George Washington Dudley was born in Clermont county, Ohio, June 8, 1839. The family moved to Clark county, Illinois, where he enlisted in Company B, Thirty-seventh Illinois Infantry. Was in battles of Pea Ridge, Prairie Grove, siege of Vicksburg, and was captured and held prisoner at Fayetteville, Arkansas. Came to Linn County in 1866 and in 1870 married Carrie Husted at her home where Centerville now stands. Their children are Mrs. Mary Cochran at Centerville; Carrie, who married George A. Dudley; and William R. who married Elisabeth Moore. During the famous debates in Illinois between Abe Lincoln and Stephen A. Douglas George W. Dudley drove with the party from town to town and heard many of the speeches. He was present when Scott Holderman was arrested and saw his accomplice Foster hanged by a mob in Sugar creek.

Reuben Lamb, one of the big Lamb family of Quakers, was neighbor to the Holmeses, and had eight children, those living here being Mary Lamb Mills, Esau, Lydia, Louisa who married Bolivar Holmes, Isaac and Josiah E. They came here in 1857. Reuben was an active abolitionist and was on the list for killing by the Bushwhackers. He was a preacher and was well known in every log cabin home.

James Campbell Stewart was born in Ireland in 1822, lived in Tyler county, West Virginia, where he married Fannie McCoach, sister to our Uncle John McCoach, who was also born in Ireland. From Knox county, Illinois, they came to Linn County in 1859. He served in the Sixth Kansas Militia. Their children were James McCoach who married Anna Waggoner, George Samuel, Mary E. who married Will Michaels, Dorothy who married George E. Michaels, Mattie who married H. C. Terry, and John H. who married Maggie Marmon.

Michael Marmon was from Dublin, Ireland, where he married Sarah Patterson and came to America in 1857, living awhile at Galesburg, Illinois, and coming to Linn County in 1870, locating in Lincoln township. Their children are Frank who married Carrie Sweetland, Agnes married Alva Canady, John married Anna Davis, Sarah, George David married Amanda Stainbrook, Maggie married John Stewart and William who married Hettie Johnson.

Michael Stroup married Mary Ann Pulse in Highland county, Ohio, and came to Linn County in 1898. Their son August Elbert married Laura Calvert who traces her ancestry back to Cecil Calvert, brother to Lord Baltimore. August and his wife live at La Cygne.

Samuel Crawshaw was born in Lancaster, England, came to America in 1852, and to Valley township in 1855, his wife being Bettie Hayworth. He was a robust redheaded beef-eater Englishman who took quite a part in the fight then going on. His son William married and their children were Matilda who married John Williams, William who married Lucretia Endersby, Edwin Richard who married Amanda West, and John Thomas who married Mary Williams.

The Hummels came through from Delaware City, Ohio, with the Elihu Ireland family. They arrived about 1867. Solomon Hummel's wife was Christina Dinward. Of their children Emma married D. King McCoach, Nettie married Al Weidman, Grace married Joe Rose, and Mattie married Ed Puckett. Daniel Hummel, brother to Sol, married Ellen, daughter of Elihu Ireland.

Benjamin Franklin Kempton and Anna Williams his wife came here in 1861. He was a carpenter. Their son L. F. Kempton married Corinne Lockwood.

The high hill southwest of La Cygne was long called "Whistling Point" because by whistling loud enough and long enough a ferryman would come and carry you over. Riley

Hensley, son of George who was son of Middleton Hensley from Missouri who was the first owner of the place. Of this family Betty married John Dillon, Riley married Mary Lingwood, Matilda married D. L. Mooney, and Mary married John Maginnis whose father ran the mill at Trading Post. Riley Hensley now occupies the old home place.

Erastus Hiram Jones is the son of Hiram Jones, a physician and Methodist preacher who died in Texas in 1860. His mother was Elmira Dennis Jones of the well known family of Dennises who located here. These Joneses originated at Dundee, Scotland, where the name was spelled Jannis. The Dennis family were from Pennsylvania to Muskingum county, Ohio, where Elmira was born. When they started West to seek their fortune they crossed the Allegheny Mountains and they all walked and carried some part of the load to relieve the team, and Elmira carried two heavy flat irons as her part. When they got to the Ohio River they built a flat boat, floated down to the Mississippi and rowed up that stream to McGregor's Landing and went inland and opened a store or trading post for Indians, which still is called Le Brand, Iowa. It was here "Ras" was born May 29, 1851. The father's health failed and they took him to Angeline county, Texas, where he died, and Elmira brought her family back to Kansas where they joined her sister, Mrs. J. M. Iliff, and other relatives, among them the Mays and Robinsons, at now the Antioch school neighborhood. The young folks had a fairly good time. They had a wonderful singing school under the guidance of John Massa Iliff and at one time took a chorus of one hundred and twenty-eight to a singing contest at Farlinville. "Ras" and a boy named Granville Robinson rode over the Mine Creek battlefield and they think the number left dead on the field was exaggerated.

The parents of Samuel Tucker, now manager of the Pleasanton Telephone Exchange, came to Linn County in 1876 and settled on a farm four miles north of Pleasanton, where they lived till 1907 when they moved to town and the elder Tucker retired from active business. They were a forceful people, John Wesley Tucker being in the Kansas legislature during the Llewellyn administration and voted for Peffer to be United States senator from Kansas. This John Wesley Tucker was born in 1843 in Ohio, attended Butler University at Indianapolis, and was ordained a minister in the church of the Disciples of Christ. In 1871 he was married to Sarah Ann Thompson at Greentown, Indiana, she being a lineal descendant of Charles Thompson of Virginia, who signed the Declaration of Independence as secretary of the Continental Congress. Another ancestor was David Thompson, an officer under Mad Anthony Wayne, who received high commendation from that officer. In 1795 he married Mary Swope, who was born September 21, 1775, in the old Fortress Monroe in Monroe county, Virginia. In 1823 they had accumulated ten children and lived in Henry county, Indiana, one of these children being Michaël Thompson, born in 1813, who became the father of Sarah Ann Thompson Tucker, who came to Linn County with her family in 1876. The children were Edgar Marion Tucker now in Pasadena, California; Charles Wesley Tucker at St. Louis, Missouri; and Carrie Lucretia, who became the wife of Edgar M. Goss. Samuel Tucker was married in 1895 to Stella B. Wood, daughter of Calvin R. Wood of Potosi township. They have one child, Clyde Ernest Tucker, who graduated from Kansas University and married Cleda Humphrey, daughter of Verner Humphrey, and now live in Pleasanton.

Albert Lemuel Humphrey was a successful cattle man, accumulating a fortune in various kinds of property. He made his home at Pleasanton, in the vicinity of which town he owned nearly a thousand acres of land. He was born in Iowa City, Iowa, in 1848, and was married there in 1870 to Jennie E. Rickford from Pennsylvania. Verner Humphrey, a son, was born to them at Pleasanton in 1872. Jeannette became the wife of William M. Laughlin; she died at her home in Blue Mound in 1914.

John D. McRae is well remembered as the old Scotchman who ran a store in Farlinville from 1865 till 1924. He was born in Vanklek, Canada West (now Ontario) in 1835, his father being Donald McRae and his mother Mary McLeod McRae. John D. married Mary Ann Aldridge from Decatur county, Indiana. They had seven children: Jennie, who married Ira Campbell, whom she survives and is now postmaster at Goodrich; Paris, who married Anna Gott; Mary Olive who married William Herrick Campbell, a brother of Ezekiel and Ira; Finley Jay who married Emma Arbogast; Walter who married Myrtle Adams; Grace who married Clarence Conrad; and Angus still single at Riverside, California.

Leon A. Luhillier came to Pleasanton in 1882 and joined Dr. Cornelius P. Lee in the drug business. He married Effie C. Lee in 1884. Their children are Marvin at Osawatomie; Harold now with his father in business; and Catherine now Mrs. Virgil Stepp.

Five stalwart young men and a sister named Fickes came to Trading Post from the family home on a farm near Bellefont, Center county, Pennsylvania, prior to the Civil War and took part in the border warfare, their names being Samuel, Jacob, John, Morgan, and William Fickes, and their sister Jane who later married William Hensley who had settled on the ridge east and north of Brooklin and had his home where the town of Barnard (now Boicourt) was located when later the railroad came. The father of these Fickes children was of a German family and was born in Virginia, later moving to Center county, Pennsylvania, where he married a Miss DeVinney at Bellefont. There was another daughter, Mary Ann, who married John Ross in the Pennsylvania home and brought a large family here in July, 1859, who are mentioned elsewhere. All these men married and raised big families, but in the early years scattered, many of them going to Colorado. Morgan Fickes married Minerva Rhodes of a very good family who lived in the valley two miles west of Trading Post. They had two sons, Lester and Edward, the latter being killed a few years ago by a tree falling on him on a farm east of Pleasanton. Lester made his home in Pleasanton many years. Morgan Fickes became a very wealthy man in land speculations and it is said nearly every abstract in Linn County bears his name. He owned a saw mill at Trading Post and furnished lumber for nearly all the pioneer homes when log construction stopped. He acquired title to the land where Pleasanton stands and when the railroad came through in 1869 he out-generaled all his rival town promoters by taking Octave Chanute into partnership. As Chanute was the chief engineer of the Kansas City, Fort Scott and Gulf Railroad he had the controlling influence that located the station and the town as is told elsewhere. Morgan Fickes built a fine big hotel, called the Gulf House, up on the side of the "Mound" at Pleasanton and it was a famous landmark throughout eastern Kansas till its destruction by fire, an event that was the beginning of the downfall of Morgan, his fortune being swept away and litigation called his presence in court at every term for thirty years, finally sending him to the "poor house" for the last four of his ninety-four years of life.

John Ross and his wife, Mary Ann Fickes Ross, brought their six children here in July 1859 and located at the Post. There were four boys, John Custer, Laird, Morgan Fickes. and Samuel. The latter died at La Cygne about 1871 while running a saw mill there. Elizabeth Ann married Henry DeWitt at Trading Post and moved to Pea Ridge, Arkansas, and their home was right in the midst of the battle of Pea Ridge and she was required to bake biscuits by the sack-full for the Confederates and later for the Federals, and on her return to Trading Post went through the same experience with the two armies during the Price Raid. Mary Ross married and moved to Colorado but is now spending her old age at Eighteenth street and Muncie Boulevard in Kansas City, Kansas, where her brother, Rev. Morgan Fickes Ross, is pastor of the Oakland Christian Church. Rev. Ross was married to Martha J. Osman at Fontana on December 20, 1875. Of their children Samuel lives at 1024 Ruby Avenue; Frank at Fourteenth and Pacific; Paul at 206 South Fourteenth street; Mrs. Mary Tibbett, 943 Ruby Avenue; Mrs. Sophia Perkins, 6401 East Eighth street, Kansas City, Mo.; and Mrs. Alice Reon, Birmingham, Alabama. This aged couple have twelve grandchildren and two greatgrandchildren. Rev. Ross was fifteen years old when the Price Raid occurred and he and his father and brother Laird were arrested with Uncle Jacky Lane and Harvey Smith and taken before General Price, a pompous person sitting in a big chair in his army ambulance. General Marmaduke told Price that the senior Ross had been an accomplice of Henry Arny, an abolitionist in St. Louis in 1858 and 1859 and deserved punishment. Ross produced papers from his pocketbook proving him to have been in Bellefont, Pennsylvania, at the date named and General Price told Marmaduke to "Take them away, I've got enough on my mind." When the Federal batteries opened up next morning the five prisoners escaped and after forty-eight hours of hunger the Rosses got a big feed at the home of their daughter and sister Mrs. Hensley where Boicourt now is. It was raining and cold that evening of October 24, 1864, and General Sterling Price was uncomfortable and out of humor when they stopped at Sugar Creek for supper. Early in the morning he hurried on in his ambulance drawn by four white mules, his two daughters occupying the rear seat. They sought a more balmy climate somewhere south, not willing to accept the warm reception Pleasanton and his men were urging upon them every minute. At the James Goss farm three miles south all the family came out and stood round the ambulance while Price inquired where he was and expressed surprise that he was in the hated land of Kansas, but he accepted a drink of water from the ladies and the driver whipped up the white mules and left. Rev. Ross later had the distinction of helping build the second home built in Pleasanton and also worked as a carpenter on the construction of the Gulf House.

James Simpson, one of the old timers of Mound City, was born in Saulsbury township, Bucks county, Pennsylvania, October 21, 1835, and died at the farm home a mile east of Sugar Mound in 1901. He came here and established a home by buying out one Jim Service and went back home and married Sarah Allen Eisenbrey of Lumberville in the old home county of Bucks. They had four sons born here, two of whom died in infancy. Orville is unmarried and is at the head of his mother's household. William N. their first born married Eleanor Hand, daughter of J. W. Hand of Paola. These young people met while students at Baker University. They had a daughter, Mary Eleanor, who married Sterling Price Williams and now live at Bloomington, Illinois, and they have

one son. Eleanor Hand Simpson remained a widow seventeen
years and then married Prof. W. A. Meyers, who is the president of Southwestern University at Winfield, Kansas. Mr.
Meyer's first wife was Bessie Capper, sister to Senator Capper,
who died about 1910. Mrs. Sarah Williams is now a greatgrandmother and remembers pioneer experiences very vividly.
When Price's rebels came through she hung blankets over
the windows so no light would be seen at night. Her little boy
Orville was hidden in a ravine overgrown with brush, and all
the family treasure, including clothing and pillows and bedding
and the silverware for the table was buried under earth.
They slept many nights with their heads on brooms instead
of pillows.

Moses Clark Butts of Virginia married Henrietta Mercer
at Piqua, Ohio, and brought their family to Linn County in
1878. Their oldest, John Wesley, married Lotta Hayes; Frank
never married; Osa Eva married Thornton C. Creager; Harry
Edwin married Eva Lingwood; Carl married Alice Donovan;
Stella married Elmer Tungett. Carl served in the Spanish-
American war. The mother of these, Henrietta Mercer, was
of the great family for whom Mercer county, Pennsylvania,
was named, and one of her ancestors rose to distinction in
the Revolutionary War. Harry Edwin Butts and his wife
Eva Lingwood have seven children at their home at the old
"Jim Parent ford".   Ernest Clark married Mary Fadelma
Conley; Lucile married Lester Shearer; and Lottie, Helen,
Hazel, Buford, and Kenneth are at home. The mother, Eva
Lingwood, wears a set of gold earrings that were worn by
her greatgrandmother Rose back in Norfolk, England. It
was Mr. Butts who helped to cut down the big walnut tree
which was shipped to Germany in 1902 after being exhibited
at the St. Louis World's Fair. It was sold for three hundred
dollars. In 1926 Mr. Butts sold a walnut tree on his own place
adjoining for two hundred and fifty dollars, this last tree being
only two feet in diameter. A short distance from their home
on the old John Hood place is the last log house built in Linn
County, now occupied by Earl Craft.

William Miller Hazlett and six of his brothers came from
Indiana county, Pennsylvania, to Linn County as early as 1855.
They were all enthusiastic anti-slavery men, and Albert the
oldest became a close associate of Old John Brown and was
with him at Harper's Ferry and was one of those hanged at
Charles Town jail. John, another brother, located two miles
south of Prescott and married Grace Lonsburg, daughter of
William Lonsburg, who lived on an adjoining farm, and have
many descendants still living in the neighborhood. William
Miller Hazlett served in a Pennsylvania regiment and married
Elizabeth Fyock, widow of Levi Fyock of Indiana, Pennsyl-

vania, and they came to Linn County in 1864 with six of the
Fyock children, two girls and five boys.   Charles Fyock, one
of these seven, had served in Company F, Ninety-seventh
Pennsylvania Infantry, joined the family here in 1866 and
married Sarah Gump, daughter of John Gump, who had come
here from Morgan county, Missouri.   Charles and Sarah had
six children.   John married Julie Scott; Cora married Case
Eubanks; William; Lester married Miss Peavy; these children
are all in Colorado; Grace married Dwight Cheever; Murray
McKinley is at home unmarried.

Kelton Wilson Harkness of Scotch ancestry was from New
York Revolutionary stock who came very early to Illinois.
There were eight brothers who settled near Peoria, and the
families were so numerous the neighborhood became noted
as "Harkness Grove", a name it still bears.   In 1857 "Kel"
as he was always familiarly known came to the southeast
corner of Linn County and as a mere boy established a
"claim" to a quarter section of land by occupying it and building a shack in which to live.   The Bushwhackers notified him
to leave, but he stayed and he owed his life to his faithful
dog who "whispered" to his master in the night and by his
nervousness told of the presence of strangers.   "Kel" was
sleeping out in the weeds and heard the posse instructed to
shoot him on sight.   Some how he escaped them and he got
that land by a patent signed by Abraham Lincoln as President,
and it is a remarkable item of history that in 1865 this Linn
County boy was one of the six selected to carry the body of
Abe Lincoln to its last resting place in Springfield, Illinois.
These six boys were each given a badge prepared by the
Government authorities to wear as active pallbearers and
that badge and the patent to the land with Lincoln's signatures
are treasures carefully kept by the family.   In 1861 when
the Civil War came on he was yet only eighteen years old.
He walked to Westport Landing and went by boat to his old
home near Peoria and enlisted with boyhood friends in the
Third Illinois Cavalry and was elected sergeant.   At the close
of the war in 1865 he returned to his old home and married
Julia White and to them ten children were born, eight of
whom are living in 1927, so that Mrs. Kelton W. Harkness
happily living in her own home is surrounded by eight children
with their families amounting to fourteen grandchildren and
seven greatgrandchildren, some record in following the Biblical
injunction.   The surviving children are Lee, who married Liza
Reeves, Minnie married Ross Kennedy, Ernest married Elvira
Ham, Jeannette married Ed Blackman, Ella married Otto
Nichols, Capitola is unmarried, Dexter married Matie Hinton,
Riley married Ella Roy.

Robert Moffett McClure came as a young man to the neigh-

borhood of Moneka, where he settled on a claim and lived
for sixty years with the love and respect of all who knew him.
In the first few years he hauled freight from Westport Landing, as Kansas City was then called, one interesting item
being the bell that is still used on the Baptist church of Mound
City. Mr. McClure was a member of that church and helped
in the erection of the bulding. He was born in Princeton,
Indiana, September 16, 1846, and his death occurred December
26, 1926, at the ripe old age of eighty years. At the age of
seventeen he enlisted in Company H, Seventeenth Indiana
Infantry and served till the close of the war in 1865. In
1866, in company with Marion Polk he came to Linn County
and they settled on adjoining claims near Moneka. In 1874
he returned to Princeton, Indiana, and was married to Miss
M. Belle Wheeler. Of eight children born to them five survive
as follows: Joseph P. McClure, Los Angeles, California;
Quincy D. McClure, Iola, Kansas; Claude Q. McClure, Crowley,
Colorado; Montague M. McClure, El Paso, Texas; Mrs. Edith
Kloppenstein, Mound City, Kansas; James C. McClure, Denver,
Colorado.

Conspicuous among the native born of our people was May
Florence Broadhead who was born May 2, 1859, in a cabin
two miles west of Mound City, as the daughter of Jabez B.
Broadhead and his wife, H. Maria Smith Broadhead, natives
of Chautauqua county, New York, who had come to Linn
County in the fall of 1858 with their first born child Ellen.
This native born child, May Florence, grew to maturity here
and was a valued member of society, a useful member of
the Congregational church. Christmas day, 1880, May was
married to Charles Wesley Forbes at the home of her parents,
the ceremony being performed by Rev. H. Robinson of her
own church. The Broadheads were from the old home of
Ezra Hanchett Smith, father of Ed. R. Smith, Mrs. Broadhead being a niece of Ezra Hanchett and cousin to Ed. R.
At the death of Mrs. Forbes on December 22, 1926, only
three were left of this prominent Broadhead family, being
children of Ellen, as follows: Miss Ethel Botkin, Mr. Clyde
Botkin and Mrs. Nell Thormley, all of Hutchinson, Kansas.

Augustus Wells Burton came to Linn County in 1857, bringing his aged parents, Mr. and Mrs. Herman Burton, with him.
They were originally from Manchester, Vermont, where A.
W. was born. Burton seminary at Manchester was established
by his ancestors. On their way west they had lived at Martinsburg, Ohio, and then in McLean county, Illinois, where A. W.
Burton was married to Sarah Hettie Hays, a native of Kentucky. Their next move landed them on a claim on the Osage,
later over into what is now Stanton township in Linn County
in 1863. All their children were born here—in 1858 Frank,

who married Jessie Mathews, daughter of L. D. Mathews of
Mound City; in 1861 Horace Ellsworth, who married Sarah
Vannetta Lake, daughter of Rev. O. E. Lake of the Congre-
gational church and Caroline Augusta who married Warren
Wallace of Prescott.

Mr. Burton became captain of Company H, Twelfth Kansas
Cavalry and had a strenuous career both in the "border war"
and the Civil War, but had a remarkable experience in the
Indian uprising in which he showed rare ability as a commander and courage to face with a small company a mob of
two thousand howling savages. This story is told in the
article on Isaac W. Marrs in this book. Captain Burton
served as special agent for the Federal Land Office in the
Dakotas and Minnesota and in the Kansas legislature and
was county treasurer two terms.

The children of Horace Ellsworth and his wife Sarah Vannetta were Willard Augustus who married Mabel Mackey and
now lives in Kansas City; Frank Madden, who married Marie
Deyone of Pittsburg; Grace Vannetta who married Wilbur
A. Potter of Lawrence; and Charles Orange, still with his
parents. Horace remembers that as a boy he saw General
Sterling Price drive by in his ambulance drawn by four white
mules, the general's daughters occupying the back seat. He
witnessed a lively skirmish at Fish Creek crossing near the
present school house of that name, where two rebels were
killed and another so badly injured he died at the hospital
in Fort Scott. Relatives of the two killed came and got their
remains some weeks later.

James Wesley Wickham came to Linn County in company
with a man named Spillard from Cleveland, Ohio, in 1868,
and brought with them some high-class breeding horses which
did much to raise the standard of horseflesh in this community.
Wickham established himself as a carpenter at Mound City
and on May 24, 1871, was married to Hannah Elizabeth Worden, daughter of Elijah Worden (who was born in New York)
and wife Mary Jane Day Worden (who was born in Ohio)
who had come here from Wisconsin, arriving September 22,
1858, locating on a claim at what is now the southeast corner
of Pleasanton. Mr. and Mrs. Wickham established themselves
in a house near the present center of Mound City and were
influential good citizens. Mrs. Wickham has much to her
credit in the preservation of local history. As a girl she began
keeping "scrap books" and now she has twelve big volumes
of carefully classified newspaper clippings that have a very
great value and should be treasured and preserved by the
county. Mrs. Wickham has a very interesting story in this
book about incidents of the Price Raid in 1864.

Dr. William Harrison Rees has been an active and highly esteemed citizen of Linn County since he graduated from the Keokuk Medical school and hung out his first shingle at Trading Post. His father, Thomas Davis Rees, from German stock which came to America prior to the Revolution, was married at Warren, Pennsylvania, to Melinda Black, whose father Samuel Black was a Kentuckian who served with General Jackson at the Battle of New Orleans. In 1832 they moved to Warren county, Illinois, where our Dr. Rees was born in 1843. When the Civil War came on he enlisted in Company B of the 102d Illinois Infantry in the Army of the Cumberland which in 1862 drove Bragg out of Kentucky and Tennessee. He was under Generals Rosecrans and Thomas and was wounded three times, at Resaca and Savannah. He went through with Sherman to the Sea, capturing Fort McAllister and Fort Magruder. Sherman sent Thomas's command back north through the Carolinas and when they arrived at Goldsborough they got the news of Lee's surrender. They were at Raleigh, North Carolina, when they heard of Lincoln's assassination, announcing which Ben Harrison told them "they have killed the greatest man that ever lived." They hurried on to Washington and were in the Grand Review. He was discharged from the army June 6, 1865, and started at once in medical school. His father and mother had preceded him to Linn County and lived on the farm two miles east of Pleasanton now occupied by his brother, Elmer E. Rees. He married Tennessee Lansdowne Hinds, sister to Wash Hinds, and in 1890 moved from Trading Post to Pleasanton. He has been an active worker in the temperance cause and in the activities of the Grand Army of the Republic. Elmer E. Rees served as county commissioner.

Ben Ellis and his brother Ike came here from Linn county, Missouri, where Ben was born October 7, 1825, and Isaac some years later. Their parents were Jacob Ellis from North Carolina to Tennessee and Temperance Cooper of Welsh birth. Benjamin's first wife was Mary Curtis, whose children were Elmer E., John Murray, now at Whitlash, Montana, and Arthur William, now a carpenter in Kansas City. The second Mrs. Ben Ellis was Sarah J. Shinn, whose surviving child is Frank B. Ellis of the Bank of Pleasanton. Ben and Ike arrived in 1856 and located on the Broadhead farm which they bought from Parks. Ben later had a general merchandise store in Mound City and was at Westport for goods at the time of Price's Raid and sold out a wagon load of tobacco to the soldiers. Ike was a wagoner in the Sixth Kansas Militia and was at the Mine Creek battle. Elmer E. now in the grocery business at Pleasanton has his son Benjamin Ray associated with him and who is married and has a child Joseph Elmer. Frank B. Ellis the banker married Adeline Golden, daughter

of Wm. and Amelia Golden, who came here from Pennsylvania
in 1880—he was a carpenter—the wedding of Adeline being
on May 19, 1904. Their children are Howard and Donald
Frank. James A. Shinn was a brother of Sarah J. Shinn the
second Mrs. Ben Ellis. He went from here to Leadville, Colorado, where he became mayor of the town, got to be very
wealthy, and served as state game and fish warden when that
state was the sportsman's paradise.

David Snider came to Mound City September 3, 1866. At
seventeen years of age he had enlisted in Company D, Thirty-
fifth Illinois Infantry and served to end of war. His father
was of the same name and of good old Dutch stock, his mother
being Sarah Tipton from near Zanesville, Ohio, from which
city they went to near Danville, Illinois, where our David
was born. He married Margaret Ellen Avery at her home
five miles southwest of Mound City in 1873. Their children
are Leora who married Charles Dwight Barnes, Bertha married Charles A. Hagan, Mosse is unmarried and a teacher in
the Mound City schools, Fred Erwin married Gussie Bowmer,
Colvin Bowman married Ethel Thomas, Ralph Waldo married
Fern Lambert. David remembers the incident of Alva Root
losing a saw-mill from its site at the state line on the Marais
des Cygnes. It was not an especially up-to-date property but
when Root returned from a trip into Missouri he brought with
him what Snider called a "real saw-mill."

Samuel Avery and his wife Malissa Bradshaw were from
New York and settled on a claim five miles southwest of Mound
City in 1864. The Avery children were Alfreda who married
H. C. McNeil, who became the owner of the Natchez New Era
newspaper; Mary Catherine married Abe Cannady; Margaret
married David Snider; Eldora married Thomas Forrester;
James DeGroat married Ella Snider; Ephraim married Josie
Stanley; Sadie died at thirteen.

James Martin was born in Tennessee in 1827 and went to
Illinois where he married Serelda Records. In 1854 he came
to Linn County and liked it so well that in 1857 he returned
here with his wife and three children they being Celia who
married Columbus Hensley, Sarah who married George Swingley, John Henry who married Dicie Workman (daughter of
Alonzo Workman who came here in 1860),—and three born
here—James who married Marie Zigler, and Orie who married
Orville Staton. Walter the youngest boy died at Camp
Funston of influenza while training for the World War. The
children of Henry Martin and his wife Dicie Workman are
Edith who married Roscoe Staton, and the unmarried children,
Howard, Dicie, George, and Opal. They live on the old home-
stead established in 1857. James Martin the first was em-

ployed at one time on the farm of Charles Hamelton the arch
murderer. He disagreed with Hamelton on many things and
once, when threatened, told Hamelton, "If you can shoot any
quicker, or straighter, than I can, come ahead."

George Washington Hinds, familiarly known as "Wash",
was long one of the principal land owners of Valley and Potosi
townships. The Hinds were a New York family and his
father Benjamin Hinds was a lieutenant under Mad Anthony
Wayne at the battle of Lundy's Lane and won personal commendation from that popular hero. Benjamin married Nancy
Fox, a Kentucky woman. There was a large family and they
came west in three wagons drawn by oxen and Wash says
they had no trouble from faulty spark plugs but it did take
a good many gallons to the mile. They came across Missouri
by way of Gasconade, Fort Osage, Eldon, and in 1854 arrived
at a spot in Linn County about a mile west of where the
Marais des Cygnes crosses the state line, and that neighborhood has been their home since. About a mile away Willis
Hill made a home on Mine Creek and in April 1855 married
Ellen Hinds, sister to Wash. The Tates and Swansons also
settled near. Neighbors were scarce and social life very dull,
but they got along handsomely. They had good feather beds
and they spun and wove cotton and woolen and linen cloth
to clothe a big bunch of people. One spring Wash killed thirty-
nine wild turkeys, so fat they would burst when they fell.
There were so many wild pigeons they would break the limbs
off the trees where they roosted. As more people came in
there were corn-shuckings, wood-choppings, quilting-bees,
rail-makings, cotton-pickings, and these events meant dancing
by the young folks, especially at the home of Alfred and Asel
Witten, where Alf. Barnes now lives. John McHenry an uncle
to Wash Hinds, was a member of the Missouri legislature from
Bates county and died during a session at Jefferson City.
They brought him home and Uncle Jackie Williams of Trading
Post preached the funeral sermon. Osage and Miami Indians
were numerous and good neighbors. Of this family the surviving children are Jane, who married Thomas Heath and lives
in Butler, Missouri; John married Hattie Potts, now in California; Sarah married John Moon of Cass county; Vernie
married James Brown; Martha married Sawyer Makinson;
Ben married Delia Allmon, sister of Frank; Frances married
Robert Barton; Tennessee Lansdowne married Dr. Rees; and
George Washington married Nettie Makinson of English birth
and after her death married Mary Ellen Fisher by whom he
had three children: Jackson Benjamin, now in Montana; Mabel
Ellen, now a demonstrator in home economics for the county
agent; and George Winifred, a teacher in Jackson county,
Kansas.

A noted preacher of the early days soon after the Civil War was Rev. Lauren Armsby who was born in Northbridge, Massachusetts, January 16, 1817. He died at Council Grove, Kansas, in 1904. He was a graduate of Amherst College in the class of 1842. He married Hannah Van Ingen of Albany, New York, and to them our well known citizen Sherman Armsby was born at their home in New Hampshire. The family lived awhile at Faribault, Minnesota, in 1856, and when the Civil War came on he became a chaplain in a Minnesota Regiment. After the war ceased he was pastor of the Congregational church at Candia, New Hampshire, and in 1870 he came to Mound City as pastor of the local church, and a few years later was called to Council Grove where he lived out a fine career.

Sherman Armsby was one of the early day business men of Pleasanton. He married Mary Belle Whitman (daughter of James E. Whitman from Greenbriar county, Virginia, to Ohio, where he married Charlotte Palmer, and to them Mary Belle was born in Ralls county, Missouri, in 1860). They came early to Kansas and made their home at Trading Post where Mary Belle went to school to Jesse Kennedy whose daughter is now Mrs. Kate Whitman living four miles northwest of Pleasanton. There were two stores at Trading Post then, one kept by the Douds and the other by Talbott and Rainwater, and a man named Ziegler had a pottery on the banks of the river south of where the bridge now is. About the time Pleasanton became a town Sherman and Mary Belle took up their residence here and raised a family consisting of Alice who became the wife of Dr. D. E. Green; Beatrice who married Thomas Saunders; and Horace Holly who served in the World War and is now bookkeeper for the Blaker Milling Company. Though Sherman Armsby died in 1888 he is still familiarly spoken of.

Benjamin Franklin Blaker, senior member of the firm of B. F. Blaker and Co., lumber and grain merchants of Pleasanton, and also one of the proprietors of the Blaker Milling Company of Pleasanton, became a resident of Linn County in 1870. He was born in Bucks county, Pennsylvania, December 3, 1844, a son of Joshua C. and Ann (Croasdale) Blaker, also natives of Bucks county. Upon his father's farm, he was reared to manhood, gaining early in life a practical knowledge of agriculture and also acquiring a fair education in the district schools. In 1871 his brother Alfred joined him and the firm name became B. F. Blaker & Co. In 1872 they commenced dealing in grain and two years later built an elevator. In 1886 they erected the mills of Pleasanton under the firm name of the Blaker Milling Company, and equipped them with all the modern improvements. The capacity of the mills is about one hundred and fifty barrels of flour per day and one hundred barrels of meal. About one-fourth of the entire amount of wheat used has to be imported as the home market can not supply the demand. The firm operates lumber yards at La Cygne, Fontana, Blue Mound, Parker, Gridley and Kincaid, Kansas, and at Sprague and Amsterdam, Missouri. They are interested in a commission house in Kansas City, where Alfred Blaker made his home and whither he removed for the purpose of being near his business.

The marriage of Benjamin F. Blaker occurred in 1872 and united him with Miss Adda Brabant, who was born in Milwaukee, Wisconsin, in 1850. They were the parents of Emma, who married Ernest T. Prickett and made their home in Kansas City, Missouri, and Pauline, who married Victor Meyer and live at Pleasanton. He was a member of Jewell Post No. 3, G. A. R., at Pleasanton having been a soldier in a Pennsylvania regiment in the Civil War, and was a pastmaster in Eureka Lodge No. 88 A. F. & A. M. Alfred Blaker's children were Ernest, who became a professor at Cornell University; Eleanor, who married Rev. Jay Withington and who has the Presbyterian pastorate at Columbus, and William W. who lives at Lawrence.

Mrs. Mary A. Shattuck of Pleasanton is one of the heroic women of the west. She crossed the Great Plains in a wagon drawn by oxen eight years before the famous trip by Ezra Meeker and now at eighty-three years young she looks fully capable of making the trip by aeroplane as Ezra did. Her maiden name was Mary Anstress Barnard and she was born at St. Charles, Missouri, October 16, 1844, the daughter of Elijah Patterson Barnard from Kentucky, and his wife Anstress Foman from New York. In 1846 when she was eighteen months old she crossed the plains in a wagon drawn by three yoke of oxen, arriving in the Willamette Valley of Oregon after six months of slow travel. The family stayed there till 1849 when they went by ship to California, and after a year there started back to Missouri by way of the Isthmus of Panama, and she remembers the trip in canoes up the Chagres river and the ride on mule back through the jungle. There were no roads of any kind. In 1851 her father started to wandering again and got to Wisconsin, but in the fall of 1852 returned to Springfield, Missouri, from where in April, 1853, they again with ox teams left for Oregon by way of Salt Lake, Utah. They went into the Umpqua Valley in the fall of 1853, where they stayed till 1859. They then had good schools in that western country. They went from there to the San Jose Valley in California. In 1860 they left Los Angeles and with horses and mules came by way of El Paso and Sherman, Texas, and Fort Gibson, Indian Territory, and landed on a claim three miles southeast of La Cygne on Middle Creek. On October 8, 1865, she was married to William Henry Shattuck, who had served as second lieutenant in Company B of the Sixth Kansas during the war. Mr. Shattuck was born in Rensellaer county, New York, and had come to Linn County in 1858 to join his sister Mrs. Loretta Smith, wife of Albert Smith who had come here with the party of Uncle Jacky Lane. She remembers the killing of Mr. Long on the prairie east of Silver Mound by stragglers from Price's Raiders in 1864. Mr. Shattuck served as county commissioner in 1874. The Shattuck children are Grant M. now in Lead, South Dakota, Alden who lives with his mother, Mrs. Jessie Frisbie whose husband was county clerk, Mrs. Nettie Calvin and Clyde of Valley township and Mrs. Ina Calvin, who lives on the old home place.

Albert H. Smith came here from Oswego, New York, by way of Grundy county, Iowa, to Valley township in 1858. In 1864 he was in the legislature and later served as county commissioner. His children were Juliette who married A. I. Trickey, Frank J., William Milton now in Denver, Jessie A. who married James McGuire, and Horace Greeley who married Clara Rush, daughter of James Rush, who came from Philadelphia in 1869. There were seven of the Rush children.

Henry Blackburn was born in England and lived in Oskaloosa, Iowa, where his daughter Josephine was born in 1845. They came to Linn County in 1858 and lived on a farm five miles northwest of Farlinville and were neighbors to the Dobyns family, who had also come from Oskaloosa, where Blackburn had served as recorder of deeds. He was a member of the Kansas legislature. Josephine married Mr. Gibbons, who served in the Ninth Kansas Cavalry. She remembers that when the party went up from Mound City to Paris to move the county records to the new county seat at Mound City a girl named Melinda living at Joel Chitwood's fought off the crowd with a broom. This girl later married Jesse Hawthorne and they moved to the state of Washington.

Joseph William Barrick, born in Mount Vernon, Missouri, September 12, 1845. His parents were from Ohio and when the father died in Mount Vernon the mother brought her children to Linn County on September 12, 1855. He was a boy standing around the polls in 1859 when he saw Montgomery smash the ballot box and he saw the two Wilhite boys, friends of Montgomery, and the party of Missourians who had illegally voted escaping in the brush. He went with "Old Betsy" when the county seat was moved from Paris. At the time of Price's Raid Joe was in the Home Guards, equipped with old guns the Indians had traded back to get new ones and hence no good. Johnny Garratt was their leader and others were young Lewis Osborn, Nick Snow and William

Fletcher. Some straggling rebels came by and he saw Jake Fleming shoot one of them. His mother's father, James Brown, came here from Anderson, Indiana, after the Civil War.

Nicodemus Snow was born in Bowling Green, Kentucky, October 27, 1826, and on July 12, 1848, married Angelina Smith, who was born January 22, 1825, in Cooper county, Missouri. They had six sons—John Marshall, Jacob, Austin B., Nicholas D., Martin S., and Ira—whom they brought to Linn County on October 30, 1857, and established a home in section 27 two miles northwest of Pleasanton, where Nathan Breedlove had previously lived—his wife Druzilla was a sister to Mrs. Snow. Linnville succeeded Paris as a town, was a stage station, had a telegraph line, and at its zenith of fame had about twenty-five houses. Among the neighbors was Johnny Fletcher, who taught a subscription school and rated a young child as a "scholar" and a boy of fifteen as a "scholar and a half" in estimating his tuition fees. G. W. Holt (father of Jonah Holt), B. F. McIlvane, whose widow lives in Mound City, George Furse, who came in 1855 (father of Samuel), William and Ike Murray, who came in 1855 from Polk county, Missouri; Old Johnny Fouts who married a sister of the Murray boys (their sons Philip and William still there) ; Willis W. Sutton father of W. L.; Enoch Estep who was probate judge; Mark Irwin, John and Charlie and Joe Barrick; and Hiram Barrick who was sheriff; and the parents of Henry Strong, were among their neighbors. Austin B. Snow still lives on the old home place. He saw Griffith hanged at Mound City and remembers that in 1864 all the women and children had gathered at his home for protection during the Price Raid and were at breakfast when Old Man Hardy appeared looking like a tramp and was almost shot by B. F. McIlvane, who took him for one of Price's men.

The leadership in cultural efforts at La Cygne and in fact throughout the north half of Linn County was for many years conceded by common courtesy to George J. Miller, and many men and women now living have a grateful remembrance of the encouragement he gave them to higher and better aspirations in life, and a reverence for the better things which they now pass on to their own children are as a benison upon the memory of this good man. He had grown up in pioneer life and all that he had in the way of education, cultural development and material wealth he got from hard laborious work. He would stop tying a package of merchandise to take up the personal problems of the boy or girl he was in contact with. A devoutly religious man, he was a power in stimulating his own church and any other that appealed to him. He was always anxious to encourage young people in good literature and music. When the winters were long and entertainment so scarce as to make a dreary monotony of life, it was George J. Miller who would give the whole town a delightful evening with one of his lectures on some of the classics. He was a profound student of Shakespeare and could take any of his dramas as a theme for an hour's happy conversation with his neighbors. The origin and development of this good man we give as follows: George Jarrett Miller was born in New Franklin, Howard county, Missouri, April 11, 1839. His parents, Henry Cameron Miller and Louisa Somers Richards, were both born in Virginia. In an early day they moved to Arrow Rock, Missouri, a small town on the Missouri river from which then as now there was no communication with the outside world except by mail and steamboat. Here they lived until George J. Miller was eighteen years old. During an epidemic of cholera his mother died and he and his sister Nancy Miller and his brother Cameron Miller were separated, George J. going to live with his uncle William W. Miller near Sibley, Missouri. He went to school at Georgetown, Pettis county, and began teaching school when only a boy of seventeen. During the early war troubles in that section he joined a company of Confederate recruits and took part in the battle of Boonville, where he was taken prisoner and paroled. During the period of parole he taught school, making his home with C. L. Lewis of Jonesboro, Missouri. In 1866 he married Lillian Leora Lewis, daughter of C. L. Lewis, the Rev. Burk, a Presbyterian minister, and Esquire Wilborn, both afficiating, as a sacred ceremony alone was not considered legal. They lived in Arrow Rock a year where one daughter, who died in infancy, was born July 30, 1867. From Arrow Rock he moved to Jonesboro (now Napton) where he engaged in the mercantile business. From there they moved to La Cygne in February, 1870, where he entered into the mercantile business with his cousin Harry B. Miller, later founding the Geo. J. Miller Mercantile Co., which continued until the year 1903. On June 19, 1879, George Jarret, Jr., was born, who survives him. His wife Lillian Leora died in La Cygne November 11, 1884. On May 8, 1887, he was married to M. Dell Petticrew in La Cygne. To this union were born Ruth Somers, John Richard, Julia Elizabeth, Mary Virginia.

When Mr. Miller came to La Cygne he at once became a leading worker in the Sabbath school. No churches were here then, but he and some other citizens soon had a flourishing Sabbath school in a small hall over a store room. There they gathered together persons of all denominations and beliefs and for many months these good people labored to improve the rough elements of society so common in the frontier towns of that early day. This pioneer work had much to do in paving the way for the churches later on. When the various churches were able to build places of worship, each gathered to itself members from the union school and from this source there sprang several large, flourishing Sunday schools in La Cygne. Then for about ten years Mr. Miller was identified with the M. E. Church, always a leader in its Sunday school. His work in this line was not confined to La Cygne alone. He was the direct means of organizing and largely maintaining many schools of a like character in surrounding country districts. He made frequent visits to these places, lectured to the people on Sunday and in every way encouraged them in this good work.

The Hensleys were Kentucky people. William Hensley arrived in Linn County about 1860. He married Jane Fickes, sister to Morgan. John Paton Hensley of the same family married Lucy Ogan and was a soldier in the Sixth Kansas Cavalry under David Goss. His son Bush had a son named Melvin, who enlisted in the Coast Artillery and served in France.

John Ogan was a soldier in the Tenth Kansas Infantry. His grandson, Thomas Kimbler, was a soldier in the World War in France.

Oscar Hoyt was the son of Ira Hoyt, born in Rutland, Vermont, and his wife Hannah Graves Fairbanks of Massachusetts. Oscar was born in Kalmazoo, Michigan, in 1846 and came to Linn County in 1874. He was married to Julia Amelia Lyman. They made their home in Liberty township. Of their children Eugene married Mary Mays, Belle married W. B. Kerr, Oscar L. married Stella Griffith, and Robert L. is unmarried.

John Byerley was born in 1846 in Tennessee and came to Kansas in time to be a soldier under Captain O. E. Morse in the Fifth Kansas Cavalry. He married Margaret Walker at the home of Jacob Ungerhire in the old Georgetown school district. She was the daughter of William Alfred Walker and his wife Susanna Sales, both from Wilkes county, North Carolina, where their daughter was born in 1856. The Byerley children were Frank who married Laura Thompson; William who married Louise Willis Hoyt; and James who married Carrie Hilyard and now lives in Osborne county.

David Sibbett had a brother named Samuel and a sister Elizabeth who married John Gates. The Sibbets were from Cumberland county, Pennsylvania.

Among the earliest of the permanent settlers of Scott township was James Cattell Marshall who in the spring of 1857 preempted a claim of 160 acres of prairie land about six and a half miles west of the present town of La Cygne.

Two years later he was joined by Lucy, his second wife whom he had previously married in Ohio, and the couple continued to live on their farm till 1874, when they came to live in La Cygne. Here they dwelt in their little cottage home in the northeast part of the town till 1883, when with their two sons Carl and Bert they left the state to make their future home in Eureka, Humboldt county, California, where ten years later they died within a year or so of each other. Few of the early pioneers of Linn County were better known than "Uncle Jimmy" and "Aunt Lucy" Marshall, as they were familiarly known to their neighbors. They had been reared in the Society of Friends or "Quakers" as this sect is more commonly known, and continued to exemplify in their lives the principles of "peace and probity" so characteristic of this peculiar sect. This was especially the case with "Aunt Lucy" whose quiet and kindly Quaker ways, soon endeared her to all who came to know her.

In his earlier manhood, true to his Quaker rearing, he had been an earnest and consistent nonresistant, holding stoutly that war could not be justified on any account. But his experience with the Border Ruffians and the brutal Trading Post Massacre in 1858, and especially his association with John Brown and James Montgomery, Ed. R. Smith and other Jayhawkers who were fighting to keep Kansas free, quickly dissipated these pacifist theories. He was fain to admit that as between war and the triumph of rampant wrong, war was the lesser evil. So when came the call to arms in 1861, and the oldest son, then but sixteen, pleaded to be allowed to enlist, both his Quaker father and "Aunt Lucy" helped to bundle him up in three thicknesses of overcoats in order that he might look big enough for the recruiting officer to accept him. And later, when "Old Pap Price" eluded the Federal generals and came racing down on his mission of invasion through eastern Kansas the father oiled up his old smoothbore musket and showed up at Mound City to do his bit as a home guard. James Cattell Marshall came of Virginia-Maryland stock, the same that produced the great Chief Justice John Marshall. The first of the family, Thomas Marshall, came to America from England in 1744 and established an estate on the Maryland shore of the Potomac almost opposite Mt. Vernon, the home of the Washingtons, with whom he and his family soon became intimate. Later William Marshall, a youthful offshoot of this family, went down into North Carolina on a stock buying errand and there became enamored of a beautiful Quakeress whom he married, thus cutting himself off from his aristocratic Virginia relatives. He became a Friend, learned the trade of a stone mason and helped to build the walls of historic Ft. Sumter during the Revolution. Later, this William removed with his family to Portage county, Ohio, where in the region known as the "Connecticut

Western Reserve" James Cattell was born in 1816. His father, Benjamin, or "Benny" Marshall as he was known in the neighborhood, "took to books" and was one of the first schoolmasters in that region. When hardly more than a boy, Uncle Jimmy managed to get a few months of study at Mount Union College, a Quaker school that I believe is still in existence in Alliance, Ohio. About 1840 James C. was married to Henrietta Fawcett, a Quaker lady, who was also a teacher. The young couple had become enthusiastic "Reformers", including temperance, dress reform, women's rights, etc., in their enthusiasm, but more particularly were they devoted to the cause of anti-slavery, then led by Phillips, Garrison, Parker, Lucretia Mott and others. James and his wife spent most of their vacations lecturing in eastern Ohio and Pennsylvania on these and other subjects. In 1848 James and Henrietta Marshall established a young lady's academy at Edinburg in the Shenadoah Valley of Virginia, near the spot where Sheridan later was to fight his famous battle of Cedar Creek and do his "twenty mile ride" from Winchester. Here the son Carl was born in 1852 and here the family remained till 1854.

In 1849 came an interesting hiatus in James Marshall's life, when he joined a company of young Virginians and sailed around Cape Horn on a ship they had chartered to try their luck in the gold fields of California. It was while on a gold-hunting trip by sea along the northern coast that James was shipwrecked, narrowly escaping with his life. Proceeding down the coast afoot he with his party discovered Humboldt Bay, the only inclosed harbor on the Californian coast north of San Francisco, and the present site of the thriving city of Eureka. James was of the party who founded this town and being a surveyor, assisted in laying out its streets. It was owing to this circumstance that he later returned to spend the remainder of his life in this place.

Returning to Virginia in 1851 little the better off financially for his adventure as an argonaut, he resumed his connection with the Virginia school, which she had conducted in his absence. In 1854 her health failed and in the hope of restoring it the school was disposed of and the family removed to Tama county, Iowa, where on October 6, 1856, she passed on. With almost her last words she solemnly adjured her husband to remove to Kansas and devote himself to the cause of winning this young territory to freedom. Their long residence in slave-holding Virginia had only confirmed their hatred for this "divine institution" and their wish to see it stamped out utterly.

On the death of Henrietta, "Aunt Lucy" assumed the care of the children, Laura a girl of thirteen, Homer eleven, and Carl four. Two years later James made a brief trip to Salem, Ohio, where he and "Aunt Lucy" were married. Soon after

and all her early and dear associations to take up the duties
of a pioneer mother in a little cabin on the Kansas prairies.
From this later union there were two children, one a boy
who died in infancy and the other Libertus Justus Marshall,
born in Mound City about the time of Mr. Lincoln's Emancipation Proclamation in 1863. The boy received his formidable
moniker in commemoration of this event. He was the lively
lad later known to his friends in the La Cygne home as "Bert."
He is now a resident of San Jose, California.

Lucy Ann Marshall, familiarly known to the pioneer settlers
of Linn County as "Aunt Lucy," was born near Salem, Ohio,
April 26, 1822. Her father was John Fawcett who was born
near Philadelphia in 1786. His father was Thomas Fawcett
who operated a grist-mill on the Brandywine River during
the American Revolution. The family were of English extrac-
tion. In 1817 while on a business trip to Virginia John Fawcett
became acquainted with Miss Ann Bayliss, a young lady of
good family and some social prominence. After a romantic
courtship, the young people were married, Ann becoming a
Quakeress and soon afterward they moved to Ohio and settled
on a farm near Salem in Columbiana county. In education,
culture and the social refinements, Ann Bayliss was much the
superior of her staid, plodding farmer husband and naturally
her aristocratic family regarded her marriage as a mesalliance
and she saw little of them thereafter. John Fawcett lived
to be seventy-six. Ann Bayliss was descended from somewhat important ancestry. Her mother was a Turner and her
paternal grandmother was a Blackburn, a daughter of Colonel
Richard Blackburn who came from Ripon, England, in 1733
as an officer in King George's army. He was afterward a
patriot member of the Virginia house of burgesses and is
buried at the ancestral home, Ripon Lodge, twelve miles
from Mount Vernon. The Baylisses and Turners as well as
the Blackburns were leading families in the history of Virginia and many of their descendants are still prominent in
social and public affairs. Uncle Jimmy and Aunt Lucy were
followed to Kansas by certain of their brothers and other
relatives. Bayliss and Branson Fawcett with their families
came respectively in 1865 and 1866 and settled on near-by
farms. John Fawcett the oldest brother and Bayliss had
served through the Civil War, John as colonel of the One
Hundred Forty-fourth Ohio regiment and Bayliss as a captain
in the Second Ohio Cavalry. Bayliss was a carpenter by trade
but cultivated a farm in the Ewing district of Scott township, where he lived for many years. Branson Fawcett lived
for several years in Scott township, then removed with his
family to Cowley county.

Bayliss R. Fawcett, a brother to Aunt Lucy Marshall, was born in Richmond, Virginia, August 11, 1827, his maternal ancestors being the Baylisses, wealthy people of some distinction, one relative being closely associated with George Washington in the Revolutionary War. His parents took him to Salem, Ohio, where he grew up and became Captain of Company M of the Second Ohio Cavalry. August 17 1862 he was married to Mary Artz, who was born at Buffalo, New York. Flora, their first child, now Mrs. Adam Stolper, was born at Salem. On their way to Kansas they came down the Ohio river and were stranded on a sandbar and Flora had the whooping cough. At St. Louis they took a stage through, arriving at Twin Springs where they joined "Uncle Jimmy" and "Aunt Lucy" Marshall, Mrs. Marshall being a sister to Baylis. Their daughter Anna was born at Twin Springs. He died at the home of his daughter Flora in Leavenworth December 4, 1892, and was buried in Mount Muncie cemetery. The children of Mrs. Flora Fawcett Stolper are Carl B. who married Lena Feris and lives in Fort Worth, Texas; William A. married Bessie Lintner and lives in Kansas City, Missouri; Louise F. married Erven D. Kohl and lives in Kansas City, Missouri; Mary H. married William A. Robie and lives at La Cygne.

Hyrcanus Highley served in the Civil War in Company C, Fifteenth Kansas Cavalry. His family came from Wythville, Virginia, where he was born August 17, 1842. The mother and several children lived at Paola. January 17, 1869, Hyrcanus married Mary Matilda Dixon, daughter of John Dixon of La Cygne, their two children being Carrie who died at twelve years of age, and Herbert Thomas who died in Kansas City at the age of thirty-six leaving a daughter, Bonita Marie, who is now in school at Fremont, Nebraska. On April 27, 1921, Hyrcanus was married a second time to Mrs. Mary Petefish. Suffering a severe injury in an accident in later years he was taken to the Soldier's Home in Leavenworth where he died June 15, 1925, leaving his wife and two half sisters, Mrs. W. J. Lane and Mrs. George Majors, both of Garnett, Kansas, and a brother Thomas M. Highley, late police commissioner of Oklahoma City. The Highleys were a forceful people leaving a record of good citizenship.

The Finches have always been numerous about Linn County and the country north of it since 1857, when Commodore Finch owned part of what is now the William Black farm north of La Cygne. They were descended from Ira Finch of New York and his wife, a Miss Buell, sister to General Buell of Civil War fame. This couple moved to Ohio and once owned the tract of ground where the city of Columbus now stands. They allowed several thousands of acres to revert to the state for taxes, and the state capital was subsequently built upon it. To them was born Thomas Samuel Finch who married Lucy Warner of German birth, and to them Charles Sherman Finch was born in Franklin county, Ohio, in 1864, and as a boy came to La Cygne and worked in the blacksmith shop of E. P. McCarty and Jim Nash who married one of the Finch girls, and for C. W. Olney. At about that time he enlisted in the Fifteenth United States Regulars and served five years. Returning to La Cygne he on June 11, 1887, married Jennie Geneva only daughter of E. P. McCarty. They had three children, Jessie who married William Bright, Lester McCarty who married Ivy Ayres, and Lucy Pauline who married Dana McClanahan. The Finches have a family tradition going back to the year 1200 when a Finch is claimed to have carried a cavalry sword into Jerusalem in one of the Crusades. This sword was brought to America about 1621 by a younger son who surreptitiously took it from the ancestral home in England. It has since been handed down to the oldest boy as a family relic and has been the object of a feud for its possession. When Thomas Samuel Finch became an officer in the Twelfth Ohio Volunteer Cavalry in the Civil War this sword was remounted by citizens and presented to him with this inscription on it: "Presented 2d Lt. T. S. Finch by the non-commissioned officers and privates of Co. L. 12 "O. V. C." If this tradition can be substantiated the Sword of La Cygne outranks the Sword of Bunker Hill and that of Damocles in historic interest. A further traditional claim for it is that at Valley Forge a Finch was a major in the Continental Army and when Washington's sword was sent to an armorer for repairs he accepted the use of this sword temporarily. Two sons of Commodore Finch, Curtis and David Mascal, enlisted in a Missouri regiment and were subsequently transferred to a Kansas regiment in the Civil War.

Mabry Madden was a Virginian who came through Kentucky to Illinois where he married Kezia Sappington, a South Carolina woman. Their surviving children were John Madden, who married Lena Curry and later he became county clerk, county treasurer, and postmaster of Mound City. Elza married John Harmant; Mary married Henry Strong, and Maria married Dr. H. H. Cox. The Madden ancestors were from Ireland.

Charles W. Libby and his wife Mary Jane Mayberry were from near Portland, Maine, and emigrated to Minnesota in 1851, then two years in Wisconsin, and to Boone county, Illinois, where Frank Charles Libby was born. They came to Kansas in 1868 and settled near Zenia in Bourbon county, but as they got water from a spring over in Linn County, they moved over and Frank served two terms in the Kansas legislature from this county. He was married August 16 1874 to Mary Ann Williams from Illinois. Frank was a big cattleman at one time and when he failed he owed the bank $5800, a big sum in those days, but they told him to go right ahead and use the bank's credit and he won out handsomely, and now at seventy-six years of age is happy and contented. Frank's daughter Cleda married Thomas Potter at Blue Mound, who is serving a second term as member of the legislature from his district.

John W. Garratt was born in Otsego county, New York, in 1809. He came to Linn County in 1857 and settled in Potosi township. He died there July 4, 1872. He married Amanda Daniels in Garrattsville, New York (the town was named in honor of his family) in 1829; she died in 1852. In 1854 he married Rebecca Carpenter of New York and she died in Linn County February 29, 1878. He left two sons, John Garratt and Neal Garratt. He served as postmaster at Potosi and in 1859 built the first sawmill in that vicinity. The son John Garratt was married October 12, 1867, to Maria B. Harris, born in Philadelphia as the daughter of John Jeremiah and Margaret Harris who later lived at Woodburn, Illinois. She was teaching school in Old Potosi at the time of her marriage and they lived there until 1881 when they moved to Pleasanton where he followed his trade as a carpenter. They had two daughters, Mrs. Cora Lockwood of Faith, South Dakota, and Elida who married Albert R. Cottle, son of Thomas D. Cottle and nephew of Dave Cottle the race horse man of Liberty township and also nephew of John David Day another famous horseman. Albert R. Cottle has been for twenty-five years a deputy in the office of the United States Marshal at Muskogee, Oklahoma. John Garratt lived in Linn County sixty-five years, having come here when he was fourteen years old. In 1862 he enlisted in Company M, Second Kansas Volunteer Cavalry, and served to the end of the war. Mrs. Garratt was one of eleven charter members of the First Presbyterian Church of Pleasanton when it was organized October 11, 1869.

Mose McGlothlin, says the La Cygne Journal of April 15, 1927, is dead, and his death marks the passing of another of the few remaining ones who knew the town in its infancy. Born in slavery, his early days were spent with his beloved Marse and Mis'tis, and many were the interesting memories he could recall of those days. At the time of the Civil War he was a boy of perhaps 14, and went through the conflict as the personal servant of Captain William Shattuck of Valley township. At the close of the war he came with Captain Shattuck to Trading Post. When W. H. Broadwell opened a drug store in that thriving little city Mose was employed by him to work around the store. Soon after that he came to the new town of La Cygne and was employed by T. N. Marshall to herd cattle. But Mose had been reared as a house servant and soon was employed as waiter at the Dixon House which was the first hotel in the town. At that time the building comprised the house as it now stands and the house just north of it which was later moved to its present location and two private residences made from the old hotel. In the stirring times of the early days the Dixon House was a busy place, and many interesting tales of the wild customs of the time when whisky was a common beverage, Mose could relate. One was of a patron who rode his horse through the wide front door and into the dining room, demanding immediate service, causing wild confusion in which Mose crawled under the table until order was restored. A few years later when the old La Cygne House west of the railroad enjoyed a flourishing business and all passenger trains on the old Gulf railroad stopped here for meals, Mose was the headwaiter and many times has entertained children of later generations by calling off the bill-of-fare and acting in pantomime his duties as headwaiter. A born mimic, characteristic of his race, he could relate stories of early events that caused his hearers to live over again with him these early experiences. He was kind and gentle and intensely loyal to his white friends. Surviving him are his wife Ruth and daughter Maude of the home and son Harvey of Joplin.

Along about 1863 a number of ex-slaves arrived at Mound City and established themselves on farms, among them T. J. Baskerville who took up a "claim" adjoining the town of Moneka and lived to a good old age. Baskerville was a very influential man among his own people and had a great reputation as a "healer", possessing a strong magnetic power which relieved those he treated of aches and pains. His fame was so great that a "beaten path" led to his door and as the law regulating medical practice prevented his receiving a money compensation for his services those whom he treated brought with them a great variety of produce and other things to express their gratitude in a substantial way until his accumulations excited much curious interest.

In 1865 Moses Ellsworth came from Sangamon county, Illinois, to make his home in Scott township. This family was quite well known, the children being J. L. Ellsworth, now of Medicine Lodge, A. L. and A. T. Ellsworth of Fontana, and E. W. of Iola, and Rhoda who married Jesse Vance in 1861 in Illinois. The Vance children were Curtis, Mary Laurett, Ann Adella, William E. and Alberta T. Among the third generation, her grandchildren, Mrs. Vance left Clyde Geer of Sterling, Colorado; Loren Geer of Osawatomie, and Earl Vance

of La Cygne, and five greatgrandchildren. This family illustrates the rapidity with which time passes. Old Moses was
a veritable patriarch, a fine example of good citizenship, but
except for this brief mention would soon be not even a memory
except to the occasional visitor at his tombstone.

Frederick W. Pollman was for many years an exemplary
and leading citizen of La Cygne. He was of German origin,
having been born at Billinghousen in Lipple Detwold. He was
an expert in making brick and was the first in that industry
in La Cygne. He was married at his home in Germany to
Amelia Brokman and three daughters and five sons were born
to them here. A son William went to Baker City, Oregon,
and is rated as a millionaire, and is president of the biggest
bank there. In 1876 the father became associated with Fred
Tilghner in the meat business, which recalls another good old
citizen long since removed.

"E. P." was another unique character familiar to everybody in the same way that "Ed. R." and "Geo. J." and "J. D."
identified other big and useful citizens. "E. P." always wore
"chin whiskers", chewed tobacco and talked incessantly for
his town and its people, his distinguished trait his faith-
fulness in his friendships. Ethelbert P. McCarty was born
April 16, 1843, at Niles, Trumble county, Ohio, where William
McKinley was born, and up to the age of fourteen years our
good citizen and the future president of the United States
were playmates and school mates. Mr. McCarty was a pioneer
in the oil business and at Mecca, Ohio, helped in the drilling
of the fourth well put down in the United States, and was an
authority on such work and in his old age did much of the
pioneer work in developing oil and gas in Linn County. He
was of the superb type of men, mentally and physically, that
made up the Union Army and in 1861 immediately answered
Lincoln's call by enlisting in Company C of the Nineteenth
Ohio, in which he served until discharged in October, 1865.
In 1862 while in the army he was married to Nancy M.
Teachout on August 31st. Four days after his release from
army service he and his wife and child and her parents left
for Kansas in wagons and located at Eureka in Greenwood
county, and engaged in stock raising but the Texas fever
killed every animal. He went then to Hartford and opened a
blacksmith shop and added a store to his business and prospered till in 1870, when a cyclone destroyed all his property.
In 1871 they came to La Cygne where he opened a blacksmith
shop and a stock of merchandise and later was in real estate
business. Of the children, Jennie the eldest married C. S.
Finch, a blacksmith and implement dealer; Howard is in business; Ernest was with his father in the real estate business;
and Frank is with the La Cygne Telephone Company.

Ira D. Bronson was born in Warren, Herkimer county, New York, October 24, 1835. At the age of nineteen he emigrated to Illinois where he taught school, first in Knox county, and later near Antioch, Lake county. At Antioch he married, on June 11, 1867, Miss Annie Webb, a native of that place. Mr. Bronson came to Kansas in 1857, located in Paris, where he engaged in the lumber business. In May 1861 he enlisted in Company F, Second Kansas Volunteers, and was mustered out of the service in the fall of 1865, as captain of Company I, Second Arkansas Volunteer Infantry, having also served as captain of Company A, Fourth Arkansas Volunteer Infantry. In March 1866, he moved to Mound City, remained there until August, 1870, when he moved to Fort Scott. Mr. Bronson was interested in numerous town sites in southern Kansas, the town of Bronson in Bourbon county, having been named for him.

Aunt Kate Long, widow of Henry Long, was one of a heroic family that lived in the Brooklin neighborhood for more than half a century, surviving her husband many years and died on the homestead she and her husband had settled upon sixty-six years before. She had reached her ninetieth year, as she was born December 17, 1834, at Salem, North Carolina, and came here in 1858 to establish a home. She was a keenly intelligent woman and was well acquainted with John Brown, James Montgomery, Dave Sibbett and other heroes of the time. She had long been an active member of the M. E. Church at La Cygne. She left two sons, Willis and Thomas, who still live in the old neighborhood.

Henry Carpenter was long an honored citizen of Linn County, having established his home two miles east of Trading Post where his youngest daughter, Mrs. Orie E. Allmon, now lives in this historic home. Henry was born February 5, 1826, at Bennington, Vermont, and by the death of his father he was thrown on his own resources when but a boy. He went to Hannibal, New York, where on March 22, 1849, he was married to Emily A. Lane, sister of the well known John S. Lane and daughter of "Uncle Jackie". Four children were born to them at Hannibal: John Wellin, Warren T., Ward J., and Frank H. At Trading Post three more children came: F. S., Nile P., and Orie E. These all married except Warren, who died in infancy. Large families were raised by John Wellin, who married Dorothy Neollsch; Ward J. who married Anna Kelsey; Frank H. who married Maggie A. Woliver; Fred S. married Ella Pierson; Nile P. who married Delia Calvin; and Orie E. who married Frank Allmon September 2, 1891. Mrs. Allmon says her mother often told her of the hardships they suffered in the first years, one incident being that of the father walking to Fort Scott and carrying home provisions for his hungry family when his horses had been "borrowed" by the Bushwhackers.

In 1859 Amos W. Long located on a claim at the northeast corner of Silver Mound east of where La Cygne now is. He brought with him his aged father Samuel Long and his brother Lewis Long. Amos W. Long's wife Lavina and four children —Lucy, Francis, Samuel and Edward—constituted his family at that time. When the war came on Amos W. Long was elected a captain in the Sixth Kansas Militia and went with his company to meet Price at Westport, leaving his family alone. On October 23 Grandfather Long went out on the prairie to drive the cows home. In the distance he saw a number of men riding toward him. He rode to the home of a neighbor nearby, finding only the wife at home. She wanted to hide him in her house, but he said no one would harm a man seventy-six years old and he would hurry on down a ravine and hide his money and valuable papers. As he emerged from the ravine the rebels rode out from a bunch of trees and shot him dead and rode away without touching the body. The neighbor woman carried the sad news to the family and the two women took the body home and cared for it. Amos Long soon after took his family to Paola, where his children grew to be highly respected citizens. Fannie Long taught school in La Cygne and many citizens will remember her. Callie Long married John Sheridan. Amos served two terms as sheriff of Miami county. Younger children were Samuel and Ben.

A noted character of Lincoln township was Stephen Weech, who was born in Summerton, Somersetshire, England, on August 25, 1837. His family came to America in 1854 and in 1858 settled two miles east of where La Cygne now is, where he had his home in a substantial stone house. He married Eliza Rose, daughter of Jule Rose. They had three daughters, Rose who was born May 27, 1864, and married George Gilliland in 1891, and to whom a son was born; Mary married a Mr. Hampton, and Lizzie married a Mr. Grisham. "Steve" was familiarly known as "Colonel Weech" in compliment of his services as marshal at Fourth of July celebrations.

Daniel Stainbrook was a real pioneer. He was born of German parents of Pennsylvania stock at Zanesville, Ohio, December 27, 1824. At twelve he was an orphan and came west to make his home with his sister, Mrs. Lizzie Nevitt in Illinois. In 1849 he drove a team of oxen through to California without losing an animal, a record at that time. He came back in 1851 to Bureau county, Illinois, farmed a while and married Mary Frances Drawyer of Bradford, who was born in Peckskill, New York. In 1866 he sold out and came here, buying out old Peter Blystone who lived on the north side of Middle Creek ford, still known as "Blystone Crossing." Susie Blystone became the wife of Capt. David Goss and is still living as are others of the Blystone family. The children of Daniel Stainbrook were Laura Ann, John Frederick who married Mollie Long, Franz Sigel who married Addie Doig, Ruhama Elizabeth who married B. W. Mendenhall, and Julia Amanda who married George D. Marmon.

Henry Dellinger, who was a prominient citizen of La Cygne, was born in Pennsylvania. The family moved to Ohio where Henry grew to manhood near Columbus. He married Lydia Pickering whose family established the town of Pickering, Ohio. Henry served as a lieutenant in an Ohio regiment in the Civil War and brought his family to Mound City in 1865, to Trading Post in 1867, and to La Cygne when the railroad came in 1869. His children were Alma who married Vinton Rockhold; John Fremont who married Carrie Emogene Lane and moved to Garnett, where John served as sheriff of Anderson county; Ida married Harry Hutchinson and moved to Salina; Grace who married Howard Dreher and moved to Salina, where Grace died; Pearl married W. J. Stites, La Cygne; Theresa married Fred Black, La Cygne.

Henry W. Woodruff was born in Farmington, Connecticut, on November 23, 1827, and died at La Cygne, December 31, 1898. He was a fine citizen who served his country faithfully in both army and civil life.

John Thomas Wilgus was born May 6, 1841, near Mount Sterling, Illinois, and came to Kansas in 1857. He served in the Fifteenth Kansas Cavalry until the close of the Civil War. He was married to Elizabeth Potts at Paola September 2, 1869. In July, 1885, the family came to La Cygne where they operated one of the leading stores of the town which is still conducted by the sons Frank and Alfred, and Miss Rena.

Selwyn Douglas began his career in the legal profession at La Cygne and later moved to Oklahoma where both he and Mrs. Douglas were powerful influences for good in the development of that new state. She was credited with the splendid work of securing the $50,000 Carnegie Library for Oklahoma City. Their son McGregor Douglas won distinguished honors at Kansas University and is now one of the leading lawyers of Oklahoma.

Over in the southwest corner of Scott township in the years before the Civil War, Levin S. Dorsey made his home, being then an aged and infirm man. He was from Spencer county, Indiana, where he had been a school mate with

Abraham Lincoln, his father being Azel W. Dorsey who is mentioned in history as "Abe Lincoln's first and only teacher." Levin, in conversation with William H. Ward who then lived at Brooklin, resented the idea that Lincoln was a "very dull scholar." "Why no!" said he, "Abe was considered smart." Levin had two sons, Truman H. and James Azel Dorsey who enlisted in Company H (afterward Company E) Sixth Kansas Cavalry. Truman was captured by the enemy July 27, 1864, and was confined in Tyler prison in Smith county, Texas, till exchanged at the close of the war in 1865 and came home to Linn County to die from disease contracted in prison. The father went out to repair a farm fence and was later found dead, and was mourned as an estimable citizen and neighbor. James Azel Dorsey studied medicine and was for a time running a drug store at Opolis, Kansas, and practicing his profession. With Truman Dorsey in Tyler prison were thirty-six men of Company E, Sixth Kansas Cavalry, nearly all from Linn County.

Among the early settlers in Valley township was Jackson Lane, long familiarly known as "Uncle Jacky" Lane. The family were originally from Derbyshire, England, and one of them, Roswell Lane, arrived in America in time to be a soldier in the Revolutionary War on the right side. His grandson was our Jackson Lane, born at Litchfield, Connecticut, September 30, 1804. He married Sally Ann Parish and they made their home at Hannibal, New York. They had two children who lived to become citizens of Linn County—Emily Almira Lane and John Sheridan Lane, the family arriving at Trading Post in April, 1860. They began to get pioneer experience at once. That was the dry year and there was no vegetation at all. Nothing grew. Garden seeds put in the ground never germinated. Families fed the straw in their bed ticks to the milch cows and finally they drove their cows down along the creeks and the river and cut down willow trees to let the cows browse off their tops, later driving all their live stock off into Missouri rather than let them starve and the Missourians were not in a state of mind to give them a cordial welcome. For fourteen months not a drop of rain fell and it seemed the end of things. Three men were hanged in the vicinity and the settlers terrorized. One dark night Mrs. Robinson came to the Lane home two miles east of Trading Post and told them the Bushwhackers were riding all over the country and that they had made prisoners of Tom Goss and Jim Martin. This brave Mrs. Robinson rode on into Trading Post and notified the soldiers stationed there, who started to rescue Goss and Martin and punish the intruders, who had gone east and at the state line had turned Goss and Martin loose. In 1861 the Civil War started in April and all kinds of troubles came to the settlers. No one thought

of undressing and going to bed for a night's rest. Only a
few old men and young boys were left in the homes and they
slept out in the fields or in the brush. All the vigorous men
were in the militia and away from home. One cheerful bit
of information was given out by a man who rode through
the settlements telling the people that Hamelton was coming
back with four hundred Indians to kill off all settlers at one
swoop. A few families left, not many. Those who stayed
would gather in groups of three or four families, the women
taking care of the young children while the old men and boys
took to the brush. General Jim Lane's regiment was located
a mile and half north of the Trading Post, and with the
scarcity of food following the drouth it was a hungry time
for everybody. One night the regiment started for Missouri
to rout a company of Bushwhackers they knew were in camp
there. They took along a regular army cannon and made a
brave noise as they rumbled past the Lane home in the night.
As usual, a spy had preceded them to the Bushwhackers' camp
and the game got away. The war activities took most of
the men on both sides of the border away from home and
the terrors of midnight murders and assaults kept up inter-
mitently until the Price raid in October, 1864. Uncle Jackie
Lane and his son-in-law, Harvey Smith, were at Trading Post
where the rebels captured them. Uncle Jackie, then past
sixty years of age, insisted they be taken to Price, and arriving
before the rebel commander he introduced Smith to Price
and incidentally gave to Price the sign of distress of a
Mason, to which Price responded by ordering them separated
from other prisoners and guarded. In the early morning
about two o'clock, the Federal batteries made it so uncomfortable the rebel guards took to their heels and Lane and Smith
found themselves free, although the rebels drove a few of
their prisoners before them as far as the Arkansas River.
The Price raiders were starved and in a desperate plight.
They began to show up about two o'clock in the afternoon of
October 23 and their twenty-five thousand men were spread
out all over the earth, no military order, every man skirmishing for himself. Every home was robbed every ounce of food
taken, and every article of value they could carry. In many
instances they maliciously destroyed things that were treasures in the homes. Old Pap Price rode at the head of the procession in his two-seated ambulance drawn by four white
mules. He witnessed the murderous conduct of his soldiers
but his influence was gone and they would have laughed at
his commands had he tried to control them. Price's two
daughters rode in the ambulance with him, witnessing their
foul insults to women. At the Trading Post they ran the
flour mill until they broke it. Nothing was left, and had not
Henry Carpenter brought a commissary wagon loaded with
food for the militia, the citizens would have been very hungry.

In the years following the war the Lane family moved to La Cygne when the railroad arrived there in 1869. John S. Lane had married Sarah Chapman and they had three children— William J. Lane who married Mollie Highley and is now a druggist at Garnett; Carrie who married John Dellinger of La Cygne who is now a merchant at Garnett; and Clarence E. Lane now living at Keokuk, Iowa. Uncle Jacky lived at La Cygne several years but finally returned to his daughter Mrs. Emily Carpenter in Valley township where he died at the age of eighty years.

Elihu Ireland was born in Ross county, Ohio, in 1818. His wife was Hannah Clopper of Fairfield county, Ohio. Elihu served in the Forty-sixth Ohio Infantry in the Civil War. They came to Linn County in 1867 and settled on Middle Creek about three miles northeast of La Cygne, where they were delighted to find an old Ohio friend in Abraham Beidler, who had preceded them.[1] The Irelands stayed through and a large number of descendants of Elihu and wife are here to honor their memory, among them Mrs. John Moncrieff; Ellen, who married Dan Hamill in Ohio; Robert Henry (Bob) our present well-known citizen; Catherine, who became Mrs. Louis Shaffer; James S. now at Mound City; and Jerry C., who a few years ago was sheriff. They were a fine pioneer family. Coming west in wagons they saw at Pleasant Hill, Missouri, a very large man with a very large wife driving a team of very large horses. Driving alongside they recognized them as the Worlands from their old home in Ohio, who became well known in Linn County by their annual visits with Irelands. When driving past where "96" school house now is Bob Ireland saw his Uncle Eli Stuckey apparently in a fight with another man but it proved to be only joyous manifestations at recognition of old friends.

Robert Alexander Campbell was a Scotchman who settled as a pioneer in Rowan county, North Carolina. One of his ancestors carried a gun in Washington's army while his boy who was too young to enlist drove an ox team. Robert A. finally reached Perry county, Missouri, where he enlisted in Missouri state militia and later married Mary Whybark whose father had been sent as a missionary to the Indians in southeast Missouri by the Dutch Reformed Church as early as 1805. In 1866 Robert A. and his wife came to Linn County and located seven miles southwest of Mound City, purchasing the claim of Ed Tucker's father. Here they helped organize the Pleasant Hill Presbyterian church with the families of Ephraim Hahn, William Smith, Victor Johnson, Peter Bolinger—all of whom were old Missouri friends of the Campbells —and also the Dunlaps and Wilsons. This church was on the

---

1. The Beidlers left here in 1876 for Colorado, and from there to Washinton.

old Sammy McGrew farm afterward owned by Tom Curry. The Campbell children were Nevlin (familiarly known as "Nev" when he was editor of the Mound City Progress newspaper) who married Dora Calvert. Rowena married David O. Markley and Robert Freeland married Inez Chenowith.

The death of Thomas Nesbit Marshall marks the passing of one of the most remarkable figures in Kansas history, both as a personage and from the standpoint of actual experience. A Scotch-Irish ancestry produces a type of men who overcome difficulties, who fear nothing, and who never know when they are defeated, a type of men who fight fairly, always out in the open, and who have a sense of personal honor possessed only by the truly great. Of such parentage was Mr. Marshall born on September 9, 1845, in Virginia, Illinois. True to this ideal type, his whole life was characterized by industry, persistence, courage and honor; and the loss of both parents before he was seven years of age did not dim the lustre of this heritage. In 1866, three years before the town of La Cygne was established, he came to Kansas and located at Trading Post where he engaged in the livestock business, which he continued without interruption for a period of sixty years. The record of his experiences in this business would make an important chapter in the history of the cattle industry of the United States and would extend from Oregon to Albany, New York, and from Texas and New Orleans to St. Paul, Detroit and Canada. Before the days of railroads in the northwest, he drove his herds on horseback for hundreds of miles to market or to the nearest shipping point. He was familiar with the cattle traffic from Texas to Abilene, Kansas, in the early seventies and knew all the big cattle men, good and bad. He delivered his live stock to Kansas City at a time when there was no established market at that point and no stock yard, his stock being delivered out on the prairie where there were no enclosures of any kind. He helped to establish the first live stock market at Kansas City and saw the building of the first stock yards. He sold live stock to the first packing house, a business conducted by a man named Baker, in a boxed-up shack twelve by fourteen feet, so located that it was necessary to swim all his stock across the Kaw river. This was not considered any obstacle, however, as prior to that time he had been swimming his stock across the Missouri river in order to get to the St. Joseph market. A few years ago he traced upon a map of the United States all the trails that he had traveled on horseback in the early days, and this map, with its crude tracings, resembles a railway map of the United States of the present day. In March, 1924, Mr. Marshall was invited to Washington before the Committee on Agriculture in the United States Senate to tell about his early experience in the cattle business, and particularly of the beginning of the

Kansas City market. His recollections as given to the Senate Committee were reduced to writing and published in book form as a part of the Senate proceedings and contain much valuable and interesting history. In 1887 he became associated with the Stoller Commission Company of Kansas City and returned to the northwest as foreman of the cattle shipping business for that company, his principal shipping points being Helena, Montana, and Boise, Idaho. In 1890 he returned to La Cygne where he continued in the live stock business until the day of his death, which occurred at seven o'clock on the evening of August 18, 1926, as his home in La Cygne. His cattle business in the northwest in the seventies and the eighties brought him in contact with much of the rough element, but his natural dignity, his courteous demeanor, and his fearless disposition afforded all the protection that was ever required. Mr. Marshall was married on December 9, 1900, to Miss Anna Berry, at the Midland Hotel in Kansas City, Missouri. His keen appreciation of her many accomplishments and her unusual business ability enriched his life to a high degree; and their beautiful modern home on Market street was the greatest joy that ever came into his life. A sketch of Mr. Marshall's life would not be complete without reference to his political and civic activities. In politics, he was an intense partisan. He never sought nor held an office of any kind, but for half a century he bore the burdens of his political party in his community. Young men might waver and neglect their political obligations, but he never did, and to him was left the chores of his party in his precinct year after year. It mattered not whether the candidate aspired to be a United States Senator or wanted to be the next constable, he received the same careful and earnest attention. In the first few years of his life here Tom was associated with his elder brother William who married Loma Colpetzer, daughter of one of the victims of the Marais des Cygnes massacre and they moved to Peoria, Illinois, where he was the head of a big cement plant.

John McCoach, who was born in Ireland, came to America and married Sarah Jane Roberts. Among children born to them were David King McCoach, born April 30, 1857, in Virginia, who married Milly Ward at her home near what is now Boicourt. Their surviving children were Clifford, who married Myrtle Duvall; Fannie who married Ben Starks and lives near Richland school house; Emogene, who married Harry Carpenter and lives in Pleasanton; and Leona who married Lovell Klick. Another son was James who married Sarah Hafley. "Jim", as he was familiarly known, learned telegraphy and was station agent at Sterling, Kansas, and other points on the Santa Fe System.

Michael Mitzel and Elizabeth Trout Mitzel his wife came from Ohio in 1859 and settled on a preemption claim near Brooklin. There were two boys, Benjamin and Abraham, who were too young to get into the military service when the Civil War broke out in 1861 and the father was too old. But the boys did their part by becoming wagoners, Ben driving a government team all over the country between Fort Scott, Fort Smith and Fort Gibson. At the battle of Cabin Creek south of Fort Scott the rebels captured all of the outfit but Ben, who escaped and rode home on a borrowed horse. Abe, the younger boy, after the war served as a wagoner under Col. Carpenter and Col Brookhead when General Custer in 1869 drove the insurgent Sioux, Arapahoes, Cheyennes and Kiowas to the number of ten thousand south from the Platte River to a place in western Indian Territory (now Oklahoma) known then as Camp Supply, where the Indians surrendered, delivering up one hundred and fifty of the ring leaders who were held a long time as prisoners of war. This campaign was one of great hardship through snow and slush and Abe Mitzel drove one of one hundred and fifty-six mule teams attended by forty ambulances. Custer's army was on the run all the time, having only one thousand men of the Tenth Cavalry, and the Thirty-seventh Infantry as guards for the train. Abe tried mining in Colorado till 1874, when he came home and married Nancy Dixon, daughter of John Dixon. They had a son, Hal John, now in Kansas City, and a girl Alpha Rose, who married M. G. Buffington and now lives at Oklahoma City. Ben Mitzel married Missouri Gudgell of Brooklin.

The numerous Shrakes of Linn County are descended from Philip Shrake who was born in Germany in 1800 and his wife Rebecca Stuart Ash of Scottish Stuart ancestry born 1803. They had two sons born near Indianapolis, Indiana: Green W. Shrake, September 24, 1835, and Newton J. Shrake, April 18, 1839, who came to Kansas. Green W. arrived in Linn County in 1860, filing on government land near Brooklin and adjoining the farm of Captain Zebediah William Leasure and served under that officer in Company K of the Sixth Kansas Militia. He married Emily Robertson and for awhile they made their home at Trading Post where Green had a saw-mill, later living in La Cygne, and in 1890 moved his furniture factory from where the Blaker Lumber office now is to Eighteenth and Grand avenue in Kansas City where he built up a good business. In 1906 it was destroyed by fire. Both Mr. and Mrs. Shrake lost their lives in a gas explosion which wrecked their home on Woodland avenue, Kansas City. They left two daughters, Mrs. Hattie Lovelace and Mrs. Lillie McCutcheon, in that city. Newton J. Shrake enlisted in Company E of the Seventh Missouri Cavalry Volunteers, in which

he served as corporal. He married Mary E. Garrett of Hancock
county, Illinois, and in 1869 with their son Charles then only
three months old they came to La Cygne. Both Green and
Newton were accomplished in music and in the "eighties" they
manufactured organs, some of which are still furnishing
melody in homes in Linn County, and when not selling organs
Newton was helping local culture by teaching old time singing
school. Their factory also turned out high grade walnut furniture which they made too good for the amount of money people
then had money to pay for. So Green took the factory to
Kansas City. The children of Newton J. Shrake were Charles
L. who married Florence Stainer of Pierre, South Dakota;
Nellie M. who died in childhood; Jessie who married James
Warren Mitchell of the La Cygne Journal; Albert L. now in
business at Topeka, and Edna O. who married W. R. Phares
and lives at Winfield. The children of James Warren Mitchell
are Eleanor who married Rudolph Rose and has two children
Meredith June and Rudolph, jr., and Louise a graduate of
Stephens College, and Marjorie.

As one approaches Mound City from the east the road runs
up at considerable elevation around a wooded hill known as
"Sugar Mound." At the northeast corner of the hill there is
a pretty grove where in 1857 Ebenezer Barnes erected his
home. A short quarter of a mile around the hill one gets
into a pretty home street that leads west down hill past the
court house and on into the business part of the town which
because of this beautiful mound is called Mound City. But
at that time it was just Sugar Mound and the home of
Ebenezer Barnes was the scene of what became a notable event
in Kansas history. On January 4, 1859, an election was being
held on the submission of the Lecompton Constitution and
for the election of state officers. Ed. R. Smith was one of
the clerks of the election and his father, Ezra Hanchet Smith,
was one of the judges. There were two ballot boxes—one for
state officers' ballots and one for the constitution votes—
just ordinary cigar boxes with a slit in the top of each to
insert the ballot. There was a ballot with the names for state
officers and two other ballots, one reading: "For the Lecompton
Constitution without the Douglas Amendment"; and the other,
"For the Lecompton Constitution with the Douglas Amendment." It will readily be perceived that both ballots read
"For". The Douglas Amendment really meant "with slavery"
or "without slavery." It was an ingenious device of the proslavers to count all the votes for the slave constitution. The
free state men were furious about it and were riding the
precincts asking free state men to see the trick and refrain
from voting on the constitution. Nineteen votes had been cast
here and most of these voters were standing around when
James Montgomery appeared on the scene. He was in a rage

and seizing the ballot box with the constitution votes held it aloft as he denounced the trick involved in the ballot. The startled voters could only see in his act a violent assault on the sanctity of the ballot and one called out, "That box is the palladium of our liberties!" Montgomery retorted, "Yes, this is the palladium of our liberties, but when it is polluted in this manner I'll show you what to do with it!" And he threw the box against the wall of the house, smashing it, and as it fell he stamped the box to splinters and ground the ballots into the ground with his heel. Ed. R. Smith was elected to carry the returns to Lawrence where he delivered a good majority for the free state ticket for state officers (who were elected) but no votes on the constitution ballot.

Andrew Chapin Doud was one of the early settlers in Valley township. He was born October 4, 1825, in Berkshire county, Massachusetts and in 1852 went to Ohio where he was married to Lucinia A. Sayre and in 1860 located five miles northeast of Trading Post and after two years of rough life on the state line he moved to the Post and opened a general store and served as postmaster. Of three children Chester was drowned in the river at the age of ten years, May married David Teachout and now lives at Douglas, Arizona, and Edgar R. died in the City of Mexico in 1908. By a second marriage A. C. Doud had several children of whom Albert now lives at Seattle and the widow lives at Monte Vista, Colorado. Mr. Doud served a term in the legislature. At the time the Price Raid poured into Trading Post Mr. Doud was carrying five hundred dollars in his pocket, four hundred of which belonged to a widow in town. Calling his little girl May, then ten years old, he led her into a barn near the house, showed her where he was burying the money, kissed her goodbye, and went into the woods south of town. As he was a known free state man they burned his store after stealing all they could carry. They took all his household goods and left him very poor indeed. Mr. Doud and his first wife are buried in Trading Post cemetery.

Edmond J. Merrill was born in Andover, Ohio, in 1826. He married Miss Morse, a cousin of Samuel Finley Breese Morse who invented the telegraph code. He and his brother, H. L. Merrill and his family moved to Kansas from Iowa in the fall of 1858. He being a blacksmith and his brother a wagon-maker, they bought a claim near Elm Creek in Scott township, H. L. Merrill taking up a claim about one and one-half miles southeast on Elm Creek. His neighbors were Sylvester Armstrong, Simeon Elliott, William Flook, Ira Lawrence, Asa Palmer, and their families. As there were quite a number of children among them the parents began to think about school for them. The only place in the neighborhood available

for a school room was a log corncrib built on the claim of H.
L. Merrill, which was cleaned up and appropriated for a school
room. Miss Olive Merrill, a sister of Mrs. Asa Palmer, was
hired as the teacher. It was a subscription school and was
taught in the summer of 1861. E. M. Merrill and Sylvester
Armstrong seeing the need got the neighbors together and
organized a school district, E. J. Merrill donating an acre of
ground from his farm on which they built a small wooden
frame and filled it in with adobe brick, whitewashed the inside,
put in long benches for seats, and a stove, and they had a
comfortable schoolhouse and community center. The Cadmus
school house stands today on the same site this first school
house stood on. The first teacher employed there was an old
gentleman named Dunn. In the meantime, E. J. Merrill built
for himself a house, barn and blacksmith shop of wood. E.
J. Merrill having grown tired of a prairie farm he moved to
a timbered farm four miles north of Farlinville early in
the spring of 1865. About that time the stage route was
changed, so it ran through his farm as it went from Paola
to Fort Scott, Merrill's farm being midway between the two
places. He built a barn and kept a change of stage horses,
and as there was a demand for an intermediate postoffice E.
J. Merrill was commissioned as United States postmaster and
his commission was signed by Abraham Lincoln as president.
The postoffice was named Ridge and was kept in his home.
Mrs. Merrill had to serve dinner to the stage drivers and
passengers, dinner to those that came from Paola at 11:30
and to those that came from Fort Scott at 2 o'clock. That
old stage coach would be a curiosity now.

Henry Newton Gaines didn't come very early but he "kicked
up considerable dust" in the days of Populism and became
state superintendent of public instruction after overcoming
what seemed insuperable difficulties in the way of obtaining
an education, becoming one of the best known teachers of
the state and finally landing the honor of a place in the state
house. He lived fifty years in Kansas, always a close, conscientious student and a model of good citizenship, and when he
moved down to Martin county, Florida, he was made chairman
of the board of county commissioners eight years consecutively,
and still comes each year to visit the scenes of his early manhood, especially in old "Swayback" school district in Valley
township where the family home first was. His parents were
James Pendleton Gaines and Martha Dyer Gaines from
Grainger county, Tennessee to Illinois, and to Linn County
in 1880. The other children were William Thomas, James
Columbus, John Robert, Anderson Talbott, Amanda Jane (now
Mrs. Hurley at La Cygne), Mary Etta (now Mrs. Highley at
La Cygne), and Ulysses Grant. All these children were well
known citizens of Linn County. "Newt" married Julia Devine

in Cass county, Illinois, five children coming to them: Bertha May, Arthur Bennett, Bessie (now Mrs. C. F. Cordrey of Topeka), Grace (now Mrs. Karl A. Menninger of Topeka), Irene (now Mrs. Robert L. McPherson of Florida). "Newt" as we all knew him was one of the foremost among the Populist orators but was almost howled down out at Kingman when the crowd was yelling for Jerry Simpson and Mary Ellen Lease. "Newt" was introduced but the crowd couldn't see him and wouldn't listen till he caught their ear with "Why, even the babies are affected by the Alliance program. Last night a child was born without socks at Wichita and they called him Jerry!" This caught the crowd and they gave "Newt" an ovation and nominated him next day for the state office, the same year Stephen H. Allen was made attorney general— two state officers on one ticket for Linn County.

Oliver Dickinson Harmon was born in Portage county, Ohio, June 16, 1828. His parents were of Puritan descent and in religion Congregationalists. His father's name was Chauncey Harmon and the maiden name of his mother was Comfort Dickinson. Leaving the school he was teaching in Kentucky, he emigrated to Kansas in the spring of 1857 and settled in Scott township, Linn County, on a claim which he preempted. In 1879 he sold his farm and engaged in the general merchandise business at La Cygne. He was assistant United States assessor for two years and deputy United States collector for three years. He was county surveyor of Linn County two years, township trustee four years, represented his district in Linn County for two terms in the state legislature in 1866 and 1867. He was a member of the Independent Order of Odd Fellows for over twenty-five years and was Secretary of La Cygne Lodge No. 66. He was an active member of the Patrons of Husbandry and was secretary of Elm Grove Grange. For seven years he was secretary of Linn County Agricultural Society and was a director of the State Board of Agriculture. He was married in Scott township, Linn County, March 17, 1858, to Miss Mattie J. Preston, daughter of Thomas Hess Preston. They had two sons, Chauncey P. who married Miss Elizabeth Hungerford, and Frank H. who married Miss Mollie Denton, daughter of Richard A. Denton.

An early arrival in Scott township was Ralph Lanning and his wife, Diana Bendy Lanning, who was of English descent. Ralph was of Welsh parentage and was born in New Jersey in 1819. They came here from Illinois in 1857 with five children who were born in New Jersey, and six additional children were born here. They had much contention over roads in those days just as they have had of later years. "In 1867 a meeting was held at the Colson school house," says A. L. Lanning. "Mound City men were present urging the issue of bonds to build a railroad by way of Twin Springs, Mansfield and Mound City. After the speaking Uncle Johnnie Gates pointed toward the Marais des Cygnes valley, saying, 'Gentlemen, if ever a railroad is built through this county it will go right down there, a natural road bed that God Almighty has made for it.' " His prediction came true. The Lanning children were Aaron L. who married Elizabeth Emma Preston, George B. who married Minnie Hinkle, Sarah E. who married Daniel Goode, Symmes H. who married Alice Paxton, Mary A. who married Paul Nungesser, John who married Bessie Shinkle, Cornelia who married Frank Bearly, and Amanda and Ella B. who never married, and Hattie who married Walter Bearly. The six children born in Scott township all became school teachers.

Abner T. Cady, the father of Samuel D. was born in Massachusetts in the year 1805, moving to the state of New York with his parents when a boy and being one of the early settlers of that state took his share of the hardships of a frontier life —in summer, clearing away the timber that had been felled during the winter and doing the usual work on the farm; in winter, hunting and trapping for a livelihood, as the state at that time paid large bounties for wild-cat, panther, bear and wolf scalps. In 1825, Abner T. Cady was married to Dolly Nudd of Steuben county, whose parents had settled in that state at a very early period. In 1835 he emigrated with his father's family and his own to Indiana, moving west with their wagons until they reached the Ohio river, where they built log rafts upon which they loaded their families and teams, wagons and cows, and dropped down the river to Madison, where they remained all winter. In the spring they located their farm thirty miles from Madison in Ripley county, where Mr. Cady with the assistance of the boys cleared another timber farm, remaining there about twelve years. Here the son Samuel D. was born February 28, 1837, and was a boy of ten when his father moved into Dane county in what was then Wisconsin Territory, and settled seven miles north of Madison, entering a half section of land which he farmed until 1853, when he moved into Mitchell county, northern Iowa. He was one of the first settlers in that county and one of the town company who laid out the town of Mitchell, the county seat of Mitchell county. In 1857 Abner T. Cady removed with his family into Linn County, within the then Territory of Kansas, where he died the following spring. His family consisted of ten children eight boys and two girls. They were reared in the habits of industry and temperance of which the father was himself a noble example, and by which they have all profited.

In May, 1858, young Sam, along with twelve others, was taken prisoner by about thirty pro-slavery men from Missouri, under one Charles Hamelton, and led out to be shot down as free-state men. In this massacre five were killed, five wounded and all supposed to be dead. In 1860 he married Frances A. Lane, daughter of Uncle Jacky Lane. In 1864 and 1865 Sam Cady traveled overland through Kansas, Nebraska, Wyoming, Utah, Montana, Idaho, Washington, through Oregon and California, returning to Kansas by way of Panama and New York. In religious matters he was a firm believer in the gospel of conduct, holding that an honest observance of the golden rule is all that is required of any man. In his business he always practiced its precepts, believing that in trade, politics, or religion, "Honesty is always the best policy." In 1866, after his lengthy travels, he returned to Linn County and was merchant, postmaster, express agent, etc., at Twin Springs, till in 1870 when La Cygne became a town, he moved his store there.

Alonzo Farlin and James Boston owned a saw mill on Big Sugar Creek and furnished the timber for the first bridge there. They had corn burrs and ground meal. Mr. Boston married Amanda Barber of an excellent pioneer family. After his death Amanda married Captain Bunn of Mound City and by a later marriage became Mrs. John Tompson and they had a store in Farlinville. Alonzo Farlin and wife left that part of the county in 1866.

Pleasant Chitwood was born in Macon county, Tennessee, February 22, 1827. He began his business life as a hotel clerk in Mississippi and in 1848 emigrated to Boone county, Iowa, where he became a farmer. He was elected sheriff of Boone county in 1852, and during his term studied law, being admitted to the bar in 1856. The next year he came to Linn County. Mr. Chitwood was married in Macon county, Tennessee, May 10, 1848, to Miss Mary Whitley, a native of Smith county, Tennessee.

In the early spring of 1857 a new personality came into notice at Mound City, very mildly at first, but with latent strength that was to expand into state and almost national fame. He was a boyish young fellow of slight figure, brown hair, with the mild sallow complexion of the student who had just finished a course in medicine and now at only twenty-two years old was a full-fledged doctor. Up to this time the leadership of affairs here had been in the hands of mature men. Montgomery was then forty-three years old and was the "whole thing" to the community. Augustus Wattles and John Otis Wattles were much older. Old John Brown was fifty-seven years old. These men were all religious, stern, puritanical in their rules of living, as were most of their associates. Yet here was a new candidate for a place as a hero who had not a thing in common with the established system. He was profane, drank like a fish, and was a gamester by nature, nervous, and "quick as a mink." His processes were different and had he gone to clean out the groggery at the Trading Post he would have been sincere in attempting its destruction but would have consumed the liquor instead of pouring it into the gutter, as did Montgomery. He would have weakened the enemy by robbing them of their wealth at the gaming table. He was a young scamp, not yet a bad man but traveling rapidly in that direction. He was a humdinger and he had come to stay. This twenty-two-year-old was Charles Ransford Jennison, who had been born in Jefferson county, New York, June 6, 1834, and when twelve years old had gone with his parents to Wisconsin where on February 26, 1854, at Albany, he had married Miss Mary Hopkins of about his own age. Early in 1857 they started for Kansas, stopping only a few days at Osawatomie, then coming on to Mound City. He was soon "Doc Jennison" to everybody and seemed destined for a successful professional career. A number of men now near their peak years were ushered into life by this doctor. He had a streak of the dramatic in his make-up and he took to the "rough-riding" of the Jayhawkers like a duck takes to water. But it was impossible that he should be assimilated cordially into a crowd accustomed to psalm-singing and prayers. There were differences that almost amounted to clashes. In a way he stole the thunder of the other fellows by leading in forays of his own till he began to be called "Jennison the Jayhawker," an alliterative title easy to the tongue and pleasing to the ear, so he built up quite a following on the glory the other fellow had earned. It was at a time when large numbers of free state people were coming into Linn County, most of them fully informed as to the needs of the time and willing to become martyrs if need be to the cause. Jennison became a daring actor and got the whoop and hurrah crowd at his heels. In less than a year he had led a crowd over into Scott township and hanged Sam Scott in his door yard a few miles west of where La Cygne now is. They went from there to Brooklin expecting to hang Rev. Long and only the influence of David Sibbet in vouching for the loyalty of Long saved his life. They went on to a farm near where Mine Creek crosses the state line and hanged Russell Hinds. In each case the provocation set up was interference with free negroes in a free state, for by this time the free staters felt confident they had control of the situation. Later this crowd went on an expedition into Missouri and burned out the store and home of Jerry Jackson a few miles east of Trading Post. These were major tragedies that were whispered about for two generations at least, and committed at the dictation of Charlie Jennison when only twenty-three

years of age. They matured early in those days. While
Montgomery would not have used these methods, he openly
applauded the hangings both in speech and writing. Jennison's career was meteoric. He was colonel of the Seventh
Regiment when only twenty-seven years old and was accorded
a place in the councils of the big leaders of the west. In
January, 1859, when John Brown was on his way to Canada
with the eleven negroes he had liberated, the runaway slave
Jane Seabury was sent down from Lawrence, she having in
some way failed to connect with the party going to freedom
under the British flag at Chatham, Ontario. There was some
concern as to what to do with her, but Doc. Jennison said
'Send her up to my house' and for years Jane Seabury was
given a home and kind treatment and only a few months ago,
at the age of ninety, she was a strong defender of this Will
of the Wisp in border affairs, testifying that he was a good
man, a good provider, and kind to his wife and friends. He
made a reputation as a stern disciplinarian and his rough
riders did many things at his dictation they would not have
done of their own initiative. But he made enemies who were
relentless and who finally hung up enough complaints to his
discredit to cause his downfall, and in 1862 he was compelled
to resign as colonel of the Seventh Regiment. Later in 1863,
through political influences, Governor Carney appointed him
colonel of the famous Fifteenth Regiment, but it is said he
was cashiered from the service and afterwards ran a saloon
and gambling house. The very few who remember him credit
him with a strong personality and regret that sinful habits
prevented his having a glorious career with rich rewards. In
the Standard History of Kansas there is this comment on
Jennison: "Jennison had been commissioned colonel of the
Seventh Kansas by Governor Robinson in the fall of 1861.
His numerous forays and plundering proclivities coming to
the attention of the authorities he was forced to resign in
March, 1862. So proficient was he in lifting livestock that
the pedigree of many a horse found in Kansas in that day
was tersely expressed in "Out of Missouri by Jennison."
After the Lawrence Massacre Governor Carney, then under
the influence of those opposed to General Lane and to the
reelection of President Lincoln, commissioned Jennison colonel
of the Fifteenth Kansas. This same influence pushed him to
the front in the campaign against General Price. He was a
Federal guerilla."

In June, 1857, several families came from Schuyler county,
Illinois,[1] to make their home here. In the party were Eli
Cox, Robert Ewing and several of his friends, William Cox
(an uncle to Eli), and a family named Huggins. At West
Point they met Joshua Sheek, who told them of the troubles

1. This story was written by Mr. Mitchell in 1895.

prevailing, and they continued on by way of Trading Post to Brooklin, where Sheek and Captain Leasure helped them to select their claims, on which they all located June 2.

At the time Cox and his party arrived the free-state men had things pretty much their own way, and Montgomery and his men were retaliating upon proslavery people by requesting their absence from the community. It was a rigorous application of the old Mosaic law—an eye for an eye, a tooth for a tooth—but more generally a horse for a horse and the owner's expulsion from the county. Cox saw several caravans of them going away grieving over their misfortunes, as they were pleased with the country.

In 1858 it was a common sight to see squads of horsemen riding over the prairie without legitimate excuse for their presence, and at such times families left their homes after sundown and slept on the open prairies, while the men would gather at the fords on the river and stand guard all night against invaders.

Eli Cox enlisted August 9, 1862, in company E, Sixth Kansas cavalry, under Col. William R. Judson, and served till June 28, 1865. Was at Prairie Grove, Cane Hill, Newtonia, Honey Springs, Maysville and Duvall's Bluff. While acting as escort to the mails between Fort Smith and Fayetteville he had a narrow escape. With him was a young man named Stevens, who enlisted from Twin Springs. They were set upon by two hundred rebels and were being chased down a road, when Cox's horse was killed under him and he was thrown quite a distance by the fall. He crowded behind a tree and a moment later young Stevens was captured right in front of him, so near that he heard every word. The brave boy surrendered and dismounted, patting his horse affectionately, when he was asked what regiment he belonged to. Upon answering the Sixth, he was riddled with bullets and stripped of his clothing in a few minutes. The party had been speculating where Cox had disappeared to, but something attracted their attention upon the road and they galloped away. Cox fled through the forest and reached Fort Smith.

The captain of Mr. Cox's company was Henry M. Dobyns, father of Frank Dobyns of Farlinville. He was killed by a party of Bushwhackers October 23, 1864, while on his way home on a furlough.

William Harrison Ward gives the following account of the loss of the horse of Eli Cox and the killing of Harrison Stevens: The fight occurred on the 12th day of August, 1864. Some days previous to the fight a detail of the Sixth Kansas Cavalry under Lieut. John C. Anderson of Company M, consisting of William Beth, Eli Cox, Chas. H. Harmon, Corp. W. H. Stevens, James M. Winn, Daniel F. Hugg, S. A. Gault, and myself of Company E and Richard Broome and John Lasear of Company

M, and two members of Company B named Stewart and
Simmons, and perhaps some others, had been sent from Fort
Smith to Fayetteville, Arkansas, to bring down the mail from
the north, which we could get only occasionally. The error in
the statement is that Eli Cox's horse was shot from under him.
Now these are the facts in the matter as I remember them:
On the morning of August 11, 1864, the above named detail,
together with a number of infantry men returning from on
furlough, nine women on horseback going to the front to visit
relatives in the army, and two six-mule teams loaded with
sutler's goods and on which were nine bags of mail. A
tenth bag, supposed to contain a large amount of money was
fastened on Eli Cox's horse as being the best and swiftest
horse in the command. Eli always kept his horse in the best
trim of any man in the regiment. We had proceeded on our
return as far as Ice's Creek in the Boston mountains, when
night came on and we went into camp at the farm of an old
settler by the name of Benjamin Hale. We resumed our march
next morning before it was fairly light and before we had
eaten any breakfast. A gentle rain falling in the meantime
caused one of the teams to stall so badly as to necessitate the
unloading of the wagon to get it up a hill which lay in our
road. From this point we had proceeded not more than a
couple of miles when we came to a small clearing, with
undergrowth very dense all around it. In this clearing was
a double log house. As we came to the clearing the enemy,
who had been concealed in the aforesaid undergrowth, charged
down on us, at the same time throwing a heavy detachment
across the road in our rear to prevent escape in that direction.
Here Sergeant Broome of M Company, an English boy, was
killed. We were now in a very narrow gorge with a very
steep hill on our left, leaving the front, which the enemy was
rapidly closing, as our only reasonable chance for escape. By
clean fighting about ten of the boys, including Lieut. Anderson
and Eli Cox, succeeded in breaking through the enemy's lines
and escaping to the front, and the rest of the boys, save
myself, abandoned their horses and took to the brush. I,
on my horse, climbed the mountain side to a distance of about
300 yards, when I reached a bench on the mountain side along
which ran a neighborhood road intersecting the main road
about a mile ahead, where the main road goes up a long
ascent out of the narrow gorge at a farm house called
Reddings. My road fell into the main road at the foot of
this ascent, Eli Cox being about midway of this ascent, with
me about fifty yards behind him. Eli's horse being pretty
well jaded by the long run, came down to a walk, and with
Eli calling to those ahead of him to "wait." Eli's horse coming
to a walk and in his excitement perhaps thinking that I was
an enemy gaining on him abandoned his horse and took to
the woods. I thought that as long as my horse could get

up a trot he could beat anything I could do afoot so I stuck
to him till I reached level road, then you should have seen
the gravel fly! The mysterious feature of this event, if we
may call it an event, was the finding of Eli's horse after the
fight. The scene of this fight was somewhere near twenty-
five miles from Fort Smith, Arkansas. Eli with the other
boys came straggling into Fort Smith a couple of days afterward on foot. Daniel F. Huff of E Company rode Eli's horse
into camp a couple of days afterward, claiming to have found
the horse tied to a tree in the woods about a quarter of a
mile from the road where Eli abandoned him, but with no
mail bags on him. The mysterious part of the affair is "Who
tied that horse to the tree?" It does not look at all reasonable that an enemy or anyone else after capturing such a
horse as that of Eli Cox would tie it to a tree in the woods
and go off and leave it. Eli as he was lying behind a tree
saw Harrison Stevens killed. There was one particularly
savage guerilla named John Schell who rode a gray horse.
Harrison was standing not far from Eli when Schell rode up
and asked Stevens what command he belonged to and on being
told the Sixth Kansas Cavalry Schell shot him through with
a musket. Harrison folded his arms and said, "Oh, Lordy!
Oh, Lordy!" and fell dead. These are the facts as I saw them
and have heard Eli relate them. Eli's horse was not killed.

The National Tribune, the soldiers' paper, gave this account
by a wagon master named Peck who witnessed the incident
from a place of concealment, of the killing of Captain H. M.
Dobyns: The captain, having served his time out, was returning home with a small wagon train load of refugees coming
north with a small escort. They encamped for the night
about forty miles south of Fort Scott and were attacked in
the morning by a band of guerillas. One of them rode up
to Captain Dobyns and demanded his surrender. "You will
treat me as a prisoner, will you?" asked the captain. "Yes",
replied the guerilla, whereupon Captain Dobyns handed his
revolver to the guerilla who took it and shot the captain right
there with his own revolver, and he died the following night.
It was after dark the second night when the refugee train
bearing Captain Dobyns' body reached Fort Scott. Joseph
B. Dobyns, one of the Captain's sons, accompanied by Peck
who tells this story, met the train as it came into town and
as the son inquired for his father he was told "Captain Dobyns
died last night." Peck let Joe have his horse to use in taking
his father's body to the family home in Linn County, where
it was buried in a nearby cemetery. The son Joe had just
returned to Fort Scott from escort duty. William H. Ward
remembers that at a Fourth of July celebration at Brooklin
in 1859 Captain Dobyns was the orator and Ward says he
had few if any superiors as a public speaker at that time.

James C. Marshall, father of Jesse and Homer and Laura, made a speech stating it was the eighty-third year of American Independence, and a young lawyer named B. F. Perkins made a speech that surprised the natives, as they had not expected the outburst of patriotism he gave them. An old gentleman named Spangler who had the remarkable accomplishment of playing two fifes at once assisted by a snare drum and a base drum made music for the occasion.

James Donaldson Snoddy was born September 11, 1837, at the foot of South Moutain, White Deer Valley, Lycoming county, Pennsylvania. He acquired a common school education in Pennsylvania and Indiana and prepared himself for college, graduating from the University of Michigan in 1859, and receiving his master's degree from that institution in 1867. He came to Kansas in February, 1861, located at Mound City. He enlisted in the Seventh Kansas Cavalry and was made first lieutenant of Company C, resigning in 1862. He was commissioned colonel of the Sixth regiment Kansas militia June 13, 1864. April 1, 1864, he with his brother Maj. J. T. Snoddy became the publishers of the Border Sentinel at Mound City, and upon the death of Maj. Snoddy some weeks later Colonel Snoddy took over full management of the paper. In 1865 he had associated with him F. B. Smythe, and in August, 1866, the paper was purchased by Joel Moody. Colonel Snoddy was a member of the house of representatives for the years 1868, 1869, 1870, 1881 and 1883, and the special session of 1884, and was speaker in 1883-'84. He was state senator in 1871-'72. He was married to Cornelia A. Baird March 15, 1865. Mrs. Snoddy died November 23, 1907, after a few hours' illness. Colonel Snoddy's home in his later years was at Pleasanton. A son James, remembered by all as "Jimmie" married Miss Bartleson of Pleasanton and they have their home at Portland, Oregon, where he is a successful lawyer.

Late in the summer of 1856 a squad of "Texas Rangers" came into Bourbon county from the south. All were well armed and mounted. The rowels on their spurs were said to be as large as dinner plates. They soon allied themselves with the Jones party, thirty South Carolinians headed by G. W. Jones, agitating for a slave state, after which, with Jones, William Barnes and Jesse Davis in command, they marched toward Osawatomie in search of Old John Brown. On about August 5 they were engaged in battle at Middle Creek in Linn County, and were defeated, fleeing precipitately to Fort Scott. The Texas Rangers were alleged never to have stopped until they got back to the Red River. This incident gave the name of Battle Hill to the scene of it. Had the Rangers only stayed it might have made quite a story as Old John Brown and Captain Shore and one of the Clines had one hundred or more men eager to make their acquaintance.

LE MARAIS DU CYGNE

A blush as of roses
  Where rose never grew!
Great drops on the bunch-grass,
  But not of the dew!
A taint in the sweet air
  For the wild bees to shun!
A stain that shall never
  Bleach out in the sun!

Back, steed of the prairie!
  Sweet song-bird, fly back!
Wheel hither, bald vulture!
  Gray wolf, call thy pack!
The foul human vultures
  Have feasted and fled;
The wolves of the Border
  Have crept from the dead.

From the hearths of their cabins,
  The fields of their corn,
Unarmed and unweaponed,
  The victims were torn,—
By the whirlwind of murder
  Swooped up and swept on
To the low, reedy fen-lands—
  The Marsh of the Swan.

With a vain plea for mercy
  No stout knee was crooked;
In the mouths of the rifles
  Right manly they looked.
How paled the May sunshine,
  O Marais du Cygne!
On death for the strong life;
  On red grass for green!

In the homes of their rearing,
  Yet warm with their lives,
Ye wait the dead only,
  Poor children, and wives!
Put out the red forge-fire,
  The smith shall not come;
Unyoke the brown oxen,
  The ploughman lies dumb.

Wind slow from the Swan's Marsh
  O dreary death-train,
With pressed lips as bloodless
  As lips of the slain!
Kiss down the young eyelids,
  Smooth down the gray hairs;
Let tears quench the curses
  That burn through your prayers.

Strong man of the prairies,
  Mourn bitter and wild!
Wail, desolate woman!
  Weep, fatherless child!
But the grain of God springs up
  From ashes beneath,
And the crown of this harvest
  Is life out of death.

Not in vain on the dial
  The shade moves along,
To point the great contrasts
  Of right and of wrong!
Free homes and free altars,
  Free prairie and flood—
The reeds of the Swan's Marsh,
  Whose bloom is of blood!

On the lintels of Kansas
  That blood shall not dry;
Henceforth the Bad Angel
  Shall harmless go by;
Henceforth to the sunset,
  Unchecked on her way,
Shall liberty follow
  The march of the day.
          —John Greenleaf Whittier.

The scene of this poem is a spot in Linn County around which will always cling the glamour and mystery and romance which attaches to the pioneer French trappers' settlements, and the glory which illumines a scene of martyrdom will make it a shrine at which all mankind who love human liberty and justice will in the coming ages pay homage. This spot which is possessed of such deep and abiding interest is the thrifty village of Trading Post. There are men still living who connect its remote and romantic past with its tragic and realistic later years when the white man broke into its peaceful solitudes with his unwholesome laws and his arts which he turned to infamous uses. Yet with all its wealth of incidents of world-wide importance it is in modesty hidden away in its beautiful environment almost without a place in written history. From a sense of duty to a generation of heroic men and women fast disappearing the writer will chronicle with some attempt at detail the story of its past, being assured that some things here recorded are not elsewhere preserved, and hoping that others may supply unavoidable omissions.

The topography of the country around Trading Post is strikingly peculiar and the landscape wonderfully beautiful. Just north of the village is a high hill of an elevation of perhaps three hundred feet, and a mile long. It is entirely covered with a heavy growth of forest which gives it the name of Timbered Mound, and around its crest is a great ledge of rock. The Marais des Cygnes river runs against the west end of the mound and turns south a quarter of a mile and then takes an easterly course, there being a series of rapids at the turn which has made it a favorite crossing place and around

This poem first appeared in the Atlantic Monthly for September, 1858.

which grouped the village. From this crossing there wound, in the early days, through the forest up toward the northeast, an Indian trail which afterward became a military road of the United States. At the distance of a mile from the river it crossed the east end of Timbered Mound at a considerable elevation through a pass left by its junction with a huge smooth hill a half mile long, on the east, called Prairie Mound. Beyond this passageway there spreads out a landscape of remarkable beauty and of unique character. For many miles to the north and east there is a flat, level stretch of prairie out of which rise a great number of mounds of an infinite variety of fantastic shapes. One of those nearest, Hay Rick Mound, is a perfect cone of a half mile in width at the base and rising three hundred feet to a point not large enough for the foundation of an ordinary house. Others are oblong and have flat tops many acres in extent, the edges being sharply defined against the sky beyond. They are all smooth and grass-covered to the extreme top, and the crests of many of them are now crowned with homes of farmers, while the flat plain below is marked off checkerboard fashion into farms. Four miles east of the Timbered Mound the imaginary line between Kansas and Missouri is drawn, but the scene beyond is a continuation of the unending variety within the range of vision.

The first authentic accounts of the Trading Post begin with 1835, when the French trappers took up their abode near the crossing of the river, and a tradition says the first was named Jean Baptiste, but it is a fact certified to by reliable living witnesses that in 1842 the proprietor of the little trader's store on the river was a Frenchman named Michael Giareau (pronounced ja-roo), from which fact it for many years was known at Giareau's Trading Post. The region then swarmed with the Osage Indians, but during that year they were crowded on south and a reservation made for the Miamis out of the country to the north. But it was for many years after the resort of the wild blanket Indian. In 1842 the United States government found it necessary to establish a military post somewhere on the frontier, and a force of soldiers in command of Gen. Winfield Scott came south from Westport, Missouri, to select a site. They built a substantial log fort to house a full company of dragoons. There was a reservation for such purpose near the Post and for several weeks the soldiers were encamped there. It was then the white men of the border line of civilization began to visit the abode of the intrepid Frenchmen, and a boy who then came to the place on business is now[1] a citizen of the village—John Courtney, who was born in Helena, Arkansas, August 20, 1832, and moved with his parents to Missouri, settling on Miami creek fifteen miles northeast of the Post in 1841, then the

1. This article was written in 1895.

extreme outposts of the settlements; and when General Scott's army appeared in the summer of 1842, young Courtney and his widowed mother carried vegetables to the Trading Post and sold them to the soldiers. It was finally decided to locate the cantonment farther south, and it became the present Fort Scott.

Two years later came the great flood that spread over all the valley, and the next spring, 1845, came the remarkable event of the visit of a steamboat to Giareau's little establishment, to bring him a stock of Indian goods and to carry away his accumulation of furs. The settlers of western Missouri were notified of the coming of the strange boat by excited Indian runners, who had seen it down the river, and all the big and little Pukes came straggling over the prairies on horseback to see the curious spectacle. There were a hundred and fifty collected on the bank inspecting the little flat-bottomed sternwheel affair that seems to have been without a name.

Courtney remembers it as a motely crowd of uncouth, uneducated men, women and children, who had never seen anything but backwoods life. While they stood looking at it they discovered that the engineer of the boat was very sick, and a report got among them that he had smallpox, at which they took to their heels and ran away much alarmed, till one of the boatmen informed them he had only a fever. The poor fellow never recovered, and was buried at a spot now in the middle of the street where the postoffice stands, a spot easily identified, as a military road had been constructed to connect Fort Scott with Westport on the Missouri river, and he was lain alongside it in the forest. His name is not remembered. The steamboat stayed at the Post several days. The military road referred to was a fine one. Andrew Wilson, an uncle of Courtney, was a member of the firm who built it by contract, and he worked on the road from Westport to Muddy creek, two miles south of the Post. There was a crossing at the ford and also a ferry near the mouth of Sugar creek.

Giareau had with him two Frenchmen and also a slave named Gabe, the latter raising a good crop of corn and vegetables on a small farm adjoining the Post. Courtney visited the one-room log houses of the French trappers and became acquainted with them. One was named Mosier and had a wife and young daughter, and lived adjoining Giareau's place on the east side of the stream, while directly on the opposite side was the house of Murier and wife, the other members of the little colony. Their houses were very neat and clean, and gay with the red blankets and trinkets from Giareau's stock of Indian finery. The Courtneys and several of their neighbors traded there regularly till about 1848, when West Point was opened as a trading place. About 1848 Philip Chouteau bought out Giareau, and he afterwards sold out to Peter Avery, but along after the opening of the Territory Philip Chouteau again got the business and was associated with Tom Polk in conducting it, and after a year or two sold it to Seth Belch, a Jefferson City lawyer, who afterwards became speaker of the Missouri house of representatives.

There was no change or addition to the buildings of the Post till along about 1856, when William Daniels and Dave Postlewaite each built a house about two hundred yards east of the Giareau post building, Postlewait's building becoming a store and the log house built by Daniels becoming a "grocery" saloon. The incessant carousals of the frequenters soon made the place a terror to the settlers. It soon became so offensive that James Montgomery came over with some of his men in the spring of 1858, and as the barrels were brought out to him he smashed the heads in with an ax, and the liquor was soon running a hundred yards down the military road. This was the first temperance crusade in Linn County.

Perhaps nowhere were the attempts to fix slavery as an institution in Kansas so unremitting and fierce as immediately around Trading Post. At other places the politicians and vocal warriors did heroic work, but here it was a constant struggle between the free-state settlers and the mercenaries of the slave powers. Ten miles away at West Point on the Missouri side of the line was a large camp of ruffians who rode about over the prairies in barbarous garb, inflicting upon the free-state men every manner of indignity. About the first of September, 1856, George W. Clarke, a short, stout renegade who had been Indian agent at Fort Scott, headed this crowd, and along in the afternoon arrived at Trading Post. On the way they committed the most atrocious acts. Several houses were burned and the settlers ordered to leave. At that time there lived just north of the Prairie Mound a man named Samuel Nickel, who seemed to be a special object of their murderous intentions. He happened to be away from his home and escaped with his life, but his family were terribly abused. Finally they passed on and encamped at the Post, but after dark fifty of them went back, led by one Captain Fisher, and burned the house and carried away whatever suited their fancy. They went to the chicken roost and cut the feet off the fowls through sheer cruelty. They burned out several other settlers in sight and went on to Sugar Mound (now Mound City) and other places in the western part of the county, committing the most terrible crimes. The Nickel family returned to southwest Missouri, but the next November Old Sammy came back to their claim and rebuilt, the family returning in the spring of 1857, as did most of the other settlers. From then on there were threats and mutterings of trouble to come, though there was very little trouble and no violence between the free-state settlers and the pro-slavery people inside the Kansas line, beyond occasional excited controversies.

At that time there lived on the Kansas side of the line three miles east of Trading Post, one Charles A. Hamelton, who had a number of slaves and kept up quite an establishment. He was well educated and of aristocratic bearing, but became brutally insolent to his free-state neighbors, refusing them the courtesy of recognition. William Hairgrove, who had known his family in Georgia, paid him the deference of a visit. Hamelton met him at the gate and was told of Hairgrove's courteous intention, but he coolly rejected Hairgrove and failed to invite him into his house.   With other free-state men he would occasionally talk when meeting them at the postoffice. "Broad Tom" Jackson, a noted proslavery man, was his nearest neighbor, till some of his mischief compelled Jackson to leave, when the present Judge William Goss, of La Cygne, took the land. With his pugnacious temperament and hatred of slavery, it is entirely probable that the fact that poverty compelled Goss to be over in Missouri most of the time teaching school, saved him from a fatal encounter with Hamelton and his men. Hamelton had a younger brother named Alvin Hamelton, studying law with Judge Barlow at Paris at the time, and an elder, Doctor Hamelton at Fort Scott. In the fall of 1857 the Hameltons found the free-state majority so distasteful that they moved over into Missouri, where for several months they associated with the guerillas.

It is interesting to observe the condition of western Missouri at that time. Nearly all the western border of that state was wild land, particularly that portion east of Linn County. The land was nearly all patented to private parties, only a very few of whom had settled on it. The land is beautiful prairie with numerous creeks trending to the southeast. In the timber along these creeks were hidden numerous cabins of squatters, but they never appeared much in evidence. West Point, in the extreme northwest corner of Bates county, had suddenly grown into a town of several hundred, but this included four hundred of the ruffians, who were not fair representatives of the Missouri settlers either in appearance or moral character. The well-known Green family[1] from Massachusetts had then long lived in their present home. George Walley had brought his free-state family of six there from Ohio in October, 1856, and brought with them the first sawmill and the first reaper ever in Bates county. The present Alvin Walley is still living upon the old homestead. The well-known free-state "Uncle Tommy" Francis family then owned three thousand acres near the line. Scattering along for ten or fifteen miles were perhaps a dozen influential families, about half of whom were free-state, while the others were slaveholders who had also the sympathy and assistance of the squatters along the creeks. Jerry Jackson then had quite an extensive farm and store two miles in Missouri on Mulberry

1. Read story of John Green.

creek, nearly due east of Trading Post. He had a number of
slaves, yet was on very friendly terms with the free-state
settlers in Kansas and showed them kindness that should give
him a lasting place in history, notwithstanding a very unhappy
termination of their acquaintance. Gathered around him on
the east were a number of well-to-do families, Judge Rogers
and the present Pierce Hackett among them. They were a
very good class of people. Hackett still lives there, and is
a most entertaining and pleasant gentleman, and his experience shows that many innocent slaveholders suffered when
the infuriated Kansas free-state men practiced retaliation.
Thus all western Missouri was apparently as open and free
and inviting as Kansas soil, but the "promised land" as they
viewed it lay across the line in the new territory. The one
great object was not land, but to make it a slave state. From
then on the trouble grew in intensity.

There was no postoffice nearer than Paris and in 1857 Austin
W. Hall wrote out a petition for the establishment of an office
and at the suggestion of Mrs. Samuel Nickel named it Blooming Grove after her old home in Pennsylvania. The petition
was granted and Samuel Nickel became the first postmaster,
opening the office in David Postlewait's store. The name of
Blooming Grove was retained till a few years ago, when it
became Trading Post.

Early in 1857 many new settlers were coming in, and a
company of Eastern capitalists were scheming to build a
railroad along the route of the military road from Kansas City
to Fort Smith. In anticipation of it, a part of them came on
and bought out Chouteau and Polk and proceeded to lay out
a large town in the name of the Montgomery Town Company.
Seth Belch purchased the store. There were 800 acres in the
proposed site, from the river eastward including Prairie
Mound and a part of Timbered Mound. A great portion of
it was platted. Many distinguished men were in this enterprise, among those here at the time being Senator Bigler and
Congressman Montgomery of Pennsylvania, Congressmen
Samuel C. Davis and O'Boyle of Indiana, and Horace G. Smith,
who became the manager of the enterprise. A steam sawmill
was in process of construction in the spring of 1858 just east
of the ford, which a man named Wing of Terre Haute, Indiana,
was superintending.

Along in the spring of 1858 there was much threatening
by the Bushwhackers just over the line, and the free-state
men procured guns and drilled as a military company with
a Mr. Tucker for captain and James M. Sayre lieutenant. They
were daily in expectation that Clarke would swoop down upon
them with his four hundred Bushwhackers and execute his
threats. But as late as the 17th of May there had been no
trouble, and on that day the company resolved to discontinue
their daily meetings and go to work upon their farms. There

was in the company one Bill Allen who immediately disappeared from the community and made a trip to Missouri and betrayed all their plans to Hamelton and his men.

Hamelton, on moving back to Missouri, had made himself the unwelcome guest of Jerry Jackson at his store, and loitered around there and West Point. At the latter place at noon on May 18, James B. Sheek heard Hamelton address the camp of Bushwhackers and ask for volunteers to go with him "down in the valley and attend to some devils down there." He particularly cautioned them that only men who would obey orders were wanted. That night these volunteers met him at Jerry Jackson's and they rode off toward the south without a truthful statement of their intentions to old Jerry.

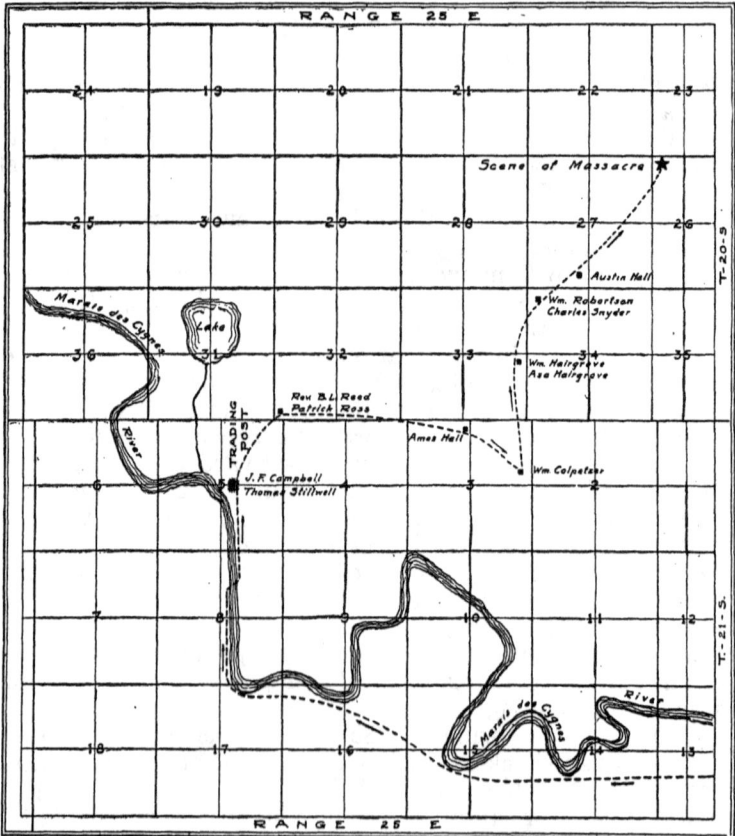

Route followed by Hamelton and his thirty-two assassins in approaching and forcibly taking charge of the eleven men whom they shot down in the Marais des Cygnes Massacre.

The morning of May 19 was beautifully bright and clear, but very warm. The settlers were all out in their fields at work, and there was no thought of trouble. About nine o'clock Hamelton and thirty-two men crossed at the ford at the Trading Post, from the south, and rode to where the new mill was being constructed. They were armed heavily, and were very boisterous and abusive in their manner, cursing the men who were at the mill and driving them off before them as prisoners. Wing, the superintendent, and the well known Samuel D. Cady, then a boyish fellow, being among them. They then went to the Giareau post building where John F. Campbell was in charge as a clerk for Belch, and added Campbell to the prisoners. There were at that time only two other buildings and the saloon at the Post, where they failed to find any free-state men, and they marched off up the military road till they got between Timbered Mound and Prairie Mound, where they released all but Campbell, whom they drove along to the house of Samuel Nickel. Approaching the house Hamelton dismounted, and with a revolver in each hand and men holding a rifle over each shoulder, he walked into the room where Mrs. Nickel sat sewing. He demanded Mr. Nickel, and was told he was away, which was true, as Nickel was one of the county judges and was at the county seat at Paris. Hamelton refused to believe it, though, and one of his men began climbing up into the loft to search, and in doing so knocked a heavy clock down on the little girl baby in the cradle. Mrs. Nickel screamed in alarm at this when one Aaron Cordell put his revolver against her and said, "Howl, damn you, howl!" But they soon left and went out a little way on the road to where Rev. B. L. Read was talking with two travelers—Patrick Ross who had come from Fort Lincoln on the Osage, and William A. Stillwell, who was from near Moneka and on his way to Kansas City to buy goods. They added all three to Campbell and drove the four prisoners a mile and a half east to the claim of Austin Wilbur Hall, who was absent, but they found his brother Amos Cross Hall, an invalid, asleep. He was awakened and made a prisoner. They drove their prisoners to William Colpetzer's, a mile southeast, very near where Hamelton had lived. Mrs. Colpetzer saw them coming and begged her husband to hide, but he assured her he had done no wrong to anyone and would not run, and the mob rode up and took him away a prisoner. They then went north again a little over a mile to the house of Michael Robertson, whom they took, and also his guest, Charles Snyder, who was visiting Robertson from his old home at Effingham, Illinois. They then went a mile northwest to the house of William Hairgrove, whom they took prisoner, and also his son Asa. They now had ten prisoners, who were taken entirely unarmed and with only their rough clothing of plowing time. They started off towards the northeast driving their prisoners like brutes, and often forcing their horses against them. On the prairie near Hay Rick Mound they met Austin

W. Hall returning from Capt. Eli Snider's blacksmith shop with a plow he had had sharpened. Hall was driving the yoke of "brown oxen" of Whittier's poem and was so nearly blind with sore eyes that he could not tell the character of the mob till he was added to the prisoners, who were warned on pain of death not to speak to each other. Once one spoke to their captor saying he was hungry, and the reply was the captors expected "fried scalps" for dinner. Then as they crossed a brook another asked permission to drink and was told to "wait and get it in hell!"

They were driven about a mile to a spot up on the hill about a quarter of a mile from Snider's shop where Hamelton formed the prisoners in line and told the ruffians to guard them while he took four men and went to capture Snider. They saw them go down the hill and across a ravine and up into a peculiar cove where Snider had built his forge. It was a deep draw open toward the south with the shop built into the eastern bank, the door facing west. For some purpose Snider had built a stone wall down through the middle of the draw, nearly to the road. Hamelton dismounted and walked up to the door and pointing his gun at Snider said with an oath, "I've got you now!" A remark of Hamelton's men caused him to take his eye off the sight for an instant and in a flash Snider had a double-barreled shotgun bearing on Hamelton, with the remark, "Don't be too sure, Captain Hamelton!" Hamelton then jumped aside and got on his horse and with his followers, who were his two brothers and two others, rode up on the hill back of the shop.

Simon Snider, a brother of the blacksmith, and a son of Eli Snider and John Robinson were in the shop, and Eli asked his brother and son to go to the house a hundred yards up over the hill and get their guns and he would walk out and protect them from the men who were riding around to get on the hill. They started and as Eli stood in the open he began to retreat to the stone wall a hundred feet away and just as he went over it a volley of buckshot struck him in the back and ankles. Hamelton and his men were up on the hill back of the shop. Hamelton dismounted and rested his carbine on his horse, so that it received in the neck a charge from Snider's gun. By that time Simon Snider and the boy had got to the house and opened fire on their assailants, and wounded one Bloomfield. The attacking party then retired.

In the meantime the prisoners, a quarter of a mile away, were witnesses of the battle at Snider's, and when Hamelton returned he was much enraged. He hurriedly ordered them to march, and led the way to a spot a quarter of a mile northwest of Snider's shop, up a ravine on the side of the mound till near the top of it. The ground was smooth and covered with grass. When the ravine had narrowed so there was only room for one man to walk in it, he ordered them to

halt and form in line facing east. They obeyed their over-
powering captors in dignified silence. The eleven men covered
thirty feet of space in this way. The first on the right or
lower end was Campbell and then Colpetzer, A. W. Hall, the
two Hairgroves, Amos Hall, and the other five in unknown
order. Hamelton was all the while cursing and ordering his
men to separate each side of the line of prisoners, which they
did on horseback, the slopes of the ravine on either side making their horses' feet higher than the prisoners' heads and
about twenty-five feet away. Hamelton and his brother Al,
the two Yealocks, and Hubbard, all of whom had had a neighborly acquaintance with the prisoners, were in the party facing
them. The only words spoken by the prisoners, were by
William Hairgrove, who said, "Gentlemen, if you are going
to shoot us, take good aim." Hamelton ordered his men to
get ready to fire when one, "Fort Scott" Brockett, wheeled
out of line with a curse and said he would shoot in a fight,
but he would have nothing to do with such an act as that.
Hamelton cursed him and with difficulty brought the balance
of the men into line and gave the order "Fire!" The volley
was full and fatal. Austin Hall, the only present living survivor, says that as they fell he saw on Colpetzer the hue of
death, and it came like an inspiration to him to fall flat with
the others and feign death. Nearly all the assassins scampered
away at once, but Hubbard called out. "They are not all
dead; let us finish them," and dismounting with one or two
came back and went down and kicked the victims to see if
they were living, while Alvin Hamelton sat on his horse and
fired his revolver among them. Patrick Ross was shot again
to make sure of him, Austin Hall (who had not been hit at
all) was kicked and pronounced dead, and as Hubbard saw
Amos Hall breathing he told another to "put a pistol to his
ear; I never knew that to fail." Instead the pistol was put
against his cheek so that his tongue was nearly cut off and
he retained the bullet in his mouth, spitting it out after the
assassins left. They hurriedly rifled the pockets of several
and fled.

As soon as their horses' footsteps died out Austin Hall, who
was unhurt, turned and called to the others. He was answered
by two of the wounded who begged him to keep quiet for
fear they were being watched. Hall, however, crawled up
and looked over the crest of the hill when he saw the murderers
in a crowd on Spy Mound a mile away, curiously looking back.
He returned to Mr. Campbell, who was mortally wounded in
the bowels, and fixed him so he could talk, and Campbell gave
him some messages to write his friends, and told him about
some of his employer's money he had buried for safe-keeping,
and gave him a twenty dollar gold piece left in his vest pocket.
Austin Hall then ran down the ravine and met Snider and his
three companions, who did not understand the tragedy they

heard going on, and the five hastened toward Trading Post.

A short distance out on the prairie they met Mrs. Hairgrove and Mrs. Colpetzer and her twelve-year-old son Frank. They suspected Hamelton's intentions, and had yoked up a team of oxen and loaded the wagon with bedding and water and followed. The men told them the particulars and hurried on for assistance. They soon gathered about twenty-five men and started back, meeting the two women bringing in the wounded on their wagon. The men brought the dead from the place of slaughter, which was literally drenched with blood. William Hairgrove, one of the wounded, had bled terribly. The dead were Colpetzer, Campbell, Ross, Stillwell, and Robertson. They were taken to the house on the north side of Timbered Mound, recently owned by William Goss. Doctor Ayres, of Farlinville, attended the wounded.

The sole survivor of the family of Rev. B. L. Reed, one of the victims of the Hamelton massacre, is Mrs. Ellen Brockett, living in 1927 with her daughter, Mrs. William Persinger, four miles northwest of Pleasanton. Her father, William Lewis, was from Wisconsin, and had one child, Ellen. When the father married again to a woman named Palmer, Rev. B. L. Reed and his wife wanted Ellen and adopted her with the consent of the father. The Reeds had lost three children before this. Ellen was still only a child when the massacre occurred in May, 1858, but she remembers many interesting things of the time. She says Rev. Reed was a Missionary Baptist preacher, born and raised to manhood in Connecticut, where he married Sarah Beckwith and came west into Missouri where he worked among the Indians till in 1857 when he came to Linn County, and took up an intimacy with the Indians here, preaching to them and teaching. Ellen remembers that on Christmas Day they would visit him bearing gifts of furs and foods, expressing their sincerity each with a kiss upon his cheek. Ellen remembers that when the victims were fired upon Rev. Reed fell unconscious. Hamelton insisted they make sure to kill "that damned preacher," and the crowd fired a second volley into the body of Pat Ross, thinking he was Reed. To correct this mistake one of the mob got off his horse and turned Reed over and fired with his gun against Reed's body, the charge and the force of the explosion tearing a great hole in his side from which his bowels protruded. In the excitement, fearing a return of the murderers, the rescuing party placed Reed on a pony with a crude bandage to cover the gaping wound and the pony was led to a cabin in the brush a mile away. A woman appeared and Ross swooned and fell into her arms, her hand by accident entering the wound in his side. She was an heroic woman who knew how to act and taking Reed into her humble home nursed him through an awful sickness from the wound and shielded him from evil men who surrounded the home in the night intent on completing the crime against his life. The name of this woman cannot now be established and she must remain thus without a place in printed history. But she did nurse Rev. Reed back to an almost complete recovery and he preached and worked in the service of his church till about 1890 when he died and was buried alongside his wife at Osawatomie. Ellen the adopted daughter married William Brockett who had come from Illinois. They had several children, the survivors being Phebe who married William Matthews of Trading Post, Thomas still unmarried, and Ora married Ed Plant from Kansas City, who now gives a home to the aged mother. The vindictiveness of Hamelton in ordering the destruction of Reed is said to have been because Reed had gone to Westport Landing and brought down fifty Sharps rifles which were distributed among the settlers to aid them in protecting their families.

This monstrous crime was purely a political assassination, instigated and executed by the proslavery mercenaries. The victims were all of American birth, of respectable ancestry, and of gentle breeding. They had been inoffensive and courteously polite to those who differed with them. Rev. B. L. Reed was a missionary Baptist preacher. Stillwell was a Pennsylvanian who lived over near Mound City. Patrick Ross was from Fort Lincoln on the Osage, traveling through the Post. Hairgrove was a native of Georgia, but had moved here from Macoupin county, Illinois, and his family were people above the average in intelligence, the son Asa afterward becoming state auditor. William Colpetzer was from Pennsylvania, and was perhaps the brightest man intellectually in the community. He was of cool and deliberate judgment, honest, courteous, polite, and brave to fearlessness. Robertson was a peaceable man, who had recently moved into the community from Effingham, Illinois, and Charles Snider was a young man visiting with him from the same place. The Hall brothers had lived on their claim nearly a year, having come from their birthplace at Eden, Lamoille county, Vermont. Austin W. was twenty-six, and his brother two or three years younger. They had never known any life but the peacefulness of their New England village. Samuel Nickel, whom the murderers failed to get, was a noted character, and commanded high respect for his honor and bravery. He was a pronounced blonde, over six feet high, and minus one eye. He had eleven children, all boys but one, ranging from infancy to mature manhood. He and his wife were from Blooming Grove, Pennsylvania, had lived in southwest Missouri since 1838, and had arrived on their Kansas claim on New Year's Eve, 1854. By a long subsequent residence they proved to be people of excellent character, and the son John is still living within a few miles of the place. The lives of all of these men prove that the murderous attack on them was without the excuse of private malice, and that they became martyrs to the cause of freedom.

The most intense excitement followed. Free-state men from far and near gathered to offer assistance. R. B. Mitchell and James Montgomery each came at the head of a strong party, but the assassins had fled beyond reach. Four of the dead—Colpetzer, Campbell, Ross, and Roberston—were buried in a common grave on the north side of Timbered Mound. Stillwell was taken to Mound City for burial. The five terribly wounded recovered, and Amos C. Hall joined the party two or three weeks later who went over into Missouri to arrest the assassins, and helped to capture and bring back Matlock, who was taken to Paris and put in charge of Deputy Sheriff Colby, who allowed him to escape, it is supposed through sympathy. The fact that such desperate characters could escape punishment from proslavery officers shows how badly the free-state settlers needed such heroic characters as James Montgomery and his associates. The terrible tragedy was telegraphed all over the Union, and became a great factor in crystallizing public opinion against slavery. Whittier immortalized it in his poem.

A most singular and important thing is the subsequent close relation of Old John Brown to this little community, and the utter absence of a reliable history of his life here. The writer is aware that what is hereinafter stated is at variance as to dates and circumstances with several able writers of that period, but as Brown had reason to conceal his real acts and intentions, there is every probability that the testimony of honest, intelligent men, who have lived right upon the spot ever since they were the companions in arms of the immortal John Brown, is a truthful statement of important historical facts.

The scene of the Marais des Cygnes massacre is now owned by a man who came to it while the blood of the martyrs was still fresh upon the sod where they fell, and who has continuously resided there since. The land is technically described as the northwest fractional quarter of section twenty-six, township twenty, range twenty-five, Linn County, Kansas.

Charles Hadsall, who became an associate of Old John Brown a few days after the massacre, was born in Northmoreland, Luzerne county, Pennsylvania, April 14, 1825. He is of Dutch ancestry. He removed to Illinois in 1846, made a trip to California 1852, and came to Kansas in May, 1858.

Hadsall came down through Bates county, Missouri, where he fell in with one of the assessors, named Bushon, who told Hadsall if he would help him write out his report he would assist him in the selection of a claim which Hadsall was looking for, so that after a day or two they were riding around over the country together. At one place they met a fellow named Matlock, who was boasting about how he and some of his friends had killed a lot of "abolitionists" a few days previous over in Kansas. The fellow's details of the crime were revolting to Hadsall, and he made notes of what he heard. The next day they were at the house of Thomas Francis, where they met Captain Weaver and Eli Snider, the blacksmith. Assessor Bushon was visibly excited at meeting Snider, and soon left. Hadsall then told Captain Weaver about Matlock and where he could be found, but Weaver paid no attention to him, but on leaving invited Hadsall to accompany him over into Kansas, and on the way told Hadsall he had already sent men after Matlock, and sure enough they had him a prisoner at the Snider place when they arrived.

Mr. Hadsall cannot tell the exact date, but distincly remembers that the ground was still red with the blood of the victims. It is reliably fixed at about the last week in June. He says that John Brown had already begun the erection of the fort and had purchased the claim from Snider. Brown

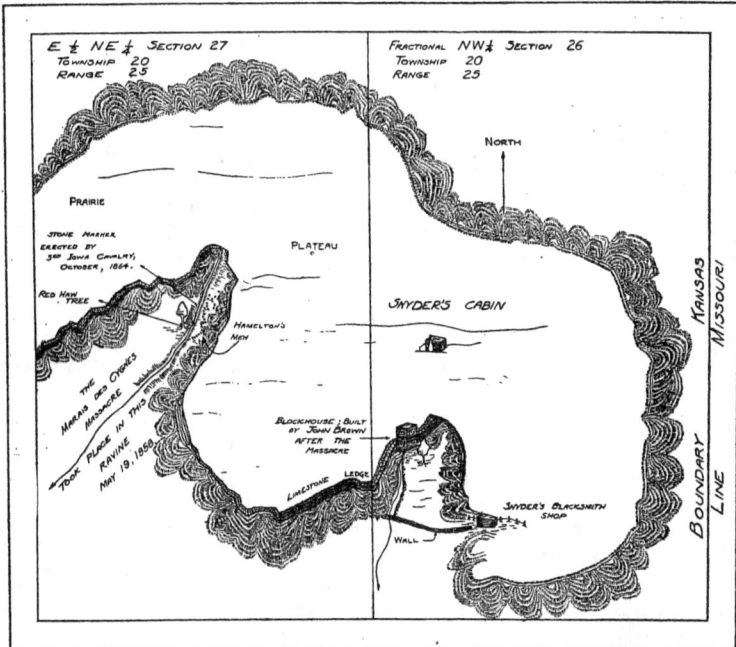

Scene of the Marais des Cygnes Massacre as sketched by Major L. R. Roberts who was topographical engineer for the Roy Chapman Andrews Expedition into the Gobi Desert in Central Asia. The two-story fort erected by Old John Brown is shown where now stands the stone house erected by Charles Crystal Hadsall, who spent the summer there with Brown in 1858.

had a company organized and the place was maintained in
regular military order. From that on Hadsall became a daily
associate of Brown and had every opportunity to learn his
doings. Above all he admires Brown's military genius, as
in fact do all those who were with him in those days. He
showed great skill in the construction of the fort, and at the
expense of tediousness his description is related.

The site of it was in front of where Snider had his shop.
It was in a little cove in the south end of the mound which
extended back about a hundred yards from the road at the
base of the mound. At the head of this was a spring of good
water, all around rather steep slopes. About fifty feet from
the east, north, and west wall of the little inclosed valley
Brown built out of hewed logs a two-story house eighteen
by twenty feet square, with a flat roof. There were numerous
portholes on each floor, which made it easy to observe the
approach of anything from any direction. To the height of
a man's shoulders on the outside a stone wall three feet thick
had been constructed, and the water from the spring ran
through the house and into a pit three feet deep at the southwest corner on the outside, at the foot of a fine oak tree.
Brown usually took water from this place, and was proud of
the arrangement. At the east end of the fort there was
another handsome spreading oak under which during the
summer he cooked and ate and carried on the business de-
volving upon him as commander.

Nearly all his followers were there at first, among them
John H. Kagi, Stevens, Tidd, Leeman, Anderson and Hazlett,
several of whom were afterward with him and died with him
at Harper's Ferry. So far as the claim and the fort could
belong to any one it belonged to Old John Brown individually
by purchase from Eli Snider, several eminent historians to
the contrary notwithstanding. Brown busied himself with
the preparation of manuscripts, and as Hadsall sat and talked
with him he asked Brown what his plans for the future were.
For answer Brown passed over to him the manuscripts, and
upon perusal Hadsall found them to be an exhaustive treatise
on military science and rules of war. It was a high moral
code in its provision as to the treatment of conquered enemies,
and required soldiers to abstain from pilfering and robbery,
but permitting them to take their substance from the enemy
during active war.

Beyond allowing Hadsall to read his writings Brown never
communicated his plans to him. At times he would entertain
them with descriptions of great battles of the world and the
strategies used by successful commanders. Brown seldom had
more than half a dozen men with him at the fort, but all along
the Missouri line sentries were posted, and men reported to him
regularly at various hours. No one was permitted to enter
the Territory without satisfactory evidence of good intentions.

Frequently prisoners were brought in and a courtmartial assembled at which Old John Brown sat as president. If the prisoner was adjudged all right, he was released, but if there was a doubt about him, he was marched to the Missouri line and told to travel east. At one time an ignorant squatter from Missouri was brought in, and after it was decided he was harmless, Brown invited him to dine with him, and asked him if he would have a glass of "abolition milk," which the fellow said he would, but showed that he was suspicious by the way he tasted it, and remarked, "Why that 'ere tastes like cow's milk." Brown laughed and told him it was cow's milk from James Montgomery's cows.

Things went on this way till July 25, when Snider proposed to Hadsall that he purchase the place from him and say nothing to Brown about it. Hadsall expressed some surprise, and told Snider he would do nothing of the kind, and soon after told Brown of Snider's proposition to him. On that occasion Brown showed the only anger that Hadsall had ever witnessed, but walked away without saying much. Shortly after he told Hadsall that he was content for him to have the place, but he, Brown, wanted to reserve all privileges of military occupation at his pleasure. It seemed that Brown had not made all his payments to Snider, who in a way not unusual to him was trying to get some money from Hadsall. That day Brown wrote out and signed the bill of sale to Hadsall and signed it in his own name, and Snider, after turning over to Hadsall his three yoke of oxen, cows, wagons, and plows, received six hundred dollars from Hadsall and added his quit-claim to the bill of sale. Hadsall lost this precious bit of paper during the war.

The only member of the Hamelton gang of murderers ever brought to justice was one William Griffith, the story of whose apprehension, trial and execution is taken from Ed. R. Smith's story written for the Mound City Clarion as follows:

"Wm. Griffith prior to the time of this massacre lived near the state line in Missouri and was known to the settlers on both sides near the line as a stupid, ignorant and harmless kind of a man. But he was 'swooped up and swept on to the whirlwind of murder' under the influence of bad whisky, coupled with the intense excitement of the times roused to a white heat by the inflamatory speeches of Hamelton and many others made at a big meeting of the proslavery propagandists and Kansas refugees held near Papinsville, Missouri, on the 18th of May, 1858, when and where it was resolved to invade Kansas on a tour of extermination and from where an army, or mob rather, numbering full five hundred, marched to the state line east of the Trading Post in Kansas, arriving there at about midnight between the 18th and 19th of May, whereupon a halt was made to rest, arrange and dress up the line, prior to their descent upon the unsuspecting people of the beautiful valley surrounding the historic old Trading Post. Judge J. H. Barlow, a former well known resident of this county, had been sometime previous to this notified by Captain Hamelton to leave the Territory as on a certain time the Missourians were going into Kansas on a hunt to 'kill snakes' and that they would treat everybody they found there as a 'snake' and their enemy.   Judge Barlow upon receipt of this message went down into Missouri and was present at the big meeting above referred to and was a member of the committee on resolutions.   Disagreeing with the committee as to the time and practicability of the contemplated invasion he presented a minority report advising against it and in a speech before the meeting against the attack upon the settlers in Kansas as illtimed and necessarily disastrous to the attacking party. He assured his friends that the Jayhawkers under Montgomery were armed with that most dreaded of guns, Sharpe's rifles and Colt's revolvers.   That shot guns and squirrel rifles were no match for such weapons, that the free-state settler was better prepared to withstand and repel an invasion than they had ever been.   But his efforts were fruitless and availed him nothing.   The mob marched and as related halted at the state line, where Judge Barlow again addressed them to more effect.   It was midnight and the stars shone down upon them in cold, cheerless light.   They had ridden many miles across the prairies and were tired and hungry, with no blankets nor food for man or beast, and then they were at the threshold of hated but dreaded Kansas.   They knew that Montgomery could not be far away and 'snakes' might be more plentiful than desirable.   At any rate a wrangle ensued among them, threats and loud and lusty cursing was much indulged in.   At last in the early morning hours of that most eventful day so full of horror and death to the unsuspecting people then wrapped in peaceful slumber in their humble cabin homes scattered here and there over the valley, Captain Hamelton, disgusted with the cowardice of his drawling associates, mounted his horse and rode out of the mob and called on his chosen band, the 'Bloody Reds', to ride to the front and follow him.   Thirty-two as bloodthirsty wretches as ever 'cut a throat or scuttled a ship' rode out and away over the border after their hot-blooded commander.   The remainder of this aggregation of border ruffianism like the wolves of the border that they were before daybreak disappeared and were heard of no more.   The sortie of that awful day has been so often told and is so well known as to need no repetition to our readers now. William Griffith played his part in that bloody tragedy and was gone, none could tell where.

"Afterwards, in the spring of 1863, 'Old Man' Hairgrove, one of the victims of the massacre, then a soldier on duty at Ft. Leavenworth under command of General R. B. Mitchell, was across the river in Missouri and became aware of the

whereabouts of Griffith, which fact he promptly reported to
General Mitchell, who as promptly sent a sergeant and squad
across the river under guidance of Hairgrove, and they found
and arrested Griffith. He was then sent to Mound City and
turned over to E. B. Metz, the sheriff of this county, and
was by him guarded until his trial came on in October of
that year before Hon. Solon O. Thatcher of Lawrence, then
judge of the district court for this county. Judge D. P. Lowe,
then a resident of Mound City, was assigned as counsel for
the defense of Griffith. The court house was then the City
Hall. On October 3 a jury was empaneled and sworn to try
the cause consisting of Jacob Holderman, John Purdue, Josiah
Sykes, James Barrack, Wm. Crozier, John P. Wheeler, W. T.
Smith, Wm. Farris, Perry Blair, Ira Haight, Amos Durbin
and Ben Bunch. A verdict was reached on the second day
of the trial of 'guilty as charged in the indictment.' The usual
motions for a new trial, etc., were filed, argued, overruled, and
Judge Thatcher pronounced the sentence of death upon the
poor, friendless wretch, who received it with much greater
composure than it was delivered. It was 'That Wm. Griffith
be hanged by the neck until he be dead, on the 30th day of
October, 1863, between the hours of 10 o'clock A. M. and 2
o'clock P. M.' It was further ordered by the court that the
sheriff take him into custody and closely guard him, and that
he furnish the prisoner with necessary clean clothes at the
expense of Linn County.

"We had no jail then; no such capacious and secure citadel
as now stands in our town, a frowning menace to evil doers
and consequently a detail was made from several militia companies and put under the command of Lieutenant Dennis Gray,
who came to town and established their camp in a vacant building on the spot where Mr. Goodwin now lives, known then as
the Boyer house, and who took charge of Griffith. The doomed
man made no effort to escape. He sat around the camp, ate,
drank and smoked with his guards, told the story of his part
in the massacre and appeared careless, if not oblivious of the
swift coming day of his ignominious death. His wife toward
the close of his time to die came to see her husband. She was
a small, apparently frail person, and was heart-broken at the
approach of the day when her husband must die, and she returned alone to her fatherless children. October 30, 1863, was
a beautiful day. James D. Snoddy was then lieutenant-colonel
commanding the militia of this county, and called out on the
day of the execution Campanies "A", Captain Charles Barnes;
"B", Captain Knight; and "C", Captain Wilson, with the detail.
No less than two hundred men were under arms, Col. Snoddy
commanding. C. S. Wheaton was deputy and acting sheriff.
Griffith was mounted in a wagon and seated upon the coffin
that his body soon after filled. A hollow square was formed
about it by the militia and in this order moved from the

prison camp, up Main Street and down to the mill, across the creek into the woods then standing over there, where a gallows had been erected, consisting of two uprights some eight feet apart and ten feet high, across the top of which was thrown a cross beam, through the middle of which was a pulley. A well prepared rope ran through the upper beam out over the top to the post half-way down which was attached to this rope a large box filled with anvils to a weight exceeding four hundred pounds. This weight was fastened with another rope binding it to the post. At the other end of the rope suspending the weight, dangled a hangman's noose. Beneath this gallows stood Griffith apparently as unmoved as any of the hundreds of spectators present. The militia formed a hollow square about the gallows facing outwards. Sheriff Wheaton nervously read the warrant for this execution; bandaged the arms and legs of the condemned man; pulled down the black cap shutting out the light from eyes never again to be opened on earth.

"During all this time of preparation there stood, silent and grim, an old man, with head uncovered, his long white hair hanging down upon the collar of his old soldier coat, his stern eye and countenance as set as death, fixed upon the proceedings, awaiting the signal for him to perform his part in this legal tragedy. It was 'old man Hairgrove," the same William Hairgrove, one of the eleven unoffending defenseless men who on the 19th day of May, 1858, were 'from the hearths of their cabins, the fields of their corn, unwarned and unweaponed the victims were torn.'

"The same dauntless old veteran who, there with clenched hand and set teeth, stood in that line of death, where 'With a vain plea for mercy no stout knee was crooked; in the mouths of the rifles right manly they looked.'

"The same old man on that day dropped upon the bloodsoaked earth with a load of buckshot in his breast. The same man who survived to devote his remaining years of life to bringing to dire punishment his would-be murderers. There, like an avenging Nemesis with a bright keen bladed hatchet in hand uplifted and ready, the old man stood and awaited the signal. It came and with all his force he drove the sharpened blade of steel through the suspending rope deep into the post. The box of anvils thus freed fell to the earth with a crash and poor Griffith was instantaneously jerked into the air, and falling back, hung suspended and dead. An involuntary groan escaped from nearly all present at the horror of the dreadful act. One man in the ranks of the militia fainted and fell to the ground. There were dozens of women present who witnesses this execution and stood their ground as bravely as the best of the supposed sterner sex. So far as known, Griffith was the only one of the thirty who participated in the massacre of the Marais des Cygnes ever brought to justice or whose whereabouts were ever afterwards known," except the subsequent story as told elsewhere by Gen. John H. Rice (see index).

Along the latter part of the summer of 1858 Brown's sentinels were withdrawn and his company returned to their homes. Brown then was at the place only at intervals, but Mr. Hadsall remembers he was often there after cold weather. During his absence he was at Montgomery's fort, and in December was down on the Osage in Bourbon county.

During Brown's stay at the Snider place Hadsall was impressed with the utter absence of selfishness or egotism or vaingloriousness in Brown. He was modest and unassuming. All his orders were more like requests, and implicitly obeyed. He frequently visited Austin Hall, Dr. Massey, and others, and was well known to them, much of his talk being very prophetic of subsequent events. Among strangers he generally passed by an assumed name, usually as "Captain Walker," but his men addressed his as Captain Brown. This great character—one of the world's heroes—left a reputation here without the stain of a single act of wrongdoing.

In after years Mr. Hadsall built a spacious stone house over the spring, the first floor opening on the sward where Brown's fort stood, and the second at the little plateau above. He was married November 27, 1864, to Miss Sarah Walley, of the noted Missouri family, and they took up their residence here. It is to be hoped that this scene of martyrdom may always be possessed by such estimable people. Scattered about, used in cribs and in supporting hay shelters for stock, are many pieces of the hewn timbers of the fort, which otherwise has entirely disappeared. Two stones set in the ground during the war by an Iowa regiment to mark the scene of the massacre have been reduced by relic hunters from a height of four feet to mere projections above the ground, and a hawthorn tree which has grown on the line to six inches in diameter is literally covered on trunk and branches with carved initials of visitors. There is a well worn path to the spot, and at times parties numbering as many as fifty visit the place and hear the story from Mr. Hadsall, who is very courteous to visitors.

Things went badly with the Missourians after the Marais des Cygnes massacre. Hamelton and his men went back to Jerry Jackson's place, but stopped only a few minutes. Hamelton shouted a few words to some acquaintance and rode north to Kansas City and was never seen here afterward.[1]

Pierce Hackett says old Jerry Jackson deplored the crime and rebuked the evildoers. There is everything to prove him a good, kind man, for several of the murdered men owed him money for goods purchased at his store, and it is said Col-

1. For history of this man Hamelton see index—John H. Rice.

petzer's debt to him was over a hundred dollars. But he was given the reputation of harboring bad men, and was terribly persecuted. It all terminated very sadly. Sammy Nickel and Hairgrove called on him a day or two before the next Christmas, and a truce was entered into for mutual protection. They were to restrain evildoers and notify each other of danger. But on Christmas eve, Jennison the Jayhawker, who either did not know of the agreement or violated it, surrounded the place and burned the handsome big house Jackson had just completed, and destroyed and carried away all his property. The bravery shown by Jackson in defending his property is still spoken of in admiration by those who were told of it by the attacking party. Jennison was able to walk around, but could not sit in a saddle for a long time afterward, and it is generally conceded that two or three Kansans who went over there came home only for secret burial. The exact truth of this was never known. Old John Brown was not connected with this incident, but it is reasonably sure that Snider piloted the party to the place.

Austin W. Hall and his brother were soon after compelled to go back to Vermont, that Austin might be treated for sore eyes. He was very slow in recovering his sight, but April 14, 1865, he returned here, was married to Miss Caroline Fisk November 28, 1869, and they took up their home at Trading Post, and three children born to them are living, Amos Homer, Carlton Fisk, and John Austin. Mrs. Hall died several years ago, and Mr. Hall subsequently married an accomplished lady of Vernon county, Missouri, Miss Edith Hill, by whom he has one child, Clyde William Hall.

From the penniless boy who walked from Kansas City in 1857, Austin W. Hall has grown to be one of the largest landed proprietors in the county, and has large mercantile and milling properties. He is a man of affairs and honored and respected. Within sight of his home a handsome monument has been reared to the memory of those who fell on that fatal 19th of May, 1858. He is the only survivor of that terrible tragedy, and the tender care of that sacred spot shows his love for their memory.

During his absence in the East many great events and many new people came to the Trading Post. The old Giareau building became the property of Doctor Massey, and it sheltered Old John Brown as his guest. Doctor Massey was forced by the war to abandon them, and an estimable widow, Mrs. Matilda Tubbs, occupied the buildings with her family, and to their kindness many sick and wounded soldiers owe the preservation of their lives, and have since written their gratitude from all parts of the Union. A son and daughter of Mrs. Tubbs are still living at the Post—Miss Addie and Mr. Amos Tubbs.

Company B of the Sixth Kansas Cavalry was organized at

Trading Post, commanded by Captain Orahood and Lieutenant David Goss. Company D of the same regiment was very largely made up of Trading Post men, Old Sammy Nickel and four sons going into it—William, John, Ben, and Newton —and William and Ben died in the service. Two others of the Nickel boys—Robert and Jasper—were in the Fifteenth and Ninth respectively, Jasper dying in the service.

During 1858 Joseph Goss and several sons followed the elder son, William, and located in the village. Joseph is now a nonagenarian of good physical and mental strength. He was born in Rowan county, North Carolina, October 21, 1804. When the Price raid came tearing through the little place in 1864 with forty thousand men his house was shot almost to pieces and everything of value carried off— a common experience of the settlers. A talk with him brings up the names of many good men who were his neighbors in these troublesome days—John R. Williams (Uncle Jacky), Jackson Lane, S. R. Hungerford, and interesting Uncle Johnny Baeritz, and William Crawshaw, who was captured by Clarke's raiders, and carried to West Point and tortured for informa- tion against his neighbors, which he heroically refused to give. Crawshaw was an Englishman by birth and had been a big railroad contractor at one time.

In 1860 John Fickes and his brother Morgan, now of La Cygne, put in a dam at the ford and beside it a big mill, which has always been a noted institution. It has passed through various hands and kept constantly growing, the present owner, Austin W. Hall, having recently doubled its capacity and put it to running night and day to fill orders. It has both steam and water power, and a big sawmill is operated in connection with it.

Amos C. Hall, after the war, settled at Helena, Montana, where he became very wealthy. He died about 1893.

In 1870 an iron bridge was put over the river by Oscar F. Dunlap, who was captain of Company H of the Fifteenth Kansas Cavalry. Soon after, the old Giareau buildings began to succumb to decay and now are entirely gone. With a big mill going night and day the Post is fast becoming a thrifty modern village. May its memories be ever preserved.

Some enlightenment as to the character of the men who came up from Georgia with "money and men" to drive the free state people out of Kansas and fix the slave institution here is given in a letter written by General John H. Rice, then of Fort Scott, as follows:

"Fort Scott, July 7, 1892.—Hon. Joel Moody: Dear Sir: In reply to your inquiry concerning the Hameltons I state: I became acquainted with Dr. Thomas Hamelton in 1847. He was an eminent physician. As a physician and scholar he stood far above the average of his class. His sons were

Charles A. Hamelton, born about 1822; George P. Hamelton, born about 1826; Algernon S. Hamelton, born about 1828. Doctor Hamelton the father died in Rome, Georgia, in 1857. In 1854 Milt McGee of Kansas City came to Georgia soliciting money to make Kansas a slave state. He made a speech at Cassville. Dr. Thomas Hamelton gave him his check for $1000. Charles A. Hamelton was a planter, as they were called. George P. read medicine. Algernon S. never followed any special pursuit. Capt. Charles A. and George Peter came to Kansas to carry out the old doctor's sentiments. I do not remember exact date; I guess about 1855. They left Kansas and returned to Georgia in the fall or winter of 1857 and 1858, I think. I was practicing law in Rome in 1858 and at the September term of court, 1858, Capt. Chas. A. Hamelton came to me and said he was bankrupt, insolvent, and was under arrest then for debt. Imprisonment for debt was in vogue then and we had a state insolvent law similar to the last national bankrupt law. Under certain circumstances the debtor would file a schedule of property and take an oath that released him from arrest.

"I filed proceedings for him—filed his schedule; as well as I remember now it contained one item, a watch. And the court on my motion ordered the oath administered and Hamelton released. When done he said to me: 'I will see you at your office directly after dinner' (not a word had been said about fee). About 1 o'clock he came into my office and said: 'General, you did me a great favor and I am free; and now I start again in the world' (and he shed tears freely). 'Here is all I can give you as compensation for your trouble' (and he threw down on my table four $20 gold pieces). 'I am going to Texas—start in an hour—good-bye.' That was the last I ever saw or heard from him except from hearsay. He however went to Waco, Texas, lived there until 1861, raised a regiment and joined Lee in Virginia; lived through the war; returned to Texas, lived there till about 1878, when he returned to Georgia and lived in Jones county, where the old Doctor his father was born, and died about 1881 of apoplexy. He stood about 5 feet 10 inches, weight about 180 pounds, of a florid complexion, was intellectually and physically an active man, and was one of the handsomest men I have ever seen. George Peter Hamelton on returning from Kansas went to Mississippi, where he practiced medicine and died there (so I have heard.) Algernon S. Hamelton went into the Confederate army and was killed in one of the Virginia battles.

"Old Doctor Hamelton was my father-in-law's family physician. I knew them all well. They were a very 'high-strung' family—aristocratic, rich, haughty and domineering. In 1850 there lived in Cass county, Georgia, Col. Lindsay Johnson and his two sons, Jefferson and William. They were rich and imperious also. But we had great political excitement then. The two parties were then 'Union' and 'Southern Rights'. The Johnsons were 'Unions'; the Hameltons 'Southern Rights' or 'Fire-eaters'. There was an election for a state convention. Colonel Johnson was the 'Union' candidate. Old Doctor Hamelton was the 'Southern Rights'.

"Jeff Johnson said something about Doctor Hamelton. The Hameltons heard it. Charlie Hamelton said 'I'll make one of my niggers cowhide Jeff Johnson.' Johnson heard that and on next Saturday the three Hameltons and three Johnsons and friends met at Adairsville for public speaking. No sooner on the ground and Jeff Johnson knocked Charley Hamelton heels over head off of a high porch, and then he stood still. Hamelton rose, pistol in hand. Johnson drew his (and he was a noted dead shot). Hamelton fired and shot Johnson through his groin. George P. Hamelton who was off to one side fifty yards drew a pistol and shot five times, thrice at Jeff Johnson on the porch, and twice at Bill Johnson who came in the meantime between them—hit nobody. While George P. Hamelton was firing Charlie was prevented by one or two persons from firing a second time at Jeff Johnson; but when George P.'s five shots were out, Jeff Johnson dropped his pistol as deliberately as if shooting at a mark on Charley Hamelton, and shot him through the left breast. The shot whirled Hamelton round, and in the next moment he shot Hamelton in the back—coming out on right of right breast—and Hamelton fell. As he struck on his knees with his rump toward Johnson and head directly from him he shot him again a raking shot that tore along his back, as coolly as shooting at a mark. He turned half round and as George Peter, who had emptied his pistol, came up with a long dirk, shot him in the side, which whirled him half round; and then Johnson and two Hameltons, all badly and as a dozen doctors said fatally wounded. Unfortunately for the world and the peace of society, all three got well.

"Then Doctor Hamelton challenged Colonel Johnson to fight a duel. Johnson accepted—to fight with broadswords. Dr. Hamelton refused to fight because Johnson being forty pounds the heaviest man had chosen 'an unusual weapon'. Then Doctor Hamelton indicted the Johnsons for 'an aggravated riot' which under the code was a penitentiary offense. I was a Union man and was Johnson's right bower in all the fight and I defended the Johnsons in the most exciting trial of a week I ever saw. They were acquitted and the Johnson mob in spite of the sheriff and court rushed in, took the jurors on their shoulders and carried them in a triumphal march around the public square. The Hameltons got out of sight, fast.

"I always wondered and never knew why Charles A. Hamelton came to me to get through the insolvent court. All I ever knew was, he did. Johnson was elected. Much of this is outside of the history you asked for, but I thought it might interest you. A little more of the same sort in parenthesis: I said unfortunately they did not all die. The Hameltons lived to perpetrate that most murderous, damnable massacre at Trading Post.

"Bill 'Eorpi' of whom you have read shot William Johnson, Jeff's brother, dead. Jeff killed a man in Chattooga county, Georgia, after the war, and a year or two after was shot from ambush and killed. His oldest son wantonly shot a negro, was tried, convicted and hung at Rome, Georgia, (the first white man ever hung in Georgia for killing a negro), and his second son was hung to a limb in Arkansas a few years after for some devilment. Thus went these six men and the world would have been none the loser had they never lived.

Now, Joel, I really have no pen to write with; could not write much better if I had. And it is too hot to spell correctly or think. So if you read this you are a good scholar. Your friend, etc.—John H. Rice.

General John H. Rice was as he states in his letter a native of Georgia himself. Prior to 1884 the author of this book knew General Rice when he was the publisher of the Paola Republican at Paola in Miami county. He had as a rival one L. J. Perry who published the Paola Spirit. There was a fierce newspaper row between them. Perry traced back to Georgia and accused Rice of certain treasonable publications. Rice sued Perry in the district court for damages. About that time this writer went East as a compositor or typesetter on newspapers and the first person he worked alongside of was Charles R. Hanleiter, then a very aged man and too feeble to be working. He was interested in me as a Kansan and asked if I knew a John H. Rice. Conversation disclosed that he had been Rice's partner in the publishing business down in Georgia and that they had issued a geography for use in the public schools of the rebel states. This geography was a humdinger. The map of America in brilliant colors showed the "Confederate States of America" covering all of the country except a small spot in green stowed away back of Wisconsin up against the Canada line labelled in small letters "United States of America". When a copy of this was obtained and produced in the district court at Paola General Rice dropped his suit against Perry and sold out and moved to Fort Scott. He later moved to Sedalia and published a daily newspaper devoted to changing the state capital from Jefferson City to Sedalia. He was resourceful and showed great strength of character. This was his last great effort. He had four sons and a daughter who have attained to highly honorable stations in life.

As related in the story of John Brown's stay during the

summer of 1858 at the scene of the Hamelton massacre, where he erected a substantial fort and had an organized company for its defense, he spent much of his time writing and planning the great event that was to bring him to an ignominious death without shame and to take upon himself the undying, endless fame given to him as a martyr. This old hero stayed at the murder farm till late in September. There was no renewal of violence. His fame and his presence was a shield of defense for the entire border. His active mind was preparing for other scenes of action. About the first of October, 1858, he returned to his old haunts about Fort Brown west of Mound City. He was in constant association with Montgomery and with Wattleses and other leaders of Linn County. He was always modest, deferring to the authority and leadership of others. During the fall there were appeals for protection for settlers on the Little Osage river in the northern part of Bourbon county and Kagi and several of his immediate following were with him when he accompanied Montgomery to their relief. While on this errand of mercy a negro named Jim came to Brown's camp and begged for help, saying his family was to be sold and probably separated for life. The result of this was that John Brown and Kagi formed two parties to go over into Missouri and carry away these slaves. In John Brown's party were twelve men, in that of Kagi eight only. The Brown party went to the place of one Hicklan, the master of Jim, and liberated that negro and four of his family. From there they went to Isaac Jarne's place and released five more, taking Jarne along to prevent alarm being given. Kagi went on the south side of the Little Osage river to the home of David Cruse who raised his rifle to fire but was shot dead before he pulled the trigger. Besides Brown and Kagi there were eighteen men in this raid, not one of whom has ever been mentioned to my knowledge, but I imagine their names appear somewhere in this book. It is a fact, though, that this was all done without the knowledge and consent of either Montgomery or August Wattles, the latter upbraiding Brown for his violation of a truce then supposed to exist between Missouri and Kansas. As it was just about this time that Jennison and his crowd went over and burned out Jerry Jackson in violation of an acknowledged truce with the people of the vicinity of Trading Post it is easy to see there were people willing to practice retaliation at the risk of renewing the bloody feud. But they got away with it and drove home into Kansas carrying the rescued black people in a slow moving wagon drawn by oxen. They arrived at the Wattles home at Moneka in the night time and in reply to an inquiry as to what it was all about John Brown replied, "See, I have carried the war into Africa."

To this final visit of Brown to his staunch friend Wattles especial interest attached, for it was at this time that he produced the "Parallels" published in the New York Tribune and elsewhere, which attracted great attention and are more often quoted in connection with Brown than anything else except his final address to the Virginia jury. Mr. Wattles had severely censured his old friend "for going into Missouri contrary to our agreement and getting these slaves." He replied, Mr. Wattles testified in 1860: "I considered the matter well; you will have no more attacks from Missouri; I shall now leave Kansas; probably you will never see me again; I consider it my duty to draw the scene of the excitement to some other part of the country." Montgomery and Kagi were parties to this discussion of the storm his raid had created. Brown had been writing letters as they talked. Finally, turing to the others with a manuscript in his hand he said: "Gentlemen, I would like to have your attention for a few minutes. I usually leave the newspaper work to Kagi, but this time I have something to say myself." He then read the "Parallels" which he had dated at the Trading Post, lest the usual date line, Moneka, prove a cause of trouble to the staunch Wattles household. They are as follows:

"Trading Post, Kansas, January, 1859.—Gentlemen: You will greatly oblige a humble friend by allowing the use of your columns while I briefly state two parallels, in my poor way.

"Not One year ago Eleven quiet citizens of this neighborhood (viz) Wm. Robertson, Wm. Colpetzer, Amos Hall, Austin Hall, John Campbell, Asa Snyder, Thos Stilwell, Wm. Hairgrove, Asa Hairgrove, Patrick Ross and B. L. Reed, were gathered up from their work and their homes by an armed force (under one Hamelton) and without trial or opportunity to speak in own defense were formed into a line and all but one shot, five killed and five wounded. One fell unharmed pretending to be dead. All were left for dead. The only crime charged against them was that of being free-state men. Now, I inquire, what action has ever, since the occurrence in May last, been taken by either the President of the United States, the Governor of Missouri, the Governor of Kansas, or any of their tools, or by any proslavery or administration man, to ferret out and punish the perpetrators of this crime?

"Now for the other parallel. On Sunday, the 19th of December, a negro called Jim came over to the Osage settlement from Missouri and stated that he togther with his wife, two children and another negro man were to be sold within a day or two and begged for help to get away. On Monday (the following) night, two small companies were made up to go to Missouri and forcibly liberate the five slaves together with other slaves. One of these companies I assumed to direct. We proceeded to the place, surrounded the buildings, liberated the slaves, and also took certain property supposed to belong to the estate.

"We, however, learned before leaving that a portion of the articles we had taken belonged to a man living on the plantation as a tenant, and who was supposed to have no interest in the estate. We promptly returned to him all we had taken. We then went to another plantation where we freed five more slaves, took some property, and two white men. We moved very slowly away into the Territory for some distance, and then sent the white men back, telling them to follow as soon as they chose to do so. The other company freed one female slave, took some property, and as I am informed, killed one white man (the master), who fought against the liberation.

"Now for a comparison. Eleven persons were forcibly restored to their natural and inalienable rights, with but one man killed, and all 'Hell is stirred from beneath.' It is currently reported that the Governor of Missouri has made a requisition upon the Governor of Kansas for the delivery of such as were concerned in the last-named "dreadful outrage". The marshal of Kansas is said to be collecting a posse of Missouri (not Kansas) men at West Point in Missouri, a little town about ten miles distant, to "enforce the laws". All proslavery, conservative free-state, and dough-faced men, and administration tools, are filled with holy horror.

"Consider the two cases, and the action of the administration party.

"Respectfully yours, John Brown."

Indubitably the parallel was an effective one. The theft of black human property was always the most heinous offense known in the South during slavery days; and although he had expressed due horror at the Hamelton massacre Governor Denver had neither requisitioned the Governor of Missouri for the delivery of Hamelton's criminals nor offered a reward for their apprehension. Now, however, the case was different. Governor Medary sent a message to the Legislature on January 11 denouncing both Brown and Montgomery, refusing to give the names of his informants as to their movements in Linn and Bourbon counties and asking the legislature to act at once, besides repeating his offer of $250 reward each for the arrest of Brown and Montgomery. To this a committee of the legislature made a remarkably spirited and able reply. While censuring Brown and Montgomery, and attributing to them "the ruin and desolation" that had "settled down on two of the most beautiful counties in Kansas," the committee was "clearly of the opinion that all armed bands should be dispersed and the law should be sustained. Kansas has too long suffered in her good name from the acts of lawless men and from corruption of Federal officers." As to the Federal governor's offer of a reward the committee was emphatic in its stand that this policy would not succeed. "The man of Kansas," it said, "that would, for a reward, deliver up a man to the General Government, would sink into the grave of an Arnold or a Judas. . . . Such has been the acts of the general government in this Territory that public sentiment will not permit any person to receive the gold of the General Government as a bribe to do a duty." There being a minority report of a different character the legislature referred the whole matter to a select committee, which brought in a harmless report that the legislature should uphold the Governor in enforcing the law.

Montgomery promptly wrote, on January 15, a long letter to the Lawrence Republican setting forth actual conditions and saying, among other things: "For Brown's doings in Missouri I am not responsible. I know nothing of either his plans or intentions. Brown keeps his own counsels and acts on his own responsibility. I hear much said about Montgomery and his company. I have no company. We have had no organization since the 5th day of July." Montgomery with splendid courage followed this letter up in person arriving in Lawrence on January 18 and boldly walking into court in the afternoon surrendered himself to Judge Elmore, by whom he was turned over to the sheriff. As the only indictment pending against him was for robbing a postoffice, this border leader was promptly released on four thousand dollars' bail. Two days later he spoke for nearly three hours before a large audience in the Lawrence Congregational Church, detailing the whole history of the border troubles. Frequently interrupting him with applause the audience at the conclusion of his story gave three cheers for him and three more for "Old John Brown"! The next day Montgomery went back to the south, where he continued his efforts in behalf of peace. On February 2 he returned to Lawrence with six of his men who likewise surrendered to Judge Elmore, to Governor Medary's great satisfaction.

As for John Brown he was now ready to leave the Territory for the last time. Of constructive work there was no more to his credit than when he left the Territory in 1856. The terror of his name undoubtedly acted as a deterrent while he was on the Missouri line. But there had been peace in Linn and Bourbon counties and would have been had he not appeared, until Montgomery wrongly or rightly assumed the offensive in November,—except for the usual lawlessness of a frontier where the courts are not respected. As Montgomery said, Shubel Morgan kept his own counsels and went his own way and the sole act of any significance to be credited to him during this six months in Southern Kansas is the capture of the slaves. On the other hand, his presence in Linn, after deducting properly the numerous activities wrongly attributed to him and his men, was in itself the cause of excitement and strife. It was an incentive to men of the Weaver type to spread stories of impending trouble for their own ends. Certain it is that the Missouri raid, in violation of his agreement, caused many peaceful free-state settlers to flee their homes for fear of violence, and might have resulted seriously but for the efforts of certain Missourians to keep the peace and for the pusillanimity of those who wished to retaliate but feared the consequences. In Missouri, however, that raid had caused sufficient alarm to convince Brown again of the telling effect upon the crumbling foundations of slavery of a similar undertaking on a large scale. "All the slaves in the thickest slave settlements in Missouri for twenty or thirty miles have been carried into Texas or Arkansas or are closely guarded by a large force every night", reported on January 15th, a Tribune correspondent from Lawrence.

For several days the eleven black fugitives were hidden until the storm about the incident subsided. **Brown visited** many places those days, for the last time. He went over to the fort at the murder farm and visited Charlie Hadsall. While there he did considerable writing and gave Mr. Hadsall the "Parallels" to read, and went on to Trading Post and showed them to Dr. Massey. He took supper at the Tubbs home and had Amos play religious tunes on his violin, expressing great pleasure in the music and giving to Amos a most interesting personal memento. From there some twelve miles he went back to Wattles' and got together his **equipment for** carrying those eleven black people to the protection of a foreign flag which then meant more as a guarantee of freedom than did the Stars and Stripes. It was then midwinter.

The next heard of John Brown was at Harper's Ferry. With twenty-one men—most of them very young and one of them right off a farm down near where Prescott now is— he had entered and taken possession of the United States arsenal with all its stores of war materials at about midnight. They sent out parties who brought in prisoners until a dozen prominent citizens were crowded into the little brick house used for a fire department. At daylight came assaults from the militia of the town and defensive firing by Brown's men. No new recruits came. The uprising did not uprise. The black people who had promised to respond to call did not show up. They had been told all these things would happen on the 24th and this was the 17th, as circumstances seemed to urge haste on the part of Brown and his men. By the early morning light an old physician of the town named Beckham,[1] on his way to visit a patient, came within range and was killed by a bullet. This incensed the town and soon the whole community was shooting at the little group in the engine house. The government at Washington was notified by telegraph and at 12 o'clock noon a train with a company of militia arrived, and later another train with Governor Wise and Colonel Lee (the latter only two years later to engage in a much greater crime than John Brown could have ever been capable of). Brown's party were overpowered and the incident is familiar to everybody. Whole volumes have been written upon it—too much to give in this book—but every citizen of Linn County should be familiar with this great incident that had its origin here. One of our own boys was there, and fully half that little group of men had fought here in the border wars for freedom!

Brown was brought to trial—a mere formal affair—in which he was found guilty of treason against the state of Virginia. Two men were assigned to defend Brown, but there could be no defense. A verdict of guilty was inevitable. Brought before the court for sentence he made this remarkable speech:

"I have, may it please the court, a few words to say. In the first place I deny everything but what I have all along admitted: of a design on my part to free the slaves. I intended certainly to have made a clean thing of the matter, as I did last winter when I went to Missouri and there took slaves without the snapping of a gun on either side, moving them through the country, and finally leaving them in Canada. I designed to have done the same thing again on a larger scale. That was all I intended. I never did intend murder, or treason, or the destruction of property, or to excite or incite slaves to rebellion, or to make insurrection.

"I have another objection, and that is that it is unjust that I should suffer such a penalty. Had I interfered in the manner in which I admit, and which I admit has been fairly proved— for I admire the truthfulness and candor of the greater portion of the witnesses who have testified in this case—had I so interfered in behalf of the rich, the powerful, the intelligent, the so-called great, or in behalf of any of their friends, either father, mother, brother, sister, wife or children, or any of that class, and suffered and sacrificed what I have in this interference, it would have been all right. Every man of this court would have deemed it an act worthy of reward rather than punishment.

"This court acknowledges, too, as I suppose, the validity of the law of God. I see a book kissed, which I suppose to be the Bible, or at least the New Testament, which teaches me that all things whatsoever I would that men should do to me,

---

1. The worst "cussing out" the writer ever got was by a man of this family when he learned I was from Kansas. "Yes, sah, by Gad, sah, the home of Old John Brown, sah! That old hoss thief and murderer, sah! Kansas—by Gad, sah!" Then it was worse when I mentioned I lived near Trading Post. Finally he held his breath a moment and said "By Gad, sah! You are a gentleman, sah! I have no right to talk this way to you, sah! And I apologize, sah!" This happened in a dining room in Washington in 1884. Afterward this family entertained me at their home in Harper's Ferry and the whole family went down and got me a brick from the engine house. And I never once lowered the flag of Trading Post. This refers to the Beckham notation on page 225.

I should do even so to them.   I endeavored to act up to that instruction.   I say I am yet too young to understand that God is any respecter of persons.   I believe that to have interfered as I have done, as I have always freely admitted I have done, in behalf of His despised poor, I did no wrong, but right.   Now if it is deemed necessary that I should forfeit my life for the furtherance of the ends of justice, and mingle my blood further with the blood of my children and with the blood of millions in this slave country whose rights are disregarded by wicked, cruel and unjust enactments, I say let it be done.   Let me say one word further.   I feel entirely satisfied with the treatment I have received on my trial.   Considering all the circumstances, it has been more generous than I expected.   But I feel no consciousness of guilt.   I have stated from the first what was my intention, and what was not.   I never had any design against the liberty of any person, nor any disposition to commit treason or incite slaves to rebel or make any general insurrection—I never encouraged any man to do so, but always discouraged any idea of that kind.   Let me say, also, in regard to the statements made by some of them that I have induced them to join me.   But the contrary is true.   I do not say this to injure them, but as regretting their weakness.   Not one but joined me of his own accord, and the greater part at their own expense.   A number of them I never saw, and never had a word of conversation with till the day they came to me, and that was for the purpose I have stated.   Now, I have done."

There is little more to be said.[1]   John Brown died as he had lived—brave, and free from fear of any kind.   On the morning of his execution he took a tender but cheerful farewell of his comrades in bonds and in arms.   He gave them each a small coin, except Hazlett.[2]   He visited Stevens last: "Good bye, Captain" he said; "I know you are going to a better land." "I know I am," replied Brown.

John Brown was put into a furniture wagon, in which was his own black-walnut coffin; the jailer, Mr. Avis, who had been very kind to Brown, and the driver, a man named Hawks being the other occupants.   The wagon was surrounded by cavalry which escorted it to the field where the gallows was standing, something like half a mile away.   Here then were a large number of soldiers going through military maneuvers, and assembled to prevent the rescue of Brown.   He was calm, perfectly self-possessed.   He was asked if he thought he could endure the ordeal, and replied, "I can endure almost anything but parting from friends; that is very hard."   In

1.   The following two pages are taken from Oswald Garrison Villard's "John Brown" a book that should be in every library in Linn County.   As Mr. Villard copied from my writings, and properly credited them, I feel justified in borrowing this much from him.

2.   Hazlett had escaped arrest but was later apprehended at his old home in Pennsylvania.   He was taken back and was hanged March 30.

speaking of fear, on the road to the scaffold, he said: "It has been characteristic of me, from infancy, not to suffer from physical fear. I have suffered a thousand times more from bashfulness than from fear." "You are a game man, Captain Brown," said an attendant. He replied, "Yes, I was so trained up; it was one of the lessons of my mother; but it is hard to part from friends, though newly made." "You are more cheerful than I am, Captain Brown," said his friend. The stern old hero replied, "Yes, I ought to be."

The wagon halted at the scaffold and the troops opened file. Brown descended from the wagon, saluted the Major and Mr. Hunter, and ascended the scaffold stairs. I shall let an eye-witness describe the execution.

"His demeanor was intrepid, without being braggart. John Brown's manner gave no evidence of timidity. He stood upon the scaffold but a short time, giving brief adieus to those about him, when he was properly pinioned, the white cap drawn over his face, the noose adjusted and attached to the hook above, and he was moved, blindfolded, a few steps for-- ward. It was curious to note how the instincts of nature operated to make him careful in putting out his feet, as if afraid he would walk off the scaffold. The man who stood unblenched on the brink of eternity was afraid of falling a few feet to the ground!

"Everything was now in readiness. The sheriff asked the prisoner if he should give him a private signal before the fatal moment. He replied, in a voice that sounded to me unnatur- ally natural,—so composed was its tone, and so distinct its articulation,— that it did not matter to him, if only they would not keep him too long waiting." He was kept waiting, however; the troops that had formed his escort had to be put into their proper position, and while this was going on he stood for some ten or fifteen minutes blindfolded, the rope about his neck and his feet on the treacherous platform, ex- pecting instantly the fatal act; but he stood for this com- paratively long time upright as a soldier in position and motionless. I was close to him, and watched him narrowly to see if I could detect any signs of shrinking or trembling in his person, but there was none. Once I thought I saw his knees tremble, but it was only the wind blowing his loose trousers. His firmness was subjected to still further trial by hearing Colonel Smith announce to the sheriff: 'We are all ready, Mr. Campbell'. The sheriff did not hear or did not comprehend, and in a louder tone the same announcement was made. But the culprit still stood steady until the sheriff descended the flight of steps, with a well-directed blow of a sharp hatchet severed the rope that held up the trapdoor, which instantly sank sheer beneath him. He fell about three feet and the man of strong and bloody hand, of fierce passions, of iron will, of wonderful vicissitudes, the terrible partisan of Kansas, the capturer of the United States Arsenal at Harper's Ferry, the would-be Catiline of the South, the demigod of the abolitionists, the man execrated and lauded, damned and prayed for, the man who in his motives, his means, his plans, and his successes, must ever be a wonder, a puzzle and a mystery. John Brown was hanging between heaven and earth."

This was written by J. T. L. Preston of the Military College of Lexington, Virginia, a few hours after the execution. He adds: "In all that array there was not, I suppose, one throb of sympathy for the offender. Yet the mystery was awful —to see the human form thus treated by men—to see life suddenly stopped in its current, and to ask one's self the question with answer, 'And what then?'"

John Brown's body was taken to North Elba. As it was lowered into the grave the preacher repeated the words of Paul: "I have fought the good fight; I have finished my course; I have kept the faith; henceforth there is laid up for me a crown of righteousness, which the Lord, the righteous Judge, shall give me; and not to me only, but unto all that love His appearing."

Daniel Underhill, who had his home in Liberty township, was a man highly honored throughout the county and was elected to various positions of trust and honor, being a member of the legislature in 1863, county treasurer two terms and then a member of the state senate. On April 3, 1857, he arrived where he built his permanent home in a rather lonesome neighborhood, as there were "no settlements clear down to Sugar creek" as late as 1870. On the military road Fort Leavenworth to Fort Scott a family named Clements from Illinois built three big two-story stone houses north of Sugar creek—two on the west side of the road and one on the east side. This was a pretentious community but it had no other name than the "Stone houses." When the "dry year" of 1860 happened the Clements went back to Illinois and Alec Seaman got the stone houses and made his home there. Daniel Underhill's father was Daniel Underhill from New York to North Carolina, who married Winifred Ball, and they made their home in Indiana, where Daniel was born and was married to Julia Ann Richart, who was born in Ross county, Ohio. They had three children, Laura Evelyn Underhill, who became the wife of Thornton Daniel Keller; Emma Josephine, deceased; and Harlan who married Miss Frank Coe daughter of Ira E. Coe, who now live in Lawrence.

Thornton Daniel Keller who married Laura Evelyn Underhill was born in Virginia in 1853. They had two children, Ora now Mrs. Roy Parmeley at Cushing, Oklahoma, and Mary at home.

States are not great
Except as men may make them;
Men are not great except they do and dare.
But states, like men,
Have destinies that take them—
That bear them on, not knowing why or where.

The WHY repels
The philosophic searcher—
The WHY and WHERE all questionings defy,
Until we find,
Far back in youthful nurture,
Prophetic facts that constitute the WHY.

All merit comes
From braving the unequal;
All glory comes from daring to begin.
Fame loves the State
That, reckless of the sequel,
Fights long and well, whether it lose or win.

Than in our State
No illustration apter
Is seen or found of faith and hope and will.
Take up her story;
Every leaf and chapter
Contains a record that conveys a thrill.

And there is one
Whose faith, whose fight, whose failing,
Fame shall placard upon the walls of time.
He dared begin—
Despite the unavailing,
He dared begin, when failure was a crime.

When over Africa
Some future cycle
Shall sweep the lake-gemmed upland with its surge;
When, as with trumpet
Of Archangel Michael,
Culture shall bid a colored race emerge;

When busy cities
There, in constellations,
Shall gleam with spires and palaces and domes,
With marts wherein
Is heard the noise of nations;
With summer groves surrounding stately homes—

There, future orators
To cultured freemen
Shall tell of valor, and recount with praise
Stories of Kansas,
And of Lacedaemon—
Cradles of freedom then of ancient days.

From boulevards
O'erlooking both Nyanzas
The statured bronze shall glitter in the sun
With rugged lettering,
"JOHN BROWN OF KANSAS:
He dared begin,
He lost,
But, losing, won."   —Eugene F. Ware.

The governor of Virginia, Harry A. Wise, interviewed John Brown as he lay a prisoner in the engine house, and made this comment on the old hero:

"He is no madman, but the best bundle of nerves I ever saw; cut, bruised and battered, and chained beside, he showed himself to be a man of courage and fortitude. He is a fanatic, of course, beyond all reason, but he thinks himself a Christian, and believes honestly he is called of God to free the negroes. They say when one son was dead by his side he held his rifle in one hand and felt the pulse of another who was dying, all the time cautioning his men to be cool and sell their lives dearly.

"While I was talking with him," continued Governor Wise, "some one called out that he was a robber and a murderer. Brown replied, 'You slave-holders are the robbers.'

"I said to him, 'Captain Brown, your hair is matted with blood and you are speaking hard words. Perhaps you forget I am a slave-holder; you had better be thinking on eternity. Your wounds may be fatal, and if they are not, you will have to stand trial for treason, conspiracy and murder, and how can you hope to escape, when you admit your guilt?' The old man leaned on his elbow and beneath the bandages on his broken face I saw the blue eyes flash, and he answered me: 'Governor Wise, you call me old, but after all I have only ten or fifteen years, at most, the start of you on that journey to eternity, of which you speak. I will leave this world first, but you must follow. I will meet you across Death's border, and I tell you Governor Wise, prepare for eternity. You admit you are a slave-holder. You have a responsibility weightier than mine. Prepare to meet your God!' "

On November 2, 1859, John Brown was taken from the jail to the court room at Charleston, Virginia, and sentenced to be hung on the second day of December following. During this interval an undertaking was entered into in his behalf of which little is known to the general public, as those parties, with possibly two exceptions have passed from life. The purpose of this effort is to gather the fragments from the story as they drifted to me during the more than forty years that have elapsed.[1]

Early in October, 1859, Richard J. Hinton came to Kansas, visited James Hanway at Dutch Henry's Crossing (now Lane), and induced Hanway to go with him to Linn County. Arriving at Moneka they sent for Captain James Montgomery and Augustus Wattles, both of whom immediately responded, and a conference was held in a room immediately over the post-office at Moneka Hotel, then kept by Dr. George E. Denison. This consultation resulted in the planning for the rescue of John Brown. Hinton advocated an attempt by force, which necessitated the transporting of a considerable body of men to Virginia. Wattles did not approve of this, believing it impracticable, and thinking that chances of success were only possible with a carefully selected few, and the exercise of the keenest tact and highest courage. Nevertheless Hinton's idea had the right of way for the time and a list of seventy-five to one hundred eligibles from Kansas, Iowa and the East was made for the undertaking. Just when and where further consultations, if any, were held, is not now clear. Certain it is that the plan was changed. Difficulties as to funds, transportation, arms and provisions, as well as the almost certain exposure in attempting to rendezvous and handling of a large force anywhere within striking distance of the objective point, conspired to bring into play the more conservative judgment of those having the matter in hand. Hinton had returned to the East to work up the Eastern contingent, which never materialized. Hanway as far as is known took no further part, leaving Montgomery and Wattles to project arrangements. A small force was soon determined upon and a great care and secrecy exercised in their selection and moved to the East.

The success of a few men from Lawrence and vicinity a few months before in rescuing Dr. John Doy from the St.

1. This is the story of an expedition to rescue Old John Brown from Charlestown jail written by O. E. Morse of Mound City for the State Historical Society.

Joseph, Missouri, jail naturally pointed in their direction for a part of the detail. Joseph Gardner, Silas S. Soule, J. A. Pike and S. J. Willis were selected from the Doy rescuers. James Montgomery, Augustus Wattles, H. C. Seaman and Henry Carpenter went from Linn County. Benjamin Rice from Bourbon county and Benjamin Seaman, a brother of H. C. Seaman, went from his home in Iowa. Gardner, Pike and Willis (Soule had gone East earlier) went to Leavenworth. Not wishing to visit St. Joseph, for obvious reasons, they hired a team to take them to Easton, twelve miles east of St. Joseph. While waiting at the hotel for a train they listened to a thorough discussion of Kansas and Kansans, of Lawrence, and especially of the Doy exploit. They restrained themselves from taking part in the discussion and proceeded without further incident to Pittsburgh, Pennsylvania, where Soule joined them, and they journeyed together to Harrisburg. Of the southern Kansas party Wattles went in advance of the others. Under Montgomery's lead those mentioned above and Dr. C. R. Jennison (later known as Colonel Jennison) left Linn County. At Lawrence Jennison left the party and returned home. The others proceeded to Elwood, opposite St. Joseph, where letters from Major Abbott and some others secured them the assistance of Ed Russell, Thomas A. Osborne, A. L. Lee, and probably D. W. Wilder. The party reached Elwood too late to avail themselves of the ferry crossing, and crossing that night (a very dark and stormy one) was essential to the carrying out of their plans. The only rowboat at the place belonged to Captain Blackiston. The oars were carefully put away and the skiff securely locked. "Love laughs at locksmiths." So it proved in this case. Blackiston's daughter was Russell's sweetheart, afterwards becoming his wife. Through her he got the oars and key and with the assistance of one of the others mentioned of the Elwood party, the crossing to St. Joseph was safely made, though attended with many dangers in the darkness and the overloaded skiff. Some transportation over the Hannibal and St. Joseph Railroad was furnished by Elwood friends, and the additional amount necessary was put up by Major Tuttle, the agent of the road at St. Joseph, later a resident of New York, who was thoroughly in sympathy with the free-state movements in Kansas, as was Colonel Hayward, the general superintendent of the road.

The Montgomery party proceeded direct to Harrisburg without further incident of historical importance, where they were joined by the Lawrence party, by Wattles, Benjamin Seaman from Iowa, and R. J. Hinton. While there is no evidence at hand to show that Frederick Douglass joined the party at Harrisburg it is pretty clear that he was in consultation with them later in their progress towards Charlestown. It will not be understood that these men were seen in public together, or that they stopped at the same hotel, or traveled as a party on the trains. They moved apparently independent of each other, representing themselves as stockmen, grain men, laborers, land seekers, or what ever seemed best to suit the occasion or most fully obscure their real intent. They had a meeting place at the office or residence of a doctor (name forgotten), who was in sympathy with their undertaking. At these meetings plans for the campaign were made and scouts sent out; Seaman of the Linn County party and Soule of the Lawrence contingent doing most of this work. Montgomery, Wattles, Seaman and Soule, and possibly others of the party, established a meeting place in the vicinity of Hagerstown, Maryland, from which place they pushed forward their tours of observation across the river into Virginia, Seaman going to Martinsburg to examine the rough country in that region. Soule going more directly to Charlestown secured an audience with Brown under strict surveillance of two armed guards. Under these restrictions no progress could be made in unfolding or perfecting plans. No others of the party saw Brown although very direct communications were kept up through someone whose identity has been lost in the haze that passing years throws over our memories.

While preparations were going on as related, the weather changed to severe cold with a heavy fall of snow throughout the entire region, rendering traveling through the mountains impracticable. This with the strong and watchful force at the jail and the constant patrolling of the roads, were difficulties seemingly unsurmountable, and by many of the party they were believed to be real reasons why the undertaking was abandoned. The manager of the affair found in the will of John Brown a greater obstacle to their plans than snow, cold, patrolmen, or Virginia Militia. John Brown refused to be rescued. His reasons were: First, that he had been the recipient of many kindnesses from the jailer and his wife; that he had had privileges that were secured by his pledge not to take advantage of them to escape; that the jailer was a fearless official who would not be caught off his guard or give up his prisoner without a struggle, and for himself he was honor bound both to his keeper and to his friends outside to prevent further bloodshed. Second, he was strongly impressed with the conviction that death on the gallows was a fulfilment of his mission, the rounding out of his effort; the act that would make effective all his work for the freedom of the slaves. In his simple and terse way he said: "I am worth more to die than to live." For himself he may have had a prophetic vision as he neared the end, and so not far away enacted that tremendous tragedy that not only emancipated the slaves but rescued a nation from the thraldom of a terrible crime and the bondage of living openly before the world a stupendous and wicked lie, and started it on its course to be the leader and arbiter for the betterment of mankind.

What of the men who volunteered for this hazardous under-taking? With the exception of Henry Carpenter, the Kansas men returned to the Territory. Carpenter came to Kansas from Ashtabula county, Ohio, and remained in Pennsylvania when the party broke up. When last heard from fifteen years ago he was still in western Pennsylvania. Montgomery, Sea-man, Rice, Gardner, Pike and Willis enlisted in the army, Montgomery as colonel of the third regiment, Seaman as cap-tain, Rice as sergeant, and Gardner as private. In the same regiment Pike and Willis enlisted in company A, Ninth cavalry.

When in February, 1862, the third and fourth regiments were destroyed to advance the interests of a few selfish and ambitious men, Montgomery was sent to the Southern Atlantic coast to organize and command a brigade of colored troops; Seaman went with the Fifth Cavalry to which his company was assigned; Rice to the Ninth with his company; Gardner to the Tenth with his company, being later promoted to a captaincy in the First Colored infantry; Pike was made first lieutenant of Company A, and later captain of Company K of the Ninth cavalry; Willis became first sergeant of his company and later first lieutenant of Company A of the Tenth infantry.

Montgomery died at his home near Mound City, the 6th day of December, 1871, and is buried in the soldiers' cemetery at that place. Wattles died December 9, 1876, near the same place. Seaman and Soule, the two scouts, were both killed many years ago by roughs while serving as city marshals, the first at Baxter Springs and the other at Denver, Colorado. Gardner died at Lawrence in the early 70's. Benjamin Seaman died in Iowa; Rice is reported dead; Willis died at White City, Kansas, some years ago. Captain Pike, probably the only survivor, has a position at the penitentiary at Lansing. By their devotion to the cause of freedom in the early Kansas days, by their patriotic service in the army and their good citizenship afterward these men made a record that might well be emulated by any group of American citizens.

(D. W. Wilder having questioned the accuracy of the fore-going, Mr. Morse writes further, adding certain corroborating letters which are appended. To give further light extracts were appended from letters written at the time, Mr. Wilder withdrew his criticisms and returned the following:—Ed)

D. W. Wilder: In the "History of Torrington, Connecticut," John Brown's birthplace, written by Rev. Samuel Orcutt, there is contributed a biography of John Brown one hundred octavo pages long by F. B. Sanborn of Concord, Massachusetts. This biography was published in 1878. Mr. Sanborn's "Life and Letters of John Brown", 645 pages was published in 1885. In the Torrington biography Mr. Sanborn says (page 19) of John Brown's campaign in Virginia: "It was the first decisive act of an inevitable tragedy, and such were its romantic features that in the lapse of time it will no doubt be gravely expounded as a myth to those who shall read American history some centuries hence. John Brown was indeed no mythical nor in any sense dubitable personage.

O. E. Morse: Regarding Mr. Wilder's criticism on my story of the attempted rescue of John Brown, it occurs to me that his whole discussion, boiled down, simply means that what I wrote was not true because Wilder never heard of it—a standpoint from which no man is permitted to give testimony in any court in the world. I refer you to the enclosed written proofs that there was an attempt to rescue Brown. Your predecessor, Judge F. G. Adams, after making investigation, was thoroughly convinced that such an attempt was made, as indicated by his letter attached, and marked, "A"; next a copy of letter of Major J. B. Abbott, referred to in Adam's letter marked, "B", in which he distinctly states, "expedition to liberate John Brown." Surely Abbott knew what he was talking about. Note "C" is a copy of a part of captain J. A. Pike's letter written in reply to Secretary Adams who had followed Abbott's suggestion and written Pike, wherein Pike distinctly states that Montgomery and party were alone. Note "D" is a letter from Pike in which he names Brown, and in which he fixes the year 1859. Note "E" is another letter from Pike written recently in which he gives some details of their experiences, stating that Soule saw Brown at Charlestown and also that Hinton was at the meeting at Harrisburg. Now this is what Wilder asked for—written testimony of one of the participants as to the fact that an account was made to rescue John Brown and that Hinton was one of the party, and that Montgomery and his men were there. Note "F" is a letter from Ed Russell, written nearly seventeen years ago, in which he gives no dates and neither mentions Brown, Hazlett, nor Stevens. Standing alone it might apply to any or many of the transactions of that period, but when it is understood that it was in response to a request to write what he knew of the attempted rescue of John Brown and was informed that what he wrote would be used in writing up that occurrence for the Historical Society, then his paper has point and value. Now what do I know about this matter personally? First, I knew Montgomery, Wattles, the Seamans, Rice and Gardner in the most thorough and intimate way. I served as a line officer to Montgomery the first eight months of the war, and had had his confidence and friendship for more than four years before. Wattles was my wife's father, and Henry Seaman was captain and I a lieutenant in the same company, under Montgomery, and was a neighbor and friend for years before; his brother Benjamin, I knew well, but for a less time, and not so intimately. Rice and I enlisted in the same company and had known each other for three years

before. I commanded for a year the company to which James
Gardner belonged and knew him intimately. Henry Carpenter
was in the employ of Augustus Wattles for a year or more,
so his home was on the adjoining farm, where I "bached." I
hardly think Mr. Wilder's acquaintance with these men gives
him warrant to speak for them and of them as I might presume to do. What he says of knowing one of the Seamans
I think is a case of mistaken identity. The Linn County Seaman he knew probably was Alex Seaman, county treasurer
of Linn when Wilder was auditor of state and is entirely un-
related to the man of whom I wrote.

Nearly twenty years ago James Hanway related to me the
incident of Hinton coming to his place in Miami county, and
they two coming to Moneka, this county, for the conference
with Montgomery and Wattles, as related, and in his talk
of the matter it was always for the rescue of Brown—Stevens
and Hazlett were never mentioned. I submit that what Hanway remembered twenty years ago about a transaction in
which he took part is a little better evidence than Wilder's
recollections forty-five years after an event he had nothing to
do with and knew nothing about at the time.

In the plan to use a larger force I was one of those selected
for that larger force; therefore had early knowledge of the
movement. A little later Henry Seaman gave me the story
of the expedition, giving the names of the members of the
party, places visited, plans and experiences, and always to
rescue Brown. Much has been forgotten but a few things
were fixed in my memory, among them the turning back of
Jennison, the meeting at Harrisburg, the character of the
country south and the direction in which he scouted. Wattles
often referred to these matters, particularly to Brown's refusal to be rescued, or to have further risks taken on his
account. His (Wattles's) family were fully in his confidence;
knew at the time of his purpose of going east; and Mrs. Morse
and another daughter, Mrs. Hiatt, who is living with us now,
are certain that their father took part in an attempt to rescue
John Brown. If there was no attempt to rescue, what occasion
was there for Brown to say "the best use they can make of
me is to hang me", and why did he decline to be rescued?

I note what you say about straightening this up to apply
to the rescue of Hazlett and Stevens. I have no distinct data
or information upon which to base a story of that kind.
This is the story of the attempted rescue of Brown, based
upon undeniable facts. To change it to something else would
surely be a "perversion of history." Wilder points out your
duty in that line. I don't question that there was some attempt to rescue Stevens and Hazlett. I am quite certain that
there was. I think, too, that Montgomery went East for
that purpose. I had no connection or direct knowledge of
the matter, so do not attempt to write of it, which may account

HISTORY OF HENRY TRINKLE 237

for some coincidences that seem to startle Mr. Wilder.. Now, may I suggest that to yield to the criticisms or be governed by the dictates of any man, is to narrow the field and cripple the efficiency of your department.

Henry Trinkle[1] has lived in what is now Lincoln township since the fall of 1858, and has a distinct recollection of the many incidents of the early years. He came from Porter county, Indiana, where he was born December 2, 1834, and where he had known some of the Miami Indians, and visited with them when he came here to their new reservation. During that fall he was with the Geboes, and hunted a great deal with Jim Eveline, a half-breed who will be remembered by many old inhabitants. All that portion of town now north of Market street was wild prairie, with grass growing on it that would conceal a man on horseback in many places. One exciting hunt resulted in his getting a handsome buck exactly where the Rudd house stands, now occupied by M. Badger.

In 1861 Trinkle was employed by the Miami chiefs to superintend the store which they opened on the hill on the Nop-shin-gah farm, now owned by Manfred Priser. Nop-shin-gah was head chief at that time, and on his death was buried in the little cemetery still called the Indian graveyard. Ach-a-pon-gah succeeded him as chief.

A family named Splawn had opened a farm on the quarter section southeast of the Market street well, and had their residence where the Louis Volkman house now is. The Splawns subsequently sold to a family named Shuler, and they sold to Washington Gowing, Jr. The Splawns and Shulers were thus the first settlers of what is now La Cygne, and it is sad to relate that the seniors died and were buried in a little graveyard not twenty feet from the Market street well, and are at present slumbering in this unprotected ground. Subsequently other members of these families died and were buried in a little graveyard, still protected, on the James Ireland farm two miles northeast of town. They are all remembered as very nice people, but nothing can be learned of their antecedents. This brief mention is the only monument to their memory.

Mr. Trinkle remembers a character who lived in a little cabin at the ford where the fair grounds now are. He was named Graham, and the ford took its name from him, so he was probably among the "first families," though he is remembered as an indolent, shiftless, harmless, old man, quite patriarchal in appearance, with long white hair and beard. Few took the trouble to learn his name or history, and among the settlers and emigrants he was known simply as the White Pilgrim, while the Indians gave him the equivalent in their

1. This was written by Mr. Mitchell in 1895.
John W. Orahood and David Goss were officers of Company D, Sixth Kansas cavalry, not Company B. Company D was evidently recruited in Linn County, and the "additional enlistments" were nearly all men from Trading Post.

language, Wah-pe-lah-quet, which names are preserved for their poetic value, should future bards write the story in verse.

Mr. Trinkle also remembers that in the Indian language the hill north of town was called after the Miami chief, John Roubideau, Ach-a-pon-gah, meaning Big Turtle.[1]

Martin Taylor also had some peculiarities that Henry remembers, one of which was that he had a herd of swine to which he sang a song that would bring them out of the forests to their feed without bringing any of their neighbors to dinner. Martin was a neighborly sort of man, but was mischievously associated with the proslavery people on the Missouri line, and on one occasion Henry rode to the old man's place at daylight to tell him his practices were known and retribution would surely overtake him if he persisted in it. Old Martin in fear and trembling ran for the timber, and his family carried food to him for several days where he lay in a hollow log. In the meantime, some of Montgomery's men did call for him with a rope without finding him. Taylor was ever after an exemplary citizen.

In 1862 horse stealing and other depredations were so numerous that a company was organized for protection of life and property, at H. D. Ward's place a mile northeast of town (now owned by Frank Conley). Eighty men enrolled in this independent organization, with Isaac Massey captain, and Henry Trinkle first lieutentnt. M. W. Gouin was secretary of the organization. A great number of horse thieves owed their detection and imprisonment to this efficient organization.

Mr. Trinkle was not able to enlist in the regular military service by reason of having two infants to take care of, but all his spare time was spent with the army in active service. He had been with Montgomery's men on many expeditions of rescue and reprisal, and afterwards with them when Jennison commanded them. On one occasion a party of three hundred pursued marauding Bushwhackers to near Balltown, where they ran into an ambush and Ed. R. Smith was shot. Captain Williams of Mound City was along that time.

On another occasion Jennison led about three hundred against the Bushwhackers, and just over the line captured a man whom he had had prisoner once before. He was of bad reputation, and Jennison told him if he ever caught him again he would hang him, and taking out his pocket knife split the fellow's ear for a mark of identification and turned him loose. Jennison was a cruel disciplinarian, and members of his band offending him were treated unmercifully.

Mr. Trinkle's most valuable recollection of those times is his description of the invasion of the state by Price's army October 24, 1864. He was stopping out on Middle creek, east of where La Cygne now is, and heard of their coming, and rode out towards West Point and saw the rebel army of nearly

1. Read Ach-a-pon-gah's story "Naming of the River."

40,000 men scattered over all the country to the east. The rebels were driving before them all the cattle they found, and those that were exhausted by the drive were taken up and slaughtered by the rear. Some of the cattle got beyond their reach, and Harvey McDonald gathered up forty fat steers which he sold in Osawatomie for $1,600. Night overtook the rebels at Trading Post, only a portion getting across the river. But there was little rest all night for either side. John Fickes, a brother of Morgan, owned the Trading Post mills at that time, and stayed in them while the rebels ran every machine to its fullest capacity. Wagons were loaded as rapidly as possible and sent on to the advance. Three hundred beeves were slaughtered at the Post. Just at daybreak Pleasanton made so sudden an onslaught on the rebel camp that they fled precipitately, and every little camp fire had beefsteaks on spits, showing that many of the rebels left with empty stomachs. They also abandoned a great deal of clothing. Carcasses of beeves were strewn everywhere and people had to stay away for weeks for fear of pestilence.

One noticeable thing as the rebels passed through Lincoln and Valley townships on the 24th was that the Texas troops under Price marched in close ranks in military order, while the Missourians were scattered all over the country murdering and pillaging. At old Sammy Nickel's place a visitor, just after their passage, asked Mrs. Nickel how they had fared. She said the rebels took everything—all they had left was at the end of a rope at the barn. Jennison had caught one of the pillagers and refused him a soldier's death and hung him.

On the morning of the 25th Trinkle was with the Federal front, and says for ten miles it was a mad chase. Every hundred yards or less rebel dead would be found who had been stripped of clothing by their own comrades, in some cases even the wounded being deprived of covering. Mr. Trinkle thinks the number killed must have been largely in excess of any estimate he has ever seen.

Colonel Moonlight flanked the rebels on the west and saved Mound City. This tended to bring the rebels together, and at Mine creek nearly their whole army was assembled. At that time the formation of the ground was peculiarly bad for their retreat. The creek runs nearly straight east, and the north bank was for a mile or more abruptly precipitate for several feet, making it impossible for the rebels to pass it except at a little narrow ford right in the middle of the army. Price got half his army over and formed them in four successive lines of battle, but before the remainder could scale the banks Pleasanton's cavalry engaged them in a fierce battle. It is said that many of the men who had served under Jennison rode into them and with revolvers destroyed them like they were sheep. Many were forced over the bluff and crushed.

Artillery stationed on the hill where Pleasanton now is, poured shell into their thickest ranks on the opposite side of the stream. The rebels had fully three men to one Union man, yet they were so panic stricken they were mowed down in windrows. There were about eight hundred left to surrender at the congested ford. A major general, Marmaduke, and several brigadiers and minor officers were taken. Marmaduke gave his sword to a mere boy, which looked rather ludicrous in a big, pompous man of fifty. That portion of Price's army which were across the creek went pell-mell for Missouri and escaped, going down past Nevada.

The scene after the battle was terrifying. Fully three hundred horses horribly mangled were running and snorting and trampling the dead and wounded. Their blood had drenched them and added to the ghastliness of it all. One hundred and fifty Union dead were taken to Mound City for burial, and the rebels buried on the battlefield. A lady living there at the time says that three hundred were buried in one grave, while at numerous other places groups of rebel dead were interred.

There were gathered from the battle field three big wagon loads of guns of all kinds, from old flintlocks to shotguns and rifles and revolvers, and three wagon loads of saddles. In 1868, when the Gulf road was built through where the battle was fought, the plain was white with bones, some of which were of slain men.

Richard Anderson Denton has a very distinct recollection of the condition of things here in 1866, when he first came with his family. Mr. Denton was born in Halifax county, Virginia, but was taken in his infancy by his parents to Indiana. He married in Tippecanoe county, Indiana, Miss Naomi Pharer Lee, and in 1865 started west with his wife and one child, now Mrs. Ella Young—Mrs. Frank Harmon being born in Ray county, Missouri. After spending a year in Ray county, Missouri, he came on to where La Cygne now stands. He remembers the old emigrant trail to have been from West Point, Missouri, past Maddox ford on Sugar creek to Blystone's crossing, where Daniel Stainbrook now lives, then straight west to the Ballard ford. There were then a considerable number of houses between Middle creek and the river. Daniel Stainbrook and his son-in-law, Thornton Bunch, Washington Gowing, Sr., Washington Gowing, Jr., David Brewer, and one or two others, had opened farms in the prairie on this line of road.

A man named Ennis had settled upon the quarter including the Ballard ford, now the Griffin farm, and was building a mill and Denton bought him out, and after considerable trouble and expense sold the water power right and mill to Brice G. Mundell, who was soon swept out by a freshet and never was able to rebuild. Mr. Mundell lived on the property until a few months ago. Mr. Denton bought new machinery, and for several years operated it near where the fair grounds stand.

Mr. Denton took an active part in the fight against the agents for the Miami Indian lands, Col. A. G. McKenzie and General Blunt. The Indians had been given individual allotments of 200 acres per capita, and it was supposed that the residue of the lands would be thrown open to settlement at $1.25 per acre, and every available piece was eagerly seized by the emigrants. But there was a mischievous clause providing that any Indian "overlooked or unprovided for" might claim lands held by such settlers and oust them. After awhile McKenzie and Blunt found it profitable to look up and bring forward so-called heirs, and demand either the land or a cash compromise, usually $10 an acre for timber land and $6 for prairie. This was quite different from $1.25 an acre, and a vigorous protest was made. The settlers organized with Wash Gowing, Sr., president, and R. A. Denton, secretary. A committee consisting of Mr. Denton, G. Marion Moore, and George W. Moore went to Paola for legal advice, where they learned that the practices of Blunt and McKenzie were legal under the terms of the treaty.

The Gulf road was then being slowly constructed, and La Cygne was surveyed and laid off as it now exists on the map during the spring and summer of 1869. The first store was that of a Mr. Chetland, who sold general merchandise in a building near where the section house now is, in the south part of town. The settlers were becoming more and more angry over the land question, and on it becoming known that on a certain day McKenzie was coming down from Paola to see some of the land, it looked as though trouble would result. But McKenzie came and with him was Congressman Grinnell of Iowa afterward senator from that state. The settlers gathered and no doubt intended to do him violence. There was some angry wrangling, when McKenzie asked permission to address them, which was granted. He was a smooth talker and after a short talk pacified most of them and contracted with them then and there on his own terms. Only a few held out, and they finally compromised.

The road finally reached Fontana and the town began to grow. George Noble had the first drug store, but it was only a few days till J. O. Rogers and James R. Moore were selling quinine, poisons and cosmetics, and it is not necessary to remark that Mr. Rogers has been here ever since, though Mr. Moore has been in California several years. And it might be truthfully recorded here that J. O. Rogers, old Mr. Pratt, R. A. Denton, and others, used to walk to Fontana to "catch the train for Kansas City."

There was talk those days about oil and gas just as we

have it now. Daniel Stainbrook dug a well, and one of his
men carried a light down in it which ignited gas and caused
an explosion and created great excitement. The man escaped
with slight injuries. But ever since then Uncle Dan has
believed in the gas theory.

"Johnny" Young was one of the most beloved men that ever
lived in La Cygne. His entire life was beautiful and it was
a public lamentation that he was taken at the early age of
forty-three years. John Alexander Young was born April 15,
1848, in Washington county, Pennsylvania. He came to La
Cygne as early as 1871 and conducted a high-class photog-
rapher's establishment. He married Miss Ella Denton, daughter of Mr. and Mrs. R. A. Denton, and they made a place
for themselves in the affections of all the people by their
generous and untiring work in community affairs. Mrs. Young
is now living at San Diego, California, with her sister Mrs.
Frank Harmon.

It is a long way back to the days of King John of England,
but that is where we go to get the beginning of the Thorne
family of Linn County. The earliest ancestor of record was
John who lived in Pembrokeshire in eastern Wales during the
reign of King Richard the First, affectionately called the
Lion-Hearted or Coeur-de-lLeon. King John who followed
Richard put his sword across the shoulders of William son
of John and dubbed him Sir William Thorne. This was the
same year Magna Charta was signed, 1215, but there is no
record as to which side Bill Thorne was on, but judging by
his descendants we are prone to believe he was the fellow
who showed King John where to put his name on the dotted
line. There was a mess of history on down to 1635 when
the first in America was John Thorne who arrived at Salem,
Massachusetts, that year. As a family they have been represented in all wars. When King Philip had his Indian wars
both John and his brother Israel served with ability. In
Colonial days the family lived in New Hampshire and were
related to many noted men of the time, one off-shoot of this
family being Daniel Webster. In 1842 a branch of the family
lived in Illinois where our Rufus Ferdinand Thorne was
born February 20 of that year. They came early to Kansas
and took part in the border war up in Johnson county, and
when the Civil War came on "Rufe" became a first lieutenant
in Company H of the Second Kansas Cavalry when about
twenty years old. He was wounded and taken prisoner at
Chickamauga in September 1863 and was in the famous
"Libby" prison at Richmond for nine months and for eight
months was shunted around to Atlanta and Macon in Georgia
and to Charleston, Columbia and Charlotte in South Carolina
and from the latter prison he made his third attempt at escape

and succeeded, traveling four hundred miles in twenty-four days (or very likely nights) reaching the Union Army at Knoxville. He got back into the service in Company F of the Fifth Kentucky Cavalry. His story of his year and a half in the prison pens of the south make very thrilling reading. At the close of the war he came home and was married to Nancy Jane Sprague at Spring Hill April 5, 1866, and a few years later came to Linn County making their home at La Cygne where he was owner of the La Cygne House, a noon time dining station for the old "Gulf" road and entertained many notables on this line of travel. "Rufe" was a leader in public affairs and helped make and unmake congressmen, governors and senators. His last public service was as steward of the State penitentiary at Lansing. Living up to family traditions his two boys Donald and Oscar enlisted in the famous Twentieth Kansas and served under Funston in the Phillippines, Oscar being killed by a shot in the head at Caloocan on March 11, 1899. The children of Mr. and Mrs. Thorne were Stephen A. who married Edith A. Henry of Cass county, Missouri, and had two daughters—Esther and Edith Grace; Philip Sheridan served as clerk of the district court and married Maude Campbell, daughter of Ezekiel Campbell of Mound City and they have one son—Loren who married Mary Helen Kenney whose father John Kenney was a Canadian and her mother a sister of John R. Mentzer; Kate married T. E. McMasters and lives at Pittsburg, Kansas; Donald served in the Twentieth Kansas and Eleventh United States Cavalry and was a soldier in the world war, and Oscar G. was in the Twentieth Kansas and was killed at Caloocan. This was and is a fine family, perpetuating the strong character and beautiful traits of the parents. Senator John Thorne of Johnson county is the son of George, a brother of Rufus, and a very fine character.

Phil Thorne went west with a young wife into the employ of the Union Pacific, working in various capacities, and later was auditor for the Oregon Short Line in their offices at Salt Lake City. For a time he was with William Pollman in the great North Pole gold mine owned by the Baring Brothers, the great London bankers, and during a visit to the mines by Alexander Baring and his wife Phil and Mrs. Thorne became intimately acquainted with them and Phil has a scarf pin given to him by Mrs. Baring as a souvenir of their association, and an invitation to visit them in their London home. It was in this mine that William Pollman got his big start towards his accomplished goal as a millionaire. Phil Thorne afterward was assistant manager in a big real estate loan office in Salt Lake, where their son Loren was born.

Ezekiel Francis Campbell was the son of Patton Campbell who came from Scotland to near Bloomington, Illinois, in

1840, and whose wife was Emily Stansbury, a native of Illinois. In 1868 Ezekiel F. married Lillie Virginia Bunn, daughter of Ezekiel Bunn, a pioneer of 1857 who took his family up to Baldwin in Douglas county while he was in the Union army. Zeke Campbell was too young to get into the service. Lillie Bunn his wife was the only survivor of five children. She was married to Ezekiel F. Campbell March 1, 1874. Their only child was Elvira Maud (the Elvira being from her maternal grandmother, Elvira Wright Bunn) and who married Phil Sheridan Thorne December 8, 1897. Mr. Campbell was a successful business man and left a valuable estate to his family.

Ezra P. Moon, the man who walked with Ed. R. Smith and his father from Westport Landing to Linn County in April, 1857, was a prosperous and highly respected citizen. He was born in the same county as the Smiths in the town of Ellery, Chautauqua county, New York, being a descendant of Ebenezer Moon who lived in Wales in the sixteenth century. On the steamboat "Star of the West" he by chance made the acquaintance of Ezra Hanchet Smith and his son Ed. R. and when landing met Rev. J. R. Marr, who influenced them to come to Linn County. He settled on a claim on Mine Creek and on November 25, 1860, married Martha Ann Robinson and to them were born four children, the survivors being Ezra E. and a daughter Mary who married Thomas Doughty.

A particularly atrocious crime was that committed by a party of men under the leadership of Sheriff Clem of Bates county, Missouri, the last week in October, 1861, when Richard Manning and William Upton were killed at the cabin home of Manning just south of the Marais des Cygnes river near the state line. People who knew these young men testified to the excellence of their characters, and subsequent inquiry proves that their lives were innocent sacrifices to the lust of the Bushwhackers who were not yet entitled to recognition even as "rebel" soldiers. Early in the morning, while it was yet dark, the Missourians rode up to the house and called to the inmates. Not suspecting anything wrong, Richard Manning stepped outside to answer their call, when he was riddled with bullets. Mrs. Manning had arisen and at the sound of the guns, she tried to close and bar the door, but they rudely thrust her aside and attacked William Upton, who was still in bed, and cut his throat with a butcher knife, almost severing the head. Mrs. Manning not only witnessed these awful murders but the assassins sneaked away in the dark and left her alone with her dead. She never recovered from the shock and died a few days later in premature childbirth. The crime caused great excitement among Linn County people. Morgan Fickes, then a leading citizen of Trading Post, sent out runners for volunteers to follow and punish the murderers. From Farlinville quite a number responded, including Byron M. Corbin and his three brothers, Sumner Botkin and Sidney Fairbanks. Murray Botkin and Owen Botkin of near Mound City were with them. About sixty men assembled at Trading Post. They elected Byron Corbin to be commander and started on the trail. They rode straight through Butler without resistance and on to Pleasant Gap, a village some ten miles beyond. There they met a Bushwhacker force of about a hundred. It was to be a battle, so the Kansans dismounted, each fourth man holding the horses, one of these being our crippled man, Sindey Fairbanks. The little army of forty-five men lined up in open order and started for their antagonists, when by a clever strategy the Bushwhackers fired the prairie grass and with the wind against them the Kansans were forced to their horses to get around the end of the fire line. It was a melee on horseback. Five horses of the Bushwhackers were running around riderless and the field was soon abandoned to the Kansans, who found only a woman to confront them. She said a number of Missourians were killed—seventeen she estimated. As the Kansans started westward toward home two Bushwhackers were riding parallel to them, apparently to head them off at a ford. Sidney Fairbanks claimed the right to first shot and saw the lead horseman double up in his saddle and turn to join his companion, who steadied him on his horse till they got over a hill out of sight.

This crime was described in an interview with Hiram Speaks written by Ed. R. Smith for the Linn County Clarion December 18, 1891, as follows: "William Upton and Richard Manning were two genial, honest young men, well known and honored among the free state settlers along the line who had taken claims and were trying to establish homes on the free soil of Kansas lying between the Marais des Cygnes river and Mine creek. Dick Manning was a royal good fellow and for so young a man, a prominent free state man. He was married and had a small log cabin fairly well 'chinked and daubed' on his claim and a few acres broken and fenced. 'Bill' Upton was younger than Manning and unmarried, making his home with the Mannings. In May or June of 1862, Ex-sheriff Clem of Bates county, Missouri, with a posse of some fifteen or twenty 'border ruffians' crossed the line in the night time and silently stole into the little scattered settlement in this county in the forks of the Marais des Cygnes river and Mine creek. About the break of day this gang of desperadoes rode up to the cabin of Manning and hailed the house in the usual manner of the times. Manning got up, hastily pulled on his trousers, took down his gun, unbarred his door and standing there in the open doorway, asked: 'Who's there' and 'What's up.' His reply was a sally from the rifles and shotguns of Clem's gang. Manning fell dead across his threshold. The brave wife of the murdered husband sprang out of the bed and tried to drag the dying man into the cabin and bar the door. Manning's murderers were too quick for her, for they made a rush for the cabin before the door could be closed and resistence was useless. The poor woman was rudely thrown back into her bed. In another bed in the corner opposite lay doomed Upton. Knowing resistence to be useless, Upton, instead of getting up flattened himself out in his bed, hoping that in the darkness and confusion he might escape the fate of his friend. It was not to be. The bed was searched, the man was found and riddled with bullets where he lay. These human wolves of the border then piled the two corpses on the floor, robbed the humble cabin of such bed clothes as were not soaked in human blood, took the arms of their victims and left the poor widow alone with her dead. There by the side of her murdered young husband, when the morning came, the neighbors found her senselss, prone across the breast she could not warm to life again. Poor woman! She died soon after in premature childbirth.

"Clem mounted his command and as the morning light broke over the land, robbed the unprepared and defenseless settlers as he came to them. Among others, he took from 'Uncle Tommy' Speaks, his horses and such articles from the house as they fancied. Next they visited Hiram Speaks, who lay sick in bed. They gathered about him and drawing their pistols swore they would kill him anyway, but better council prevailed. After robbing his house of bed clothes, knives, forks and spoons, they took four head of good horses and left him. By this time the news had spread through the settlement that Sheriff Clem and his gang was over the line murdering the settlers. Clem was hurrying the horsemen, riding about and preparing for his flight. But he had waited too long. Two brave boys, Joe Speaks and John W. Speaks, one a son of 'Uncle Tommy' the other his nephew, hearing of the murder of Manning and Upton, mounted their ponies and sped away to the 'Ruse ford' on Mine creek. Crossing over to the Missouri side of the stream, they took up their position to await the coming of Clem. They had not long to wait for soon came the gang riding helter skelter into the stream, where they stopped to water their horses. As little as did their victims a few hours before, so did they as little expect that death was so near them, for they no sooner got huddled into the stream than the two Speaks opened fire on them with double-barreled shotguns loaded with buckshot. At least four of them went down to death under that deadly fire. Scarcely realizing from which side of the stream this attack came, they rushed madly out for the Missouri shore, and blindly returned the fire. Another victim was there added to their list of murders, for here Joe Speaks received a wound from which he died on the spot. Thorougly frightened Clem

gathered his dead and wounded into a wagon and furiously
fled away into Missouri."

The story of Winnie Campbell and her husband Lewis
Campbell persisted for many years as a thriller among stories
of negro adventure. Winnie was a capable, intelligent woman
of vigorous physique who at thirty years of age found herself
a "free woman" down in the Red River country of southern
Arkansas, down where the most inhuman of slave masters
practiced their fiendishness. It was the land where Simon
Legree and his breed lived—whom literature has accepted
as monsters unrivalled for brutality. A kindly old couple
approaching their death gave to faithful Winnie all the rights
they could confer in the words "free woman". Winnie had
been for more than ten years the wife of a slave man, "Lewis",
who was owned on a plantation miles away. They had a
boy born to them who was ten years old when the mother
received her freedom and as usual the boy took his station in
life from his mother and was also "free." But in a slave country
free negroes were not desired nor were they long tolerated.
Their presence made the black people wish for escape from
slavery. So stringent laws were enacted forbidding the
presence of "freed" negroes in the country unless they had
some representative citizen—of course a slave owner—to act
as sponsor for them, a situation possibly worse than slavery
itself, as the sponsor had no property rights of his own to
protect. Failure to comply with this law meant that Winnie
and her boy, Elias, would be put on the block and sold back
into slavery. Deep in the religion of the black people was a
belief in the "promised land" and the forbidden word "Kansas"
was magic to them. They heard their boastful masters tell
of the great open spaces where they were to set up new
plantations. But even in that dark, benighted country, there
were sources of information from which the ignorant slaves
derived understanding and comfort—a sort of freemasonry
that guarded precious secret knowledge of what was doing in
the world of white people. So in mysterious midnight whisperings Winnie Campbell heard of a rough trail up north, past
Fort Smith, on to Fort Scott, to an open prairie country
where white people believed in free negroes and accepted and
protected them. She talked it out with Lewis. She and the
little boy Elias would go first—five hundred miles through a
hilly country with practically no people, either white or black.
There were many Indians to be encountered, days without
food, hiding from chance travelers for fear of apprehension,
sleeping wherever darkness found them—five hundred miles
entirely on faith! Emerging from the rough hills, she and her
little boy came to a grassy country with the smile of sunlight
upon it. There were settlements where she met her own black
people—slaves who must not harbor "refugees". But the

freemasonry of slavery whispered to her to go west into Kansas, and leading the little boy by the hand she appeared at the door of Simon McGrew, who had just established a home five miles southwest of where Mound City now stands. When her story was heard, Winnie and her boy were domiciled in the smoke house and given employment.

In about a year Lewis her husband came up that long, dreary distance. He traveled as a runaway slave, always in fear of apprehension. Tortured by hunger and the fear and uncertainty of his fate he stumbled through the rough forest, afraid to be seen on such roads as were then in use. As he emerged into a country peopled with whites and black slaves, instinct told him that Kansas lay west of them, and the slaves gave him what they could without detection. And so on a bright day—shall we call it Providence or that influence called "instinct"?—he rapped at the door of a small house and as it opened there was disclosed to him his wife Winnie and boy Elias. They lived several months in their happy reunion till late one night the McGrew home was surrounded by a mob and the United States Marshal from Fort Scott (the Federal Court at that place worked hand in hand with the proslavers) announced that he was looking for a runaway slave named Lewis Campbell, who was dragged out and placed astride a bareback horse, his feet being tied beneath. There was much rough talk and the suggestion was made that they "go to Smith's" (meaning the home of Ed. R. Smith, where a young negro refugee named Jim Titsworth was given a home). Old Simon McGrew heard this and ran about the place like a crazy man till chance offered when he took a bee-line for the Smith home two miles away, where he finally arrived puffing badly but shouting "Up! Up! Up!" "Up! Up! Up!"— which had much significance to a member of Montgomery's Jayhawkers. Hurriedly explaining, he got a good horse and started due east about three miles to Mound City. In the excitement at the McGrew place the boy Elias slipped away and got to the home of Samuel McGrew a half-mile east who quickly saddled a horse and with a Sharp's rifle started for Mound City. At a point half-way to town he heard a horse running furiously and where the two roads merged into one he could in the starlit night see a rider lying low on his horse and urging it to greater speed. Taking deliberate aim he called, "Stop or I shoot thee!" and as there was no stop he blazed away. Three times he called out and fired at the fleeing figure who drew away from him toward the town. A few minutes later, an improvised cannon was fired three times—a signal for all the men within hearing to assemble—and soon they were arriving from every direction. They started for the Simon McGrew place and arriving there learned the "posse" had shown signs of nervousness and hastened off toward Missouri by way of Fort Scott. The Linn County men followed them across the line but could not catch up to release Lewis Campbell, who was taken back south and served his master all through the Civil War, when he came back to his wife and child at Mound City. Elwood Smith made them a present of forty acres of land and they were till the end of their days the object of kindly solicitude to their white neighbors. As a solemn old Quaker, Sam McGrew was chagrined to learn he had three times tried to put a Sharp's rifle bullet through his brother Simon.

Another noted ex-slave is Jane Seabury who was born in 1835 on the farm of Horace Herndon in Platt county, Missouri, who sold her for $700. Soon Simeon Scruggs, son-in-law of Herndon, bought her back into the old family, and she proudly relates that he refused $1500 offered for her. Scruggs took her when he moved to Leavenworth county, Kansas, in 1858, and she ran away in the night, reaching Lawrence just as the Underground Railway was starting two companies for Canada, one being conducted by Old John Brown with thirteen black people and the other by a man named Dewey, with whom Jane Seabury was to have gone but missed connection somehow and she was taken by a man named Stewart to Mound City where Dr. Charles R. Jennison met the party on the street and directed that Jane Seabury, then about twenty-three years old, be taken to his home, where she for several years had a home and protection, and now (1926) at the age of ninety-one and entirely blind she praises the name of Colonel Jennison and his family. She proudly asserts that she was regularly married at Mound City to Thomas Marrs and that it is so recorded in the county books. Marrs had been a slave at Fayetteville, Arkansas, who saved from his wages at extra work enough to buy the freedom of his mother and himself. The party under Dewey with whom Jane was to have gone was captured and taken to Weston, Missouri, where a cannon was fired and their captor shouted, "Come and get your niggers!"

Jim Titsworth who lived at the Ed. R. Smith home was at Lawrence during one of the raids and was killed by a Bush-whacker.

George Fletcher Hamlin conferred considerable distinction on Linn County when as our member of the state senate he introduced the amendment to the State Constitution in 1878 which brought about the abolishment of the liquor traffic. This evil was so firmly fixed that it required great courage to stand up in the open and fight for its extinction. Every town in the county except Mound City had from four to five saloons which put up a bold fight against any interference. It is now recognized that every crime of those days was the result of drunken carousals many of which ended in murder. Mr. Hamlin fought it out and was a winner, the amendment being adopted, giving Kansas great acclaim throughout the nation. While it did not for years suppress the liquor traffic it gradually grew in strength and popularity until now we have a new generation which never saw a saloon. Mr. Hamlin was a leader in all local affairs and was the mainstay of the Methodist church, being of a deeply religious nature. He was one of the organizers of the La Cygne Exchange Bank and served for years as its president. For years he conducted a grocery store, had a lumber yard, handled grain and carried on extensive farming enterprises. Mr. Hamlin came of distinguished ancestry and was a cousin to Hannibal Hamlin who was vice-president of the United States with Abraham Lincoln and named his eldest son after that distinguished statesman. George Fletcher Hamlin, our distinguished citizen, was born at Hillsborough, Hillsborough county, New Hampshire, June 3, 1823. He was of English descent on both sides, tracing his father's family back to his grandfather and his three brothers who were named Europe, Asia, Africa and America. Vice-President Hannibal Hamlin was the son of Africa, and Joash Hamlin, the father of our George Fletcher, was the son of Europe, who was a soldier in the revolution and afterward a prosperous New England farmer. The mother of George Fletcher was Lefy Murdough Hamlin, who produced twelve children. He was married twice, his first wife being Julia A. Brown, to whom he was married April 19, 1846, in Ross county, Ohio. She bore four children, Charles J., a merchant of Philadelphia; Hannibal F., who lived in La Cygne and married Miss Lizzie Hughes; Mary B. and Scott, all of whom were well known throughout the county. By a second marriage to Miss Elizabeth Williams in Fairfield county, Ohio, March 25, 1861 there were two daughters, Minnie E., who is now Mrs. Thad Rex, and Lefy E., who died in 1922 as the widow of William A. Chick.

James P. Way was born at Winchester, Indiana, September 8, 1826. The Way family were Friends from the earliest period of which history or tradition gives any account. The family settled in America before the Revolutionary War and there is tradition that General Nathaniel Greene of Revolutionary. as well as Quaker fame was related to the Way family. The parents of James P. were Matthew Way and Hannah Martin. There were five sons and three daughters, the subject of this sketch being the oldest. Four of these sons were in the Union army. Miss Amanda Way, one of the daughters, was distinguished for her deeds of philanthropy and especially for her noble work as a lecturer in the cause of temperance. Armsby Diggs Way, a brother, lived at La Cygne and married Sylvia Richardson, sister to Mrs. Frank H. Davis; they had a daughter now Mrs. C. E. Conley at Paola. James P. Way came to Kansas in June, 1861, locating in Linn County. He held various local and school offices. In 1863 he was elected county clerk in Linn County and held that office one term. In 1866 he was elected a representative in the state legis- lature from Linn County. In 1871 he was elected county treasurer and in 1875 he was again elected to the same posi- tion. He was a member of the Masonic fraternity, of the Odd Fellows and the Good Templars. He was married at Win- chester, Indiana, October 3, 1849, to Miss Thursey A. Hiatt. She was a member of the Friends and was well educated. They had four children. The survivors are Mary Bonita, who was a graduate in music under Professor Bartlett of Lawrence and was pianist of the Handel and Haydn Society of Lawrence. Arthur Perley graduated from Kansas University.

Martin Funk was the head of a family of good citizens of La Cygne. He was born in 1832 near Berlin, Germany. After coming to America he was married in Cleveland, Ohio, to Elizabeth King, who was a native of Switzerland. In 1858 they located in Kansas City and owned 40 acres where the Live Stock Exchange now is and after two years sold it and moved out to Shawneetown, and in 1869 came to La Cygne, where he was for forty-seven years a part of community life. Martin was the life of the village band and was an artist with the tuba horn. Their children were Henry, now deceased; Martin, who married Little Shrake and had one boy, Clifton; Elizabeth, who married William Repp and had two children; Charles, who married Mamie McKinney at Brookfield, Mis- souri; Edward, now living at Topeka. Martin, the father, served in the Union army.

The Eli Babb family originated in Maryland where the first of this name lived and afterwards moved to Ohio, where his son, Joseph Waddell Babb, was born in 1817 at the place where Phil Sheridan got his appointment to West Point. In 1821 the family went to Delaware county, Indiana, where Joseph Waddell Babb grew to manhood and was married to Mary Ann Weeks, who had come there from Orange county, New York. They brought their family to Potosi township, arriv- ing March 11, 1858, and located a mile and a half northeast of where Pleasanton now is. Their children were Susan, who had preceded them here in 1857 as Mrs. Josiah Cummings, who died some years ago in California; Mary Alice who married Henry Gibbons from Nova Scotia; Eli Scotten, born in Madison county Indiana, who married Mrs. Eva Probasco; Edgar Sisson now in Spokane, Washington; and Emma Ernestine. Another Eli Babb, twin brother of Joseph Waddell and uncle to our Eli Scotten, incurred the active enmity of the Missouri Bush- whackers who placed a good price on his head and was frequently shot at. Once when he and King Powell were setting a steam boiler for a saw mill at the Carmack ford across Big Sugar creek they were attacked by Hamelton and two companions. A Sharp's rifle bullet was put through Hamelton's blanket roll and he dropped it and fled, leaving the blanket as a trophy which Babb preserved many years. Our Eli Scotten Babb and his wife have taken part in all public and social affairs.

One of the noted and honored characters of the years immediately following the Civil War was Judge David Linton who bought in 1868 a farm of six hundred twenty-eight acres in the vicinity of Farlinville and made it one of the show places of the county. He had a fine herd of Durham thoroughbred cattle and Saxony sheep and made a success of scientific farming. He was a very positive character with ample courage to back up his convictions. He served a term as probate judge and then the "crime of '73" came along and he went off on this blind lead and never got back. Very few now know what that political upheaval was. Following the Civil War the country was on a paper currency system of money. There were all kinds of inflations of values just as we have had following the World War. But the paper money had no guarantee back of it, yet believing the "fiat" of the government could make money out of "chips, whetstones or paper" a great organization called the Greenback party was built up and ran Horace Greeley for president against Grant. Old John Sherman was secretary of the treasury and bluntly said "the way to resume is to resume" and with that put the country back on a gold basis of values. It was a tremendous incident in national history and the wisdom of the Grant administration was established in history. But David Linton brought up a fine family of boys and girls who have won success from the prairies of old Paris township. Always public spirited, he joined with Bob Mitchell and Alonzo Farlin and James Boston and Bill Sutton in putting in a good bridge over Sugar creek near where the town of Farlinville grew up and was named after Alonzo Farlin who started a store there. Ill health soon took Mr. Linton out of active life, his later years being spent as an invalid in Pleasanton where he died in 1899.

The Linton family had an interesting origin. John Linton came to America with William Penn on his second trip, located in Philadelphia and was an influential member of the Society of Friends. Six generations down from then our David was born in Ohio on January 30, 1815. In 1839 he graduated from Miami University and it will interest many of our college boys and girls to know he was one of the founders of the fraternity Beta Theta Pi. He practiced law in Wilmington, Ohio, and was a member of the Ohio state senate for two terms. On

July 27, 1841, he married Ann, daughter of Reverend Thomas
Thomas and wife Elizabeth Robinson Thomas whose parents
came from London, England, to Cincinnati where Ann was
born in 1820. The children of David and Ann have reflected
great honor upon their parents by their success in educational
lines. They were Laura who married Captain Eli C. Lowe
and took an active part in local politics and published the
Mound City Torch of Liberty; Elizabeth married Captain
Myron M. Corbin and their children have been particularly
honored as told elsewhere; Horace married Sarah Brockman
of Illinois; Clara married Captain Robert E. Brewster of Pleasanton; Clarence married Eva Jane Griffith of Linn County;
Emma married John B. Hill of Ohio; and Mary married Robert
Fisher of Kansas City and after his death David Hunter of
St. Louis.

The surviving children of Myron and Lizzie Corbin are
Dr. Alberta Linton Corbin of Kansas University where they
not only conferred the degree of Doctor of Philosophy upon
her and made her a member of the faculty but built a magnificent dormitory for girls costing $500,000 that has the name
of Corbin Hall in her honor. The boy Arthur Linton Corbin
is now the senior member of the faculty of the law school of
Yale University and was appointed by President Angell as
the first Sterling Research Professor in Law created by the
will of John W. Sterling, a prominent New York lawyer.
Arthur is relieved of all teaching that he may devote his time
to investigation and writing. He is given a separate office
with a working staff.

Captain Robert E. Brewster who married Clara Linton is
well remembered as the miller in charge of the Pleasanton
Roller Mills. He was a lineal descendant of Elder Brewster
of the Mayflower party. Among his collateral relatives were
President Zachary Taylor and General Winfield Scott. They
had one child, Helen Barten, who took quite a part in the
campaign to secure the ballot for women, both in Kansas and
in New York. She became the wife of Professor F. W. Owens,
now head of the mathematics department of Pennsylvania
State College at the town of that name.

Emma received the degree of M. D. and married a doctor;
they have had their home at Oswego. Their daughter Helen
is the wife of Professor C. F. Craig of Cornell University. This
completes a remarkable record of one family starting from
a farm in Paris township.

Very prominent in the business life of the county was Henry
Albert Strong who organized the H. A. Strong Mercantile
Company at Mound City and developed it into a big business.
His father Lyman Strong and mother Hannah Montague were
Massachusetts people, whose first American ancestor arrived
at Northhampton in 1636. Lyman moved to Stevenson county,

Illinois, where Henry Albert Strong was born in 1844. An uncle had urged them to "come out on the prairies where you don't have to clear the land", so Hannah the wife and mother was left at Rutland, Vermont, till he was established in Illinois, when she joined him there, but in September 1858 they came on to Kansas Territory and Lyman was very active in the work of guarding against the Bushwhacker raids. In 1860 they bought a claim with a house and a good crop of potatoes about four miles north of Mound City. O. P. Watson was their nearest neighbor, who later was a merchant in Mound City, and Pleasant Chitwood, a pettifogging proslaver lawyer lived near. When a school was started Henry Strong was employed as teacher and among his pupils was Joel Chitwood and his mother. This woman had not had opportunity for an education in her younger days but side by side with her little boy she studied and became a well educated and useful member of society. When Mansfield was given a postoffice Lyman Strong was made postmaster and the son Henry deputy. The stage ran from St. Joseph to Fort Scott, with four horses frequently changed. At 11 p. m. the stage from the north arrived and the bag had to be opened and the mail worked and at 2 a. m. the stage going north arrived and the mail had to be opened and worked again so that Henry had a real job as deputy postmaster. In 1862 at seventeen years of age Henry enlisted in Company K Twelfth Kansas Cavalry under Captain Sears from Mound City. Captain Sears was promoted to be major of a colored regiment and was succeeded by Lieutenant Miserez from Germany. Captain A. W. Burton's company was in this regiment but as they had been captured by Quantrill and paroled they could not be used in the regular service so they were sent out to Fort Larned to control the Indians as told in the Isaac Marrs story. After the war Henry Albert Strong and Mary Madden were married. They had a daughter Loie who married Ralph Waldo Moody, and their children are Henry Strong Moody and Kathleen M. who married Dr. Charles Jennings Carey.

Silas Smith and his good wife Mary (Vermillion) Smith came from Marion county, Illinois, in 1866, bringing three small children, Charlie, Clara and Minnie, and bought a settler's claim to one hundred and sixty acres seven miles southwest of La Cygne in Scott township, where for thirty years the family maintained one of the homes noted for hospitality. Seven other children were born here, two dying in infancy, and George who married Hettie Colliver and had three children. George died in 1912. All the other children survive, being Charles who married in Colorado and now lives in Denver, Clara who married George Kuhn and lives in Colorado Springs, Minnie who married Elias Grandon whom she survives and now lives in La Cygne, Walter who married

Katie Thomas and lives in Pueblo, Colorado, Cora who married Frank Preston and lives at Pratt, James Frank who married Garrah Marsh and lives in Kansas City, and Jessie who married Dr. H. P. Dooley and lives at Akron, Colorado. Their Scott township home was in the Ewing or Prairie Home district, their neighbors being the Leasures, Creagers, Prestons, Carothers, Merrills, Ewings, McCartys, Coxes, all influential pioneer families. Silas the head of the household added to his holdings till he had a whole section of highly improved land and carried on farming, stock raising and feeding on a large scale. He was just naturally a "justice of the peace" and held that office about all the years he lived there. He was of a deeply religious nature and hundreds of young couples considered it an honor to have "Squire Smith" perform their marriage ceremonies. In 1896 Silas found most of his children married and scattered so he sold the farm and with his wife and Jessie made their home in Colorado Springs. James Frank Smith stayed in Linn County and became the owner and editor of the Pleasanton Observer and was honored by President Roosevelt with appointment to be postmaster of that town. In 1900 he was married to Garrah Marsh, daughter of Edward L. Marsh of Mound City, three children coming to them, all schooled at Kansas University, Marsh the son now in business at Chicago, Ruth who married Kenneth Goodell and lives in Chicago, and Rebecca who is at home with her parents. J. Frank Smith is a spirited, vigorous man who has exerted a tremendous influence in his time. Leaving Pleasanton he was for a time in charge of the Kansas good roads association with an office at Topeka till his conspicuous ability brought him an invitation from the Chamber of Commerce at Kansas City to take charge of the Missouri campaign which resulted in the vote of the people to issue sixty millions in bonds to build permanent roads and "take Missouri out of the mud." This was one of the really great things of recent years. Missouri, a naturally backward state, became a conspicuous leader in the good roads movement and in the expenditure of one hundred and twenty millions of money placing Missouri at the lead in highways there was never a hint of dissatisfaction and a great pride in the fact there was never a word of scandal in the handling of this huge sum of money by an organization of which Theodore Gary was the head. Mr. Smith made a study of the school system and of dairying, advocating the consolidation of school districts by which children were given larger and better housing and more competent instruction and more accessible schools because of the improved roads, and converted many farmers to the practice of dairying as a source of cash money on the farm every month. To prove his case Mr. Smith took a trainload of farmers and bankers to Wisconsin and on a week's trip demonstrated that land with much less fertility there was earning twice as much as were lands in Missouri. His book on the facts of that trip is now valued as a text book.

Sylvester Ward, who brought his family here in June, 1857, had a strenuous career. His father died in North Carolina where he was born May 15, 1820, and Sylvester became a "bound boy" to James Brown who moved to Gibson county, Indiana, in 1825. Thus at the age of five years Sylvester was separated from his mother Betty Ward and sister Letitia whom he left in North Carolina. He grew to manhood in Gibson county and in August, 1841, was married into a very good family, his bride being Martha Crowder, daughter of Nehemiah and Artelia (Paskel) Crowder from Henry county, Tennessee. To them was born several children, among them William Harrison Ward, who first saw daylight on December 6, 1842. When they came here in 1857 they made their home on a "claim" near Brooklin and saw all the "border warfare" following that date. Paris and Brooklin and Trading Post were the only towns then in existence. Joseph H. Barlow[1] and Pleasant Chitwood practiced law at Paris. Dr. John H. Umphrey and Dr. Stewart attended all the sick. Barlow owned several slaves and Robert Pamplin who lived a mile west of where Boicourt now stands owned a "wench" as they then called slave women. James Fox who started the town of Paris brought slaves with him in 1855. The "climate" became too hot for Fox and he went back to the Bushwhacker camps in Missouri in 1858. John Hood succeeded to the postmastership and also became a successful merchant, later being in the Hood and Kincaid bank and store at Mound City.

A young man named Wilburn Weaver started a store at Brooklin. Among the neighbors was McDonald Osborn who practiced medicine during the week and preached the Gospel on Sunday. John Weddle was another settler. Ignatius Turman who lived in the neighborhood had two sons, one of whom, William, commanded a band of guerillas over in Missouri, and David the other son died a Union man in Texas during the Civil War. Rev. William Long, another settler, had three sons, Enos E., John and James, in the Union Army, and another son Bloom in the rebel army. Rev. Long was a North Carolinian by birth and was suspected of harboring proslavery spies and but for the active protection of David Sibbett, then postmaster of Brooklin, Rev. Long would have been hanged by the same party who hanged Sam Scott. Another man rather liked as a neighbor was Thomas Smith, son-in-law to Ignatius Turman, was driven out and he settled several miles west of Butler, Missouri. A party of Kansas men followed him with the intention of hanging him but

1. Judge Barlow had two sons—Robert and William—who returned to Kentucky and enlisted in the Confederate army. Robert was killed in battle and William became insane from wounds.

on entering his house they found him dying from sickness. Smith left two sons, Stephen and Ignatius. Some time later raiders from Kansas attacked the camp of Capt. William Turman on an island in the Marais des Cygnes a few miles east of Trading Post and Stephen Smith, who was visiting his uncle, was taken prisoner. He was taken to Trading Post, where he was tried by court martial, sentenced to death and executed by shooting in the fall of 1863. Many of his former neighbors about Brooklin were saddened by Stephen's fate, thinking he was the victim of evil associations.

On one occasion after a raiding party had been into Missouri a young man named Peter McNew received a yoke of oxen as his share of the spoils which seemed to create dissatisfaction. "A few days later", says Mr. Ward, "my mother saw Peter going west past our place afoot. Not long after, she noticed two men following Peter on horseback, and later saw all three going back eastward. That was the last ever seen of Peter McNew alive." Some three years later W. B. Carager was hunting in the bottoms near the state line when his dog became excited at a big hollow tree, the cavity in which was piled with chunks of wood. Closer examination disclosed the skeleton of a man and by the cloth of the trousers was identified as that of McNew.

John Rowan Bailey met with a tragic fate as the result of his proslavery sympathies. He lived on a claim adjoining the Ward home near Brooklin. His young wife was a most estimable woman and the baby that came to them seemed to assure a happy future. In the heat of the partisan strife just preceding the Civil War they moved back to Missouri. In the winter of 1862-3, the First Iowa Cavalry was stationed at Johnstown on the eastern side of Bates county. It seems that Bailey had become almost blind and partially demented. He was caught between the two armies and charged with stealing horses. One of the Iowa soldiers had married the daughter of a Mrs. Wiggins. A slave named Adam Cooper, but commonly called Ben Dobbins after his former owner, was working for the Wiggins home. One night the family had retired and as Ben sat by the fireplace a knock at the door came, and a man all bloody was seen when the door was opened. He insisted on coming in, saying he had been shot for stealing horses of which he was innocent, and that he was mortally wounded and wanted to be allowed to lie before the fire and die. A son-in-law in the bedroom heard the talk and slipped out and reported and a short time later a squad of soldiers came and took him away. Next day the old black man saw a fresh grave between there and the camp and felt sure it was the last resting place of "Row" Bailey.

In the spring of 1860 Cyrus Hays a justice of the peace and George W. Huff, a young man of the neighborhood, became involved in a dispute and they agreed to meet next forenoon at a definite time and place and settle with their guns. When Huff arrived at the spot he found Hays already there behind a rail fence with a shotgun, with which he wounded Huff severely. Huff emptied his revolver shooting at Hays but without effect and so the battle ended. A young woman named Mary Griffin, who happened to be passing, witnessed the fight. Huff recovered from his wounds and served during the war in Company E, Sixth Kansas Cavalry. He was a fearless man and for his participation in the running down of Scott Holderman, who was wanted on a murder charge, he incurred the enmity of a brother, Guilford Holderman, who was shot from ambush and killed not long afterward. It was proven that Huff was not in the party which killed young Holderman.

George Washington Moore who lived three miles southwest of where now is La Cygne, was of a remarkable family. He was named after George Moore, an uncle who was a soldier under General Andrew Jackson at the battle of New Orleans. George W.'s father was James who was born in Wilson county, Tennessee, February 1, 1815, and had twelve children and all arrived at maturity and had families of their own before a death occurred. George W. was born in Lawrence county, Illinois, April 21, 1842, to which place his father James had come from Tennessee with his wife and children, carrying all of his earthly possessions in an ox cart. George W. became an apprentice to Tarleton Baren and married Baren's daughter Melana who gave birth to eight children, as follows: Carrol died in infancy; George Marion; Ezra Baren died in Washington; Squire Dillon now living at Prescott; Cornelius Ades died in infancy; Rowena Alvira married Frank Allen, nephew of Governor Allen of Ohio—she died in Spokane; and James Knox, now in Atlantic City, New Jersey, who married Isabel Labadie, daughter of Peter Labadie, who married a Miami Indian woman. In 1850 George W. made a trip to California returning by way of Panama. In 1854 to Clay county, Illinois, and in 1856 moved to Linn County and on August 7 camped where La Cygne now is, crossed the river at Graham's Ford and found his claim three miles further on.

George Marion Moore was married February 13, 1862, to Emma DeVilliers at his father's house. Her father was recently from England. They had eight children: Clara who married Cameron L. Hafley; Charles W. died in infancy; Mary Melana now at Slater, Missouri; George H. now in Kansas City; Maude who married John Todd; James Frederick lives in Rosedale; and John Stanley a druggist in Wichita. George

Marion served as trustee of Lincoln township, as register of deeds in 1873, was postmaster at Pleasanton five and a half years, and was probate judge two terms.

Robert Epps and his wife Elizabeth Bales moved from Tennessee to Indiana, where Caleb Talbert Epps was born February 16, 1852. The family came to Linn County in 1858 and located four miles southeast of where Pleasanton now is, joining John Hau and Carter Hau who had preceded them. John M. Seright married Rosetta Epps. When Price's stragglers were passing through they had put their movable baggage in a rock quarry and they sought to evade questions but old Grandma Kennon was too truthful and told them where her trunk was and they ransacked it and everything else.

John C. Quinn was born September 1, 1808, in Preble county, Ohio. In 1838 when he was thirty years of age he married Louisa D. Everding and they made their home in what is now Scott county, Iowa. His wife died in 1860 in Ashtabula county, Ohio, leaving him with nine children to care for. A comfortable fortune he had accumulated was swept away. He came to Kansas and enlisted in Company M of the Fifteenth Kansas Cavalry, and upon his discharge came to Linn County and married Mrs. Amanda Lamb, who bore him four children. In 1865 he was a member of the legislature from this county, in 1867 was a county commissioner with D. A. Crocker and J. H. Jones. In 1869 Daniel Underhill resigned as probate judge and Mr. Quinn was appointed by the governor to the vacancy, and was reelected in 1870. In 1873 he removed to California to join his children there and passed away November 9, 1887.

Robert Cornelius Garratt was a Potosi township settler who got nearly all the thrills passed around in border days. He was a traveled and experienced man, having gone to California in 1850, where he mined till 1858 when he came here joining his brother John W. who had come direct from the old home at Garrattsville, Otsego county, New York, where Robert was born September 7, 1821. He went back to his boyhood home in 1860 and married Miss Catherine Hawk. They were driven from their home in 1862 and went to Mound City where he was associated in business with O. P. Watson. He died at the age of seventy-six years in 1898.

The town of La Cygne was organized in 1869 when thirty-five people arrived at the townsite from Madison, Wisconsin. They were a notable company. The leaders were Dr. A. H. Davis and B. S. Heath. Dr. Davis bought six hundred acres and soon from his old home in Wisconsin came Lucius Cor

nelius Cary and wife and two boys Harry and Fred; John
Phelps Kenea and wife and her mother, Mrs. Gilson; Dr. Rudd
and wife; A. E. Foot and wife and son Rev. J. I. Foot; J. J.
Starks who became a merchant and had a wife and two sons
Albert and Johnnie; C. W. Olney and wife and son Charles;
Mr. Copp and wife; Franklin Richardson and wife and daughter Sylvia; Franklin H. Davis and wife. This strong company
was joined by Major B. S. Henning, then superintendent of
the old "Gulf" railroad, and Wallace Pratt of Kansas City
and Col. A. G. McKenzie who had been prominent as
an Indian agent with office at Paola. The La Cygne Journal
was started in 1870 by Kenea and Cary and A. E. Foot became the first mayor. It was then only five years after the
close of the Civil War and the country was settling up as
fast as the newcomers could be taken care of. They had
previously been coming in by wagons but now the railroad
put them down right at the spot and a string of box-cars
would hardly be "set" on the siding till a team and a cow
would be led out, the parts of a wagon put together and loaded
with household goods and with mother and children on top
would drive off to their new home. It was a wonderful scene
of activity to everyone and seemed to presage the building
of a metropolis at this beautiful place. The Methodists built
up a strong church organization, and the Presbyterians
followed. The Baptists came but didn't stay long. The
Christians or Campbellites as they called them then, made
a brave showing. The Catholics had a church on east Market
street, but soon there were only three or four families left
and their church was abandoned. It was the first time I
had ever seen a Catholic and I have sadly felt the loss of two
or three good boy friends. La Cygne got the cream of the
Trading Post population, Henry Dellinger coming up with his
harness shop and John Sheridan Lane came up to run the
new flour mill, and the Fickes boys ran the saw-mill. Enterprise and high resolve carried everybody along buoyantly. The
virgin soil gave wonderful crops and grain was sold and
shipped at first but later stock raising and feeding brought
in what was then "big money". Though the town never got
much more than a thousand people it was a lively place when
the entire farm population came in on Saturday to mingle
together in a social way and get supplies for another week.
They were all a superior people of culture and refinement.
There were men who could get up a good quartette to sing
the real masterpieces of music or organize a good chorus.
There were at least twenty men in the town who could hold
the enthusiastic attention of the entire population with an
address on Shakespeare, or Burns, or Washington, or Napoleon,
or any subject suggested. The town had a band and orchestra
that brought home from the state fair everything offered in
the way of honors. A county fair was organized and liberally

patronized.   There was really an exalted spirit among the
people.

The more elaborate social events were formal dancing parties
or "grand balls" as they were termed on the invitations.
Guests from Paola or from Barnard and Pleasanton and
Prescott could come and get home on the train, but those
from Mound City or Trading Post, or from the numerous
country homes, necessarily were entertained by friends.   And
these events were rather large affairs with a notable company.
I recall one at La Cygne which assembled within its guest
list representatives of many noted families of Europe and
America in the past seven hundred years.   It was following
closely after the Civil War and the gallant men still carried
themselves with military precision that gave them a distinguished air on the dancing floor.   They still had the courtliness of the early days and it was a common thing for a
man to profoundly bow to a young lady with his right hand
flat on his left breast as he very formally asked her for "the
honor of the next dance."   I recall many of these characters.
One was a graduate of West Point who had lived in the White
House when his grandfather was President.   He was a Cavalier
by the blood line and remembered that his ancestor had served
on the jury of Charles I and had signed the death warrant
of that tyrant, and that another had been president of the
house of burgesses in Old Virginia and had signed the Declaration of Independence, and another who had a glorious record
in the military service had become President of the United
States, and our hero modestly remembered that as a lieutenant
he had ridden side by side with Lieut. U. S. Grant at the
battle of Chapultepec and as a conqueror into Mexico City.
There was another there who had come straight down from
Stephen Hopkins, the old Quaker who was chief justice of
Rhode Island and a signer of the Declaration of Independence.
There was still another whose ancestor served the Continental
Congress as its secretary during its entire existence and signed
the Declaration of Independence as "Charles Thompson, secretary."   There were families represented who came through
with Daniel Boone into Kentucky on the first adventurous
trip into that country with the Lincolns and the Hanks, and
who were blood relatives of the Emancipator.   There was a
first cousin of Old John Brown who was also a nephew of
Bronson D. Alcott and hence a first cousin of Louisa M. Alcott
who wrote "Little Men" and "Little Women."   There was the
staid old "singing master" who had sat as a pupil beside Abe
Lincoln when his father was Abe's "first and only teacher."
There were young men whose ancestors had been gentlemen
in the house of the first Charles back in 1649.   There was
a tall slim man, beloved by the entire community, who carried
the same blood that animated John Marshall, our first chief

justice, and whose own grandfather had helped to build Fort
Sumter, and whose maternal blood line went back to John
Randolph of Roanoke.   There was the man who invented
the "knot" that made possible the harvester as a labor-saving
machine.   There were lineal descendants of the parents of
William Penn when they were a part of the royal household
in London and whose ancestors came to America on the good
ship Welcome.   There were those whose ancestors had landed
at Plymouth Rock only a few years after the Mayflower.
There was a soldier whose father had furnished the commander-in-chief with information that saved one great battle to
the Union.   There was a very tall young man with almost golden
blonde hair and full beard reaching almost to his waist who was
a cousin to and had the same name as the vice president who
served with Lincoln.   There was one man intimately associated
with old John Brown and who had been a member of the
expedition which purposed to liberate him from Charlestown.
There were at least three in this company who in later life
became millionaires and of great influence in the commercial
world.   There were a young man and his sister who were
lineal descendants of the family of both Meriwether Lewis and
of George Rogers Clark.   There was the first cousin of Alice
and Phoebe Cary and of Edward Eggleston who were then
at the height of their literary fame.   There was a boy who
a few years later was an employee of the White House, and
another who was later managing editor of the Chicago Tribune
and later of the New York Times.   There were many pretty
women in the costumes of that time which were quaint and
so different from the later years.   There was actually there
then a very young girl who was talking about her little boy
friend Billie Bryan, back in Mason, Illinois.   And the little
girl baby who was later to achieve fame as the inventor of
the "B. V. D." garments for men was represented at this
party by her parents.   And there was the young lady who
was the first woman to be admitted to the practice of law
in the state courts of Pennsylvania.   Three gallant youths who
subsequently served in Congress from Kansas constituencies
were "cutting pigeon wings" in the solo part of the balance
all, and the newly elected sheriff was dreaming of "millions"
to come to him from High Church members of his family in
England.   There was a young man whose ancestor had
marched into Jerusalem with the Crusaders!

And the dance!   I can feel yet, though then a small boy,
the beauty and the rythm of the music as the violins and
the cornets gave out the air of the "grand march" in which
all, even the "old folks", took part, the great resonant double-
bass fiddle accentuating the time with sonorous cadences.
When the march had gotten everybody on their feet and the
ball room space was all taken they were "squared off" into

sets for the quadrilles and the whole room was a scene of "tripping the light fantastic toe" as they executed the figures called off. In turn these gave way to merry couples dancing the polka, mazourka, varsouvienne, schottische, and waltz, alternating with intricate square dances till midnight came, when a Virginia reel or the Lancers brought the old people back onto the floor to warm up for supper and seek an excuse to go home, leaving the young people for several hours of enjoyment.

In those early days horses were an important part of each man's life. They furnished his only transportation and made it possible for him to have bread and meat. Naturally men recognized the importance of the horse as their ally in all their undertakings. During the war oxen, the faithful friends of the pioneer settlers, had become too slow for the necessities of the time, and the horse became a prime favorite both for service and pastime. Better care was given him and better breeding improved his race. He furnished the sport for this new breed of sovereigns. Racing became the great social pastime and for a quarter of a century every gathering of people for whatever purpose had a horse race on its programme. Soldiers returning from Kentucky and Tennessee had brought through with them horses of eminently respectable pedigree in the equine world. Kansas men had already become experts in the study of horsemanship. In many of their forays into Missouri intent on punishing some band of murderers they found after a swift chase of forty miles that their own plow horses were winded and to be safe they must select swift transportation for their return home. This judicious selection of horses had greatly improved the local stock.

Some of our horsemen became famous in their generation, and tales are still told of their cleverness. One of these men was John David Day of Liberty township. He had a brother named John Milton Day and they invariably addressed each other by their full formal name. John David Day had by some process become possessed of some of the best horses of Kentucky blood and appearing at a race he would in an innocent, uncouth, unsophisticated way express a desire to try his luck in the speed ring, and usually came home with a pocketful of money. John David Day had heard of a man up at Topeka who had a stallion that had never lost a race and his winnings had made his owner a rich man. John David Day wanted some of that money, so he and John Milton Day prepared old "Mammy" for the biggest race of her life. All ready, they arrived at Topeka and went into camp at the outer edge of the town. John David Day sent John Milton Day into town as a scout to size up the situation and give the Topeka stallion a good looking over. John Milton Day returned and John David Day asked him, "Well, John Milton, did you see that hoss?" "I sure did," said John Milton. "What do you think of that hoss, John Milton?" "He's some hoss!" said John Milton. "Will we have a race, John Milton?" "Well, you go see that hoss, John David." So John David went and saw that hoss and on his return said, "We won't race that hoss, John Milton, but we will mate with him." So from that mating a little scrawny leggy colt came into the world about 1870 and had the name of Little Pete bestowed upon him. At maturity he developed wonderful speed. It was a common thing in those days for a man who had a swift horse to go about looking for "matched" races and Little Pete made the circuit of Colorado, Nebraska, and Iowa and brought home a pile of money for John David Day. In 1876 Little Pete had acquired wide fame and a man named Johnson took him to the Centennial Exposition at Philadelphia where he won everlasting fame for Linn County by capturing a gold medal and a big cash prize as the fastest quarter horse in the world! Johnson brought him back to Linn County where he became the sire of a great number of celebrated horses, among them John Red owned by John Dellinger and a roan mare, Lucy Poe, owned by John Umphrey, who took all the money offered in a trip through Colorado. Some of his daughters were mated with Sleepy Jim and their daughter Lucy Day owned by John David Day was the winner of the biggest money ever known in the west. Lucy Day took all the money at Kansas City, St. Louis, Memphis and at all the Texas towns. Her last owner was Ben Phillips who ran a livery stable in La Cygne.

Another famous horse was Sleepy Jim owned by John Dellinger in La Cygne, a lovable big brute who always approached a race in such a slovenly awkward way that he required no tag to identify him. It was always easy to find men who had money to put up against him. He was the most intelligent horse ever known here and could run a race without a rider and keep within the rules. In scoring at the start he knew what the recall bell meant and would voluntarily turn round and line up again. When they were off Sleepy Jim would look around and switch his tail and romp and hug the inside track till he reached the last quarter of the mile race when he would stretch out into a long red streak that set the crowd in the grandstand wild with enthusiasm. Not much was known of his origin except that he was brought from Kentucky by Ned Orendorf about 1878. He was a big chestnut sorrel, the first thoroughbred in Linn County, a consistent winner at one mile and at one mile and repeat. He sired more winners than any horse ever owned in Linn County, among his children being Lucy Day, John Day, Bay

Jim, Jucalia, Peanut, Limber Jim, Gildersleeve, Jim Trimble, Bald Hornet, Gray Dawn, and many others who still live in the affections of this generation of horsemen.

A contemporary of Sleepy Jim was a big bay gelding named Ace of Diamonds, owned by Dave Cottle of Liberty township (a brother-in-law of John David Day), a nervous, irritable, vicious brute, crazy on the track and who had to be blindfolded to get him started, but he was a whirlwind known at all race-tracks in Kansas and won a fortune in purses. Bill Collins a bowlegged colored boy living at La Cygne was his rider.

It was all clean sport and a high code of honor prevailed. Ed. R. Smith was the dean of the racers and always the guiding and presiding genius. Dressed in a black alpaca suit with white linen and a black tie and shiny shoes he looked and was equally well fitted to grace a pulpit and deliver a funeral oration or perform a marriage ceremony, but really more at home on the throne in the grandstand starting a bunch of swift animals. Elim W. Bartleson was another of the real sports in those days, and Smiley Barnes and Charlie Barnes of Blue Mound and Alf Blaker and Barb Snow, son of Old Nick Snow, were owners and patrons of the sport, while many boys deserve a place in history as riders, among them Gus Tutt, a colored boy of La Cygne who rode John Dellinger's Jucalia, and Lewis Allen of Pleasanton who rode Bay Jim for Dave Cottle. George Allen another colored boy at La Cygne rode many fast races, as did Grant Ogan of that town.

In the early eighties there was frequent competition between Gray Leaf, Sorrel Nell, Dandy Jim and Nigger Baby. Following them was Black Joe owned by Ben F. Blaker and raced by John and Frank Phillips, a great horse at a half mile or a half mile and repeat. It was about 1883 that David Carson and his brother William Carson came down from Shenandoah, Iowa, with Siroc, a dark bay stallion with both beauty and speed. Barb Snow owned a great half-mile horse, Lee Snow, a sorrel gelding born and raised on the old Nick Snow homestead, later sold to parties who took him to Missouri.

Pleasanton's biggest horse event was the first novelty race ever pulled off here. It was in the fall of 1884. It was a big money event for a mile and a half with the money in three parts for the winner at the first half mile, the mile and the mile and a half. The horsemen were divided into two factions and for three days before the race there was rank partisanship. Siroc was a Pleasanton horse and was loyally sustained by local sports. Newt Campbell was his rider, then seventeen years old and weighing in at one hundred and five. The other horses were from the west side of the county and three days before the race two-to-one money against Siroc was flaunted in the face of all comers—Pleasanton had to put up or shut up—and she put up handsomely. The horses entered by the west siders were Bay Dode for the money at the first half mile, Bay Jim for the mile money, and Linden C. was to take down the mile and a half purse. Fully an hour was consumed in scoring or getting started, the west siders using much strategy to wear down Siroc before the start, but finally they were off and at the half mile the West Siders lost their money, and at the mile post they again lost it, and breathlessly awaited the mile-and-a-half—when Siroc nosed out and took the whole pot. Newt Campbell was carried about on the shoulders of men anxious to express their admiration and appreciation of their winnings. This was the epic event of horse racing in Linn County.

The last big event at Pleasanton and which closed a fine programme of races, was a "tug of war" between twelve men from the west side of the county pitted against an equal number from the east side. With thousands looking on these brawny farmers pulled against each other, anxious not only for the prestige of winning but for the nice day's wage that would come from a division of the prize money among the winners. But something happened. The west side fellows yelled about some alleged unfairness, and epithets that meant a fight were freely and promiscuously thrown about. Just at this crisis the fire bell rang and a big black smoke was seen pouring out of a small cottage on the east side of town. The whole crowd of people rushed over there in time to see a colored woman frantically trying to escape by smashing a window by going through it backwards. Willing hands pulled her out, when she set up an awful howl about her "baby" who was in the burning house, her appeals being so pitiful that several men ran in at the risk of their lives to rescue the child. Finally suspicion formed that the woman had fired the house and they seized her and demanded explanation when it was found that "she" was Newt Campbell dressed in his sister's cast-off clothing and that he had filled the cottage with combustibles including a barrel of kerosene and at a signal from a fellow conspirator on top of the hotel had lit the match. But by this time every one of the men had a bucket of water and when the hoax was understood someone yelled "He's smokin', put him out!" They deluged poor Newt. It was two blocks back to town through a gauntlet formed by the people and at almost every step Newt got a bucketful where it would make him the wettest. It is asserted he has never had any starch in him since. It was a big success as a sensational diversion and many were grateful that something had happened to stop a fight that would have been a disgrace. It has always been suspected that J. Frank Smith was in this conspiracy and that he rang the fire bell. And this is what we called "entertainment" in those days!

In 1885 harness horses with trained gaits came in. Ed. R. Smith led off in this equine aristocracy. Ed's first aristocrat was Gipsy Queen a dark bay mare who could trot any of them out of their money. She was a consort of Harry McGregor, son of Robert McGregor (one of the aristocrats of horse-flesh in America who sold for the princely sum of thirty-three thousand dollars down in Kentucky where horse value is known). Harry McGregor was a favorite for many years and he left a lot of children to sustain the family pride. Col. Ed. R. probably got the greatest thrill of his life while driving Harry McGregor. Elim W. Bartleson never bet on his own horse in his life and when he entered his son of Smuggler (who was the fastest horse of his time) Elim called him Hopeless. He was a big bay gelding. Another famous harness horse was Harry Phillips, a beautiful bay stallion owned by the Barnes brothers at Blue Mound. He was the champion double-gaited horse of the state, winning as a trotter one day and as a pacer the next. Smiley (S. E.) Barnes drove him as a trotter and Charlie Barnes handled the ribbons when he paced. L. A. Luhillier of Pleasanton had a remarkable double-gaited horse in Happy Riley, son of Riley Medium. Happy made a record of 2.05¼. He left many colts that became famous both as trotters and pacers. In those days the Grand Circuit started at Detroit and included Indianapolis, Cincinnati, Louisville, Covington, Nashville, Chattanooga and Memphis, and many Linn County men and their horses made the circuit year after year. It was such glorious sport one regrets that the Ford was ever invented. In those days they still had the high wheels on their sulkeys, the nifty bicycle wheels coming in much later.

There was one race at La Cygne along in the late seventies that will be recalled by a few men who were mere boys. At the south side of town there was a quarter mile stretch along the fence on the west side of the old Volker farm. In dry weather it was a delightful stretch of smooth dirt road, the wagons passing over it having barely cut through the turf. A matched race had been arranged on a day late in summer. The worm fence of rails made a convenient grandstand for onlookers and about two hundred were perched on the top rails while the horses were sent to the south end to be started. The betting was lively and as we then had four or five saloons in the little town there was both real and stimulated enthusiasm. In the crowd were two short stout baldheaded foolish old men at least sixty years old, both under the influence of artificial enthusiasm. Having no money to bet they got to quarreling over their favorite horses and soon were fighting. Neither had skill to defend himself and one would receive a smashing blow on his nose in utter surprise and walking up to his antagonist would return the blow by this time in extreme anger. Both spouted blood and soon were sorry sights to look at. The crowd on the fence applauded and the men on the ground milled around and whooped and hurrahed. Nothing was barred—the fighters hooked, gouged and scratched as they could. Their shiny bald pates still glistened. As they approached exhaustion they grappled and floundered and fell into a thick growth of wild roses whose thorns tore and cut the scalps on those glistening bald heads till the bloody sight caused some to try to separate the fighters. "Let 'em alone!" yelled some of the tough element and Wad Pinneo, a real bad man who knew he was bad, drew a six-shooter more than a foot long and yelled for the crowd to stand back. A half dozen other pistols were drawn and it looked so bad that we two hundred on the rail fence simultaneously fell backward and after striking the ground with a "plump" not one was six inches thick as we watched in a scared way through the lowest fence crack. John Lindsay was city marshal then and because he was a goodlooker and well dressed the tough element looked upon him as a grandstander and questioned his courage. Up in the town John saw pistols waving and on his big dapple-gray horse he came thundering down like the Light Brigade and pulling up his horse he lit on both feet alongside Wad Pinneo and took that warrior's gun away from him and remounting marched Pinneo up to the police judge and fined him. We climbed over the fence and surrounded the two old men who were now covered all over with bloody mud. Released from the tension of fear the crowd roared at the ludicrousness of the incident and the saloons were soon filled with men who drank bad whisky and told the funny side of the fight. I do not recall that those two foolish old men were ever again seen about town. Of the pistol toters of that day several turned out badly. Pinneo figured in several disturbances and finally died with his boots on.

Nearly all the troubles of the town came from the saloons. La Cygne had the reputation of being the "toughest" town in Eastern Kansas. At that time it was a common thing for quarrels to end in shooting. An awful fight happened in a saloon where Hesser's furniture store now is. Bob Simmons owned the saloon and Dan Glasscock was his bartender. Joe Rigby was a swarthy blacksmith from Highgate near London, England. He was short and powerful. Boss Nabors was another blacksmith who was a crony of Rigby. He was short and stout and both were drinking. They had a grievance to settle and went into Simmons' saloon for trouble. I stepped into the back door just at the climax of the scene, passing

Bob Simmons who left with drawn revolver. Dan Glasscock threw a heavy beer mug or "schooner" at Rigby which "cupped" over his left eye making an awful wound and Rigby fell as though dead. Boss Nabors was bellowing with rage and coming at Dan with a knife. A heavy iron poker was thrust through a hole in the floor into the earth. Seizing the handle of this Dan swept it through the air in a wide arc and crashed it onto the head of Nabors, literally burying it in his brain. Nabors fell in a heap and was in convulsions and soon died. He was carried on a board to his home where a postmortem was performed by taking off what was left of his cranium. Joe Rigby recovered and lived to a good old age out in Oregon. As I worked on the La Cygne Journal then with Martin Funk we felt a distinct sense of duty in being on the scene when things happened. When Keller was hanged by a mob at the Huff ford a mile north of town Martin and I were up on the limb of a big sycamore tree and when a hog wagon was driven under us the prisoner was placed on it and a noose quickly placed round his neck and the rope thrown over the limb between us, so that when the wagon drove out from under Martin and I bobbed up and down with the poor wretch whose life was going out. We were leaning out of the printing office window when Larrie McKenzie shot Charlie Johnson immediately beneath us. Larrie was city marshal and was nervous and afraid of the boy. It was all the harvest reaped from five saloons whose only excuse for existence was that they paid a hundred and twenty-five dollars a year in license to the city. All of these young men would have been a credit to their families and their town had there been no saloons.

At such events there were very frequently men noted in the annals of crime. The Younger boys were there several times, well dressed, smooth, sleek fellows who looked like successful professional men. At different times there were men at the fairs or races said to be the James boys, and Tim Lawhead entertained two men at his home north of town for several days whom he took the trouble to identify as Jesse James and a companion, and there was a peculiar coincidence in their presence and the return from Kansas City of James Glasgow Black after he had marketed several carloads of premium cattle. It was thought they meant to rob him. Lawhead went to Kansas City and called on Mrs. Jesse James who said it was her husband and showed him a letter from Jesse telling of being at the Lawhead place. Grant Gillette the notorious swindler in cattle deals lived at Twin Springs and was a frequent attendant at sporting events.

Newton M. Campbell was born in DeWitte county, Illinois, October 7, 1864, and came with his parents to Linn County in September, 1868, and located at Linnville where Judge Barlow and John Hood were their neighbors. The Campbells were of course Scotch, Newt's great grandfather being the first of this family in this country. At Linnville an old man named Judge Farris was their neighbor. He was a veteran of the Black Hawk war and had a gruesome souvenir of that historic campaign. Farris had seen his brother killed and scalped by an Indian, and when he in turn killed the Indian he secured the scalp taken from his brother and kept it till his death when it was placed in his coffin and was buried with him in Richland graveyard. The Campbells were fond of horses and Newt became a noted jocky and was in the confidence of the big horsemen who followed the grand circuit. At seventeen years of age Newt "weighed in" at one hundred five pounds. He is now an employe of the Blaker Mills and when you mention the old days and the names of some of the great race horses of Linn County Newt rises like a bass after live bait.

In March of 1857 I left Fayette county, Iowa, and joined the great rush of emigration to Kansas.[1] Political strife over slavery had precedence over all other activities. Joining the side of the antislavery movement I enlisted, with so many young men from the northern states, and in the early spring of 1857 I arrived at Leavenworth from St. Louis by the old steamer Emigrant, afterwards sunk and abandoned on a sand bar in the Missouri river below Boonville. In company with two other young men I started on foot for Lawrence, where we arrived the first day (thirty-five miles) a little footsore. We first made the acquaintance of Jim Lane, afterwards general and senator from Kansas. He sent us to Wakarusa to join a colony under the leadership of Augustus Wattles and destined for Linn County with the intention of building a town at Moneka in the center of the county, and making it the county seat. We put our knapsacks in the wagons and walked the first day, when we fell in with J. C. Anderson and two of his brothers-in-law by the name of Smith. They were headed for the Neosho but we persuaded them to turn south with us, and a few days later we took claims in the valley two miles west of where Pleasanton now is. We claimed each a quarter section in a square shape, and at once began to improve forty acres in the center so as to join fences and give us ten acres each. This was perhaps the first real improvement on the open prairie in Linn or Bourbon counties, except where the places adjoined the timber.

Our party came with horse teams and hauled feed along the road before the grass was up. In the latter part of May

1. The writer of these sketches (A. H. Tanner) was born in Ruggles, Ashland county, Ohio, in July, 1836. Living on the farm with his parents till 1855 he left home to seek his fortune in the West. Going to Fayette county, Iowa, he remained there until the spring of 1857.

and from that on during the summer a steady stream of immigration came into Linn and covered all the prairie in the eastern part of the county and much of Bourbon county. Prior to that time the settlements were confined to the creeks in these counties and consisted largely of people from western Missouri, except a colony of about three hundred Southerners from Alabama, Georgia and the Carolinas sent there by an appropriation from Alabama. These were young men under the command of Colonel Buford and had pulled in at Fort Scott. Most of them secured claims in Bourbon county after the few free-state men that had settled there had been driven out or had abandoned their places in 1856 by reason of the strife between the opposing sides on the slave question.

But it is necessary for me to recall briefly the history of Kansas in order to make things a little more comprehensive. I shall be obliged to repeat history well written by others, but it will be brief, and after this I shall confine myself to what I was personally familiar with in Linn and Bourbon counties. Immediately after the passage of the Kansas-Nebraska bill, which recognized slavery in Kansas, many emigrants from the south came to Kansas and perhaps were in a majority during 1854 and 1855. Slaves were brought in but in very small numbers. The administration at Washington was always friendly to slavery and in fact we all thought President Pierce's term of office was dictated by Jefferson Davis and Buchanan's term shared the same influence. The Territorial elections were always computed to give proslavery majorities until the fall of 1857. The governors were appointed from Washington but after remaining in Kansas a few months they always resigned rather than do the dirty work required of them. The northern states with a population at that time of about twenty millions, as against four or five million whites in the South, naturally furnished most of the emigrants to Kansas and the balance of power soon gravitated to the side of freedom. But the South had complete control of the administration at Washington and used that power to help prolong the struggle which otherwise would have ended very shortly. But they had trouble to keep their appointees in line and their governors resigned one after another. The troops kept at Leavenworth became disaffected and their officers and men were unwilling after the summer of 1857 to help enforce the Bogus Laws and subjugate the majority to the will of the minority.

The free-state men, by reason of the heavy immigration during the spring and summer, were in a large majority, and proslavery leaders had publicly acknowledged that the cause was lost in Kansas—that they were outnumbered three to one. Montgomery in company with others had organized a squatters' court in Linn County. The reason for this court can be seen when it is remembered that all the laws passed by the Bogus legislature had been repudiated and there was no recognized law in Kansas. Montgomery with a small force of men had driven out settlers who were occupying claims from which free-state men had been evicted the year before. It has been said that they were robbed and plundered by Montgomery's men. I was with him on some of these occasions and I never saw anything taken or destroyed.

Things had quieted down and the people were at work as only pioneers can work to make new homes for themselves. But the ends sought by certain parties at Washington had not been accomplished and by these the fight was kept up and urged upon the few that were here. The marshals and deputies and camp followers at Fort Scott and a United States court presided over by Judge Williams were still there. These patriots were mostly without visible means of support unless they managed to keep up strife through the federal court. They tried hard to keep troops from Fort Leavenworth but only a handful could be got and they were mostly in sympathy with the settlers.

Before this the "Wide-awakes", a secret anti-slavery order, had been organized and spread to Kansas and absorbed every free-state man in the Territory. The army officers, including Captain Lyon (afterwards general), Colonel Sumner and many others as well as many of the rank and file were initiated into the order. I was present when many of them took the oath. If warrants were placed in their hands for the arrest of free-state men it always happened that they arrived at a man's cabin just after he was gone.

But let us get back to Fort Scott and see what the faithful band of deserted heroes is doing. They needed money and whisky, for they were a convivial lot. Warrants were continually issued from Judge Williams' court for different settlers and the marshals were always trying to make arrests and often tried to get the soldiers to help. This was slow business for the reasons mentioned above. The favorite charge was cutting timber on Indian lands, and about every man in Linn County was guilty for they had anticipated the opening of the land office and settled before the Indian title was extinguished. Only the wealthier classes were arrested, for money was what these men wanted and a man too poor to pay a fine was exempt. So contrary to the rule of the present day the little fellows escaped and the "higher-ups" were obliged to come across.

This thing went on in a small way until the winter of 1857-58, when the marshals and their deputies summoned large parties and organized a good-sized army with the avowed purpose of capturing Montgomery and his "outlaws." These posses kept up their work during the entire winter but accomplished little. A few skirmishes with small armed bodies occurred though but few prisoners were ever taken; and finally towards spring the new legislature passed an amnesty act and all was peace once more. But the marshals continued to harass the people and seek to make arrests. On one occasion in the summer of 1858 a marshal, Campbell, and his deputy Dimon, came up into Linn County to make arrests. They stopped at the hotel in Mound City to feed and get dinner. Their mission leaked out and Montgomery was in town, whether by design or not I do not know. He was informed on the subject and went at once to the mill to confer with the proprietors, who were good old Pennsylvania Quakers and were prominent in free-state counsels. The writer, then twenty-one, was there with another young man hauling logs. We were asked to take part and help capture the marshals, which we did, upon being supplied with ponies to ride. Like many others in those days we had our own revolvers. We were sent north to the house of Henry Seaman, about four miles out. We found him at home and his brother Ben was also there. We soon arranged to start back towards Mound City, intending to intercept the marshals in the open prairie where there could be little chance of escape. Myself and one of the Seamans were personally known to one of the marshals and we fell back far to the rear, but near enough to assist if necessary. Riding leisurely along they soon met the marshals and after saluting and passing they dropped to the ground and called from behind their horses and ordered the marshals to halt. Marshal Campbell informed the boys he was a United States marshal and it was treason to interfere him and a very grave crime, punishable by death. But his dignity counted for nothing and both were ordered to shut up and dismount and come forward one at a time and deliver their arms. By this time the two of us in the rear were approaching with revolvers in our hands. The marshals did as they were told and came up and handed over two nice new navy revolvers. I don't think those men ever saw those guns any more. They were just what the boys needed and were very hard to obtain. Their warrants (about sixty) were also taken, together with a memorandum that directed them where to stop overnight and be with friends. These things were kept for future use, but their money, over a hundred dollars, was returned when they were finally released. The prisoners were then taken back to Mound City. Their horses, tied together, were led by one of the boys and the others rode behind.

I don't believe the boys were unduly rude to those dignified officials, but the way they gave command left little room for parley or doubt as to their intentions. They made the prisoners remove their boots and tied them to their own saddles to guard against escape. Upon arriving at Mound City we met a crowd of perhaps two hundred which had gathered and which was constantly augumented by fresh arrivals. Our ponies were the only telephones we had; but the people were

274 COLLECTING TAXES FROM HAMELTON

easily awakened and it is surprising how quick they came to
a call of that kind. A meeting was held in the street and
Montgomery made a speech, others talked and Doc Jennison
got off a little of his bravado. I never liked him over well
for he deserted a crowd of us youngsters once on the eve of
what we supposed to be a conflict of arms. He could do the
talking for a company and the rest might do the fighting; at
least that was what we thought he intended for us to do.
After talking matters over Montgomery compromised with
those two marshals and gave them back their money and
horses and all that belonged to them except their guns and
papers. On their part they signed an agreement to keep out
of Linn County and arrest no more free-state men. They
insisted on an escort as they had been disarmed, but Montgomery told them they were safer without arms than with
them, and finally gave them a passport and himself accompanied them a few miles, as far as his road home followed
them south. Thus ended another of the "outrages" of Montgomery and his outlaws.

But I must turn back to the early spring to speak of the
Marais des Cygnes murders which occurred near the Trading
Post on May 19, 1858. Prior to this, during the spring, myself
and Ira Bronson had been acting as deputy under C. H.
Stilwell, the treasurer of Linn County.

We were instructed to assess any property that had been
overlooked by the assessor, as some had been absent the fall
before and had returned in the spring. In this class were
the three Hamelton brothers, who had claims on the state
line east of the Trading Post. They had wintered over the
line in Missouri and came back to plant a crop, with a view
of selling their claims later. Our lands could not be entered
for the titles of the Indians were not extinguished.

I called upon Captain Hamelton but he refused to submit
to taxation and told me if I were older I would know better
than to make a man pay tax on property he didn't have and
could not have or keep in the Territory. They had their slaves,
and public opinion and the risk of losing their chattels had
driven them to send them back to Georgia. His argument
at this distance looks to be sound enough, but we concluded
to exact the money, perhaps ten or twelve dollars, and Mr.
Bronson and myself went together and succeeded in persuading him to dig up an old tin box and produce the gold coin
necessary to get his receipt. This was perhaps a month prior
to the murder.

Some have thought that this urged them to commit the
foulest murder in the history of all time. But I do not believe
it had any influence. The truth is they were bitterly disap-
pointed all around. They came here from Georgia two years
before with the Buford gang that came to Fort Scott. They
supposed the slavery question had been settled in their favor

and they would obtain large tracts of lands and make slave plantations here.   They were from wealthy families and when they found their friends leaving and themselves could stay no longer and had to go without even selling their improvements, they became desperate.   A large colony, estimated at over one hundred, had started to leave the Territory and headed down the Marais des Cygnes toward Jefferson City. They went into camp near Papinsville near where Rich Hill now is, and after holding a counsel a party headed by Captain Hamelton came back and proceeded to do the job.   It was for revenge alone, as all hope of their cause had been abandoned and they were then on the road to their old homes in the South.   It is my opinion that they made their way back to the extreme South and two or three years later engaged in the War of the Rebellion.   The Hameltons abandoned their claims shortly after the tax trouble and it was reported that they had marked several men for revenge, but we all carried arms and kept a lookout and continued to work as we had before.

From this time on things warmed up and trouble of much portent seemed imminent.   Sheriff Walker came down from Lawrence with a good force of men.   Montgomery accompanied him to Fort Scott, believing that the murderers had their origin there and some of her prominent citizens were responsible for them.   They made several arrests and left the prisoners in the hands of the authorities there, but had scarcely left the fort when the prisoners were released on their own recognizance and nothing more ever came of it. This shows the one-sidedness of things at Fort Scott where the proslavery party, with the help of the federal officers, had managed to retain legal power up to this time.   In June Governor Denver came down to Fort Scott and made an arrangement with the free-state people to withdraw the troops under Captain Lyon if they would keep the peace.   He came back through Linn County and held a conference with Montgomery which resulted in placing Captain Weaver on the Linn County border, the Missouri line, with a force of sixty militia, where I think he remained during the entire summer of 1858.

George W. Clark, receiver of the land office at Fort Scott, was the worst border ruffian of these parts, and now became alarmed for his own safety.   Wishing to get away from Kansas he was appointed by Buchanan as a purser in the United States navy and Kansas was well rid of him.   But peace was not yet.   Judge Williams' court was still there with its quota of marshals and deputies and official idlers who infested Fort Scott.   They also had a proslavery sheriff, for Bourbon county was one of the very few places in Kansas that had a majority of that party at the 1858 election.   However, since the election free-state men had come in by the hundreds and so the settlers were antislavery by a very large

majority. Warrants continued to issue from Judge Williams'
court and the officers, still in need of something to do for a
living continued to make arrests and stir up trouble. Ben
Rice of Bourbon and John Hudlow of Linn were arrested in
defiance of the compact made with the governor. They were
confined in the old government building at the north corner
of the square. This was in the fall. They were chained to
the floor with only quilts sent in by their friends for bedding.
Winter was coming on and their friends demanded trial or
bail. Both were denied. Excitement grew and it was the
opinion among free-state men that they should be released
by force if necessary. At a public meeting at Rayville
attended by both Linn and Bourbon county people it was
voted to proceed to Fort Scott and release them. So much
opposition developed that the project was abandoned. As the
prisoners were in the hands of the federal authorities many
declined to take the risk. But cold weather was near and the
situation called for action and secret meetings were held in
both counties to determine the proper course. Montgomery
finally decided to call for advice from other parts of the Territory. Men were sent to Lawrence and Emporia for advice
and assistance and the leading men concluded to get together
a sufficient force and go and do the job. Help came in a small
squad from Lawrence under S. N. Wood; one from Osawatomie under S. S. Williams; and another from Emporia which
I afterwards learned was headed by P. B. Plumb. They met
at Fort Bain near the head of the Osage in Bourbon county
and were joined by Montgomery and a band from Mound City.
Capt. Sam Stevenson from the head of the Osage and Captain
Barnes from farther down towards the state line joined them
at a lone house on the prairie about eight miles northwest
of Fort Scott. The whole force, now numbering seventy-five,
was placed under the command of Montgomery, and I think
this was by far the largest force ever placed under his command at any time previous to the war. Of this force probably
thirty lived along the Osage in the north part of Bourbon
county. Just before leaving camp for the last start John
Brown came in with four or five men. He wished to take
command and some say a vote was taken to see if he should
be chosen to lead. But he was not wanted at all and he left
and refused to take part unless he could command. He
wanted to burn Fort Scott but Montgomery was of a different
mind. He promised us that no damage should be done and
that it would be a bloodless affair. I believed then and still
believe that he (Montgomery) had a secret understanding
with the guard. I don't know if they were United States
soldiers or a militia posse but I still think they were our
friends and were expecting the raid.

The start from this camp was made to bring the party to
Fort Scott at daylight. The Marmaton was crossed at the

old military crossing, two or three hundred yards above where the National avenue bridge now is. The horses were left near the river and six or eight men were left there, which may explain the difference in the accounts of the numbers. Most writers give it as sixty-eight, but at the last camp there were just seventy-five. From here the advance was made in three columns and was very rapid, almost a trot. The prisoners were kept in the old government building, afterwards occupied by Judge Margrave as a residence, and though built about 1844 it is still standing in very good repair. A man named Cleveland was in the lead and forced the door in with a single push and there was no resistance from the guards. Their arms were conveniently stacked and were taken possession of at once and every man in sight was taken prisoner. No one would have been hurt except for the foolhardiness of Deputy Marshal John Little. He kept the old sutler's store and was staying there with George A. Crawford. As the posse passed his store he opened the door and fired at short range into the crowd with No. 2 buckshot, wounding Ben Seaman and J. H. Kagi, a German military officer afterwards hung at Harper's Ferry with John Brown. After the shot Little went to a side door and looked out through a transom and being noticed by a member of the posse received a bullet from a Sharp's rifle and was instantly killed. This episode spoiled the arrangement for a bloodless affair as had been promised but the rest of the program went through without a hitch. The killing of Little was called murder by the proslavery folks but the other side called it self-defense, which is nearer the truth, for armed men seldom fail to return a shot when fired upon. Some paragraphers have stated that Little used duck shot as he had been out duck hunting the day before. This is a mistake; he had been up on the Osage hunting men with a posse and had been in a skirmish at Fort Bain, where they were repulsed, and he had returned probably in a bad humor. I helped to remove some of the shot from the wounded men and I know what they were. I have been told that the intended raid had leaked out through some one and that the Fort Scott men expected it and had agreed that each man should fire from his house and do what they could in that way, thinking to drive the posse off, but they had made a bad guess and failed.

The two prisoners were soon released. Their chains were cut by a member of the party, a blacksmith named Dorey, the father of Charlie Dorey, now in Fort Scott. They were armed and were soon in the ranks, standing guard over the men who had been guarding them. There were also many others under guard—Judge Williams of the federal court, old Judge Ransom, and in short about all the marshals and deputies and court lackeys in Fort Scott, with many of the

citizens. They were hustled out into the square and a Sharp's
rifle pen was formed around them, and as it was frosty
(December 16) a fire was built for the comfort of the prisoners. The furniture of Judge Williams' office and all his books
were used for fuel. Judge Ransom and Marshall Campbell
complained bitterly and protested that it would go hard with
us for handling United States officers in such a manner, but
the boys ridiculed them and one little insignificant fellow,
Avia Flint, ordered them to keep still and pushed them around
with his little old squirrel rifle. He was a very small, cadav-
erous-looking fellow, weighing not over one hundred pounds,
and ex-Governor Ranson was far above six feet and portly
and he made a ludicrous spectacle marching at the command
of such a very inferior guard. Judge Williams was jolly and
good-natured and asked the boys to spare his fiddle and ward-
robe, which they did; but his court and all the belongings
were literally destroyed and he was compelled to witness it.
He ran away down through Missouri and I don't know when
he came back, but I think he was there a year later.

The accounts written in regard to the looting of Little's
store are quite absurd. Some say $7,000 worth of goods were
destroyed, but I think $700 would have covered all there was
in that little shack. It contained whisky, tobacco and a few
groceries. As soon as possible Montgomery ordered the store
nailed up and the looting ceased. Some of the fellows were
helping themselves to whisky and tobacco and perhaps other
things. No doubt there were men there that would steal;
but for the most part that crowd was composed of the best
men in Kansas and nearly all of them afterwards joined the
Union army and many held offices all the way from lieutenant
to brigadier general. And later the state of Kansas as well
as Linn and Bourbon counties elected them to the best offices
in the gift of the people. One member of the company became
treasurer of Bourbon county and another was United States
Senator for a long time and if I am not mistaken one was sent
to Congress from this district. I was only twenty-two at the
time and the leaders of that force were nearly all men of
mature years, but I had a speaking acquaintance with a good
many of them, including the Bains (two of them) the Thomas
brothers, Maynes, Stevenson, Stewarts, Steel brothers, Barnes,
Dentons, Hazlets, Seamans and many others. Only three
or four of that party ever went wrong that I know of. In
fact they were just the rank and file of good citizenship and
led by a man that historians have failed to do justice to.

Ben Rice served through the Rebellion in the Union army
and after the war went to California, married and raised a
family, and died at a ripe old age, after carrying an ounce
ball in his hip fifty years. His partner in misery remained
in Kansas for twenty years but is now a resident of San
Francisco. I am in correspondence with him still and he tells

me his wife still lives, that they are both well and hale, that
they have six children and about twenty-six grandchildren
and great-grandchildren and that he still works at his trade,
although eighty-one years old. He has been a steadfast member of the church all his life.

James Montgomery lived on his little farm after serving
as a colonel through the war. He lived the life of a consistent
and honest Christian and died at a good old age, and I am
only too glad to speak a word in his praise after a lapse of
over a half century. He was universally liked, a man of strong
intellect and a clear perception that marked him as far above
the average. He was a fine scholar, a pleasing and convincing
speaker and almost a prophet in his own county. It was my
privilege to hear him address a very large outdoor meeting
on the occasion of the hunt for the Marais des Cygnes murderers. He said that the disunionists, if they ever developed,
would be in the South and not among the free-soilers of the
North. At that time all antislavery men were branded as
disunionists by the proslavery party. He said that it was
such crimes as this that would free the slaves and holding
one hand above his head he added: "You can count on the
fingers of one hand all the years that slavery has to live. At
that time there will be no slaves in Kansas nor South Carolina
either. These men are digging a grave for slavery."

Here is an echo from that long distant past, a voice that
tells you of many conditions under which the early pioneers
lived their days and acted their parts in a great drama that
will always be studied with interest. The Botkin family were
all above the average in intelligence and appreciation of events
and their values. So the following pages by Judge Theodosius
Botkin[1] on the homely subject "Among the Sovereign Squats"
will give many side lights on early development in social and
political life. It was among papers filed with the State Historical Society:

The newly appointed district judge had arrived at the little
western city that nestles at the foot of Sugar Mound to hold
his first term of court and was being introduced to the members of the bar, court officers, and the curious throng of jurors,
witnesses, and loungers who filled the one-roomed, old wooden
structure that served justice for a temple. It was his honor's
first trip to the historic old storm-center around which clus-
tered the names of John Brown, James Montgomery, Charley
Jennison, and Nathaniel Lyon, and a score of lesser lights,
whose friendly rays were a guide to their neighbors in the
old, troublous time. At last the jurist was introduced to
the venerable spectacled clerk of the court and after the
usual formal salutation inquired, of course (for who ever in
those days met an old-timer and omitted such question?)
"How long have you resided in Kansas, Mr. Smith?" "Oh,

I am one of the 'Sovereign Squats,' " was the reply that was
intended to even if it did not convey the information that
the gentleman who kept the records and wore spectacles was
one of the first and early settlers in the Territory of Kansas.
The judge had in this wise run amuck with a term that
had not heretofore formed any part of his vocabulary, and
the suddenness of the shock made him hesitate. The sheriff
actually ceased for a moment the taxation of "fees for mile-
age" on the backs of the bunch of writs before him, and
muttered to the bailiff, "A tenderfoot, by thunder!" The laugh
was on the jurist, but he proved equal to the emergency.
Tossing a bill to the bailiff, he said: "Spend that for cigars
for the crowd, and while we smoke I'll get this Sovereign
Squat to confer a degree or two upon me."
There were others beside himself in the crowd who had
never learned the mysteries of the degree asked for. Of
course, the reader used to know what Sovereign Squat means,
but he may have forgotten. It is an echo of the great
Lincoln-Douglas debate, and a reecho of the clash of political
dogmas and antagonistic institutions along the Kansas border
in Territorial times, when the free-state settlers upon the
one hand and the proslavery settlers and their Missouri allies
on the other contended for supremacy in the then young Territory. That struggle intruded itself into the contest
between the two great political gladiators, upon the
issue of whose contentions hung the fate of time
honored institutions, and, as it proved, the destiny
of the republic. Who should settle the question of slavery
in the territory? Should Congress? Mr. Lincoln held to
the doctrine, and won, that the constitution vests in Congress the sole power to decide all questions of policy re-

1. Theodosius Botkin was born in Clarke county, Ohio, June 25, 1846. At
the age of fifteen he enlisted in Company F, Forty-fourth Ohio Infantry and
served through the war. In 1865 he came to Kansas and settled in Linn County.
He taught school and in 1870 located at Pleasanton, where he organized the
city schools, of which he was principal for four years. In 1875 he located at
Mound City and was admitted to the bar. He served as probate judge of Linn
County and police judge of Mound City. He was appointed judge of the Thirty-
second district by the governor in March, 1889, and removed to Stevens county.
He passed through all the turbulent times of that region, and it was in his
court that Samuel N. Wood was assassinated in June 1891. Impeachment proceedings were brought against Botkin, but on all the charges he was acquitted.
October 11, 1892, he resigned as judge and settled in Hutchinson. In 1896 he
was elected to the house of representatives in the state legistlature from Reno
county. In 1897 he was made commander of the Grand Army of the Republic,
Department of Kansas. In 1901 he settled in Salt Lake, Utah, where he practiced law.
Jeremiah D. Botkin was born in Logan county, Illinois, April 24, 1849, the
son of Richard and Nancy (Barr) Botkin. In 1866 the Botkins moved to Linn
County, settling four miles east of Mound City. Here Mr. Botkin grew to manhood, taught school, united with the Methodist church and made his first efforts
at preaching. In 1870 he returned to Illinois and entered the M. E. conference
there. While absent from Kansas he attended De Pauw University and in 1882
was transferred to the Southeast Kansas conference. Upon his return to the
state he became identified with public affairs and was a candidate for governor
in 1888 on the Prohibition ticket. In 1894 he took the stump in the interest
of the People's party and reform and was that year a candidate for Congress
from the third district. He was defeated but two years later was elected by
a large majority. Mr. Botkin was married three times; first to Miss Carrie
Kirkpatrick, who died early; second, to Miss Laura Waldo; they had a son,
Ralph Waldo. Mr. Botkin's third wife was Mrs. Mary E. Monroe and they had
three children, Mildred Ninde, Frances Willard and Paul Oliver.

lating to the territories. Douglas espoused the doctrine
that the citizens who in good faith had "squatted" or settled
within the territories should themselves decide the great
question that divided them, and that soon thereafter attempted
to divide the Union. This doctrine the.Little Giant was pleased
to call "squatter sovereignty." The free state settlers in
Kansas, ever prone to grasp and utilize the ludicrous in an
opponent's position, caught up the Douglas idea, and making
a personal application of it to their own case called themselves
and each other Sovereign Squats, in derision of the Douglas
proposition.

A frontier settlement is always full of surprises to the
uninitiated, or, to use the frontier classics, to the "tenderfoot,"
and most fortunate is that stranger who can master at all
time his curiosity, and neither ask questions nor manifest
a too inquisitive spirit. In his own case the writer was on
his first appearance among those people extremely fortunate
in having old and very excellent friends among them, who
took upon themselves to fortify him against the excesses
of a longing desire to catch on quick. "Now, see here,"
said one of these, "don't you go to showing your ignorance
the first thing. Keep your eyes and ears open, and your
mouth shut." On that very day I noticed a nice cake of
fresh maple sugar in one of the stores, and to my inquiry,
"How much is that worth?" I received the explicit information, "Four bits."

Oh, ye gods and little fishes! What a predicament was
this for a youngster gifted with an investigating spirit, and
who had learned the sterling table, about farthings, pence,
and shillings, but who had never been fortunate enough to
have struck anything of the "bit" kind, except bridle-bit,
brace and bit, etc. But I remembered my friend's admonition
in time to save my social standing, what little there was of
it, from complete wreck. My good angel came to my rescue,
and I said, "Well, I'll take it." Now, I did not want that
sugar. I had no use for it, except that I might carry it
six miles on horseback and present it to my sister. My
purse was well supplied with dimes, quarters, half-dollars,
etc. (the old shinplaster scrip), but I dared not risk making
payment of the mysterious four bits with any of these.

The merchant returned to my presence with the sugar
neatly tied up, and I handed him a five-dollar bill. Surely,
thought I, that will be more than four bits, and I can count
the change. "Have you nothing smaller?" he asked, as he
picked up the bill. "I am getting short of change." Lord,
forgive me! I did not care to retain any of the three or
four dollars' worth of shinplasters in my purse. I had no
particular use for that much small currency about my person.
But I did not know how much United States money there
might be in a bit, and I wanted to know—in fact, was just

crazy to learn, and durst not ask. So, like the moral coward I was, I replied in a sweet, innocent way, "No; I believe that is my smallest money." He gave back $4.50. He was a very careful man about making change. He laid the pieces down separately, and counted them over twice. So I knew he had made no mistake, and that four bits was the equivalent of our half-dollar back in Ohio. "Let's see," I said mentally. "If four bits is a half-dollar, then two bits would be a quarter and a bit would be 12½ cents." Something like that operation was takng place in my mind as I began placing the change in my scrip-book. Then my good angel touched a sensitive spot on my conscience and remembering the complaint about the scarcity of change, I said: "Here, Mr. Way, I find I have a whole lot of scrip. I beg your pardon. Let me exchange it for bills and replenish your stock of shinplasters." He accepted my offer and my conscience felt easier. I also felt that I had done a very smart thing. I had learned the trade value of a bit by artfully deceiving the merchant and compelling him to make change for a five-dollar bill. Had, hey? Deceived that quiet, unpretentious man?

It was nearly twenty months before I entered that man's presence again. The war was over and I had returned to settle in that community. I approached him and holding out my hand said, "How d'ye do, Mr. Way; do you remember me?" "Well, I think I do. You're the fellow who made me change a five-dollar bill so you could find out what four bits was without asking the question."[1] Here were a few reefs taken out of my sails of self-conceit. This quiet, un-ostentatious frontiersman had read my little deception like a primer, and at the same time my effort to conceal my ignorance for a frontier form and custom had enlisted in my behalf his entire sympathy and respect, and he was ever afterward my friend.

It was in August, 1865, when after almost a week spent on the road from Leavenworth to Sugar Mound, helping the mules or horses of the Overland Stage Company roll their cumber-some load through horrible knee-deep mud as far as Paola; then, the Marais des Cygnes ferry-boat being swept away by the flood, wrestling with corn bread, sliced tomatoes, rancid bacon and hard-luck coffee at the Torrey House for two days and nights, and then setting off with a few companions to cross over the raging river in a skiff and trust to luck for a conveyance on the other side to carry us on to our destina-tion, I found myself, for better or for worse, among the Sovereign Squats, and was generally referred to by them as "that newcomer."

That was as wet a week as mortal ever spent on the road in Kansas. The mud was axletree deep, and our dozen passengers on the overland stage out of Leavenworth soon

1. This was James P. Way.

learned the always anger-provoking fact that they had really
paid the company's agent for tickets the possession of which
entailed the duty of helping the mules along with their load.
This meant that everybody aboard, except the one imperial
woman and her elegantly dressed and royal husband, should
crawl out and climb down at the foot of every hill and
push, pry and pull at the stage until the summit of the next hill
or ridge should be reached, when they might crawl in or climb
up again and ride down hill. It is strange how inconsiderate
of other people's rights and feelings under these circumstances we soon became. From the driver we had received
the information that the royal gentleman mentioned was a
brigadier general recently discharged. That was most welcome news. Here was ten of us, each of whom carried on
his person or in his grip, an honorable discharge from the
army. Here was the opportunity for which, for three or
four years last past, we had prayed diligently and fervently.
We then and there remembered the promise of Holy Writ
that "The prayers of the righteous", etc. The Lord had
kindly sent us a balm for all the ills we had suffered at
the hands of brigadiers and other commissioned trash during
our term of service.

The next getting-out and getting-down place was at the
beginning of a long and most terribly muddy stretch. There
was a burst of offended royal indignation, followed by an
explosion of imperial horror and defiance, as one of the
passengers poked his head into the coach and emphatically
commanded: "Here, you fellow, you pile out of there! You
are no better than the rest of us; out with you." The
reader need not be told that the "fellow piled out of there,"
nor that he did not "pile in" again until we reached the summit of the next ridge. He was then a sight to move the
pity of the gods. His silk plug was even bespattered. But
our fun at his expense was over. At the first farmhouse
he had the stage stopped and he and his imperial spouse
alighted to wait for the coming of some other stage whose
passengers would prove more congenial to their aristocratic
feelings and possibly more sympathetic with a once haughty
nabob who suddenly awakens to the fact that he is once more
nothing but a common citizen with no further power or right
to command or exact the menial services of others. That
was the only fun we had on the trip; and we could not help
feeling that it was extremely unkind for him to abandon us
in that manner and wholly deprive us of the further pleasure
of his society.

But, kind reader, we were considering the wetness of the
weather when we struck that brigadier. Every prairie branch
was putting on the airs of a full-fed creek; every creek was
swelled up with the majestic pride of a haughty river that
has turned itself loose for a high old time; and the Marais

des Cygnes was possessed of an uncontrollable spirit to widen
its influence and extend its operations. It was unanimously
in favor of expansion. But Torrey's supply of bacon and
alleged coffee had become exhausted, and as no freight wagons
could pull through the mud that lay between Paola and the
Missouri River the dealers were unable to replenish their
stores. The missing flat-bottomed ferry boat was lodged in
a tree-top five miles down the stream and it would take
several days before it could be brought back and set to work
again.

Of the ten ex-soldiers who had come thus far on that ever-
to-be-remembered stage journey the destination of six of
us lay beyond the impassable river. But we were tired of
delay. George Elliott, the kindest and most generous-souled
stage driver who ever swung the Overland company's whips
to touch up "soldiering" leaders, hauled us down to the
northern bank or verge and left us there to barter our way
across in the leaky old skiff of the sallow-complexioned, red-
eyed and ague-stricken owner. He would land us on the
other side, two at a time, for six-bits apiece. It was then
9 a. m. The last boat-load was landed on the south side
at twelve. Three hours to make the three trips; yes, and
mighty good time for the task required under the existing
conditions. But the history of our long hunt south of the
river for a conveyance and driver to carry us on to the foot
of Sugar Mound and the incidents of the journey would be
as tiresome to the reader as the trip was to us. It is about
thirty miles from Paola to Sugar Mound. It was 7 a. m.
when we drove out of the former behind George Elliott's
"four white mice", as his superb double team of snow-white
ponies were called by every Sovereign Squat between Fort
Scott and the Big Muddy. It was 11 p. m. of the next day
when the last end of the thirty-mile journey was reached,
and we did not fool away any time either. Such were some
of the conditions that beset travelers in 1865 in this region
were the raging elements of discord had but recently ex-
pended their fury.

A stranger traveling today along the country roads in any
of the old border counties of Kansas and Missouri from
Leavenworth and Kansas City to Fort Scott or Nevada, and
viewing the thousands of well-fenced, well-stocked and well-
kept farms, and the tens of thousands of elegant and happy
homes, and the numerous and thriving cities and towns that
dot the land, would see nothing in this year of grace 1899
to remind him of the awful storm of human passion that
once swept over these fertile prairies. But he who rode along
these same highways and viewed these same sunny hill slopes
and pleasant valleys at or soon after the close of the civil
war in 1865, and who threads the same localities now, will
be prepared to fully appreciate the poetic maxim that "Peace

hath her victories no less renowned than war." Never did
war-hoofs beat harder upon Assyrian soil than upon the face
of this rich and inviting section of the great West. Never
did all the elements of discord revel in a more frenzied de-
bauchery of blood and suffering and destruction in the palmiest
days of the Saracen than along this border during the struggle
which began in 1854, only to end in 1865. The world for
ages has stood appalled at the thought of a ten-years war
around the beleaguered wall of ancient Troy, and the carnage
and misery resulting from that conflict. Ten years! Ay,
it is a long, long period for men and women to hug the horrid
form of fear to their bosoms before even a ray from the efful-
gent sun of peace, so long hidden by the dense clouds of
conflict, can penetrate to the earth with its inspiring messages
of hope. But there are still living a few of the men and
women of Kansas and Missouri whose humble lives were spent
in the midst of scenes enacted along this border from thirty-
four to forty-five years ago who can recite you tales of
heroism, of tragedy, fortitude, and endurance, of sufferings,
and of mingled emotions of hope and despair, which, if told
by annalist or poet, would transfer that table land of the
future from the Scammander to the banks of the Marais des
Cygnes.

These few survivors are fast tottering down into the shadow
land of forgetfulness; but they are passing away amid the
incalculable triumphs of peace which their industry and fortitude planted, and whose budding shoots they watered with
their blood and tears during eleven long years of heartbreak-
ing discord. Some magician's wand waved over their dwelling of log or clapboards has changed them to costly, beautiful
and commodious edifices. Where the cavalry stretched their
picket ropes the chapel stands; and where the battery guns
belched and thundered the stately temple of learning rears
its spire to the clouds and proclaims the eternal triumph of
the free school over the institutions whose adherents sought
to bar from these lands the spelling book and the primer.
Each of them feels that his own life-work has entered into
and forms an integral part of the happy result of the long
contest, and that whether arrayed upon one side or the other
he has in some way helped in the immense advancement over
which he rejoices exceedingly. He points to the evidence
of thrift, of progress, of culture and of social order about
him, and joyously exclaims: "Us old settlers set the pace
for all that." And they did! Those old settlers were once
the most zealous people on earth—zealous not only in their
political and sectarian spheres, but doubly zealous to plant
in this Western wild the very best of everything worth
preserving in their childhood homes. "That apple," said an
old settler near Pappinsville, pointing to a wagon-box filled
with very large and delicious fruit, "that apple comes from

a tree raised from the seed of an apple that I brought with me when a young man from my old home in Maryland."

Think of that, will you, as an example of American resolution. Carry a single apple on a journey of nearly 1800 miles, by rail to the Ohio river, then by steamboat down to Cairo, and by steamboat up the Big Muddy to old Westport Landing, and then by ox team and on foot 100 miles or more along the primitive highway, until at last the claim shanty on the Marais des Cygnes is reached—a journey that took at least a month! Save every seed of the precious apple! Plant them with care in the richest of black earth! Cultivate and prune and protect! For one of these days, when peace finally comes to this borderland, some fruit-loving settlers of Kansas, thirsting for the Bellflower and Maiden Blush of the old childhood home, will come this way, and, paying the price will drive their wagon under the boughs and freight them deep and high with the offspring of grandfather's old orchard on Antietam creek.

A day or two after his arrival in Kansas in the summer of 1865 the writer and a companion were riding down the "old wire road" and approaching the now long-vanished town of Moneka. A two-story frame building, 18x32 feet, stood all alone on the prairie, a furlong away from the next nearest house. "What building is that?" I inquired. My companion cast upon it a look of loyal pride and nearly paralyzed me with his answer: "That is the academy." Laugh not, gentle reader, at the humble pretensions of those old settlers. It was their ambitious spirit which laid the foundations of a commonwealth that has more schoolhouses, more advantages for a higher education, more newspapers and whose people read more periodicals than any other people of the same number on earth. The little town with the Indian maiden's name has faded from the map. "The academy" was trundled on trucks, long years ago, to a newer town ten miles away, and did duty for a quarter of a century as the office of the most renowned banking firm in eastern Kansas. But the impulse to Western civilization by the founders of the old settlement lives and shall continue to live in the institutions of the state and in the peculiar genius of its people while time lasts.

Almost at the very moment when Moneka resolved upon building "the academy" their neighbors in another settlement, forty-five miles away, concluded to build a "college." Neither town could claim any advantage over the other as to numbers, wealth, prospects, zeal, or intellectual abilities. In either community there were men and women who could discuss Euclid, translate Caesar, read Homer, or call the stars by name, and talk familiarly of plant life. Yet it is one of the peculiar illustrations of the mutations of fortune of the frontier that while "the academy" is the vanishing fabric of a dream, and its old-time site a modern corn field, the "college" grew and expanded into a university, and is today hailed as "Old Baker" by every church-loving Methodist in the West.

Something has already been said about fruit. It was one of the most noticeable things along the border at the close of the Civil War that scarcely a settler had neglected to plant and cultivate an orchard. Those in Missouri had the advantage of time, having planted several years earlier than those in Kansas, and consequently were more abundantly supplied with apples and pears at the period of which I write. But in the matter of peaches, grapes and berries the Kansas people were far in the lead. It is very doubtful whether any other section of our great country at that time could compete with western Missouri in the quality of its apples. It was the writer's fortune during the fruit-picking seasons of 1865 and 1866 to visit a large number of orchards in Bates, Henry and Cass counties, in that state, in quest of fruit for Kansas consumption, and he can testify from personal observation that only the very best varieties had been planted or were permitted to encumber the orchard lands.

For some unaccountable reason the successors of the old settlers in eastern Kansas have permitted themselves to allow one very great misfortune to creep over their affairs. The only potato that was ever sure to make a crop in all seasons in that limestone country, and which was always mealy and toothsome, was propagated by one of the Sovereign Squats near Moneka. It was round and smooth, and its coat was as red as a Winesap. Its average size in full maturity was about the dimensions of a baseball. It is possible it may have had equals; it never had a superior. If the grand old Irish justice of the peace, "Squire Sessions", had never done any other service for the country in its dark days of trial than evolving the "Sessions" potato, he would be still worthy of a place in history and a monument to his memory. And he who by his genius will give back to the country that most perfect potato, in all its old-time perfection, shall be called blessed. Another of those in that vicinity whose genius and culture gave to the West one of its choicest and still existing blessings, was good old Dr. S. M. Brice, who propagated the beautiful, delicious and favorite early peach known as "Brice's Early." The excellent taste and flavor it leaves in the mouth are not sweeter nor more delicious than is the remembrance of the grand old man that dwells in the bosoms of all who knew him.

These instances will serve to illustrate the general characteristics of a large majority of the Sovereign Squats in respect to material things, and will also show that they were a people of much culture, extensive intellectual attainments, and of a zealous ambition. Many an unfortunate but well-meaning stranger presumed too much upon their isolation from the trade and news center of the country. And it did seem that, everything considered, one might safely presume some things from that isolation. They were seventy-five miles by stage or wagon from the nearest steamboat landing, and the same distance or more from the nearest railroad station. The highways were beset by many difficulties and dangers. And yet they were content with their present conditions, coupled with their unbending resolution to reap the full fruition of their hopes and plans for the future. The daily stage left in its wake the Chicago Tribune, the St. Louis Democrat, the Cincinnati Gazette, and the New York Tribune. These papers, it is true, were several days old when they reached those outlaying communities; but their contents were devoured and discussed with an extra zest arising out of the fact and news that was only three days old was "fresh news" and appreciated.

The writer took up his residence in the fall of 1865 with a family into whose household both the St. Louis and Chicago papers came with the setting of each day's sun. Early the next spring two highly respected citizens and cattle-dealers from central Illinois came to visit and spend a few weeks looking for bargains. George Elliott stopped the "four white mice" at the foot of the lane and let them alight from the stage. After the usual greetings of long separated acquaintances, one of them opened his satchel and said: "Here, Murray, is a bundle of back numbers of the Chicago Tribune. I know your sickness must necessarily confine you to the house, and I thought you would like something fresh to read and post up on what is going on in the country." Just then I returned from the Moneka post-office and threw into my brother's lap a regular daily issue of that paper, which was actually two days later than the latest issue our friend had so kindly carried for our benefit all the way from Bloomington; and he learned from my brother's lips, for the first time, of very important events which had occurred near his own home in Illinois since his journey began.

But "How did those people subsist during all their years of strife and isolation, and so far from any market?" is the question that naturally arises. In the first place, the great fertility of the soil should not be forgotten. With the exception of the period during the great drought of 1860, that soil always responded luxuriantly to the plowman's toil. Then there were literally their "cattle on a thousand hills." A pair of three or four-year old steers would readily sell on the overland freighter's market at Atchison and St. Joe, and bring a cash price that would turn a modern drover green with envy. There was always enough of immigration to furnish a ready local market for every surplus bushel of grain the farmers could raise. Then the civil war came on, and, in its train, a greatly augmented demand for everything that was needed to supply the army, some portion of which was ever present in the vicinity of each neighborhood. Prairie hay, the best of forage, could be easily put up and the quartermasters were always ready purchasers. At the time of my arrival there, corn was worth $2.50 a bushel at Fort Scott, and prairie hay was worth $8 a ton. Any one with a team and a wagon could always find employment in freighting for the merchants, who paid from $1.50 to $2 per hundredweight to have their goods brought down from Kansas City or Wyandotte. It took six or eight days to make the round trip when the roads were good. When the roads got bad everything had to wait until they got passable again.

From these sources and by these means these people managed to have plenty of money for all their uses. There were a thousand things about modern ways of living that never troubled the Sovereign Squats in those days. One of these was the item of furniture. Now and then some family was found which was pretty well supplied with chairs. There was in every family the mother's or grandmother's rocking chair; but, aside from that, soap and cracker boxes supplied the seats of most people and their guests. Their tables were always well supplied with substantial articles of food. There was no want.

The family's chief method of travel was by two-horse wagon. There was but one buggy in all the borders of Linn County as late as the autumn of 1867, and it was made at Moneka by the owner several years before. That fellow was regarded as an aristocrat. Next to him were owners of spring seats for the two-horse wagons. These were the only real aristocracy, and a man was rated by the spring-seat test. There were three grades. The one who did not have a spring seat for his wagon was "ordinary;" the fellow with one spring seat was "good", and the chap who had two spring seats was "excellent." Wealth or the lack of it did not figure in the ratings; and it is very doubtful whether the plans of rating now pursued by Dun and Bradstreet have made any improvement over the spring-seat plan. If they have, then in what respect?

There was one inexorable social rule among those people that no one might trifle with. If Smith built a house, the whole community insisted on the right to have it dedicated by a dance before he should move into it. And everybody— that is, most everybody—attended; and those who could not or would not dance, and of such there were very few, spent the night in visiting, playing games, or settling questions of social and political importance. It was nothing unusual in those times to meet at these dances families who resided twelve to fifteen miles away.

I am reminded right here of an incident in connection with

one such social gathering that further illustrates what has already been said about the means of travel. One of our prominent Sovereign Squats had recently married and was getting down to housekeeping on his own homestead a few miles out of Mound City. Of course he gave a ball, to which everybody was invited. A young merchant of the town had engaged the company of one of our society belles for the occasion, but he overlooked on some account the altogether essential matter of getting there. The afternoon of the important day arrived and bethinking him of a means of conveying his girl to the dance, he discovered, to his chagrin, that every team and vehicle had been engaged by others. He flew about from one man to another of those who had engaged the teams, and was further mortified to learn that there would be no room for himself and partner with any of them. Here was a situation that drove him almost frantic. In his distress he unbosomed himself to Uncle Bob Garrett. "Why, said he, "everything on wheels is engaged except Brook's water-cart." "Why not get that, then?" was the reply. In a moment the distracted fellow was off to lay the situation and the suggestion before his girl. She thought that would be just the thing to do. So, just after dark that evening, one of our most cultured society belles and her lover might have been seen perched on top the rectangular water-box of Brook's one-horse water-cart, driving merrily and happily to the country ball, where their dilemma had already been discussed and laughed at by those who supposed themselves more fortunate. Their appearance in the reception-room was greeted by a storm of applauding questions, and, when the truth became known, this couple were looked upon as the heroes of the day.

The very first "woman's crusade" against the liquor traffic of which the writer has ever heard occurred here at the foot of Sugar Mound. It was, and ever has been, an unwritten law of that community that the open saloon should not exist or prosper there. Some time during the Civil War this sentiment was defied by a couple of men who seemed to have the protecting influence of the military officers then in command of the troops stationed at and in the vicinity of Mound City. Those men opened a doggery on Main Street, in the very heart of the little town. It was not long before it bore fruit. A drunken soldier, crazed by the liquid lightning that had been dealt out to him, proceeded to paint the town and the camp in deep carnation colors, and several persons narrowly escaped death from his flying bullets. This and other cases of similar character following in quick succession aroused the indignation of the Sovereign Squats, particularly the women, and it soon became evident that something would be done—but what? Most of the men able for military service were in the army, and the remainder were too few to cope with the arbitrary power of the military officer mentioned. Things were getting worse from day to day. The doggery was an intolerable nuisance to the citizens. Some of the otherwise very best soldiers that ever served their country had already found themselves in the most serious difficulty on account of their conduct while under the demoralizing influence of the drinks obtained there.

But the women of Kansas never were at a loss for a plan of action in any emergency. One morning a wagon-load of women from the vicinity of Moneka drove into Mound City. They were amply supplied with axes and hatchets, and were soon joined by a squad of their sisters of the "Mound". They marched straight to the open door of the saloon and began filing in. Just then the military officer rode up and, hastily dismounting, made a move to interfere with the women. Hovering near by was a Sovereign Squat whose keen eye and quick perception caught the full meaning of the officer's presence and action, and just as the latter was in the act of interfering in a rude and boisterous manner he was confronted by the muzzle of the Sovereign Squat's heavy Colt's revolver and brought to a statue-like posture by the emphatic, direfully freighted message, "You interfere with those women by word or act, or move a muscle until I tell you, and I'll blow your head off." He knew his man, and he did not need to be told that his sole source of personal safety lay in strictly observing the injunction that had been given him. The women drove out the bartenders and the loungers and then deliberately broke every bottle, glass, and decanter, and knocked in the heads of every barrel and keg. Having completed their work, they filed out again and proceeded to their homes. Mr. Officer was given his liberty in due time with the further advice: "If you would consult your own advantage, you will carry yourself mighty straight in this community hereafter."

That event resulted in a prohibition that prohibited for many years without any assistance from courts or statute. The great wonder is that the experiment of the female Sovereign Squats has not been more frequently tested on a much larger scale. No dramshop can long exist in the presence of the mothers and wives of any community who will muster enough courage on their own responsibility.

Such were some of the representative people whose courage, loyalty, and genius founded our Western empire and institutions; and such, feebly portrayed, were some of their ambitions, conditions, and circumstances of life. Many other pages might be filled with incidents and anecdotes relating to the Sovereign Squats that would be of interest and profit to the average reader, but space here forbids.

There was one phase of social life among the Sovereign Squats at and for some time after the close of the Civil War that was not long in impressing itself upon the attention of the newcomer. There was little social affiliation between the

families of the old free-state men and those of the proslavery
party. Social divisions were nearly as distinct as party
divisions, and whether caused by that fact as many believed,
were traceable in great part by political lines. Each group
had a well-defined center. Mound City was the social, commercial and political capital of one, and Paris of the other.
These towns had for years been the storm-centers of fierce
contending partisans. In their respective origins may be
found the key to most, if not all, the subsequent history of
that section for twenty-five years.

The first colony of Southerners to pitch its camp on Kansas
soil in southern Kansas did so on the hill south of Parent's
ford, on the Big Sugar, in about 1854. Here they surveyed
and platted the town that was to be the salve-dealer's Mecca
in the new territory and the political capital of the new county.
Their town they named Paris, in honor of the well-known
city in Kentucky from which their leaders had come. From
this point they distributed the frequently-arriving proslavery
immigrants along both sides of Big and Little Sugar creeks,
and settled them on claims that would command the best of
the timber and the available crossings. The leaders at Paris
organized Linn County, secured control of all the offices, and
made their town the county seat.

Their chief hetman, or alcalde, was Judge J. H. Barlow,
who became the probate judge or principal judicial officer
under the territorial government. A finer specimen of the
affable and suave Southern gentleman never trod Kansas
soil. He illustrated in his every walk in life the old text,
"Be yet wise as serpents and harmless as doves." He was
a non-combatant, except on the forum and in the political
councils of his partisans. He was as clean-minded as a
devotee of human slavery could possibly be. On one momentous occasion his non-interference, when but one word
or hint would have sufficed, resulted in the most damnable
tragedy of Kansas history. Two days before the Hamelton
massacre, Judge Barlow was present at the caucus of Missouri
slave-owners, at Pappinsville, when the question of forcing
all free-state men to forthwith abandon Kansas soil, in Linn
County and on the Little Osage in Bourbon was the object
of the meeting, and the chief subject of discussion. All the
hot-heads of Bates county were there. But, principally
through the oratorical and persuasive talents of Judge Barlow,
the meeting voted down the proposition looking toward
measures of extermination. Before anything further could
be decided upon Captain Hamelton, who was there with his
followers, recently expelled from Kansas in force, virtually
broke up the meeting by brandishing his revolver and by
making profane and savage threats against further opposition to his plans, and by calling upon his "bloody reds"
to follow him. Soon afterward Judge Barlow proceeded to

his home at Paris, and on this journey back to Kansas he displayed that moral cowardice from whose blighting shadow he was never after able to extricate his good name. He dropped no hint, he sent no word, to warn a living soul of Hamelton's savage purpose against the free-state settlers at and near the old Choteau trading post. No one believes that Judge Barlow ever had murder in his heart, even by freely consenting to so foul a deed. His laches can only be accounted for on the theory of a moral cowardice that paralyzed his better nature. His nearest and easiest way home from Pappinsville was by way of Trading Post; but, to avoid sight of the doomed men, and, in case a warning should reach their ears from some other source, to avoid any suspicion that he might have betrayed his Missouri friends, he made a wide circuit around that settlement and left it to its awful impending fate. That Judge J. H. Barlow was not hung by Capt. James Montgomery and his free-state company for that great neglect of manly duty is one of the greatest mysteries of modern times.

The first free-state men to settle in this area of storms and blood found their lodgment near or at Sugar Mound and along Little Sugar above that point. Already a few of the proslavery men had gone into that vicinity, but even in 1855 these found themselves outnumbered by an increasing population of their opponents, and like the sensible men they were, subsided into quiet, good-natured and inoffensive citizenship. The free-state settlers at this point were all men and women of good education, cultured habits, and irreproachable lives. "York State", New England and Ohio each contributed about equal proportions of their number. Each was a walking compendium of American political history and knew every argument that had ever been offered in favor either of slavery or emancipation. They were, in short, the very kind of people it would have been necessary to kill off before human slavery could have found a home in the Territory. But they were not willing that any should kill them without first paying dearly for the privilege—a truth which on occasion they impressed indelibly upon the history of the times.

Choosing the gentle slope that stretches down from the base of Sugar Mound to the south bank of Little Sugar Creek, they laid out their town site and proclaimed to the world that they were there to welcome people of like views and to defy their foes. Mound City thus became a center of free-state activities. A mile north on the stage road was the old town of Moneka, at and around which had gathered another settlement of free-state men. Between these two towns there was a common bond of political interest, although rivals for political and commercial favors. Both were imbued with a common hatred for their neighbor on the hill near Parent's ford.

Moneka was more of a storm center in territorial days than was Mound City. There was enough of the Quaker element in the latter to avoid haste in entering into quarrel, while the friends of Moneka always adorned their shoulders with the traditional chip. For this reason Moneka, up to the beginning of the Civil War, was a sort of headquarters for all those uneasy spirits who could little brook the more sober ideas of their Mound City brethren. A Mound Cityite might argue with an obstreperous enemy an hour to avoid being the aggressor, but would fight him to a finish afterward. A Monekaite would start the combat at once, and do all the arguing afterward—if at all. If Capt. James Montgomery wanted a platoon of the friends of Mound City to accompany him on a foray across the border, or to go hang some scoundrel, he would first have to make them a speech. If he wanted help from Moneka he got all he wanted instantly, and could defer his speech until his return and disbandment —or omit it. Moneka therefore monopolized much of the notoriety of that section and era.

Andrew Stark was the patron and promoter of Moneka, but his ideas concerning public utility were much too conservative for his neighbors. Both Moneka and Mound City were united in the determination that the county-seat must be removed from the proslavery town of Paris; but as Moneka had no living water-supply and Mound City had, it became apparent to everybody except Andrew Stark that Moneka must sooner or later succumb and vanish from the map. Andrew held on, however, until it was discovered by Murray Botkin that there was a serious defect in the Moneka town-site papers at the land office. Murray filed a contest and pre-emption claim on the town-site, and Andrew Stark awoke to the fact that his town must soon become a "has been."

Then in 1859 Mound City opened the county-seat question, and the result of the ballot was a small majority in its favor. Paris set up a howl and announced its intention to contest the election. After the result was known the friends of Mound City, with a plentiful supply of teams, and accompanied by Colonel Jennison, with a howitzer and a band of determined horsemen, appeared on the public square at Paris and moved the county-seat down to Mound City. This coup d'etat was the death blow to old Paris. Judge Barlow knew that the prejudice against his town was too intense to permit it to recover its lost prestige, but he would not let his hopes die without a telling blow. He bided his time and finding a favorable opportunity, laid off a new town site adjoining the old, and called it Linnville. He reopened the question at a time when very many of Mound City's friends were in the army or out of the state, and when the military, too, were gone, and succeeded in establishing Linnville as the county-seat. But the close of the war, the return of the veterans and the influx of immigrants during the next two years again gave Mound City the advantage, and Linnville joined the procession of defunct towns.

I have thus referred in a general way to much of the past, to be able to impress more clearly my meaning when I said at the beginning that social divisions at and for some time after the close of the Civil War were nearly as distinct as party divisions, and were traceable in great part by political lines. For instance, with only a few exceptions, a dance at Mound City or in the Moneka neighborhood would be a Republican affair, while one at Paris or Linnville, or in that vicinity, would be a Democratic affair. The two communities did not mix or affiliate in anything. The antipathy between them was very marked on occasions.

In February, 1864, with a veteran's re-enlistment furlough in my pocket, I made a flying visit to my brothers and sisters in Linn County. I had heard in Ohio that, while they still got their mail at Moneka, they had moved onto a ranch near Paris, and close to the stage line. We reached Paris at sunrise and stopped to get breakfast and change mules. After I had paid my bill I inquired of the landlord how to get to my destination, at the same time giving him the name of my people and the well-known name of the farm where they were living. His reply was: "I don't know any one by that name and there is no such farm or ranch as that in this country." Just then the stage-driver came out of the dining-room, and in time to hear the landlord's reply. "Old Dan," for it was that famous driver, asked me who my folks were. When I had told him, he turned on that hotel-keeper and gave him such a cursing for his lying as would excite the envy of a ship's mate. Then "Old Dan" turned to me and told me to crawl up on the driver's seat, and he would show me where my brothers lived. We had but a mile and a half to go before he pointed to the house, a half-mile off the road, and let me off. But in that short ride "Old Dan" managed to tell me more history about old Paris than I had ever supposed a town could have. I learned from my brothers that "Old Dan" was right; that that landlord did, indeed, know them well, and that he had once lived on that very farm. His only reason for vowing his ignorance of them and the place was that they did not "move in his set." I afterwards became intimately acquainted with that landlord, and found that under the veneering of his political and partizan prejudices, he was a most kind, generous and honorable man. My own people got their mail at Moneka, seven miles away, rather than patronize the Paris office, which was only a mile and a half away.

Before I leave the subject, I must relate that, in 1877-'78, while I was probate judge of Linn County, I undertook to sort over and classify the old territorial files of that office.

In doing so I discovered the oath of office which Judge Barlow took when entering upon the discharge of his duties at the organization of the county. It was written on parchment foolscap, and was in the judge's well-known handwriting. Here is a true copy of the body of that oath:
"Territory of Kansas, County of Linn, ss.

I, J. H. Barlow, do solemnly swear that I will support the constitution of the United States and enforce the laws thereof, particularly the law known as the fugitive-slave law. So help me God."

The original afterwards disappeared from the files in 1880 during the incumbency of Judge Aiken D. Hyatt. Whether it ever again came to light I cannot say.

The Marais des Cygnes massacre threw a blight upon the proslavery cause and an odium over the friends of that cause in southern Kansas that could never be eradicated or glossed over. On the other hand it caused an influx of free-state settlers that soon placed the latter cause on triumphant ground. These last-mentioned settlers were all cast in the same partizan mold and became immediately identified with all the struggles in which their predecessors had been and were involved. In Montgomery's measures of retribution for the Marais des Cygnes massacre, and for the brutal evictions on Mine creek and on the Little Osage these fresh arrivals were a welcome host and bore a conspicuous part.

About the same time Dr. Charles R. Jennison established himself at Mound City, and soon gathered around him a band of adventurous spirits whose religion was the hatred of everything connected with slavery and the state of Missouri. If Montgomery and his company forgot, overlooked, or omitted anything in the way of retaliatory measures, Jennison and his followers recollected, picked it up, or attended to it. But between James Montgomery and Charles R. Jennison there was very little in common. The former was cast in the mold of a Puritanical leader without having any of the Puritan bigotry or pig-headedness. He was conscientious, honest, tender-hearted toward those in distress, but exacting along the lines of decorum. He would have given his last cent to relieves a settler's wants; but would have as readily hung that man for stealing a neighbor's log chain or sod plow. On the other hand, Jennison was a moral vagabond, cruel, heartless, and conscienceless. But there was a certain glamor about his enthusiastic hatred of everything pertaining to slavery that drew men to him as moths to a light. His name soon became a terror to the people in Bates and Vernon counties in Missouri, and he used to boast in the adapted language of old Richard Coeur de Leon that "the Missouri mothers hush their children to sleep by whispering the name of Doc. Jennison"! That was no idle boast, either. Both Montgomery and Jennison were at times inspired with the spirit of prophecy in relation to the approach of hostilities between the North and the South and the results of the war.

On the Sunday before his death in December, 1871, Montgomery preached a sermon at Trading Post, the scene of the Hamelton or Marais des Cygnes Massacre. It was my privilege to hear his discourse. I sat near the front, with Austin Hall and Amos Hall on the one hand and Mr. and Mrs. Harvey Smith upon the other. The Halls were of the number of Hamelton's victims who fell at the first fire and escaped by feigning death. Mrs. Smith was formerly Mrs. Colpetzer, wife and widow of one of Hamelton's victims. In the audience were children of various ones of that immortal eleven who were "Swooped up and swept on to the low, reedy fen-lands, the marsh of the swan," on that tragic morn in May, 1858. There were also a score or more of the men present who had stood around the bodies of the slain with Montgomery, and applaudingly shouted "Amen" when the renowned leader there and then registered his vow that the blood of the dead and the tears of the widows and children should not be shed or wept in vain. There were a score of daring men there who had ridden with Montgomery on his forays of retaliation and vengeance, and who afterwards followed Cloud and Moonlight and Jennison in the larger cause of a nation's redemption. It was an audience worthy of the distinguished hero who was about to address them with a message from Holy Writ; and only a James Montgomery in spirit and action was worthy of such an audience. As he arose to begin the services, and fixed his gaze upon the familiar faces of those who had suffered and whose sufferings he had so fully avenged, a gleam of joy and satisfaction seemed to blaze from his penetrating eyes, and thrilled the audience into perfect accord with the spirit of the great thoughts which at that moment filled his bosom. He hesitated but a moment, and then requested all to arise and sing "The Battle Hymn of the Republic." The noble thought of that grand hymn stirred the crowd to the deepest depths of feeling, and it fairly seemed as though the building vibrated with the harmony and power of the music.

The text was in keeping with other features of the meeting and occasion "Be not deceived. God is not mocked; for whatsoever a man soweth, that shall he also reap." His theme was the accountability of communities, institutions and nations to the same laws of God that govern the individual. The discourse was logical, powerful and impressive. Before us stood the tall and slender form of that greatest man, if history were written true, in all the sanguinary struggles that preceded the Civil War. His shaggy shock of long, black hair and his shaggier black whiskers united to entirely enclose in a circle the forehead, the eyes and nose, but left enough exposed to reveal the deep and sincere earnestness and enthusiasm of their possessor. He seemed to fairly vibrate with the importance of the great truths that filled his bosom. With his first sentence he was not only in elbow touch with his hearers, but enchained them with his magnetic manner and qualities. I remember but one of the several climaxes in his argument that would have any bearing here. After having illustrated how God's will has been worked out by men in our own national affairs, and how at times men, without realizing the fact, have uttered prophecies that were fulfilled to the letter, he broke out with substantially these words: "I call upon my old friends in this audience, and upon Brother Austin Hall, particularly, to remember what I said to you at a certain sorrowful meeting nearly fourteen years ago, when I prophesied that the remaining years of slavery could be numbered upon the fingers of one hand, and that in that period I would lead a host of negro soldiers dressed in the national uniform, in the redemption of our country and the negro race from the curse of slavery." It was an impressive scene and occasion, and being the old hero's last sermon (for he died a few days afterward), it was a memorable one.

On the other hand, Jennison's military order freeing the slaves of the Jackson and Cass county rebels, and its rescission by a mandate from Washington, gave the impulsive colonel the excuse for saying to Mr. Lincoln, when they met soon thereafter (and I quote Jennison's words as he told them to me): "Mr. President, I bow gratefully to your will in the matter; but please to remember that when you shall issue your own proclamation of emancipation, as you must before this war is over, I shall claim 'royalty' upon the measure."

Not all the proslavery settlers were vicious toward their free-state neighbors. In sober truth, many of them never gave just cause for a single word of complaint. And the outrages of 1856, 1857 and 1858, when so many of the free-state settlers were burned out and driven off, or threatened with death if they did not leave the country, created such a general and strong feeling of revulsion in the bosoms of very many of the proslavery class that, when Montgomery started on his memorable raids of retaliation, the guilty ones found little or no sympathy from many of those of like political views, whose hearts revolted over the crimes that had been done in the name of their party.

Peace was a welcome guest, but its seductive power and influence could not smother the eruptive fires of memory which blazed forth here and there on occasion, throwing their lurid light far back through the years, revealing to the newcomer many of the exciting and ofttimes tragic scenes and events of the past. Here and there some quiet and unostentatious individual would be pointed out as one who had been a heroic actor, and who had won renown in some one or more of those awful hours of trial. And one substantial fact about such individuals has ever impressed itself upon my mind, and that is this: The real heroes of that bloody border war have persistently been the most reticent ones in relation to their experience. But here and there some glib-tongued, empty-nail-keg orator, at the country store or corner grocery, would loudly boast to the tenderfoot of how "we used to raid the Missourians," and how "we made Kansas free," and how "we used to ride with Montgomery," etc., etc., ad nauseum, to boaster's past like a primer, and remembered that he had opposed every effort that had been made to check or turn back the tidal waves of proslavery aggression. I witness several scenes wherein the boasters came into direct contact with the quiet fellows who had done the deeds which the boasters at the time opposed; but I think the most amusing incident of the kind was one which occurred at the Moneka store and post-office one afternoon soon after my arrival in the community. I shall relate it not merely on its own account, but because it throws light upon an event which has been erroneously narrated as having taken place at Montgomery's house, and accredited to that leader.

I called at the postoffice for the family mail and, being a newcomer, I at once became the target of the interest and solicitude of one of the gentlemen loafers present, who was hailed by the highly pleasing appellation of "captain". In fact, he had borne a commission of that rank in a Kansas regiment. No candidate for a position as janitor of a city school building ever buttonholed an indifferent voter with more alacrity and perseverance than the captain displayed to impress men, then and there, with his devotion to the free-state cause and his pugnacity toward its enemies during the period before the war. I was rapidly coming to the conclusion that but for him the whole scheme to make Kansas a free state would have quickly gone to the "demnition bowwows", when I was saved from that delusion by the timely entrance of one of the Corbin boys, whose appearance on the scene acted like magic upon the captain's conversational powers. He shut up as quickly and as tightly as a clam. Of course I noticed the fact and at once began to wonder what historical incident lay back of it. I afterwards made inquiry, and got the following story from a Sovereign Squat.

A number of warrants had been issued for the arrest of the leading and most aggressive of the free-state men in the vicinity of Moneka and Mound City, but something in the then recent events had so impressed the proslavery sheriff and deputy marshal with a sense of extreme danger to them down in that vicinity that none of them would undertake to make the arrests. The captain concluded that right then was his time to make a name for himself that his descendants would be proud of. He had been boasting all his life, and as no one had ever put him to the test he had necessarily con-

cluded that he was a hero in fact, and that it was his duty
to demonstrate the fact to the neighbors. And thus it came
that he loudly boasted at the store and blacksmith shop and
hotel that if the proper authority were given him and the
warrants placed in his hand he would make the arrests, and
he "would not have to have no posse to help him neither."
It took no great while for his boasting to reach the ears of
those most nearly concerned on both sides, and it was no
joke that both sides hoped he would attempt the task. The
authorities sent for the captain, and duly authorized and
empowered him as a deputy United States marshal to serve
the warrants. Equipped with the majesty of the law, placing
the writs in his inside pocket, he mounted his horse and proceeded Moneka-ward. In a certain place his road wound somewhat irregularly down a slope studded with trees and rocky
ledges. As the captain came along at that place and turned
a somewhat short curve he found himself confronted by one
of the Corbin boys—the one I have already mentioned. Something like the following conversation took place while the
captain looked into the muzzle of a big revolver: "Captain,
I'll trouble you to hand over those warrants, and be quick
about it. Not a word of back talk, sir. There, thank you.
Now, go straight home, captain, and not a sound out of you
louder than thunder, hereafter. Do you hear? Well, then,
remember it. Good-by, captain. I hope I'll not have to mention this matter to you hereafter."

The captain went, a much wiser man. I was
never able to learn that he made any official report, or that
he ever told his most intimate friends what had occurred.
But he never again attempted a part in the play until the
coming of the Civil War and the influence of Gen. Robt. B.
Mitchell secured him a commission. He was a good citizen,
and discarding his disposition toward self-laudation was an
exemplary man.

It was not with the captain's class alone that memory
played havoc in the years following the advent of peace. There
had always been a conservative element among the free-state
people, and these at times were able to shape destiny. Some
among them had on occasions let their conservatism run riot
with their better judgments, and had never been forgiven by
the radical elements, with whose plans of retribution they had
interfered. On several occasions these conservative ones had
even gone so far as to array themselves temporarily against
the free-state leaders, and under the pretense of "law and
order," permitted themselves to perform and attempt acts
that were troublesome to them afterwards. One such example
will illustrate my meaning, and will give me the excuse for
referring to some exciting episodes wherein the conservative
and radical elements came very near to disastrous conflict,

and afterwards furnished some very warm material in Linn County politics.

Late in the autumn of 1865 county politics became suddenly very interesting. One party had renominated the then acting sheriff, D. F. Park, who resided south of Little Sugar and a few miles west of Mound City. He belonged to the conservative, non-combatant wing of the old democratic party, and with his father's family had located in the settlement early in territorial days. He had displayed loyalty during the Civil War, and was accredited with a bold and dangerous reconnaissance against General Price's advance guard of scouts when he was severely wounded in the hand a short distance east of Mound City, in October, 1864. He was an exemplary man and citizen in every respect, and made an excellent official. The other party (Republican) nominated Hon. Edwin R. Smith, who had also come to Kansas with his father's family in an early day, and who was a near neighbor to the Park family. Ed. is so well known in Kansas that I scarcely need to say that he, too, was worthy of every confidence. He had been most radical and active during the Civil War, and held a high office in the "raging tads," or Kansas militia, during the Price raid. He had the happy faculty of always enlisting the very greatest enthusiasm of his friends when fighting the political battles of others, but the unfortunate ill luck of calling out the most determined and uncompromising opposition whenever he became a candidate himself. Ed. should and would have made a noble mark in Kansas state politics but for the incident which I shall relate before I close this chapter. His radicalism and enthusiasm, together with his intense loyalty and active participation in certain events and dangerous excursions during the Civil War, of which I had heard accounts, had predisposed me very warmly in his favor. But all at once I noticed that some of the old Moneka radicals were unfavorably discussing his candidacy. I had not long to wait for the solution of the political puzzle here presented. Ed. had once upon a time been a voluntary member of a posse assembled to arrest James Montgomery for assault and battery upon the Sugar Mound ballot-box. Other men, members of that same posse, had been forgiven by the Montgomery partizans, but Ed. at the time had made, or was accused of having made, an imprudent remark about what he intended to do personally to Montgomery in case he should get within Sharp's rifle range of him, and it was for that alleged remark, in November, 1858, that he was now, in November, 1865, and many times thereafter, to be called to account. It defeated him. And this brings us face to face with one of the most thrilling and eventful episodes in the territorial struggle, and which has often been mentioned, but always neglected, by those who have written our Kansas histories.

The Territorial politicians along the Kaw had by their bickerings and quarrelings, in 1857, thoroughly discouraged many of the rank and file of the free-state party, and the idea of "resistance against illegal authority was being abandoned everywhere," except in that storm-swept district between Paola and Fort Scott, and stretching from the Missouri line to the head waters of the Sugar creeks and the Little Osage and Marmaton, where the free-state cause was most fortunate in the fact that it was so far removed from the influence of those dissensions. In all that region there were but two recognized free-state leaders, James Montgomery of Little Sugar and Capt. O. P. Bayne of Little Osage; and neither of them cared whether the balance of the world recognized him as a hero or not. Each was in the fight purely for the sake of the cause and not for glory or political leadership. On the other hand, we have the picture of deplorable divisions and distrust among the leaders along the Kaw, in the letter of June 3, 1857, from Augustus Wattles to John Brown, alias "James Smith," at the very time when every free-stater's home in southern Kansas was in jeopardy, and when Montgomery and Bayne were rallying their partizans to cope with the storm of pillage and rapine that was raging in their respective localities. If there was doubt and hesitation elsewhere, here there were unity and courage. Then came the October elections of that year. Linn County had set its teeth, and the "loafers" from Missouri, Georgia, South Caroline and Alabama took to the woods. The result was 214 free-state votes and 178 proslavery votes—A. Danford and R. B. Mitchell being elected to the legislature over Judge J. H. Barlow and J. E. Mooney. So much was due to the influence of the men who, night and day, hunted the scoundrels into hiding or flight.

Then followed, in quick order, the discussion of the question about voting for officers under the Lecompton constitution. Montgomery and his partizans were opposed to giving that compact the recognition that would logically follow such voting, and opposed holding an election. His blood was up and he was dreadfully in earnest; but he kept his own counsels. The months of November and December (1857) were busy ones for him. The swaggering fire-eaters whom he and Bayne had driven out were congregated at West Point, at Marvel, at Balltown and at Fort Scott, where the "blue lodges" flourished, and from which flying raiders emerged to harrass the free-state settlers on Mine creek and along the Little Osage. Almost daily reports came in of some outrage committed by "the Missourians," and the free-state men would ride upon errands of swift retribution. Upon such an errand the doughty warrior had gone to the vicinity of Barnesville, in the last week in December. Having straightened up affairs in that community, he rode with his men to Potosi on Mine creek, upon a like errand, and thence proceeded up that stream to reassure the friends in the neighborhood of McAuley's Gap. The next day, January 4, 1858, he proceeded leisurely toward Sugar Mound. It was the day set apart for the election under the Lecompton constitution. He had knowledge that his neighbors were voting at Sugar Mound. He timed his return so that he would reach the polling-place late in the afternoon, perhaps between 3 and 4 p. m.

As one approaches Mound City from the eastward and enters the timber at the eastern end of Sugar Mound he will see if he uses searching eyes on the left of the roadway the evidences that there was once a blacksmith shop there, and one or two other buildings which have long since vanished. That was the historic spot known in Kansas annals as Sugar Mound (or Little Sugar) precinct. It was there that the conservatives of both parties assembled that day to cast their ballots for officers under the Lecompton constitution. Among them were men whose influence was ever of the largest in that community and who were ever on the side of right. They believed it for the best interests of themselves and their community that they should participate in that election and beat the proslavery party at the polls, even if the officers chosen should never be called upon to take their seats under the Lecompton infamy. They were strictly for law and order, and the ballot-box was to them as a pure and sacred shrine, not to be polluted by fraud nor soiled by violence. And it may as well be said right here, for it is historic truth that defies successful contradiction, that from that October day in 1857 when liberty won its first decided triumph there, through every contest that has ever been waged at the polls, no matter what the issue, to the present day, the records of elections in that community have been as free from fraud as in any other precinct in all the broad land. So much for the influence of those first early settlers.

Capt. James Montgomery and his platoon of men came along after most of the votes had been cast. There was still a considerable crowd standing about the polling place. Montgomery halted his men and walked up to the table where the election officials sat. He made some inquiry about the election, its purpose, and the number of ballots cast, and then startled everybody by reaching over and seizing the ballot-box. He held it up before the astonished spectators, uttered an imprecation against the Lecompton constitution and the effort that was being made to mislead the people, pronounced an anathema against that particular box for being the instrument of such unholy deception, and then hurled it upon the ground and stamped the box into splinters and the ballots into pulp. The deed was so unexpected, so audaciously, so courageously done, that most of the bystanders stood mute with amazement; those who were self-possessed enough to comprehend the situation and its significance were prudent enough in presence of the armed squad to make no demonstration of resistance or interference, and the occasion passed without further incident.

I might add in this place that without the votes of Sugar Mound precinct the free-state ticket was beaten in Linn County by a majority of twenty. The ballots in that box would have again given the victory to the free-state people; but defeat at the polls was more than compensated for by the effect which Montgomery's mad act had upon the pro-slavery partizans. They saw in that act, or thought they did, the evidence of a determination on the captain's part that made them shudder. Here was a leader who meant just what he said; and who would brook no opposition or trifling of whatever sort to his measures for the advancement of the cause he espoused. But the conservatives at Sugar Mound were sore. They looked upon the ballot-box as "the palladium of liberty". It possessed a sanctity in their eyes and minds whose pollution called for their protest; but affairs were in such state that it was not politic to protest just then; so they nursed their wounded feelings and kept their pent-up wrath warm for a more suitable time.

Montgomery was too busy watching the common enemy of them all to pay much attention to the outraged feelings of his neighbors. The "blue lodges" at Paris and West Point and the nest of vipers at Fort Scott were actively engaged in planning and executing new designs of vengeance, and constant watchfulness was required from all.

The act of Montgomery on January 4 was the first of the many startling events which made up the bloody and other-wise awfully dramatic and tragic record of the year 1858 in that stricken section of the territory. Events followed each other so rapidly and so dramatically that little time was left for the discussion of factional divisions or differences. In truth none but the cowed partizans at Paris had leisure for such recreation. Late in the fall, when every other com-munity was absorbed in excitement on account of the almost constant raidings and skirmishes, a proslavery grand jury at Paris found an indictment against Montgomery charging him with interfering by violence with the election at Sugar Mound ten months before. It was at a time when the sleep-less vigilance and every resource of Montgomery, Bayne and John Brown combined were required and put forth to protect the settlers against the "wolves of the border". Montgomery learned of the grand jury's action in November and on the 13th moved in force on Paris in search of the indictment and warrants. Brown and his men accompanied the raid; but there were no results. A few days afterward the law and order conservatives at Mound City held a meeting and decided that the election laws must be vindicated and that they would join the sheriff's posse in an attempt to apprehend and arrest Montgomery. The sheriff came with his warrant, the posse assembled in large numbers from both political parties, and after some foolish and imprudent speech-making sallied forth on its mission. But it so happened that on that very day Montgomery with his company were down on the Little Osage to right and redress fresh wrongs and of course the posse missed their game. They returned and disbanded and have been explaining and excusing their action ever since.

I have given the history of the ballot-box episode from inception to conclusion in conformity to the facts as they have been related to me by eye-witnesses and participants, and I have been as faithful in the narration as the lapse of years and memory will permit.

One amusing feature about the use of these facts in Linn County politics since the Civil War has been the zeal with which leading Democrats have on the stump urged "membership in that posse" as an argument against certain politicians; and I have known that to be done by men who in 1858 would have voluntarily served as hangmen or faggot-lighters to strangle or burn James Montgomery if they had the opportunity—and enough help.

Before I quit the subject let me say in justice to those same Mound City conservatives that they all without exception so far as I have ever been able to hear, learned to look upon James Montgomery as the one always-safe leader in their troubles and to do full honor to his exalted memory. They respected and loved him more as they understood him better. Time may not have wholly justified his violence on that January day at Sugar Mound but both time and circumstance have proven his act to have been prompted by the very highest and purest consideration for the cause whose battles he was fighting and for the people in whose behalf he was playing so dangerous but disinterested a part. He had nothing of the demagogue about him. He cared no more for popularity or popular applause than he did for the whims of his opponents. Devoutly religious, opposition to the extension of human slavery was to him the cause of God; and when once his judgment was formed he drove straight to the conclusion that his highest and holiest duty was to consumate that judgment. Yet he was always considerate towards others. He joined reluctantly in the hollow mockery of peace which the conservatives patched up at West Point after the Marais des Cygnes Massacre, knowing or believing that a few days or a few weeks at most would suffice to show the conservatives that the proslavery leaders were incapable of sincerity. Descended directly through a long line of military ancestors from the Scottish chief of olden times whose name he bore, he was as tactful and full of resources in the field as a Francis Marion or a William Wallace. "Captain Montgomery," said

John Brown, "is the only soldier I have met among the prominent Kansas men. He is a natural chieftain, and knows how to lead."

Hannah Worden was then a little girl who had a nutting holiday spoiled by the running battle. As Mrs. Hannah Worden Wickham she now tells about it as follows: On the morning of the 24th of October I went with my grandmother and sister to the Marais des Cygnes, at the mouth of the Big Sugar creek to gather hickory nuts. About four o'clock in the afternoon we heard what we supposed was thunder, but the air soon became full of smoke and hurrying out of the woods into the road we saw two merchants from Trading Post who told us to hurry to a place of safety because there were thirty thousand rebels at Trading Post who were killing every one and destroying every thing they came to. So we commenced unloading our wagon to make it lighter and hurried the horses on but soon one of the wheels broke down and we were compelled to abandon the wagon and take the horses to the timber. Then we went to the home of Mr. Huff and by that time the rebels were seen coming out of the timber and scattering in all directions all over the valley. About twenty-five rode up to the door and Mrs. Wm. Baugh went out and asked if that was the militia. They answered, "Yes"; and she said: "You almost scared us to death for we thought you were rebels." Then one of them asked if there were any men or guns about the place and on being told there were none they said, "Well, come on if you want to see the rebels eat" and then they jumped from their horses and entered the house.

Mrs. Huff had just churned and baked a large pan of biscuits which they helped themselves to until there was not a drop of buttermilk nor a biscuit left. Then they took everything eatable from the house, and all the men's clothing and then asked what we were crying for. Mrs. Baugh said: "Oh, just see what the rebels are doing over at my house," which was half a mile distant, and they told us if we had any homes we had better go to them and save everything we could. So I started home with Mrs. Baugh and the rest stayed with Mrs. Huff. We had gone only about half way when we met five rebels taking a young man with them. We asked what they were going to do with him and they said he was their prisoner and that we could consider ourselves prisoners and they would send a guard with us to the house. So two men were sent with us and when we reached the house we found it broken into and almost every movable thing taken out or destroyed. The fields were full of men, some digging potatoes, some pulling cabbage and corn, some killing hogs and chickens. It was soon dark and the men told us to fix our fires and go to bed, which we did, first fastening the doors with fence rails and chairs. We sat up in bed all night for we could not sleep.

Mrs. Baugh and I being alone with two little children, one and two years old, who were crying for something to eat. About 4 o'clock next morning, October 25th, the rebels demanded us to open the doors and let them in. About thirty came in and asked me to mix some bread for them, but I told them I had nothing to mix it in so they got an old tin wash-pan and one man poured in flour and another water and I mixed it with my hand. They would take it as fast as I mixed it and cook it on sticks over a fire or on hot coals.

After they had finished eating I went to the door and saw a crowd of rebels tearing down the fence and asked the men inside what was going to be done. One of them answered: "We're going to have a little fight—do you care?" We asked what we should do and they said: "Take some fire and quilts and go down under the bank and stay till the battle is over." We did not wait for any fire but took quilts and hurried to the bank and laid there till the skirmish was over. When we came out in the afternoon we saw some Union soldiers and they helped us over to the bluffs west of Pleasanton.

We went to the home of Mr. Baugh's father and got something to eat, the first we had had since early the morning before. At night we went to our home and found it almost entirely destroyed, and the sides of the house torn down and every hogs and chicken killed and the fences destroyed. There was not even a hill of potatoes left on the farm. We had to come to Mound City to get something to eat and beds to sleep on. We then lived on the Al. Umphrey farm north of Pleasanton.

At the time of the battle of Mine Creek the farm right at the ford on the creek was owned by John Palmer,[1] whose daughter Barbara Jane was one of the eye witnesses and gives the following account of her experience: Just before the battle began, while the men and wagons were hurrying along, I noticed an old man riding a poor tired-looking horse, with his long, gray hair streaming in the wind. On the back of his saddle he had tied a live goose and two hens and they would flop their wings every time the old horse made a jump. As he passed the house the old man leaned forward and urged on his horse with a stout stick. I heard him say to a companion: "We must hurry up or they will get us yet." Although it was not a time or place for mirth I had to laugh.

Early in the morning, sometime before the battle, while the house was full of men and they were taking everything they could lay their hands on, I was sitting on the side of the bed. A rebel officer came and sat down beside me and

1. John Palmer was from Ohio and his wife was Rebecca Hart of Louisville, Kentucky. They were an unusual family in culture and intelligence. Barbara Jane, their daughter, who tells this story, married Melville Cox Dolson in Scotland county, Missouri, in 1859. They made their home here and have one surviving child, Mrs. Albert H. Mantey, now living at Mound City, where Mrs. Dolson still maintains her own home.

commenced talking about the men taking our things.   He
said it hurt him greatly to see such things, but under the
circumstances it was impossible to control the men.   If one
did not get them another would.   While we were talking an
Indian—the only one I saw in the house—reached under the
bed and pulled out a box that I kept my children's clothes in
and emptied them all out.   I begged him to let them be as
there was nothing that he could possibly use.   He paid no
attention to me, but when the officer spoke to him in a very
positive tone and said: "You put them back where you got
them", he readily obeyed and went away.   Then the officer
took a sheet from someone and put it around my shoulders,
remarking that I might be able to keep it as a shawl.

A big, rough-looking fellow sitting near by dressing his
wounded foot, noticing as I supposed the officer's kindness to
me, said to him: "I would kill all the women and children
I could get my hands on if I had my way."

"But," replied the officer, "you don't have your way.   Old
Pap Price is the commander of this army and you know that
he expects every man to be not only a soldier but a gentleman as well."   Just then some one at the door called out that
there was going to be a battle and in the confusion that followed I lost sight of my rebel officer, as I called him.

The battle of Mine Creek was fought on October 25, 1864.
I was then living on my father's farm four miles east and
one mile south of Mound City.   The advance of the rebel army
(a squad of Shelby's men) reached our house just as breakfast was ready.   The few who came in first sat down to the
table and went to helping themselves.   The house was then
soon full of rebels.   I went to the door and looked out; the
whole valley seemed full of men.   The first that passed seemed
to be marching in some order.   At the head of the column
was an old rebel flag all torn in strips, fluttering in the wind.
But as they came on they seemed to be in more and worse
confusion, and traveling faster, until as the last wagon train
passed they were in great confusion and going at a dead run.
This was the supply train which they were anxious to save
from the attacking Union forces.

Soon the cannon began to boom and we could see the rebels
forming in battle line just north of our house, and only a
few rods distant.   Standing in the north door I could see
a great mass of men and horses coming swiftly on; soon the
rattle of musketry was so great I could hear nothing else.
I could see the cannons a mile away belch out their flames
and smoke but could not hear them for the noise of the small
arms all around me.

As soon as the firing ceased mother and I went out to see
what we could do for the wounded.   Some of the soldiers
warned us that it was not safe as there were still a few shots

being fired. But the call for help was so great that we went on over the field, doing what we could. Some of the surgeons seemed to be doing all they could, others seemed to be unnecessarily rough and even cruel. One in particular I went to was working over a man who was shot in the breast. He was probing with some kind of an instrument in the bullet hole. I saw at a glance the man was dying and asked the surgeon what he was doing. He said he was trying to find the bullet. I begged him to quit, as it made no difference to the man whether the ball was found or not, but he paid no attention, and kept on probing until the man was dead.

By this time the ambulances had come up and began to gather up the wounded and Union dead; they left the rebel dead on the field. We showed the men with the ambulance where the wounded were. They had fallen all about the house and crawled away to fence corners or brush, where we had found them, carrying water and doing what we could for their comfort. When all the wounded were taken from the field we went to the hospital which was established in a vacant cabin north of the creek before carrying them to Mound City. Here indeed was a sickening scene. Men wounded in almost every way imaginable. Some were bearing their pain without a murmur, some groaning, some crying, some praying and some dying. I often wonder how I could bear to look on such a fearful scene, much less to try to care for the poor fellows. I certainly have no desire ever to see such a sight again. But as it had to be, and so close to me I am glad I had the strength that fearful day to go on the field and to the hospital and do what I could.

When we got home we found two wounded men in our house, one a Union man and one a rebel. The Union man was wounded quite severely. He was very quiet and seemed to want to make as little trouble as possible, while the rebel, though but slightly wounded, was very noisy, not I suppose because he was a rebel, but he seemed to be a man who could not bear pain. They both stayed all night at our house and we treated them both alike, and tried to care for them the best we could, but we had very little to give them, as we had nothing left in the house to eat but a few pounds of shorts, and we owed that to the kindness of a rebel officer, who early in the day tucked it under the head of the bed where my baby was sleeping and the men seemed to respect the baby and did not disturb the bed, and so we lived on the shorts for three days. The ambulance came the next morning after the Union man. He was carried out on mother's lounge and put in the ambulance upon it and brought up here to the old stone school house, then used as a hospital. I afterwards got the lounge and have it yet, as a memento of the battle. They came after the rebel the same day but they put him in a government freight wagon and brought him to Mound City too. They both got well and may be still living.

I know that this was a small affairs compared to the great conflicts that occurred in other parts of the country, but no one can see an entire battle. There are so many actors on the stage and the scenes change so quickly one can see but little that happens immediately around them. Just before the battle closed and while they were fighting all around the house I noticed a Union soldier, a mere boy, mounted an a magnificent iron grey horse, dash up in front of a squad of eight rebels, and hurl his revolver at them. My sister called to him: "Oh! don't shoot." At that moment my attention was called to something else, when I looked back a moment after, one was lying on the ground and the other seven had dropped their guns and were marching to the rear. So one can see but little that happens close to them.

Mrs. Virginia Dix tells this story of what she saw two miles south of Mine Creek: Alone in our little home on the morning of October 25 and two miles south of where the battle was fought (for my husband had gone at the call for troops to help keep General Price from our borders); alone except for our two children, I had prepared breakfast and we were just seated at the table when we were greeted by a party of men who proved upon acquaintance to be the advance guard of Price's army. After making myself and two little boys get up from our breakfast without eating anything they seated themselves and ate theirs; then ordered me to cook which I did as long as I had anything to cook. I used four bushels of flour just brought home from the mill two days before for our winter's supply. Before noon that was all gone, also every particle of provision we had in the house, and neither myself or children had a morsel to eat for forty-eight hours. By the time the cooking was done I could see a neighbor coming across the prairie with her two children—she also was alone—and just as she stepped in my house a shell struck hers and set it on fire. We stood in the door and watched it burn up; there could be no help for it and all her household goods and clothing were burned.

By this time we could see the army passing on the run. They left two wounded men at my house, the fruits of the battle that was raging on Mine Creek. My only light that fearful night after the battle was to put the end of a rail in the end door of the stove and when it got to burning to open the front. You may judge what a night I passed, two wounded men in the house, no food for them or my children. As soon as it was light enough to see, in company with an old lady, we started to try to find something for our hungry children. Every few rods we came upon wounded men unable to walk or even crawl, dying of hunger and thirst. To reach

a neighbor's house we crossed the battlefield.   It was strewn
with dead and dying.   Oh! the horror of that day! It silvered
my hair at the early age of twenty-five years.   I can not
recall it without dread and fear at this late day, suffering too
great to be described.   Others perhaps can describe it—I can
not.

The grandest sight I saw that day, as the last of the rebels
passed up one mound with the rebel flag, all on a run, was
the Glorious Stars and Stripes at the head of the pursuing
troops coming down the hill on the other side of the valley.
So the fearful struggling armies passed, leaving want and
suffering in their train.   The pinching hunger, the lack of
every comfort, no one can realize who has not been through it.

On the morning of October 25, 1864, Moonlight's weary
command after two nights and a day of incessant marching,
together with militia which had joined him on the way, appeared in Mound City.   Already the boom of cannon and the
rattle of musketry were heard to the east.   There was no
time to stop for rest or rations, but that they might not go
into battle quite famishing the women of Mound City had
made what preparation they could and many stood out on
the street with large pans and bread bowls filled with bread
and biscuit that the men might take a piece in their hands
as they rode by.   All night of October 24 in many homes
the fires had been kept burning while panful after panful of
biscuit or bread had been prepared for the morning's need.
Conspicuous among those willing workers was Amanda Way,
well remembered by all old settlers.   She had spent most of
the preceding three years in the hospitals and on the battle-
fields of the South.   As she stood there giving "aid and comfort" to those hungry men, an officer from the battlefield rode
up in haste and accosting her said: "Madam, the ambulance
is coming here with wounded soldiers.   The command has
neither hospital stores nor nurses; can the women of Mound
City supply them?"   She answered, "They can, and will be
ready as soon as the ambulance arrives."   All the stores on
hand had been loaded into wagons and sent to the west part
of the county for safety.

The first wounded were brought there.   Later the east
half of Sweeny's carriage shop (then Atkinson Brothers'
store) was appropriated and then the old stone school house,
not yet finished but with walls, roof and one floor.   The Union
wounded were taken there, the rebels occupied the other two
buildings.   The homes of the town were levied upon for contributions of beds and bedding, and necessary appliances for
attending the wounded: of course there was need for much
more than could be furnished in the village and messengers
were sent to the farm houses in the neighborhood, returning
with wagons piled high with hay-filled beds, and bedding,
beside contributions of canned fruit, vegetables and anything

which could be found for the sick and wounded. Truth compels me to say the offers of help for the rebel wounded were not so numerous as for the wounded Union soldiers, though many tendered care and aid alike for all.

Miss Way, by reason of her experience in the army, was made head nurse and head of the commissary department also. And when the first ambulance load came, she was ready to bestow them and provide the necessities for their care. The resident physician assisted the surgeons in their work and the women of the town and county lent willing and efficient aid while the heroes of the battlefield were being cared for. In the absence of a hospital kitchen the kitchens of resident families were freely used. Almost every family assisting in preparing food for the patients and bring it as needed to the hospital. Wounded were taken into private houses where there was a room to spare. Within a few days the hospital was supplied with government officers and equipment though the citizen nurses were kept several weeks. There were about sixty Union and sixty-five rebel wounded to care for, and from among these some were cured and returned to their commands rejoicing, some sent home on sick leave, some transferred to the hospital at Leavenworth and some laid to rest in the little plat of ground north of town, so that when the March storms came the hospitals were empty.

In the spring of 1865 there came to Mound City a government agent whose duty it was to transfer the buried soldiers in this vicinity to the Mound City cemetery. Bodies were moved from Barnesville and other points where soldiers had been stationed. The plat of ground now occupied by soldiers' graves was secured and laid off. At that time the head boards were erected and names, company and regiment and state painted thereon. In 1885 these were replaced by the marble head stones and in 1889 the beautiful monument which now stands guard above the silent dead, having been secured to this cemetery by the efforts of Senator Plumb, was erected, and on the 22nd anniversary of the battle of Mine Creek, with appropriate ceremonies, the monument was unveiled in the presence of one of the largest audiences ever gathered together in Linn County. The following is the official record of interments:

Soldiers Buried in Government Cemetery, Mound City:

Jno. McSweeney, 4th Kan. Cavalry
A. G. Newton, 4th Kan. Cavalry
V. R. Teeter, 5th Kan. Cavalry.
E. D. Buck, Sargt, Co. G, 5th Kan. Cav.
Jos. Abbott, Co. C, 6th Kan. Cavalry
Clayton Kille, Sergeant, Co. E, 10th Kansas Infantry

J. L. Vanwort, Co. G, 10th Kan. Inft.
G. T. Bell, Sargt. Co. M, 15th Kan. Cav.
J. E. Higgins, Corporal, Co. K, 15th Kansas Cavalry
G. E. Wessburg, Corporal, Co. B, 15th Kansas Cavalry.
Calvin Vaugn, 15th Kansas Cavalry
J. G. Groash, Co. H, 4th Mo. S. M. Cav.
John Poor, Co. A, 2nd Mo. Cav.
W. H. Yager.
S. Winterton, Co. C, 17th Iowa.
H. W. Curtis, Lieut. 4th Iowa Cavalry
17 U. S. Soldiers unknown.

Soldiers Buried in Government Cemetery Since the War:

James Montgomery, Col. 3rd Kansas Regiment, later of the
34th U. S. Colored Troops.
S. R. Smith, Co. B, 20th Iowa Infantry.
John Hannant, Co. C, 27th Ill. Inf.
David Hill
Henry Chastiene, Corporal Co. T, 44th Illinois Infantry
F. C. Provost, Co. A, 83 Illinois Inf.
C. G. Irish
Peter Nicely, Co. H, 189 Ohio Inf.

Soldiers Buried on Family or Individual Lots:

J. T. Snoddy, Major 7th Kansas Cav.
J. F. Broadhead, Capt. Co. E, 10th Kansas Infantry.
John W. Flora, Sargt. Co. E, 10th Kansas Infantry.
E. Bunn, Captain Co. G, 12th Kans. Inf.
Chas. Montanye, Penn. Heavy Art.
G. W. Sands, Captain Co. E, 83 U. S. Colored Infantry.
G. W. Ball, Co. K, 12th Kansas Inft.
G. H. Crane.
A. F. Ely, 12th Penn. Infantry and 8th U. S. Colored
Fredric Mantey, Wisconsin Regt.

Father King was for many years the most noted personage
of Linn County. In fact he was eagerly sought after and
courted by all the savants of eastern Kansas. He was a
Spirit who for untold thousands of years had inhabited the
Celestial regions, and when he deigned to visit or communicate
with earthly people he made his headquarters in Paris township, of course, for that was where most of the first "old
timers" met. Being of the spirit world he made no contacts
in the flesh but many were the interesting conversations he
carried on through the media of Ezra Tippie and John Morrison. Along about 1870 there were mysterious gatherings
at the home of Morrison on the hill north of Brooklyn on
the road between La Cygne and Mound City. Men would
go there and come away amazed at what they heard, till
finally the place began to be crowded. Morrison was the

personal representative of Father King and to relieve the
pressure of the crowd on his modest home a "round house"
was built in his yard some two hundred feet from his residence. It was a perfectly round structure about fourteen feet
across, ten feet high, with a perfectly conical roof running
to a peak. There were no windows, the only opening being
a door which fitted so closely it was airtight when closed.
Morrison was just an ordinary man without education whose
manner of living had won for him a little bit more than the
average of respect and confidence among those who knew him.
Ezra Tippie was a near neighbor, a man of easy going habits
and of such mild and inoffensive nature that visitors who
went with much skepticism to the seances came away mysti-
fied and dumbfounded by what they experienced. On one
occasion Ed. R. Smith, then clerk of the court at Mound City,
and a companion, started horseback in midafternoon in a
winter storm to investigate this mystery becoming famous
among men. When they arrived at the end of the twelve
mile trip they found assembled quite a crowd of people,
curious like themselves, a number being women of well known
families. They asked Morrison "How about this?" and he
said he could not answer, that he was under the control of
some power which he obeyed because overwhelmingly im-
pelled to. He said when he complained that his home was
being overrun by people, Father King had commanded that
he build the round house that he might more conveniently
carry on his communications with people of the earth. There
were so many present that at this time Morrison suggested
that those living nearest give way to those from Mound City
and other distant place, which was agreeably done. With
much of a "goose-fleshy" feeling they went out to the temple
of the spirits and when the door opened they could see all
there was in the interior—a number of rough benches to seat
a dozen people and in front of them a table above which was
a frame on which were a number of musical instruments including cornets and fiddles and banjoes, and hanging at each
end was a snare drum of the rather noisy variety left over
from the war, and resting at the top a long six-foot dinner
horn of a type then very common. Without any formality
they took their seats, bashfully wondering what was to
happen. By common consent Ed. R. Smith was made spokesman for the crowd. The door was closed and there was a
moment of intense quiet in the stifling darkness when a
regular bedlam of noise broke out. The horns tooted, the
banjo and fiddles played, and the devil's tattoo was beaten
upon the drums hanging at each end of the frame, and a
big booming voice spoke through the dinner horn bidding
them Good Evening. Ed. R. began by inquiring whom they
had the honor of conversing with, the reply being "They call
me Father King. I lived on earth thousands of years ago."

"Where are you now?"

"I am in the spirit world."

"Can you tell us about our friends gone on before?"

"They should converse with you."

"What about Jesus Christ?"

"He is here; I see him frequently. I helped to roll away the stone from His sepulchre."

"Do you know about the plan of our promised salvation?"

"That curtain has not been removed."

"How do you estimate time there?"

"A thousand years to us is as a day to you."

Night after night such conversations were carried on, a soft, vibrant, rather booming voice answering from the darkness. Ladies present asked personal questions, one wanting to know if her new suit would be exposed to a rainstorm on the way home and she was advised to start early and go fast.

The mystery grew. Noted men came under assumed names and went away nonplussed. At each seance Morrison and Tippie were present as the media through which spirit connections were established. Yet the language and the voice of Father King could not be that of either. James C. Marshall (so long known as Uncle Jimmy) became a regular devotee at this shrine and promised on his deathbed twenty years later that he would come back in the spirit and make himself known. Ed. R. Smith believed till the day of his passing that voices came to him from beyond. No fees were asked those who came and were refused if offered. Morrison said he did what Father King told him and was powerless to do otherwise. Tippie said there was a mystery about it he could not solve. In the course of a year several hundred visited the place until the Spirit grew negligent and many times failed to respond to visiting parties.

On New Year's Day, 1872, a freight train was thrown into the ditch at a point about a mile north of Barnard (now Boicourt) caused by an obstruction of ties placed on the track. The engineer and fireman were killed. There was no clue to the criminal. It was decided to appeal to Father King. He told them to go to the scene and to set up a dark chamber with blankets and with the musical instruments as usually placed. It was a miserably dark winter night when the party of men went down, and they recognized various marks given them by the Spirit to identify the spot, and having arranged a dark room they spread their blankets over a frame of poles and placed the drums and instruments and waited only briefly when the bedlam of sound came and the Voice, telling them that he could do nothing for them as he was leaving this part of the universe and they would hear of him no more.

So the round house fell into decay and Father King became only a haunting memory. Two of the best men I ever knew believed with an implicit faith that they had talked with a

mortal gone beyond the curtain. And all of my childhood
that old decaying round house was a ghost mansion.

Along during the latter part of the "nineties" Congress
authorized the construction of a number of first-class battleships, one of which was to be named the "Kansas" in honor
of our state. It took several years and millions of money to
build it so it was "some boat" as the sport now praises his
automotive wagon. The legislature of Kansas provided money
to purchase for it the finest solid silver dining set that could
be found, and following that came the great event of the
launching of the big ship and the bestowal upon it the name
with a christening. A charming young woman was selected
to stand sponsor for it, she to crash upon its snout a bottle of
wine as it moved down the ways to its berth in the water,
affectionately shouting "I christen thee Kansas!" This part
of the programme was all worked out on paper when protests
began to come against a prohibition state like Kansas using
at the docks in Philadelphia what she could not use within
her own borders. A loud kick was made against the use of
intoxicating liquor. The governor was perplexed, realizing the
inconsistency of the situation and sought a way out, and Linn
County furnished the solution. Some one whispered to the
governor a beautiful thing to do would be to obtain water
from the John Brown spring at the scene of the Marais des
Cygnes Massacre, a fluid that would be symbolical of all that
Kansas stood for and sure to make a good story in the newspapers as an innovation. The idea was enthusiastically accepted. A special train was made up at Kansas City waiting
for Governor Hoch's party with the young lady, Miss Anna
Hoch, his daughter, and the wives of the governor's staff consisting of Adjutant General Hughes and something like a
dozen colonels all togged out in shining new uniforms. But
that bottle of water had to come from Trading Post, and it
had to come at once to be carried in that special train. So
a telegram was sent to a big politician at Pleasanton telling
what was wanted and how badly they wanted it to come on
that afternoon train. The big politician got busy and soon
had two young men on the way in the best buggy with the
best horse flesh obtainable. These young fellows got all
swelled up over the importance of the event and began discussing battleships and other nautical matters. It was an
interesting subject to them as they had heard all their lives
that Jennison had drank enough whiskey to float a battleship.
When they crossed the raging Marais des Cygnes the swirling
waters made them dizzy and they drove up to the filling
station at the Post. Now in those days when you got filled
up at a filling station you were full. They began to sing sailors
songs and take on the spirit of the thing. "Rocked in the
Cradle of the Deep" was worked out and then they tackled

"Nancy Lee"—"See where she stands and waves her hands, Yee-ho! Yee-ho!" When they got to the spring and filled the bottle it was safely stored under the buggy seat, and they drank some water but it failed to satisfy. They hurried to the filling station at the Post and filled up and were full. They didn't have the Short Line pavement in those days—nothing like it. The road wound around through the willows right down on the flat and they traveled almost as far up and down as straight ahead. Roaring out a gallant old sailor song they drove up to the station at Pleasanton with the smoke of the train in sight a few miles down the track. The big politician reached for the bottle—and found it was cracked and empty! He said not a word but ran into the drug store and grabbed a quart bottle of distilled water and ran with it to the station whittling off the label, in place of which he licked and put in place a gummed paper with a beautifully penned legend certifying the contents to be from the shrine of liberty made famous by Old John Brown, and in appreciation of their services the names of the young men were put on as witnesses to his signature. And thus was the battleship Kansas christened by distilled water from Missouri! Those boys still get seasick when the incident is mentioned. Just now I read the newspaper accounts of that event in Philadelphia on August 15, 1905, in an old scrap book, telling how Governor Hoch had worked an elaborate scheme of secrecy about the use of water instead of wine. A line was secured to the rigging up above the ship's side and at a proper place opposite the ship's side the bottle—with a beautiful bow of white ribbon about its neck—was fastened by a cord to the line, the end of which was in Miss Hoch's hand and by swinging it outward and then back against the ship she made a beautiful smash of it.[1]

In 1871, when the writer was ten years old this story of the naming of the river was heard from an authoritative source. In company with Johnnie Geboe and Will Peery, two Miami Indian boys of my own age, we were in the big forest about two miles south of La Cygne. We were admiring a beautiful thing of nature, a big forest tree literally covered by a wild hop vine in full flower. It was a marvelously beautiful sight and as we were discussing it in boy fashion there came to us out of the forest a tall fine looking man. He was John Roubidoux,[2] the head chief of the Miami Tribe which had previously owned all of what is now Lincoln township and also Sugar Creek township over the line in Miami county as a reservation. Roubidoux was a full-blood Indian and a

---

1 A similar situation developed when the "Kentucky" was christened with water from the spring at Abe Lincoln's birthplace. Senator Joe Blackburn showed up drunk and threw a flask of whiskey at the wet spot—the only time he was ever known to use water with whiskey.
2 Roubidoux's tribal name was Ach-a-pon-gah, meaning Big Turtle. I am glad to give him a place in this book. Johnnie Geboe is still living near Miami, Oklahoma.

very handsome man. He had been highly educated and nearly
always dressed in a tailor-made suit of black broadcloth. He
was a preacher in the Baptist faith and very sociable and
clever in conversation. As conversation lagged Johnnie Geboe
said to him, "Tell Billie about the naming of the river," and
he sat down with us and told this story with far more charm
than I could give it in repetition: "There has always been
curious inquiry into the origin of the name of our river. It
is an Indian legend based in part on a pathetic chapter in
American history. The story is authoritatively given as
follows: In 1756 the British carried away bodily the French
people in the settlement of Grand Pre in Acadia, a colony since
peopled by English and called Nova Scotia, a tragedy of such
great pathos and beauty that it was used by Longfellow as
the theme of his poem "Evangeline", the heroine being a real
character in life who came into the western country in search
of her lover, Gabriel Lajeunesse, who with others of the
Acadian village had been carried to the shores of Louisiana
on the Gulf coast. She, bewildered and wondering, set out
through the Canadian wilderness, past Quebec, on to Pierre
Marquette and down the lakes and the Illinois river to the
Mississippi, up the Missouri to the Osage.

"It is not so recorded but it is entirely presumable that
Evangeline was accompanied by men of her own nationality
in this prolonged adventure. In seeking information from
the native Indians as they proceeded up the Osage river there
was always the alluring story of a great "summer village"
at the head waters of that stream and which they finally
found at what is now the lake country at the mouth of Big
Sugar creek. This country had long been French territory
and by the elders of the tribe familiar with French agents
and their language, they were made welcome. A tepee was
set aside for Evangeline and she became intimately associated
with the women of the tribe. Her story became their own
romance and they eagerly sought information for her from
the "runners" who were constantly passing through from one
tribe to another, even locating the spot on the Gulf coast
where the unhappy Acadians had been turned loose in a
wilderness and eventually were mourned as a 'lost people.'
One day, during the routine of village work, Evangeline saw
several young boys and girls approach Sona the Wise Mother
of the tribe and in excited whisperings were telling of some
unusual event.

"'They have seen Coman and Osa,' said the Wise Mother.

"Evangeline sensed a tribal romance and to the Wise Mother
she said, 'Tell me about it.'

"'It is,' said the Wise Mother, 'a long story of long ago.
It estranged two big tribes who have never since been friendly.
It is the story of a young war chief of the greatest prairie tribe
and a beautiful young princess of our people. Coman was the

young chieftain and he celebrated the close of a great buffalo
hunt by appearing at our village with twenty of his young
and handsome braves, all dressed in feather bonnets and
beaded finery and mounted on powerful horses. They carried
ceremonial banners, signifying peace and joy. Their visit
was a great event, all our young people, especially the maidens,
dressing in their finest to do honor to their proud guests.
Osa, our princess, granddaughter of White Hair, was the
comeliest among the maidens, young and pretty and arrayed
in the finest new buckskin decorated elaborately in bead designs designating her royal station in the tribe.

"'Coman was entranced by her. He sought her constantly.
Osa manifested her admiration and attachment for him. They
made it a long and merry season and when the frost came
and the visitors must return to their prairie tribe, the parting
was not a happy one, as White Hair refused to give Osa to
the great prairie chief. Osa rebelled and threatened to follow
him. The winter was a bad one and our young people hard
to manage after their great festival with the visiting braves.
But when the flood waters were running out, and there were
flowers and green leaves everywhere, on a bright May morning
there appeared on that bank across the river twenty horsemen in war bonnets and carrying beautiful ceremonial banners.
At their head was Coman dressed in his proudest trappings.
He led a beautiful horse without a rider, and a second glance
showed it was to carry a woman. Coman gave that beautiful
and graceful salutation known as the "peace sign" and dismounting, got into one of our canoes to cross over to us.
With some difficulty he got across, but showed that he was
better as a horseman than as a boatman.

"Osa was radiant as she met him. Her luggage was brought
and Coman insisted they go.

"Coman was exultant in his triumph and addressing White
Hair, he said:

"'Coman is a great chief of a great people. We have the
Land of the Sky. We have the great high mountains where
Manitou makes his home and mixes medicine for all his people.
The eye never sees the end of our domain. Our warriors
vanquish all opponents. Our lodges are filled with a great and
happy people who own the hordes of buffalo on the plains,
which give us both meat and clothing. Our war horses are
numberless. When the Comanches put on their war bonnets
it is a sight to thrill the world. Our people offer a royal welcome to Osa as the bride of Coman.'

"But White Hair was not convinced and said:

"'It is not wise that it should be so. Osa is a daughter
of the forest. Her home is in a land of plenty. The land
produces corn and melons, and as the seasons go there are
berries, persimmons, pawpaws, grapes and plums. The whole
tribe could live on the pecans, walnuts and hickory nuts the

forests give to us. The great trees shelter us from the storms
and the heat of summer. They furnish fuel for our fires in
winter. There are buffalo and deer and bear, and fish in the
waters. The Osages are rich and happy and grow wise in
their contentment.

" 'Why should Osa go to your country where you see far
and see nothing? It is a deceptive country which smiles in the
spring time and then burns up the grass and leaves the earth
bare. It frowns in the winter and covers the earth with
snow. It has no trees. It has no water. The buffalo and
deer desert it.

" 'Your people are cruel and blood-thirsty because of the
cruel country you live in. Osa should not go to live among
you. The Great Spirit has placed this river between us and
the sullen roar of its flood waters voices his anger.'

"Osa had an expression of dismay as she witnessed the
dignified refusal of her grandfather, but stepping into the
canoe she showed her decision to go with her chosen man.
Coman turned the canoe into the stream and the waiting
people on each side were thrilled with the beauty of the
scene and its significance. With strong confident stroke
Coman forced the canoe into the flood when some angry
thing below seized the boat and drew it downward out of
sight. In a flash the two lovers disappeared. No trace was
ever seen of them or their boat. As the horrified people looked
upon the scene, a miracle happened. At the place where the
lovers disappeared there was seen on the water two great
white swans which swam away together through peaceful
waters under a canopy of vines and flowers and wild rice.

"These swans were seen today by the children. They always
return here. Their story in the great epic poem of the
Osages."

The assemblage of young people, who always listened to
this story when told by the Wise Mother arose and beckoned
them to follow, going to the great cliff at the top of Timbered
Mound, from which Evangeline, as she looked over the shim-
mering waters of lakes and river and the green valley, spread
her arms as though to embrace them and said:
"C'est le marais des cygnes."
It is the marsh of the swans

Linn County got its name from Dr. Lewis Fields Linn who
represented Missouri in the United States Senate from 1833
to the time of his death October 3, 1843, at Ste. Genevieve,
Missouri. He is affectionately recorded in history as "the
Model Senator", and a biographical sketch gives him a most
interesting personality. Linn was born near Louisville, Kentucky, on November 5, 1795, the son of Asael and Ann
(Hunter) Linn. In 1809 he went to Missouri to visit his sister,
Mrs. McArthur, and his half-brother, General Henry Dodge,

both of whom had moved from Kentucky to Ste. Genevieve, Missouri. During Dr. Linn's stay in Ste. Genevieve the War of 1812 broke out and he was accordingly appointed surgeon of the troops commanded by General Dodge. At the close of the campaign he returned to Louisville, continued the study of medicine for a time, and later entered the medical college at Philadelphia. In 1816 he returned to Ste. Genevieve and began the hard and ceaseless labor of a pioneer doctor. In 1833 an epidemic of Asiatic cholera swept over Southern Missouri and his heroic work as a physician among the afflicted won the affections of the people. As United States senator he took a leading part with the political giants of those days. When Senator Benton, his colleague, introduced the bill by which Missouri annexed the "Platt purchase" the credit of its passage was given to Senator Linn. The acquisition by the United States of the Oregon territory was another measure brought almost entirely by the efforts of Senator Linn. "This monumental piece of statesmanship", says his biographer, "in its results gave to the United States the vast Oregon country which today forms the states of Idaho, Oregon and Washington. No wonder that Senator Linn was hailed as the 'Father of Oregon'." So Linn County, Kansas, got its beautiful name from a grand and honorable source even though it did come by way of Missouri.

La Cygne of course took its name from the river.

Pleasanton was named after General Alfred Pleasanton who commanded and set his batteries on the hill at the battle of Mine Creek.

Hawkswing is another lost community, probably a poetic name bestowed by Indians in the northeast part of the county from where they enlisted in Captain Leasure's company in the Sixth Kansas.

The first of the townships named was that of Paris, the name being conferred upon the town of that name which was the headquarters of the proslavery element, who were from Paris, Kentucky, and thus perpetuated the name.

Some one started a town a half mile east and a mile south of where Pleasanton now is and called it Potosi, probably naming it after the old Missouri community of that name. The town never had more than three houses, but it was the earliest definite settlement and gave the name to Potosi township.

Centerville had a postoffice of that name in the Territorial days with James M. Arthur as postmaster, from which the township was given its name.

Scott township was named after Samuel Scott, a very early proslave settler. Scott was hanged in his front door yard by men under Jennison, one of the tragedies growing out of the slavery question.

After the Civil War the increasing population required

more definite administration of laws and new townships were cut out. The northeast corner had been recently recovered from the Miami Indians who were moved into the Indian Territory and the township set up was named after Abe Lincoln.

The northwest corner was named Liberty township voicing the sentiments of the people then living there.

The southwest corner was called Blue Mound after the beautiful hill distinguishing it.

Valley township is in the valley, Mound City township from the new town then on a boom; Sheridan township is a monument to General Phil Sheridan at the suggestion of Columbus Williams and Stanton township is in honor of Edwin N. Stanton of Lincoln's Cabinet.

Marais des Cygnes, read Indian legend "Naming of the River."

Boicourt was originally called Barnard till a duplication of the name brought a request from the Postoffice Department for a change. A man named Boicourt owned several thousand acres of pasture land there and gave his name to the station. Later the discovery of coal brought the Vernon Coal Company to mine it, giving considerable growth to the village. Vernon was an Englishman, a model John Bull—in velvet short pants, high-laced boots, velveteen hat and monocle he was a picture for us boys to look at.

Farlinville was so named in compliment to Alonzo Farlin who lived on a farm some distance west of town. He had a daughter Alice and two boys.

Cadmus was named after the Greek philosopher.

Goodrich was named after Samuel Goodrich, a prosperous farmer and leading citizen of the western part of the county.

Old Coonville was at the state line on the Market street road due east of La Cygne. It had a store and blacksmith shop and several small houses for men who worked in the coal mines. The early settlers here were Tom Gage, Isaac Bennett, Arthur Van Tuyl, W. A. Gage, William Henderson, Eli Brayton, Calvin Reed—now all gone but Bennett and Van Tuyl.

Critzer was named after a Missouri Pacific engineer, who later went to the state of Washington.

Twin Springs in Scott township was a station on the military road and had a store which sold groceries, dry goods and drugs.

Ballard's Ford a mile southwest of where La Cygne now stands, was on the old emigrant trail and was a gathering place for shooting matches, horse races and such social events.

On the old James Wishart farm south of Cadmus in Scott township a thing of world-wide importance happened. There was a broom factory there owned and operated by William

Padley and James Wishart in the early days. A young man
named Appleby came from the east to spend the winter with
his cousin Mr. Wishart, and worked with them at the factory.
As he worked with the brooms an idea persisted with him
that he wanted to improve upon and perfect the knot used
in tying together the assembled material. Going to the barn
he got some bundles of oats and after weeks of patient practice
he found the way to bind a bundle with cord and draw it taut
and fasten it with a knot. Further patient work perfected a
mechanical device which tied this knot at the right tension
and cut the cord, releasing the finished bundles and repeating
this process as the "reaper" moved along. Appleby obtained
a patent on this idea and he soon put it on the market as
"Appleby's Binder". Before arriving at perfection, however,
and getting it to a technical completion that would make his
patents a perfect defense against infringement, Appleby returned to the Wishart farm and resumed his studies on the
machine. On one occasion he registered at the old La Cygne
House and retired to his room. He failed to appear at breakfast, but no importance was given to his absence as in those
days many hotel patrons were "sleeping off" the effects of
dissipation. The second morning, however, alarm was felt
and when no response was given to knocks at his door it
was forced open and they beheld a haggard man sitting at
a table with many papers scattered about on which he had
made tracings of his machine and technical descriptions that
would protect him. He succeeded in this and in 1884 I saw
his big factory at Minneapolis. The device was the beginning
of the "harvester" as an improvement on the reaper which
had been automatically dropping loose bundles for the worker
to pick up and bind together with wisps of straw. Appleby
finally sold out to the big McCormick harvester makers and
it revolutionized the wheat business. Appleby grew to be very
wealthy. In the meantime Wishart was "getting along" slowly. He had nothing to worry him except a mortgage for a
thousand dollars which seemed to have roosted on his house
to stay. Appleby remembered the household that had given
him a home during a winter and wrote his cousin asking how
he was prospering. Wishart replied that he was just doing
fine, markets were good and crops generous, so that all he
had to keep him hustling was that mortgage that seemed
doomed to stay with him. The next mail brought a draft for
$1000 from Appleby with instructions to cancel the mortgage
at once. The Wishart family still live on the old homestead.
This romance of the harvester has never been given much
space in industrial history, yet it equals if not exceeds in importance the invention of the cotton gin by Eli Whitney which
made the cotton states of the South so wealthy that they
sought to dominate the world. It is a queer thought too that
this came out of Kansas right where they tried to impose

their infamous institution. Joseph Van Hercke, now running
a filling station and store in the old Austin Hall building at
Trading Post, is quite a character in his way. He was born
in Kansas City and married Anna Speilbach of Shawnee
Mission. Their children are Mamie who married Ernest
Maginniss, Elizabeth married Richard D. Moore, Arthur
married Ethel Pine, and Jerome is single at home. Van Hercke
was salesmanager in Linn County for Ben Appleby's Binder
and went on the G. A. R. train in 1884 to Minneapolis when
he visited Appleby at his factory. The author of this book
was on that train and remembers the ovation given to Appleby.
Van Hercke knew Appleby when he was here laboring to perfect his patent. In his youth Van Hercke received twenty-five
cents a cord for wood neatly piled, and a like amount for each
hundred rails he split out, working in the timber around
Rosedale.

The primeval forests were the glory of this country. Great
oaks, giant cotton-woods, great white "ghostly" sycamores,
magnificent walnuts, valuable hickory and ash—this original
growth of trees would more than equal the market value of
all the land in the county now. If this forest were preserved
to us now Congress would be petitioned to set it aside and
preserve it forever as a national park. If the walnut timber,
even a small part of it, had been made into furniture of the
type O. E. Morse and his brother made in their first factory
at Moneka, this furniture would be sought out to grace the
finest homes in the world. The grandeur of these trees was
sublime. From a hill-top this forest scene was wonderfully
beautiful, varying with the seasons from the delicate green
of the new leaves in the spring to the sombre shades of hot
summer and the riot of glorious colors at frost time. It was
a peace time version of "Mine eyes have seen the glory of
the coming of the Lord!" But practical man must clear the
land to make fields for corn to grow and they began to fall.
Oh! The pity of it! I remember one giant walnut tree that
stood just above the banks of Big Sugar Creek at the Jim
Parent ford. It ran straight up, as erect and stiff and proud
as the loftiest pine. Near it as though proud of the association
was a gigantic hackberry. Between the two was a miserable
shack in which lived a man who left a faint trace on the
history of his time. This magnificent specimen of God's
handiwork was sold in June 1902 for the sum of $300 to the
Hamilton Lumber Company of Fort Scott, and they sent a
force of men up to cut it down and prepare it for shipment.
When this giant was laid flat on the ground it measured six
feet in diameter at the base and five cuts ten feet long were
sawed out and one at the top eight feet long and over three
feet in diameter at the top, making fifty-eight feet of mer-
chantable wood cut into six logs; timber that has since graced

the most expensive and most beautiful homes throughout Europe. It required four horses to pull each of these logs to Boicourt, where they were shipped to Fort Scott and there squared by hewing and sent to the World's Fair at St. Louis and then to the seaboard for shipment to Germany. No wonder we had a feeling we wanted to lick Germany! H. E. Butts and Charlie King (now in California) helped in the work of removing this lovely old tree. In 1926 Mr. Butts sold a much smaller tree off his farm at Parent ford for $250.

Forestry would be a profitable study for Linn County even yet. All the hillsides are now given over to new growth which is permitted to remain in "brush." If trimmed up individual trees would grow up straight and produce a valuable crop. Around the bases of the big hills there is the wash from the uplands that makes rich soil and the moisture that assures growth. Systematic culture would enable them to produce wealth. Thirty budded pecan trees to the acre on such ground would in a few years produce more money in one crop than the present cash value of the land. I have recently gathered from the ground under one wild tree forty pounds of pecans which were worth at the lowest price four dollars, but if the meats were extracted and sold at the market price they would have a value of twenty dollars! and that from one tree out of a possible thirty to the acre! The English walnut orchards of California, selling at a thousand dollars an acre, simply could not compare with this delectable natural food product either in deliciousness or money making possibilities! And hickory is a wood the market needs. One crop of the nuts would pay several times for the land, and if some necessity required the ground for other purposes fifty trees would make fifty cords of wood worth $500 if used for fuel alone, or a much greater sum if sold for manufacturing purposes! Fifty years growth of black walnut would exceed all of them in value, and all such land would have increased grazing value. Great is the forest! Let us give heed to its possibilities as a local industry.

The man with the most experience with pecan trees in Linn County is Probate Judge T. B. Nisely of Mound City. He developed a fine grove on his farm two miles southeast of La Cygne and it is a noteworthy fact that he not only got a valuable crop of nuts from the trees but actually improved the blue grass pasture in which they grew. I remember one tree growing on his farm the crop on which he sold on the tree for twenty-five dollars. There were fully two hundred pounds on the tree, very fine nuts which would have sold readily at twenty cents a pound, which would have made this one tree produce forty dollars for the year. Judge Nisely has very kindly given us the following comment on this important subject:

"Of course it is of the wild trees only that I have any knowledge and that is the only kind that will be found in Linn County. Pecan trees are of rather slow growth, as all hard-wood trees are, beginning to bear at about the age of ten years, when they should be five inches in diameter at the base and about fifteen feet in height. If given room the tree naturally grows into a wide spreading top and one of the most common mistakes made in thinning the natural pecan groves is to leave too heavy a stand. Forty trees to the acre might be left for a few years until they had begun to bear, when they should be thinned to not more than twenty to the acre, being careful to select the ones that have the largest and best nuts for a permanent orchard. These natural groves may always be found where the pecan grows to the best advantage, that is, on the slopes at the foot of hills and most of the bottom land where in both cases the land is inclined to be of the nature of gumbo. Particular emphasis should be made on the importance of giving the trees room —lots of it—not only for the good of the trees but as blue grass always grows on this kind of land and seems to do better for having some shade, it is of much better quality not to be shaded too much.

"I would estimate a pecan tree to be at its prime at about the age of forty years and should continue to bear in increasing quantities for an indefinite number of years. A good tree at the age of forty years is capable of producing a crop of two hundred pounds. Pecans bloom late and are seldom if ever killed by frost, and I have observed that they almost always set on and seem to be going to make a good crop, but too often some kind of worm attacks the trees and it can be seen that they are eating holes in the leaves, sometimes stripping the trees of all their foliage while the nuts are just fairly formed, and of course these small tender nuts are devoured at the same time. Application of manure may be good to hasten the growth of young trees but trees that grow in a barn-lot are not of so long life as the manure— or too much of it—seems to rot out the roots and the tree will be apt to be blown down some time when the wind is unusually strong.

" While the nuts from wild trees are not on an average so large as the budded varieties grown in the South, if care is taken in selecting the trees in the manner above described all might be of good size and quality. Speaking of the quality, I think it is apparent that the nuts from the wild trees grown here are superior to those grown in Texas and other southern states. If you are fortunate enough to own a natural grove of pecan trees clean it up and have a permanent blue-grass pasture and a beautiful park; and make it a source of profit and pleasure."

J. T. Botkin,[1] formerly of Linn County, who served two terms as secretary of state beginning about 1914 wrote for the State Historical Society an account of the administration of law in this county, particularly stressing the fidelity of peace officers in the performance of their duties. He gave the following story of the crime for which Scott Holderman and Elias Foster paid the penalty of death:

"The murder referred to was committed not far from the scene of the Marais des Cygnes massacre September 25, 1865. The murderers were Scott Holderman and Elias Foster. A brief history of this crime may be of interest at this time. When I came with my parents to Linn County in February, 1866, David Goss was county sheriff. Dave Goss was a 'man of the hour'. He was fearless in the discharge of his duty, whether or not it affected friend or foe. He came to Kansas from Gosport, Indiana, in 1858. Soon after the Civil War began he enlisted in the Sixth Kansas cavalry and became captain of D company. In this company as privates were Scott Holderman, two of his brothers and his father, Jacob Holderman. The latter was a member of the jury that convicted Griffith for his part in the Marais des Cygnes massacre. The Holdermans had lived near the Missouri line before the war. They were free-state men and had suffered the usual dangers, privations and persecutions that were meted out to free-state men by lawless proslavery men like the Hamelton band.

"While the regiment was serving in Arkansas the regimental sutler was robbed by Elias Foster, a mere boy, and a native of the country. The robbery was a bold one and marked young Foster as an adept in that line. He was captured and was held as a prisoner in the regiment for several months and was then permitted to enlist in D company. He was a good soldier and he and Scott Holderman soon became good friends. There seems to have been nothing in their career as soldiers to indicate that they were to become outlaws, but as soon as they were mustered out of service they began a career of crime which though brief was more or less spectacular. They were splendid types of the desperado of the time. Both were superb horsemen and crack shots. They were as fearless and as bold and dashing as the James and Younger band of outlaws on the other side of the border, and doubtless they would have become as famous had they had the protection of partisan friends enjoyed by the James and Younger gang all the way from northern Missouri to Old Mexico.

1. J. T. Botkin was born in Logan county, Illinois, May 7, 1853. He came with his parents to Kansas in February 1866 locating on a farm near Mound City. In 1879 the family moved to Harper county. Mr. Botkin spent some time on a cattle ranch in southeastern Kansas before that country was settled. He was married to Jennie Waldren of Attica, Kansas, in July, 1885. In November 1914 Mr. Botkin was elected secretary of state and was reelected in 1916, serving the state in that capacity four years. After his retirement from office he located in Wichita where he now lives.

"Foster though much the younger of the two seems to have been the brains of the partnership and its leader. He was a born leader and a splendid specimen of physical manhood. Standing full six feet in his socks, well proportioned, straight as an arrow, and of pleasing countenance, he was good to look at even in chains. I have seen few finer looking men in my life than Elias Foster, as I remember seeing him so often in the custody of the officers. He had a happy disposition, was bright and intelligent and made friends easily. Holderman was not so attractive, either in disposition or personal appearance. He was a man of great personal courage and a very dangerous man. He married the daughter of "Uncle Jackie" Williams, and I must digress long enough to says a few words about "Uncle Jackie." Uncle Jackie Williams was an old-fashioned hard-shelled Baptist preacher. He was loved and respected far more for his high character as a man and his sincerity in the cause of religion than for his learning. He preached in that old "sing-song" style that was going out of fashion about that time. He preached long and loud. I do not remember to have heard Uncle Jackie preach more than three hours at any one time, though I am told that he often exceeded that limit by an hour or more, and that the ardor and fervor of his sermons were never abated in the slightest degree by its duration. Uncle Jackie was always going strong at the finish.

"Holderman and Foster soon became the terror of the border. They committed a number of highway robberies and holdups. One particularly bold highway robbery occurred near Paola. I think they were arrested for this crime and broke jail, but am not certain about this. At any rate, while dodging the officers on account of this crime they killed a man down on the Marais des Cygnes river in Linn County in the fall of 1865. This was a cold-blooded murder committed for money. The victim was unknown and the officers were never able to identify him. A stranger in a strange land, he met a violent death. Just another case of a man filled with hope going out into the then wild West to seek his fortune, and so far as friends were concerned never to be heard of again. Sad as was his fate there are probably none living in the world today who have an interest in this mystery of nearly sixty years ago.

"As soon as news of this crime reached Sheriff Goss a search was begun that ended only with the capture of both men and their subsequent death. Foster was captured first. He was discovered in Bates county, Missouri, and a posse hurriedly formed for his capture. Foster, who was splendidly mounted, at first laughed at his pursuers. He easily distanced all of them except one man mounted on a roan horse. Over rolling prairies, across wooded streams, up and down hilly slopes they rode, exchanging occasional shots. They rode furiously. No matter how swift the pace set by Foster the gallant roan held it and began to gain a little. Foster was heading for the town of Butler. He explained afterward that he did not want to add another murder to his list so decided to shoot the roan horse and make his escape. With this purpose in view he waited until the rider of the roan fired, then stopping suddenly and wheeling his horse he was in the act of taking aim at the roan when his own splendid mount fell dead from a well directed shot from the rider of the roan. Foster did not know that the rider of the roan carried a repeating rifle. This occurred on the townsite of Butler. I wish I could give the name of the rider of the roan but I can't. All I know about him is that he was a brave man and a good citizen. He was one of the pioneer merchants of Pleasanton, which town was started four or five years later. Foster surrendered and was taken to Mound City. There was no jail in the county at the time and he was held under guard by the officers for several months, when his case being continued Sheriff Goss arranged to take him to Lawrence and place him in the jail pending his trial.

"Late one Sunday afternoon in the latter part of the summer of 1866, if my memory serves me right, the sheriff and deputies started out with their prisoner for a drive, as was their custom. Instead of returning to Mound City, they drove toward Lawrence. Some time after dark they reached the heavily timbered bottoms of Big Sugar creek. Suddenly a mob of twenty-five or thirty men rushed out of their hiding place, overpowered the officers and took charge of the prisoner. The team of the sheriff was turned around and he was ordered to drive with all haste to Mound City. He drove a short distance, stopped, and began to search for his prisoner. I think he was not sure whether Foster was captured by his friends or his enemies. A few hours later they found his lifeless body hanging to the limb of a tree. Tradition has it that Foster was the third man to swing from that particular tree, two horse thieves having preceded him to the "Great Beyond" from the same limb.

"The search for Holderman continued, but he was wary; means of communication in the sparsely settled region of eastern Kansas and western Missouri were few and his capture seemed doubtful. It happened that William Goss, brother of the sheriff, had some business over in Missouri quite a distance from the Kansas line. He traveled horseback. One day he lost his way in the woods and found himself traveling a mere bypath that led to a lonely cabin in the midst of the forest. He dismounted, went to the door and knocked. A woman opened the door and he recognized her as Scott Holderman's wife. It was raining and this gave him an excuse to pull his hat down over his face while Mrs. Holderman briefly directed him to a road that would lead him out of the woods.

For a few minutes the life of Bill Goss hung by a very slender thread. Had Mrs. Holderman recognized him he would have been killed. Imagine if you can the feelings of Bill Goss as he walked away from the cabin door expecting every minute for a bullet to "spat" him in the back. But he was not recognized and he returned to Kansas and reported his find to his brother Dave, who with two trusted deputies, John Humphrey and a man named Huff, immediately set out for Missouri.

"There was a small country store a few miles from Holderman's cabin. Sheriff Goss took the proprietor of this store into his confidence. Holderman was not at home, but the merchant assured the sheriff that he would know when he came and would assist in his capture. Sheriff Goss immediately returned to Kansas, as both Holderman and his wife knew him very well, and to remain in the neighborhood might thwart plans for the capture. Humphrey and Huff, who were not known by the Holdermans, secured work in the harvest fields in the neighborhood and waited for developments. Holderman returned in a few days. A small posse was organized and surrounded the cabin in the early hours of morning. Before it was fairly light they called for Holderman to come out and surrender. He came out, but not to surrender. He began firing in the semidarkness and the first bullet passed through Huff's hat. Members of the posse were well hidden and protected and before Holderman could locate anyone else to shoot at, Humphrey shot him through the bowels. This ended the fight; he surrendered and was taken to Mound City as soon as he was able to travel.

"His preliminary hearing was held August 3, 1867. He was held without bond and on September 25 his trial came on before Judge D. P. Lowe, who had defended Griffith in his trial for murder a few years before. He was found guilty and sentenced to hang November 15. There was no jail in Linn County and he was taken to Lawrence and held in jail there until the day set for his execution. The sheriff, fearing an attempt to rescue the prisoner should he return him to Mound City, went to Lawrence and carried out the sentence of the court by "hanging him, the said Scott Holderman, by the neck until he was dead." Scott Holderman met death bravely, as he had often met it before on the field of battle and later in many an exciting holdup and adventure.

"It will be observed that just one hundred and four days elapsed from the day of his preliminary hearing to that of his execution. There was no new trial, no appeal, no stay of execution, or other delay so common in our courts today. I believe this execution had a salutary effect along the border. It was a warning to other criminals that the courts were working and that justice was sure and swift. I think a return to this practice all over the country would tend to check murders and furnish a just protection to honest people. At the same time it would greatly improve the population of our country by the process of elimination. After I became a man I was told by an old settler that the captain of the vigilance committee that hanged Foster was afterward foreman of the jury that convicted Holderman. Thus and in such manner did the pioneers mete out justice enforce law and restore order. So ended the career of two men who under different environment might have been good citizens. There is a similarity in their career to that of the James and Younger gang. Both got their training along the border during the great conflict between opposing factions. When the strife ended, both continued to prey on the public. But here the similarity ended. The James and Younger gang were shielded and protected by former partisans and comrades in arms. Holderman and Foster were hunted down, captured and brought to justice by their former captain and comrades in arms.

"I have always thought and I now believe that had every county in western Missouri had a Dave Goss for sheriff when the war closed the career of the James and Younger gang would have ended about the time that Holderman and Foster went out of business. But all is changed. The border war is only a memory. Where once every highway and bypath were fraught with danger, now all the paths are paths of peace. Where once the rope and the six-shooter were the chief necessities in the settlement of disputes and necktie parties were of frequent occurence, now law and order prevail. No one carries arms, and I doubt if there are a half dozen men along the border, including both sides of the line from St. Joseph, Missouri, to Galena, Kansas, who know how to tie a hangman's knot. Peace and prosperity have taken the place of strife and bloodshed. Only a few of the pioneers of the "fifties" remain. These sit peacefully in the afterglow of life's sunset, calmly waiting for the shadows. The animosities of the strife are all forgotten; the dead past has buried its dead."

The saloon was never permitted to entrench itself over at Mound City. The story of how thirty-five years before Carrie Nation smashed the bar of the old Carey Hotel in Wichita, six young women in eastern Kansas smashed a saloon, is told in an article written by J. T. Botkin, former secretary of state for Kansas and of the Linn County family of that name. The raid was in 1861. Two of the young women were cousins of Mr. Botkin. In the winter of 1861 there was in the town of Mound City a saloon owned by Eli Bradley and By Hildreth. The place had a bad reputation and its owners were without scruple as to whom they should sell liquor. Early that winter a soldier from the nearby military post got drunk in the saloon and froze to death on his way back to the post. Soon another soldier repeated the performance. These occurrences did not cause the saloon-keepers to improve their ways, nor did the Andy Moore affair, a short time later. Moore, a soldier, got drunk in the saloon and on returning to camp he fired at a nurse carrying food to some sick soldiers. The nurse's elbow was shattered, causing amputation to be necessary. When this tragedy became known publicly Mrs. Ira Height, wife of a Mound City merchant, organized a party to clean up the saloon. But the women she had called upon failed to report for duty. So she went to the neighboring town of Moneka and enlisted five young women. They were Emma, Sarah and Mary Wattles, Amelia and Drusilla Botkin. The Wattles girls were daughters of Augustus Wattles, an active free state leader in the border war days. He was one of the group which had planned to rescue John Brown from his death cell at Charlestown, Virginia, a plan which was frustrated because Brown refused to be rescued. The Botkin girls came to Kansas from Ohio in 1859 with two brothers, Owen D. and Murray Botkin. They were sisters of the late Judge Theodosius Botkin and first cousins of J. T. Botkin. The party started to Mound City early in the morning of December 10, 1861, and taken there in a wagon driven by John M. Stearns, afterward prominent as an educator in Linn County. They were met at Mound City by Mrs. Height and armed with axes and hatchets they marched silently to the saloon.

Silently they entered the place just as the first customer, Jim Tomlinson, was taking his early morning drink. They knew their business and with no word of explanation or warning they proceeded to the work in hand. Their aim was to destroy no property except such as was necessary to get rid of the liquor. They first attacked the bottled goods behind the bar. Armed with a long-necked bottle, one of the girls standing on the bar would make a swipe at a whole row of bottles, smashing them and scattering their contents over the bar and floor. They broke jugs and other containers, chopped holes in kegs and poured whisky on the floor. Bradley, one of the proprietors, said to Sarah Wattles, "If you think you are right, go ahead." Miss Wattles replied: "We most certainly do think we are right," and they went ahead. Satisfied they had emptied all the liquor in the front room, they invaded the back room. Here they found a large stock of whisky in kegs and barrels. They smashed in the heads of these and poured the contents on the floor. By this time the girls were wading in whisky almost to their shoe tops. Drusilla Botkin started to chop a hole in the floor to let the whisky escape. Bradley said to her: "Woman, you have destroyed all our goods; don't chop the house down." Miss Botkin replied: "We won't hurt your house, but if we don't let this stuff run out you will be dipping it up and selling it as soon as we are gone," and she chopped a hole big enough to let the whisky run through. By this time quite a crowd, mostly friendly to the girls, had collected. Hildreth said to Sarah Wattles: "Miss Wattles, I always thought you were my friend." She replied: "I never did you as great a kindness as that which I am doing now," and proceeded with her work.

In the meantime a whisky drummer from Leavenworth had stopped outside to watch the fun. His wagon was fitted with barrels and kegs, faucets attached so liquor could be drawn off for his customers. While the drummer was looking on Sarah Wattles quietly stepped to the side of his wagon and opened all the faucets, the whisky running out on the ground through the wagon bed. Someone called the drummer's attention to his own troubles. Approaching Miss Wattles, he cried: "I never did strike a woman, but by God I can." But Amelia Botkin stepped in front of him and threatened to split his head open with a hatchet if he touched her friend. The drummer retreated, but any frontier town is a poor place for a man to threaten to strike a woman. Scarcely had this fellow escaped Miss Botkin's hatchet until a rope was around his neck and he was being led to the rear of the building, where arrangements were being made to hang him. He begged so piteously for mercy that better judgment prevailed and he was permitted to go hence under promise never to return to Linn County. He drove out of town at breakneck speed. He was so badly frightened that he kept up this rate of speed until one of his horses fell dead about ten miles south of town and he rode the other horse into Fort Scott without a saddle.

Having cleaned up the saloon, and almost drunk from the whisky fumes, the young women returned home. None of these women were sensationalists. They were not seeking notoriety. They believed in temperance, sobriety and decency. They wanted to see their state become the home of good people, and their town a fit place for decent, law-abiding people to locate and live and rear their families. Their method may have been a little bit irregular. Undoubtedly it was heroic, but it was effective and it met the hearty approval of the good people of Linn County. Emma Wattles, now Mrs. Emma Morse who lives at Mound City, and Mary Wattles, now Mrs. Faunce, who lives in Colorado, are the only members of the party now alive.

The following story tells of the meager chances children had even as late as 1865 in getting any schooling, and yet how gorgeous even this appears compared with the Territorial days prior to 1860! This is authoritative, as it was written by a sister of Laura the school teacher:

In the spring of 1865 a neighborhood in Linn was in sore need of a school for pioneers. They like Enoch Arden had resolved to give their children "a better bringing up than theirs had been". About four miles from the center of the county on an open prairie, belonging to the Driscoll family, stood an abandoned cabin, floorless, doorless and windowless. This a few farmers "fitted up" by securing some newly sawed boards from Farlin and Boston's mill. With these they covered the ground floor of about three-fourths of this cabin, leaving bare ground in front of the poor hearthless fireplace at one end of the cabin, made a crude door and hung it on wooden hinges, fastened it with a wooden latch with string poked through a gimlet hole in the door, the only lock on the house. Then a broad board hung on leather hinges covered the space of a log left out of one side of the cabin. This was propped up on the outside of the cabin by using a fence rail provided the sky was bright but let down when it rained and this was the only window. Some long benches with rails for legs were substitutes for school desks and seats, a broad board fastened to pegs driven into the logs of the cabin supplied a writing desk—and, presto! There was a school house! Only please remember the "writing board" was so high the pupils must stand in order to reach it. And now for a teacher. Miss Laura Linton had just arrived from Ohio, fresh from its Maineville Academy. Indeed, this "school house" had been fitted up especially for her and into it she bravely went "with a heart for any fate." And into it crowded pupils of all sizes and ages, sturdy little fellows of seven to brave pioneers of eighteen or twenty armed with a revolver or two, for old settlers insisted a pretty young teacher would not be safe out on a prairie so recently the stamping ground of horse thieves and desperadoes, and still the pupils came from far and near till it was quite impossible to seat them all and the resourceful teacher selected the largest, assigned them tasks, and sent them out to study under the diminutive trees that grew a short distance from the cabin. When the little ones had recited they were sent out to play while the larger pupils came in to recite. This was on sunshiny days, but when it rained there was not room enough to seat all the children at once, moreover the board window must be lowered and then the room was so dark it was often impossible to study any ordinary print. Here again came the rare resourcefulness of that young teacher. She had a large map of the United States hung on the wall and with the larger pupils standing, often with an arm about a smaller child to prevent its falling off the bench on which it stood, with the rain pouring on the roof—(oh, how it did rain that summer of 1865) —the teacher pointed to the map and taught the school in concert to sing the states and capitals; also the rivers of the United States. When it was too dark to see the map we were drilled on the multiplication table, singing the two's and five's to the tune of Yankee Doodle; or we were told stories of the Pilgrims, or of the Quakers who lived in caves along the seashore till houses could be built in Philadelphia. On clear days at recess the boys and girls played ball together and the big boys stacked their revolvers where they could be quickly taken in case a "bushwhacker" appeared,— but he never came! However, a revolver once did valiant duty for teacher and children. Not far from this cabin quite a large sized patch of blackberries and tall weeds grew and one day the teacher discovered a large rattlesnake crawling from this patch evidently intending to hide under the school house. Luckily the small children were inside. That dauntless teacher took her pointer and accompanied by one of the big boys went calmly forth to the defense of her brood. A rattlesnake is a brave fighter and almost never runs. He coils and strikes. This one coiled, but before there was time to strike its head was severed from its body by a bullet from that schoolboy's revolver, a specimen of the frontier boy's marksmanship. The twelve weeks term came to an end and next fall there was a well-built frame school house ready, but Miss Linton was teaching in the Mound City school where there was a two-story stone building and to help her was the brave army nurse and later efficient temperance worker Amanda M. Way. And what of the pupils of so primitive a school? Much would I love to know the life work of each one. Only this do I know, one of the smallest of these pupils is now and has for many years been a successful M. D. still in Kansas.[1]

The advance of women from the position or status of a mere chattel to that of one with all the rights, responsibilities, and privileges of man, in everything that affects her liberties in the practice of the professions and in business life, in her rights to have and administer property without interference from anyone, and with full and equal power in the administration of public affairs, even the right to aspire to and be elected to any office in the land—all this has come so rapidly and so radically as to startle one who remembers that from the earliest history woman had been little better than a chattel, and even under the common law of England a woman upon her marriage surrendered to her husband all her right to hold personal or real property. Not only her individuality became merged in her husband, but he enjoyed the right of possession and disposition of her property. Her goods became

---

1. I am not sure but I think this is the same boy who was the hero of an incident in Paris township. The school was honored one day by the presence of all three members of the board of education and very proudly the teacher called her class in history to recite before them. Quite confidently she asked the boy at the head of the class "Who wrote Magna Charta?" The boy looked startled and scared and gulped and in an innocent but slightly defensive tone replied, "I didn't." A quiet moment followed when the chairman requested the teacher to have the boy stand up again. "Son," said he, "I noticed that when you denied writing that, you looked guilty. I am inclined to believe you did it."

liable to seizure and appropriation by his creditors. Through the profligacy or ill-management of the husband a woman who was well-to-do in her own right before her marriage might be reduced to poverty after her marriage. It is interesting to note the attitude of the people who were creating a new and great state toward this situation. The men of the Wyandotte convention determined that no such injustice should be fastened upon the women of Kansas, and in writing the Constitution of Kansas they framed section six as follows: "The legislature shall provide for the protection of the rights of women, in acquiring and possessing property, real, personal and mixed, separate and apart from the husband; and shall also provide for their equal rights in the possession of their children." Section nine also provided for the exemption from execution of a homestead of one hundred and sixty acres, or of one acre within the limits of an incorporated town, with all the improvements thereon, except taxes." This homestead idea is purely an American idea. The Republic of Texas first enacted in 1839, then Vermont in 1849, then Kansas. Nearly every state in the Union has since adopted it.

All this introduction makes interesting the statement that Linn County was among the very first communities in the United States to have what was then ridiculed as "Wimmen's Rights" societies. The secretary's book of the Moneka Women's Rights Association shows that at Moneka, February 2, 1858, after one of Mr. John Otis Wattle's lectures, a proposition was made to organize a Women's Rights Society. Mrs. Esther Wattles was chosen president. A committee to form a constitution was chosen, the meeting adjourned to February 13, when the meeting was called to order by John Otis Wattles. The preamble and constitution of the Moneka Women's Rights Association was then read, discussed and adopted article by article, as follows:

BECAUSE woman is constituted of body and mind and has all the common wants of the one and the natural powers of the other;

BECAUSE she is a social being and has all the relations of life to sustain which belong to an associated condition of existence;

BECAUSE she is a progressive being, ever outgrowing the past and demanding a higher and greater future, or in other words,

BECAUSE she is a human being and as such is endowed by her Creator with the full measure of human rights, whether educational, social or political, and

BECAUSE by the present arrangement of the world she is shut out of colleges and the higher order of educational institutions, thereby deprived of great opportunities for intellectual improvement, shut out from most of the lucrative professions and the mechanic arts, thereby deprived of the facilities for the accumulation of wealth and enjoyment of social life—made subject to laws which she has no voice in making and which deprive her of the ownership of property or herself, and give even her daily earnings to the control of others; dragged before courts to answer for crimes against laws to which she has never given her assent, to be tried as a criminal in halls where she can neither sit as judge or juror, or officiate as counsel; and

BECAUSE from the pulpit and the rostrum woman is called upon to give character to the rising generation and charged with the responsibility of shaping the destiny of the race,

BECAUSE she is demanded to make statesmen to wield the fate of nations, and divines to wake the world to glory:

WE, THEREFORE, form ourselves into an Association to be governed by the following constitution:

Article First.   This association shall be called The Moneka Women's Rights Society.

Article Second.   It shall be the object of the society to secure to woman her natural rights and to advance her educational interests.   In furtherance of these objects the society shall consider what woman's natural rights are and the means best calculated to secure them.   It shall also encourage lectures on this subject in the society and elsewhere; and give its support to some paper devoted to the elevation of woman.   *   *   *   *   *   *   *

SIGNED: Elvira Andrews, Esther Wattles, Elizabeth S. Dennison, Mollie A. McGrath, Emma Wattles, Pamelia Doy, Sarah G. Wattles, Susan E. Wattles, Lima S. H. Ober, Angeline P. Crystal, Rebecca E. Hulbert, Mary P. T. Snyder, Ann Schooley, Hulda A. Goodwin, Matilda L. Gibbons, R. W. Gibbons, Joseph Addis, Permelia C. Knox, Charlotte Smith, Rhoda W. Ransom, Geo. E. Denison, John O. Wattles, Hannah Strong, H. P. Danforth, O. H. Stearns, O. E. Morse, C. E. Shearer, Emma L. Burritt, John C. Anderson, R. A. Frazell, John Morrison, E. L. Taylor, Thomas J. Addis, Jr., Lyman Strong, Hamilton Schooley, J. S. Craig, Thos. J. Addis, Sr., Timothy Hulbert, P. Frizell, Charlotte S. Anderson, Aggie Lefker, Hetty Addis.

The following officers were then elected: President, Mrs. Elizabeth S. Dennison; vice president, Mrs. Esther Wattles; secretary, Sarah G. Wattles.

The following resolutions were then offered and adopted:

1st Resolved, That we will exert whatever influence we can over the public sentiment of this Territory that the constitution about to be formed may prohibit the distillation of all alcoholic liquors within its boundaries.

3rd Resolved, That Kansas cannot be truly free while the words "white" or "male" are found within the limits of her constitution.

Miss Mollie A. McGrath was then appointed to deliver an address at the next meeting on the resolution, "Resolved, that all human beings by virtue of their physical organizations have a right to as much of the earth as they can cultivate and no more."

The following was offered and adopted:

WHEREAS women can not vote and yet feel the necessity of just laws, therefore,

RESOLVED, That every woman in Kansas who believes that equal rights belong to women should consider herself a committee of one whose duty it is to do all in her power to convert to her views at least one legal voter.

The following forms of petitions were then presented:

TO THE CONSTITUTIONAL CONVENTION: We the undersigned citizens of Kansas respectfully petition the convention now assembled to frame the organic law of the State of Kansas for the citizens without any invidious distinctions.

TO THE LEGISLATURE OF KANSAS: We the undersigned citizens of Kansas respectfully petition your honorable body to enact such laws—

1st.   As will secure to woman the property which she possesses before marriage.

2nd.   Also a just proportion of the joint property of the husband and wife acquired during marriage.

3rd.   Also at the death of the husband or wife that the same laws shall govern the widow or widower in the possession and disposal of the estate and children belonging to them jointly.

4th.   That no bond or security given by the husband shall be valid without the signature of the wife.

And especially deserving of mention in the early history of Kansas is the "Ladies Enterprise Society of Mound City", probably the first woman's club organized in Kansas, and ranking in age with the famous Sorosis Club of New York City. The reason for its existence and the aims it had in view are given in the preamble to the constitution: "We, the ladies of Mound City and vicinity, in view of the great religious, educational and benevolent needs of our community, do hereby associate ourselves so that by concert of labor we may work to better purposes for these ends. As a primary measure in the furtherance of our design we propose to build and keep in repair a house to be used for religious worship, educational purposes, scientific, literary and political lectures or meetings, which building shall be called the Mound City Free Meeting House."

Following the Constitution and By-law is this list of the charter members: Mrs. Robert Kincaid, Mrs. Fanny F. Smith, Mrs. Sophia Manington, Charlotte Baird, Alice M. Trego, C. A. Baird, Ann Brooks, Rebecca S. Smith, Nettie Broadhead, Phoebe V. Deland, Emma Metz, Jane Thornton, Mary S. Blodgett, Eliza C. Young, Amanda M. Way, Tilney H. Lowe, Edna G. Lowe, Hannah Hiatt, Emma A. Dinkle, Sarah G. W. Hiatt, Maria Snoddy, Sarah M. Brown, Caroline Wheeler, Olive C. Powell, Elizabeth Scott, Laura Phillips, Susanna Scott, Sarah A. Simpson, Cordelia Bartholomew, Mary I. Coats, and Mary E. Butler.

Mrs. Robert Kincaid was the first president. She was handsome, dignified, well educated and presided with grace and distinction at the meetings. Mrs. Rebecca S. Smith was the first treasurer and Miss C. A. Baird the first secretary. The society was organized in February, 1864, the last year of the Civil War. Mrs. Caroline Wheeler was elected president in the spring of 1865, was reelected and served through the year.

In 1866 Mrs. Cordelia Bartholomew was elected president and was reelected and served the year out. In 1867 Mrs. Rebecca S. Smith was elected president and served for three years or until the disbanding of the association in 1869. Alice M. Trego served as secretary during the years 1867 to 1869.

The association was composed chiefly of young matrons who had come from the comforts, culture and refinements of civilized life to make homes in this raw new country. With families of little children growing up about them—large families were then in vogue, a new baby at least every two years—the matter of a new building for school, Sunday school, church, lecture-room, was of vital importance to them. Their husbands and brothers were interested in this work but life in the last year of the Civil War and even in the years closely following was too strenuous for them to undertake this work. But the pioneer wives—though often overwhelmed with household duties, help for the kitchen and nursery being even more difficult to obtain than today—could not see their little ones growing up without any spiritual or mental training other than a busy tired mother could give so they shouldered the burden.

The association employed as head carpenter or contractor John G. Brooks. The hall was built of native lumber, the

seats of native walnut lumber, now almost priceless. The
seats were unusual and very uncomfortable. There was no
danger, however long or prosy the sermon or lecture, of one
going to sleep on those hard unyielding benches with their
stiff upright backs.

The first funds were raised for the building by generous
subscriptions from the scant and scattered early residents of
the county. My mother, riding a vicious pony into the
country to get subscriptions, was thrown from the pony
and suffered for days with a badly sprained ankle. There
is no doubt that her colaborers sacrificed as much in different
ways for the cause. The society did not, however, depend
entirely on these subscriptions for funds, but all during the
life of the association (while the hall was building, being
furnished and adding to its attractions) there were numerous
suppers, concerts, dramatic entertainments, lectures, etc.,
given to supplement the subscriptions and raise funds for a
worthy cause.

Those early entertainments to our childish eyes and
stomachs were wonderful affairs, says Miss Jessie Smith, their
historian. The grand suppers especially appealed to us. The
tables groaned with delicious food, fried chicken, roast turkey,
pickles, preserves, jams, jellies, pies, cakes. The slices cut
from a noble pound cake with a gold ring embedded somewhere in its interior were each sold for a fabulous sum. These
suppers were a special feature of the last year of the war
when regiments of soldiers were quartered at Mound City.
The officers and men vied with each other in their appreciation
of the menu and admiration of the fair ladies who superintended the feasts. They responded nobly, heroically, to the
gastronomical and financial demands made upon them.

One of the concerts noted in the secretary's books as given
for the benefit of the meeting house was conducted by Mr.
George W. Botkin, who also had an evening singing school
in the building. Mr. Botkin always gave the key with a tuning
fork.

The dramatic entertainments consisted of a variety of
stunts. Tableaux of Sweet Maud Muller raking the hay as
the judge rode by. The judge and his proud wife, and Maud
with her husband "unlearned and poor", and the "many children who played round her door", were depicted on the stage
while the poem was read behind the scenes. We were thrilled
to our finger tips with Poe's Raven who quoth "Nevermore"
and the ravings of the "Maniac" who announced with a blood-
curdling shriek "I am mad!" The audience was always well
satisfied with the talents of our local actors and musicians.
Mrs. Henry M. Stearns at one time conducted a very successful private school in this building. On Sundays the building
was used for religious services and all religious dogmas and
creeds were expounded from its rostrum. United Brethren,

Baptist, Presbyterian and Methodist held services on their appointed days in this house. I think for religious services there was no charge made, or if any only a nominal sum, but for other meetings there was a fixed charge to help defray the expenses of keeping up the repairs, etc. At the close of the war after General Price's raid through Linn County the building was used as a hospital.

Speakers of state and even national fame talked to the citizens of the town in the "Free Meeting House", among them Judge Usher who was Lincoln's Secretary of the Interior, Judge Thatcher, Governor Robinson, and Governor St. John. A great event in the history of the town was when George Francis Train, Elizabeth Cady Stanton and Susan B. Anthony visited Mound City and addressed an overflow meeting in the Meeting House on the then fearsome subject of "Wimmen's Rights."

The pioneer women, members of the Ladies Enterprise Association, weathered with great fortitude the difficulties that beset them in this country; enjoyed to the full the festivals and other entertainments given to raise funds for the building, ignored with great dignity the sharp criticism that seems a necessary part of any enterprise, and lived to see the fruition of their fondest hopes in the completion of the Free Meeting House.

In 1869 a proposition was made by the Ladies Enterprise Association to the county commissioners that the building be turned over to the county to be used as a court house. The commissioners graciously accepted the gift and so ended the history of the building as a "Free Meeting House", and also the Ladies Enterprise Association.

Colonel James Findlay Harrison, formerly county surveyor and an old time citizen of Mound City, born March 9, 1825, in Cincinnati, Ohio, was the son of William Henry Harrison, a native of Vincennes, Indiana. His father's father born September 26, 1802, was the son of General William Henry Harrison, the paternal grandfather of our subject being the hero of Tippecanoe and later president of the United States. The father, educated in Transsylvania University in Kentucky, was admitted to the bar in Ohio in 1823. The mother, Jane Findlay Irwin, was the daughter of Archibald Irwin, a prosperous farmer near Mercersburg, Pennsylvania. On the Harrison side the family dates back to Thomas Harrison, a major general of the Parliamentary army and once colonel of the old Ironsides Regiment of Cromwell. He was one of the judges who tried King Charles and was the one who, by orders of Cromwell, dissolved the long parliament and arrested the

1. The Friends in Council of Lawrence, Kansas, was organized in 1871, while the Sorosis Club of New York City, claiming to be the oldest club in the United States, was organized in 1868. Later records show the organization of a club in Indiana in 1858.

speaker. He was hung, drawn and quartered May 10, 1660. His son Benjamin Harrison who emigrated to America on account of political differences with his father, located in the Old Dominion, and became clerk of the council of Virginia. He died in the year 1649, and left a son Benjamin; the latter was born September 20, 1645, in Southwark Parish, Surrey county, Virginia, and died in January, 1713. His son Benjamin, born in Berkley, Virginia, and later attorney general and treasurer of the colony, was also speaker of the house of burgesses and died April 10, 1710, aged thirty-seven years.

Benjamin Harrison, also born in Berkley and a son of the last named, and sheriff of Charles City county and in 1728 a member of the house of burgesses, died in 1774. His son Benjamin likewise of Berkley, was a member of the house of burgesses from 1750-1775, and was a member of the first continental congress and a signer of the Declaration of Independence. He was three times governor of Virginia and carried the popular vote of his state. His third son William Henry Harrison born in Berkley, February 9, 1773, afterward became the famous general and later president of the United States. He served as aide-de-camp under Anthony Wayne and was secretary of the Northwest Territory. He was a delegate to congress from that Territory and a brave soldier, fought at the battle of Tippecanoe November 7, 1811. He was also engaged at Fort Meigs and participated in the battle of the Thames October 5, 1812. He was United States senator from Ohio and was minister to Columbia. He became president of the United States March 4, 1841. He expired while in office April 4, 1841. His second son William Henry Harrison was the father of our subject.

Upon the maternal side the family dates back to Archibald Irwin who settled in Pennsylvania before the Revolutionary War. He was a cadet of the House of Irwin of Bonshaw, Scotland. His son Archibald married Mary McDowell, and their son Archibald married Mary Ramsey, whose father was a younger member of the Dalhousie family of Scotland. Their daughter was Jane Findlay Irwin, the mother of Colonel James F. Harrison. The parents after their marriage settled in Cincinnati, Ohio, where the father practiced law, and later died in his father's house at North Bend. The father and mother were blessed with two children, James F. and William Henry. The latter, born May 5, 1828, died in Mexico in April, 1849.

Col. James Findlay Harrison was educated in a Cincinnati college. He entered West Point Military Academy in 1841 and graduated in 1845. General Fitz John Porter was in the same class. Colonel Harrison later resigned from the Academy, but when the war broke out with Mexico volunteered in the First Ohio Infantry. He was adjutant of the same when only twenty-one years of age and served with

distinction under Colonel Alexander H. Mitchell. At the battle
of Chapultepec he rode alongside Lieutenant Ulysses S. Grant
and they rode together with this conquering army through the
City of Mexico.

He became an inmate of the White House at Washington
during the incumbency of President W. H. Harrison and was
at his bedside when that veteran soldier and statesman entered
into rest, mourned by all loyal citizens as a national loss.
This was prior to his going to West Point. After his return
from the Mexican War Colonel Harrison entered into the study
of law and later was admitted to the bar in Indiana and
practiced there for a few years. He resided in Dayton, Ohio,
from 1854 until 1864 and enlisted in three months service in
the Civil War, being Colonel of the Eleventh Ohio Infantry.
During the Chickamauga campaign he was aide-de-camp and
chief of staff to General W. H. Lytle and was covered by the
life blood of that general when he was killed in September,
1863. The friendship between Colonel Harrison and his chief
was very strong. Their fathers had been friends, tried and
true, as had likewise been their grandfathers. For a short
time Colonel Harrison served on the staff of General Phil H.
Sheridan, but after the sad demise of General Lytle resigned
from the army.

During the last call of President Lincoln Colonel Harrison
re-enlisted as a private in the First Ohio cavalry and was
transferred as lieutenant to the One Hundred Eighty-Fifth
Ohio Infantry. Later as Captain of the One Hundred Eighty-
Seventh Ohio he went to Georgia and remained until the close
of the war. During the squirrel hunter campaign in Ohio
Colonel Harrison was the recipient of the following order,
September 12, 1862: "Colonel Harrison, First Regiment State
Militia, has been placed in charge of the defense of the Ohio
river west of Cincinnati to the Indiana line. He will be obeyed
and respected accordingly. By order of Major General Lew
Wallace, Major J. M. McDowell, A. D. C." Colonel Harrison
served through the campaign and was discharged by order of
David Tod, governor of Ohio. Colonel Harrison raised a company in Dayton, Ohio, in a half hour and was placed in command of a regiment. The same day he was given charge of
a brigade, being then engaged for two weeks in the service
of the government.

In 1866 Colonel Harrison settled in Linn County, where
for many years he was county surveyor and one of the most
popular men in his locality. In the year 1848 he was united
in marriage with Miss Caroline M. Alston of South Carolina.
This estimable lady died in the spring of 1863 and the three
children of the union are now deceased. The colonel was
married again in December, 1864, to Miss Alice Kennedy, a
native of Mississippi and a daughter of John Kennedy, formerly of Belfast, Ireland, originally a Scotch merchant re-

moving to Belfast in mature life. Unto this second union were born six children, five of whom are now living: John Scott, (now in charge of government surveys in Helena, Montana), William Henry (now a successful real estate dealer at Kansas City, Missouri), Mary Randolph Farrar, James Findlay, jr., and Archibald Irwin. Colonel Harrison was a member of the Episcopal church, associated fraternally with Montgomery Post No. 33, G. A. R., of Mound City who had charge of the burial service and was laid at rest by the side of departed heroes in our beautiful National cemetery. He was a member of the Veterans' Association of the Mexican War.

The relationship between Colonel Harrison and ex-president Benjamin Harrison is that of cousin, there being relationship on both the father's and mother's side. The descendant of honored ancestry and himself personally faithful to all his obligations as a man and citizen, Colonel Harrison won a high place in the regard of a wide acquaintance and throughout Linn County, is esteemed as a man of fine attainments, superior ability and sterling integrity of character.

In September 1855 the St. Louis Conference of the Methodist Episcopal Church South sent several young preachers to organize missions among the white settlements in Kansas, among them Cyrus Robert Rice, a native of Wilson county, Tennessee. He traveled horseback and the fourth day after leaving Springfield, Missouri, he found himself among Indians naked to the waist but who greeted him in a friendly way and directed him to the double log cabin of Chief Baptiste near where the town of Paola now is. He had his first night on a bed of buffalo robes and the next day went to the settlement called Osawatomie on the Marais des Cygnes river where he met Rev. Samuel L. Adair, who told him plainly that they did not want a representative of the slave interests there. He went on to the Dutch Henry Crossing and found a cordial welcome from the proslavers and preached to a good congregation of bad people. One of the attendants is mentioned by the classical name of Philologus Thomas. He was now in Linn County on Big Sugar creek and Little Sugar creek. He met the Neiswanger family. So much of his reference to Linn County is interesting I am copying as follows:

"The next day I rode over to Big and Little Sugar creeks in Linn County. The first settlement I reached consisted of two families. The men had taken claims together and were building cabins. In the meantime they were living in tents, using wagon boxes for bed rooms. When I told them of my mission they wanted to know if I would preach for them then and there, and in a few minutes nine persons counting some children were seated in one of the tents and I stood in the door and preached to them. The poor women looked as though they were in distress and declared they did not like to leave

their good homes in Illinois and live in tents. So I read for a
text "Comfort ye, comfort ye my people, saith the Lord",
Isaiah, 41:1. The good people thanked me for the sermon
and never said a word about their own or my politics. I later
renewed acquaintance with one of the families and stopped
at their cabin more than once. They claimed the beautiful
German name Neiswanger. The other family became discouraged in a short time, sold their claim and went "back to
wife's people."

"Bidding the tent dwellers goodbye I proceeded down Little
Sugar creek and about sunset found an unusually large cabin
occupied by a family of Missourians. They had brought a
flock of chickens with them, the first I had seen on my round.
Just as I rode up to the cabin door the chickens began to fly
and cackle, and the man of the house rushed out gun in hand
calling as he passed me "Some beast is after my chickens
and I must look after them." I sat on my horse and awaited
for his return. He was back in a little while and rudely asked,
"Whar are you frum?" I told him who I was, and what I
was wanting to do, when he looked at me, I thought, somewhat fiercely, and said, "Now I know what was the matter
with my chickens; they were skeered at you. You are the
first preacher that has been in these diggins." Then he invited me to "git down and stay all night." I accepted the
invitation, dismounted and took the saddle from my horse,
tying him beside the man's team on the south side of a hay
stack. I then gathered up my overcoat and saddle bags and
followed my host in to the cabin. He introduced me to his
wife by saying "Mandy, here's a preacher cum to stay all
night with us; have you got anything for him to eat?" She
answered "Now just make yourself to hum," and went about
her evening's work.

"After supper I excused myself because I had a hard lesson
to get out of Watson's Theological Institutes, and seated by
a table with a tallow candle for light I gave some time to
reading and writing notes on the lessons. At length Mr. Long
said, "I suppose, parson, you will want to pray before we go
to bed; if so, pray now and we'll go to bed and you kin read
as long as you want to." After the prayer a ladder was
brought in and set up by an opening in the loft and the children climbed to their beds. The man and his wife retired
to a bed in one corner of the room and the preacher found
a spare bed in the other corner. The beds in the room were
surrounded with curtains.

"The man was up in the morning at an early hour and
made a log fire over which his wife cooked a good breakfast
for us. We were all up and at the breakfast before the sun
was up. For the first time in the Territory I had eggs for
breakfast. My host said if I would return and preach for
them he would not charge me for my entertainment and I

promised to return in four days and preach in his cabin. After getting the course to a settlement said to be near the head of Little Osage river I bade the family boodbye and set my face in that direction.

"I reached the locality sought by the middle of the afternoon and found a Methodist family living in a good cabin. As usual I told the man and his wife what I was there for and received their hearty cheering welcome. They urged me to stay with them over Sunday and preach for them. I consented and soon found myself comfortably situated and at my books. I was glad to have the two whole days for study. In those days I gave every possible moment to a course of study assigned to young preachers, knowing I had to stand before a committee of examiners at the next conference. I kept my library in my saddle bags, as well as my linen and underwear. I was the possessor of one suit of clothing which I carried on my body everywhere.

"Sunday, a beautiful autumn day, came and I preached to a congregation of twenty persons and organized a society of six members. I promised to return and preach again in three weeks. Mr. Johnson and his kind wife made my stay with them very pleasant. I had made an eight days' tour and reached the limit of the territory assigned to me. I had found several places for future appointments to preach and organized two small societies, and was ready to return to Osawatomie.

"On my return I preached at three places, one of them being the cabin of Mr. Long, my Missouri friend, on Little Sugar creek. He had "norated" (I use his word) the promised preaching up and down the creek and his cabin was full of people who appeared anxious to see a preacher and hear a sermon. I preached as best I could using the text "For I am not ashamed of the gospel of Christ." At the close of the sermon the people gathered about me and expressed themselves as being well pleased with the whole service and glad to know that I would return and preach again. My friend Long who had opened his cabin for the preaching place came forward and said loud enough to be heard all over the cabin, "I liked your preaching fust rate, but I thought you would pitch into me if you knew I'm a Universalist." I got the laugh on him by replying "I wasn't loaded for small game." I preached in his cabin several times subsequently and always found a good congregation for those days, and a hearty greeting from my Universalist friend. We laughed together a good many times about the trouble the chickens had over my first visit. Mrs. Long always treated me kindly and did her best to make my visits as pleasant as circumstances would allow. She always apologized for the poor fare and asked to be excused for "poor biscuits" or some other article of food.

"The next day after preaching to the Little Sugar creek

folks I made my way to Middle creek where I preached in the afternoon to a few persons. Another day of riding, lonely riding, and I found myself again at the cabin of the local preacher near Dutch Henry's crossing.

"I remained here until the coming Sunday, and I preached in the forenoon in Barnaby's cabin to a few persons. In the afternoon I proceeded to Osawatomie and preached in the evening to a better congregation than I had when I preached there the first time. A Mr. Van Horn asked me to make his cabin one of my regular preaching places and I accepted the invitation. Van Horn proved to be a very strong proslavery man. I did not know at the time of my promise to make his cabin a permanent preaching place, but some of the good people were offended and would not hear me preach again. However I made Osawatomie my headquarters for the season, and gained the good will of some of the dear people by preaching the gospel of peace and attending strictly to my business as a preacher of good will to all men.

"On my next round I made a little detour from the first and took in two points on Big Sugar Creek—Choteau's Trading Post and Brooklin—then a town of two or three cabins. I wish to mention a striking instance of that never-to-be-forgotten trip. One occurred on the old military road near the Trading Post. I had left the Post and was making my way toward Fort Scott when I met a gay company of young people who seemingly paid little attention to the stranger as they passed me; but I had not gone very far when I heard a call, and looking back saw a young man coming in a gallop, asking me to "hold on." I reined in my horse and waited with some hesitation for his coming. When he drew near he asked 'Are you a preacher?' I answered, 'I try to preach sometimes.' He instantly replied 'there is a couple in the crowd that wanted to get married, and can you marry them?' I replied in the affirmative and proposed to go back to the Post and pronounce them husband and wife. To this they said 'No, we do not want to go back to the Post if you can marry us here.' They continued, 'We are hunting for the squire, but if you can marry us it will be all right.' No license was required in those days and I began to question them concerning age, etc., when the girl broke out and said, 'I do not want to be married on horseback.' Thereupon the whole company alighted from their horses and I arranged the young people for the ceremony and proceeded to say the words that made the twain one. Thus I married my first couple, James S. Brown and Martha Hobbs, on the Old Military Road, near the Choteau's Trading Post, December 13, 1855. I wrote them a certificate on a sheet of letter paper and the company mounted their horses and rode away shouting and happy.

"Another instance shows what preachers had to meet in those days. The next day after the marriage I was stopping in the newly laid out town of Brooklin, where I found a new thing for those days, a genuine cobbler. He had his tools in one corner of his cabin, and was always ready to serve a customer. By his invitation I sat down to take off my boots and handed them to him for repairs. While he was pegging away on my boots several young men came in and seemed to have some interest in the work, but one of them kept an eye on the stranger. At length he broke out with a series of questions. He wanted to know how long I had been in the Territory? Where I had come from? Where I was going? What was my business? Was I looking for a claim? etc. The questions were all warded off by evasive answers, when the fellow seemed to be out of humor and blurted out, 'Well, you are not ashamed to tell your name, are you?' I meekly answered that it was none of his concern, and he said a hard word and left the room. His companions laughed heartily and in a few minutes the shoemaker and the preacher were left alone. The cobbler looked across his nose and said, 'that was well done.' Some weeks after that episode I returned to preach in the cabin near the town and met the shoemaker. When referring to the instance he told me the young man had worked the matter out satisfactorily to himself, and said to him, 'I know what is the matter with that chap; he is the son of the old man who was here looking for mineral and he is slipping around to get a claim before the people find him out.' I made the vicinity one of my regular preaching places but I never met the insulting and raging question mark to recognize him. He would not honor with his august presence a preacher who refused to answer questions.

"The autumn and winter of 1855 up to the 22nd of December were beautiful and pleasant, all that even a Tennessean could ask for. I had met the men of the newly laid out mission regularly and was beginning to think the Kansas Territory was all right. But on Saturday, December 22, in the afternoon, I found myself among strangers again. I came to a cabin on Big Sugar creek and asked the man if I could spend the night and sabbath day with him. He looked at me for sometime and then asked, 'Are you a preacher?' I said, 'I have preached some and expect to preach occasionally if the people will hear me.' Then he asked, 'Will you preach for us tomorrow?' I answered in the affirmative, and he invited me 'to get down and stay over Sunday.' He showed me where to fasten my horse and I soon had him beside the man's horse on the south side of the huge hay stack. Overcoat and saddlebags were gathered up and we were in the cabin getting acquainted with the family in a short time. Presently I was seated by the open door studying my lesson and making some notes for the sermon to be preached next day. In the meantime my host had gone out and was cutting wood for the big fire place, while a boy had been sent out to notify the

settlers of the promised preaching sermon. Just before the
sun went down a sudden gust of wind came from the north
and made the cabin shake. In a few minutes Mr. Thomas
came in with a 'back-log' for the fire and with a shiver said,
'I never saw it turn cold so fast in my life.' I dropped my book
and writing materials and went out to help him carry in the
wood for the night and look after our horses and see what
could be done for them. I soon had them blanketed and left
them as well sheltered as possible by the hay stack. Before
it was dark the boy came back shaking and asked his father
to put his horse away for him, saying 'I am nearly frozen.'
The wind and coldness increased every minute. Some of
the upper crevices between the logs of the cabin had been
filled with twisted rolls of hay and in a little while they began
to fall out, and the north wind came in with a rush and roar.
Soon the snow was coming in, too, covering beds and everything else in the cabin. Mrs. Thomas began to cry and sweat,
and reproaching her husband for coming to Kansas. The snow
came in more and more. At length Mr. Thomas suggested
bed as the warmest place for the night, in a little while we
were all in bed, covered 'head and ears'. The snow came
down on us all night long; I am sure it was three inches deep
on the beds and floor. As soon as it was light enough in the
morning to see Mr. Thomas was up piling wood on the fire.
In a short time his wife was up crying and sweeping the
snow in heaps. Mr. Thomas's boy and preacher were busy
shoveling the snow from before the door. It had drifted
and was piled up on the south side of the house almost to
the eaves, and was still coming down. The whole heavens
were literally full of snow. It was ten o'clock before we got
it away from the house and a road made through to the hay
stacks. Our horses would have been covered with the cold
stuff if they had not trampled it under their feet. We had
a job getting the packed snow from under them and piling
it up around to protect them as much as possible from the
cold wind. Several times during the day we had to clear
the snow away from the door and from the horses. About
the middle of the afternoon the wind ceased to blow and
we found some relief, but the snow came down straight, thick
and fast. We had our breakfast, dinner and supper about
one o'clock p. m. No one came to the preaching service, for
like ourselves all the settlers had to shovel snow as long as
they could see to work. There was no rest for the wicked,
nor anyone else, that Sunday. When darkness came on us,
and it was of the Egyptian variety, we could feel it, we crawled
into our beds again and just let it snow. I drew myself into
as small a knot as possible and wished I had never heard of
Kansas Territory. But the snow did not blow in on us, and
we slept some, being weary.

"Monday morning came and it was still snowing, the snow

had been coming down straight and fast all night, and was more than a foot deep on the level. Mrs. Thomas did not have to sweep so much as the morning before, but her husband and I had to shovel the snow away from the door of the cabin and make roads to the hay stacks and wood pile. The snow continued to come down on our poor half-frozen horses until about noon when the clouds broke away and it ceased to snow, but it was bitter cold! I had never seen so much snow, it was about knee deep to a horse, the ravines were literally full, and the hillsides were covered with great heaps of 'beautiful snow.' I sat by the log fire in the afternoon and evening, meditating on the situation and trying to devise some means to get away from cold, unhabitable Kansas Territory. I was now sure it could never be settled and improved to any great extent. Mr. Thomas and I talked the thing over and decided that no one could ever live on the wild prairies. So we were about ready to pull stakes and hurry back to our old homes. I tried to while away some of the cold time by singing 'Home, home, sweet, sweet home; be it ever so humble, there is no place like home.' But my hostess cried the more and ordered me to cease singing and we all sobbed in chorus, said our prayers, and went to bed. It was Christmas eve but we had no merry gathering, no Christmas tree, no plum pudding! We made no effort to have a Merry Chirstmas. We were in for a cold Christmas.

"So Christmas morning came with blue sky, bright sunshine, but a very cold wind from the north. After a good breakfast I saddled my horse and made a start for Osawatomie. I could see occasionally the marks of the old Miami trail on some hillside, and thus was enabled to keep my course. I rode on until about ten o'clock when in attempting to cross a ravine, my horse went down into the snow up to his sides. He could not move a leg, so I got off and with my hands pulled the snow away from the poor fellow until he could struggle out. Neither horse nor rider had ever had such experience before. After that cold hard struggle I was afraid to cross a ravine unless I could see the tops of the grass, so I turned my course and followed the divide between Big Sugar and Middle creeks until I found my way to the old Pottawatomie Agency. A Missourian by the name of Tucker had bought the buildings of the agency and was able to give me and my half-frozen horse better shelter than we had had in Kansas. We enjoyed our comfortable quarters for two days and nights. Mr. Tucker asked me to leave an appointment for preaching some future time, and I did so. He said he would take that for pay for my entertainment."

One of the beautiful characters of Mound City and who contributed greatly in a cultural way to his time and his community was Zarobobel Mentzer. He was of high class

German descent, one of his ancestors having been General John Rolla Mentzer of the Continental Army. Mr. Mentzer was born at Listenburg, Maryland, October 23, 1830. He was a devoted member of the German Lutheran Church and had always been the leader in its musical programmes. In his early life he became the employee of a prominent contractor in his native town of Listenburg, and was familiar with large affairs in business. This employer was a Mr. Bartleson, father of our Elim W. Bartleson of Pleasanton, and as a result of this association he was married on July 13, 1853, at Listenburg, to Margaret Parker Bartleson, a daughter of the house. Seven children came to them—Ida B., Lucy May, Charles Lee, Esther Allen, Mary Ellen, John Rolla and Jesse Blanche, all of whom have been exemplary, useful, successful citizens, of whom we have this record—Lucy May became the wife of George B. Dunbar of Cedar Point, Iowa; Mary Ellen married John W. Kenney of Mound City; John Rolla married Lilian Edith Lamoreau and have for many years made their home at Kansas City where John has had connection with high class bond houses; Jesse Blanche married George N. Roy of Mound City. These children gave to their distinguished father fourteen grandchildren and three great-grandchildren. The mother had died in 1874 at Cedar Point, Iowa, where they had gone after his service in the Civil War as a soldier in Company C of the Sixteenth Iowa Infantry, finishing a veteran enlistment which took him with Sherman to the sea and into the grand review at the White House in Washington. Zarobobel Mentzer was of charming personality, gifted mentally, resourceful and helpful to his fellow men, and giving to his children much more than the material comforts of life with which he surrounded them lavishly, for he was a successful man and acquired a competence. His life span measured eighty-four years when he passed away May 15, 1914, at the home of the daughter Mrs. Ellen Kenney in Mound City.

This family tradition is beautifully carried on by John Rolla Mentzer, named after the Continental General, who married Lillian Edith Lamoreau and who after successful newspaper work in his home town moved to Kansas City where he has been associated with high class investment houses and has maintained a handsome home. Their children are Lucile, who married J. D. Smith, Jr.; Donald L. who married Helen M. Dawson; and Maxine Lamoreau who married Allan G. Buckley, son of Arthur Buckley who built the Union railway station, the Commerce Building, and other large structures in Kansas City.

John William Clapper who worked on farms about Lincoln township around 1880 married Julia Crow and they had a boy born to them whom they named Raymond. They moved to Kansas City where the boy learned the printer's trade and married into a very good family. He made up his mind that he needed a university education, so they were invited to live at his parents' home and they carried their luggage as they trudged off together afoot to Kansas University. He took three years in the journalism course and is now one of the principal men in the offices of the United Press at Washington, D. C. He was detailed to travel on the train with Harding during the presidential campaign and represented his company at the Kansas City National Republican convention nominating Hoover, and left there to do the work at the Houston convention. His Grandfather Clapper was brother to Mrs. Elihu Ireland, but never came to Kansas, keeping his home at Van Wert, Ohio. With Emma Lou Martin going to the national capital from the dairy maid contest this family has a generous share of honors.

A family named Miller came here from Zanesville, Ohio, in the early days and settled in the southeast part of the county. The father was serving in the home guards when the Price Raid went through and Mr. Miller was killed on the Osage river, three rifle balls through his body showing how fierce had been his encounter. He left a large family. A son Elijah Miller lived at Prescott and married Nancy Kinder, both born in Zanesville, Ohio. Of their children Phebe married H. M. Grigsby, William married Lina Hill, John married Emma Sellers, Ida married Earl Horn, Maggie married Louis Torrey, Albert E. married Bertha Torrey, Ode married Florence Bowers. Henry and Frank, brothers to Elijah Miller, served in the Sixth Kansas.

John Sellers from Madison county, Indiana, and his wife Elizabeth Railsback from Wayne county, Indiana, were the parents of Emma who married John Miller. The other children were Lucullus Railsback Sellers who married Alice Goss, Estella married O. Manlove, Viola married Fulton Coon, Elvira married T. R. Reddick, Lena married A. J. Jackson, Alma never married, Ora married Dr. J. J. Workman.

They grew to mature years here. In 1923 Johnnie Mentzer wrote a sketch of the useful life of F. C. Bacon who was then ninety-five and his good wife still with him was ninety-four years old. Mr. Bacon was born at Charleston, Massachusetts, and she at Garland, Missouri, but by some strange romance they were married at Whitensville, Massachusetts, January 1, 1855, and lived a while in New York City before coming to Linn County in 1857. What a wonderful period of human history was encompassed by their lives!

Alfred Culbertson, who lives southeast of Goodrich, recently plowed up three very handsome flint spearheads about eight inches long, probably used in hunting buffalo on horseback.

We have a representative in the diplomatic service of the state department at Washington in the person of Julius C. Holmes, now vice consul for the United states at Smyrna, Asia Minor. He is the son of James Reuben Holmes, son of Boliver Adams, who married Louella J. Trussell. They make the family home at Lawrence where "Jim" is the head of the J. R. Holmes Investment Company. They are very patriotic, having three sons carrying commissions under the military arm of the government. Charles Boliver is a graduate of Kansas University, served as captain in the World War; Julius C. a first lieutenant; and the youngest boy James Willis is now a druggist at Lawrence and is a second lieutenant. A daughter Opal Ailene married Frank D. Scanlan. The mother of James Reuben was of the Lamb family.

In the early days, as late as 1872, buffalo hunting was a popular sport. Joshua Shaffer and his son Lewis went out to where Wichita now is and brought home a fine lot of buffalo meat for winter and a lot of hides and several buffalo calves which they kept on the farm. They trained a pair to work in the yoke as oxen and excited much interest as they drove them about, especially at the county fairs. They were finally taken to Coney Island, New York. Joshua Shaffer was from Van Wert, Ohio, where he married Catherine Hagerman. Their children were Lewis N. who married Catherine Ireland; Sarah J. married Thomas Fife; Martha married Joshua Perkins, Elizabeth married Sylvanus Perkins and Ellen married James Ireland.

Robert H. Ireland, son of Elihu, married Emma Doig. Their children are Louise, and Lorene who married Monroe Martin son of Al Martin who lived east of La Cygne. Emma Lou Martin, who won the prize of a trip to Washington from a dairy convention in 1927 at Fort Scott and was shown a royal good time by Kansas representatives and senators, including a visit to President Coolidge in the White House, is the daughter of Monroe and Lorene.

The Calvins of Valley township are prominent land owners and tobacco growers. Jackson Calvin married Elmira Taylor, both from Indiana. Their children are Elmer who married Nettie Shattuck, Otis who married Maggie Church, Alonzo married Lenora Shattuck, Dillard married Ina Shattuck, Ed married Effie Williams, and Willie who is unmarried. Elmer has a son Lee who married Flossie Tyler.

Over in Centerville township lives Samuel Thomas McCarty

who came from Keokuk, Iowa, when only fourteen years old. He married Martha Glenn of Johnson county, Missouri, and their children are Sherman who married Alice Henry, Burton married Mabel Holloman, Lottie Ann married Charles Jones, Olive married Thomas Cochran, and Orlo Sheridan married Cora Cooper.

One of the early settlers of Linn County was Simon B. McGrew, who was born October 22, 1810, in Sewickley Township, Westmoreland county, Pennsylvania, and was the fourth in line of twelve children born to his parents, James B. and Isabella McGrew. The McGrew family came to America from County Tyrone, Ireland, in 1726, and were all followers of the Quaker faith when not orthodox Presbyterians. Simon B. McGrew was married May 22, 1833, to Ura Marsh, daughter of Cooper and Martha Marsh, at the old Quaker church still standing in Sewickley Township. He moved to Jefferson county, Ohio, in 1844, where he built and operated a flouring mill for a number of years, and in 1852 moved to a newly formed Quaker settlement at Salem, Iowa, where the family (now consisting of seven children) resided till 1857, when the head of the family first visited Linn County and erected a log cabin at the head of Elk Creek, three and a half miles southwest of Mound City, on what was afterwards known as the Curry farm. Returning to Iowa the family was moved to the new home and a larger two-story log building was erected the following year in which the family continued to reside until the fall of 1864. A younger brother, Rev. Samuel B. McGrew, located on an adjoining claim to the east. A son, Abner G., located a claim on adjacent land and remained several years when he left for Chicago and graduated from Rush Medical College and was for many years surgeon for the Chicago and Northwestern Railway Company. One daughter, Jane, became the wife of Col. Ed. R. Smith, and Elizabeth married Dr. Hugh McKean of Iowa and their son, Dr. James W. McKean has been for forty years a resident of Siam as physician to the King and a world known authority on leperology, having built and still superintends a large leper colony at Chaingmai. Isabella, another daughter, married Herbert Capper who then resided at Mapleton, but they later made their home at Garnett where was born their son Arthur, who became Governor of Kansas in 1914, and is now junior Senator from Kansas in the United States Senate. One other daughter of Simon and Ura was Martha who died in 1863 and was buried in the little cemetery near the old homestead.

Simon McGrew was well known as a radical outspoken free state advocate and by reason of his activities was often marked as a subject for punishment by the Border Ruffians but fortunately escaped personal injury. He was ironically called "the Fighting Quaker" from the fact that he used the plain language, as some of his descendants still continue to do. While religiously opposed to war, with a good pair of Colts Navy revolvers he was always ready to protect himself and his family. Being trained for a surveyor, he and John Brown became intimate friends and they did surveying work together, and when Brown left Kansas, McGrew purchased Brown's surveyors' compass which is now deposited with the State Historical Society in Topeka as an authentic relic and reminder of the early days.

Simon McGrew was a giant in stature, being six feet three and a half inches tall in his stocking feet and was widely known for his great physical strength. He had a strong personal resemblance to Abe Lincoln and his portrait was often mistaken to be a picture of the Emancipator because of the strong resemblance.

The family was possessed of more than the ordinary means of the average settler, but owing to the impossibility of purchasing anything but the barest necessities of life, and that no nearer than Westport Landing, the family suffered all the hardships and privations of other pioneer families. Owing to failing health and advanced age, Mr. and Mrs. McGrew with the two sons, James B. and Charles F., removed to northern Iowa in the fall of 1864, where he died October 18, 1874, and is buried in the cemetery at Wyoming, Jones county, Iowa. Charles F. McGrew, the sole surviving member of the family of Simon who helped to settle Linn County, now lives in Los Angeles, California.

Isabella McGrew Capper, daughter of Rev. Simon McGrew, raised a family of six children who have reflected great credit and honor upon the family name. Herbert Capper, whom Isabella McGrew married in 1862, had a most interesting career. He was born in 1839 in Longton in Staffordshire, the great pottery district of England, his parents being Thomas and Elizabeth Capper. In 1842 the parents brought him to Philadelphia where they became actively interested in the abolition of slavery. The men of the family were metal workers and Herbert was employed in a tin shop in his boyhood, and after the death of his father he moved to Circleville, Iowa, where he followed the metal worker's trade. But in 1857 he wanted to be in the thickest of the fight and he started for Kansas. Arriving at Westport Landing (now Kansas City) he made the acquaintance of J. P. Harris and the two walked from that town on the Missouri river to Ottawa in Franklin county, where "Jack" Harris located and became a prominent citizen, having been nominated on the Republican ticket for Congress in 1898, and his son Ralph Harris now is owner of the Ottawa Herald newspaper. Mr. Capper took a homestead on Pottawatomie Creek near the boundary line

between Anderson and Franklin counties. After their marriage Isabella and Herbert lived for a time in Mapleton and
later moved to Garnett where they had their home for more
than forty years. They had six children: Mary who died in
infancy; Arthur, born July 14, 1865, who served the state as
governor and is now in his second term as United States
Senator from Kansas; May born in 1868 and now residing
in Chicago; Bessie who married Prof. Homer S. Myers then
of Baldwin (her death occurred in 1910) ; Edith married Fred
L. Eustace and they now have their home in Chicago. The
youngest child was Benjamin who died in 1891. Herbert
Capper was one of the first members of the city council of
Garnett, where he operated a hardware store. About 1872
the family went to Elk county where he engaged in farming
and stock raising for several years, helping to found the town
of Longton in that county which he named after his birthplace in England. They returned to Garnett and lived out
their lives in their first home. The success of the boy Arthur
has been remarkable. He learned to be a printer, graduated
from the Garnett high school in 1884, and immediately sought
employment as a typesetter on the Topeka Capital, and was
soon in line to serve as reporter, city editor, managing editor,
business manager, and in 1905 became owner. He now owns
the Kansas City Kansan and a half dozen of the leading farm
papers of the United States. Arthur was the first native
Kansan to be elected governor. His wife was Miss Crawford,
daughter of the noted war governor and soldier Samuel J.
Crawford.

L'Amoreaux is the way the family name was spelled when
Isaac was born in France in 1744 in a Huguenot family and
he married Elizabeth whose family name is not given. John,
their ninth child, was born June 10, 1794, and married Edith
whose family name is not given and their son Daniel R. was
born November 10, 1829, at Central Bridge, Schoharie county,
New York. The family were very early colonial settlers in
America. Daniel, who was to become a highly prized citizen
in Linn County, was married first to Catherine M. Lamont
by whom he had no children. His next marriage was December 29, 1857, to Sarah L. Ives, born Cuyahoga county,
Ohio, by whom six children came to him, being George W.
Lamoreau who married Nellie Connor of Holden, Missouri;
Charles N. married Ora Davis; Lilian Edith married John
Rolla Mentzer; and John H. married Rose Clarke; Kate
Claribel married Roy Hawkins; and Howard E. married Nellie
Osborn. The name became Anglicized so it was Dan Lamoreau
to us. Dan learned the trade of carpenter and joiner. In
1855 he went to Walworth county, Wisconsin, where he oper-
ated a sash and door factory. When the Civil War came on
he enlisted in the Thirteenth Regiment of Wisconsin Volun-

teers and was in Sherman's famous march to the sea and
Mr. Lamoreau's capacity to handle big affairs is proven by
his having charge of the seventy-five thousand horses on that
great military expedition. Governor Alexander W. Randolph
of Wisconsin signed his first commission as captain. He was
mustered out in 1864 but was called back to serve a veteran
enlistment and in 1866 President Andrew Johnson signed a
beautiful commission making him a major. In 1890 he enum-
erated mortgage indebtedness of Linn, Miami, Bourbon and
Franklin counties for the census bureau and served as sheriff
and other local offices. He brought his family to Linn County
in 1864. He was a true type of the heroes of the Civil War.

When a new town was started it simply doubled or more
greatly multiplied the work of the capable men in the community. So when Prescott got agoing in 1870 it asked Levi
Hart Lane to be mayor and justice of the peace in addition
to running his drug store, and as the place was small the
Missouri River, Fort Scott and Gulf Railroad (commonly
called the Gulf Road) announced that it did not feel able to
keep a salaried agent, so to save the young town from embarrassment this same Levi Hart Lane acted as station agent
without compensation, getting up at unearthly hours to sell
tickets to parties going on the early train, lugging mail bags
to and from the postoffice, pushing a freight truck to get
freight and baggage in and out of the weather and added to
these activities were his duties as postmaster all the years
of his residence in the town. In addition to all this he was
the great humanitarian of the town, helping financially many
who could never repay. In 1872 a cyclone swept the town,
reducing a number of good frame business houses to a greater
number of separate pieces than the carpenters used in putting
them together originally. This storm was a sensational thing
and almost every Prescott home has a set of photographs
taken of the "remains." It wiped out much security for Levi
Hart Lane's generous loans but he never winced. He took
on more local burdens by being elected to the legislature taking
part in the election of John James Ingalls over S. C. Pomeroy
as United States Senator. From this you get the idea of
what Mr. Lane was—a really high class man. He was born
in Louise county, New York, April 1, 1830, son of Lyman
Lane and his wife Hancy Hart. The Lanes came from Scotland, intermarried with the families of Stephen Hart and
John Lee who came from England to Connecticut as early
as 1634. These early pioneers were real fellows serving in
the Continental army and holding various public positions. Our
Mr. Lane in 1854 married Emily Jane Kendrick whose father
was a Congregational minister after graduating from Harvard
University and serving a time on the Harvard faculty. The
four children of L. H. and Emily Jane Lane were Edwin

Carlos (well remembered as Ed. C.) now at Clarinda, Iowa;
Charles Edward who was editor of the Prescott Eagle and
deputy county clerk under John Madden, and who married
Mary Burks of Prescott (and had four children: Roy E.,
Frances E., George M., and Josephine, the last two born in
Illinois. This child Josephine has the distinction of being
the first woman in the state of Illinois to hold the combined
offices of clerk of the circuit court and county recorder, in
Kendall county.) Another child of L. H. was Frances who
was with her father at Prescott and married John W. Shirley,
the station agent and who in after years was an important
employee of the Santa Fe system. Frances and her husband
had seven children (Maurice, Edna, Edith, Linda, Harry,
Charles, and Frances G.) A brother-in-law of L. H. Lane,
Asa Deland Perrin, also brought a good family to Prescott.
Their son Herbert L. Perrin now lives at Fort Scott, after
many years in Prescott.

In the capitol building at Washington there is a large room
just off the great rotunda set aside for the placing of the
statues of two men whom the legislature of each state should
vote to be their most distinguished citizens, hence this room
is called Statuary Hall. Virginia of course led off with the
statue of Washington and most of the other states have exercised their privilege in this matter. It has been thought
by many Kansas people that our state had placed there as
one of our representative men of distinction an effigy of Old
John Brown. This is an error. In 1895 the Lincoln Soldiers
and Sailors Monument Association, a national patriotic order,
wanted to honor John Brown and asked permission from the
State of Kansas to furnish the statue of our old hero, and a
joint resolution of the two houses of the legislature was passed
and forwarded to the capitol authorities asking that the
Lincoln Soldiers and Sailors Monument Association be given
the privilege to place the statue in the name of the State of
Kansas. That is as far as it ever got, the monument association failing to use the opportunity thus given.

Jacob Stites was the son of Johan Stites and his wife Ruth
Moore, both natives of Germany. They settled in New Jersey
where Jacob was born in Somerset county in 1801 and married
Ada Ayres of Sussex county that state, born 1805, daughter
of William Ludlow Ayres from Devonshire, England, son of
Mary whose mother was Mary Gomo (accent on the last syl-
able) and the great great grandmother being Susan Thorp.
Jacob Stites pioneered in Stark county, Illinois, in 1840, and
their son William and daughters Isadora and Lucy were born
there. William came with his family to Linn County in 1858,
accompanied by his sister Isadora and her husband William
Hudson. Lucy Stites married Richard Hill in Illinois and they

came on to Linn County in the spring of 1859, and the parents, Jacob and Ada, came that fall, with Mary and her husband William Thompson. These people were all very active and useful citizens. Lucy had the distinction of being the first school teacher regularly employed in Scott township. Her husband Richard Hill will be remembered by a few as a big hearty man always wearing a full beard and of very pleasing personal appearance. He served as county coroner, was then county clerk two terms, and when a candidate for the legislature was beaten by O. D. Harmon by a majority of just one vote. He was a thoroughbred Englishman and his parents were in the East Indian Service when he was born in Belarum, Province of Madras, India. At the time of the Price Raid he was serving in the Sixth Kansas Militia, taking part in the fight at Trading Post and Mine Creek. This superb man died in 1911 and Lucy is now living at Greenfield, Monterey county, California, as Lucy Hill Crawford. Speaking of pioneer days Lucy tells this experience: "My sister's husband, William Thompson, was in the regular army. Things were pretty hard for us women folks, left alone. One of their horses died, leaving her only horse—and a team was an absolute necessity. They had a three-year-old colt that had never had a bridle on and we said 'We will have to break that colt to harness.' We tied her to the fence and put the harness on, and had some trouble getting the bit in her mouth, but at last we had her hitched to the wagon alongside her mother. I said 'I will do the driving, for if either of us must get killed it will be better for me to go as you have three children and I have none.' She hung on to the bits till I got a good hold of the lines and got my feet well braced, and then I told her to let go. We expected her to rear and plunge and wreck things all over the neighborhood, but instead she walked off as calmly as an old animal. The next day we drove down on Big Sugar Creek to get a load of wood and the crooked branches we piled on looked like a crow's nest, when I saw a rick of cord wood. Sister did not want me to take any but I threw out the trashy stuff and loaded up with good regular four-foot split cord wood, and when we got home sister seemed to enjoy sharing that wood. So you see we who stayed at home did heroic things as well as the men at the front." William had a son named Webster J. Stites who was married three times, first to Miss Ladenia Stewart, then to Mrs. Bettie Harper, and later to Mrs. Pearl Dellinger Kennedy. He died at La Cygne April 20, 1928, leaving four sons and the widow.

Among the cultured men of the early days in Mound City was Joseph Harrington Trego, a son of the eldest sister of Thomas Elwood Smith who married John Howard Trego back in Bucks county, Pennsylvania, hence belonging to that famous family line descended from the William Penn family of the court of Charles the First, one of whom was knighted by Charles the Second after the Restoration. Our Joseph Harrington was graduated from the Phildelphia Medical School and practiced here all his life. He married Alice Mannington, born in Oneida county, New York, of English descent. To Joseph and Alice were born seven daughters who married as follows: Kate to Courtland L. Long and Eleanor to William B. Helm, both these couples making their homes down in the Seminole Nation before Oklahoma became a state; Helen married Robert K. Fleming the noted cattleman; Rebecca married Joseph Norris and made their home at Spokane, Washington; Sophia married Rodney W. Riggs and now lives at Fresno, California; Louise married William B. Helm of Wellington, Kansas; Sara married John O. Morse, the lawyer at Mound City; Octavia married Irving Smith and made their home at Kansas City; and Martha married William W. Thayer and makes her home at San Francisco.

Alfred Latham of Pleasanton was one of the notably successful men who started as a clerk in a store at Mound City in 1870, then drove all over the country with a peddler's wagon drawn by a span of mules selling tinware and other household necessities taking farm produce in payment, afterwards establishing a produce house in Mound City which outgrew the town and he moved to Pleasanton to get better shipping facilities, organizing his business under the name of the Latham Commission Company which had probably a hundred branch houses and shipping stations scattered over Kansas and Missouri. He had reached the ripe age of nearly eighty-two years when on a business trip to New York City on October 28, 1927, he was found dead in his bed in his hotel room, and Linn County records the loss of a fine citizen. He was married November 26, 1874, to Frances L. Bartholomew, daughter of Mr. and Mrs. N. E. Bartholomew who were early pioneers in Mound City. To the Lathams were born a daughter, now Mrs. L. A. Holbert of Kansas City; J. W. Latham of Pleasanton; George Latham who died about 1926 at Ottawa; Mrs. Harvey Lincoln of Pleasanton; and Mildred who died in 1908 at Mound City. In writing his obituary some friend said: "Know you today, that a great man and prince has fallen."

Isaac Glucklich and A. Friedman, two Austrian Jews from Kracow, came to La Cygne in 1871 and entered into a partnership that lasted until 1909, after which Mr. Glucklich carried on the business. They were good citizens and acquired and retained strong friendships among our people and accumulated a comfortable fortune. In 1874 Mr. Glucklich was married in St. Louis to Miss Rose Swartzkopf who lived here until her death in 1915, affectionately regarded by everyone. Roy their oldest son was with his father in the business, and Hattie the eldest daughter married P. B. Leivy, and Sadie is a highly prized teacher in the schools of Salina.

J. H. Matthews and wife have lived in and about Boicourt since 1867, although there was no town there then and no roads and no bridges, so he can marvel at the changes that have come when some friend takes him for a ride over the ribbon of concrete known as the "Short Line." He helped to plat the present Trading Post Cemetery and to remove the bodies of the victims of the Marais des Cygnes Massacre to their permanent resting place where a beautiful monument commemorates their sacrifice. The Matthews children are Artie, Harry, Walter, Ora Falletti, Sylvia, Stambough and Ersie.

A lovable character of Lincoln township was Edward Holden Minton, born in England in 1835, and who came to Linn County in 1859. He married Addie Spencer, daughter of Elias Spencer and sister of Samuel who became state oil inspector. They had a daughter Neda, still living. Later he married Almeida Burgess, daughter of a Baptist preacher who lived in Lincoln township, and they had eight children named Nellie, Maude, Minnie, Meda, Beth, Thomas, Stella, and Verne.

"The world was young in those days", and being young it was beautiful and fresh and attractive and it ever beckoned on to new scenes the courageous souls who became acquainted with it. No wonder the wanderlust possessed so many, urging them on to new experiences and new conquests. We thought we had found the prize winner in Mrs. Shattuck of Pleasanton, who crossed the western half of the continent twice before the famous Ezra Meeker got started, but now we have found a strong contender for the championship. In the early "fifties" (probably 1854 or 1855) then about twenty years old, there came from his birthplace at Chambersburg, Pike county, Illinois, Edward Boyd Metz. He was a pioneer by experience, as his father Benjamin Blackford Metz had gone from New York State in those very early days, as his son Edward Boyd was born there in 1835 and at the age of twenty had married Emily Chambers Middaugh (or Gilbert, as there seems to be some confusion and uncertainty as to her family name) and they came to Linn County and took a full part in all that was going on. I don't find any trace of him in the Territorial days but in the troubled times of 1863 he was sheriff of Linn County, one incident of his term being the capture and trial and conviction and hanging by the neck until dead of one Griffith as a member of the crowd of thirty-two cutthroats who committed the Marais des Cygnes

Massacre. That was a tremendous incident in a little frontier
settlement during the feverish anxiety of the Civil War, and
in addition to his work as sheriff this young fellow only twenty-
eight years old was enlisting Company M for service in the
Fifteenth Regiment, of which company he was elected captain. This regiment did important service out on the plains,
acting as convoy to wagon trains and in punishing renegade
bands of Indians. For a time Jennison was colonel of the
Fifteenth, but got into difficulty and was cashiered. There
were a lot of men in that regiment who later came to Linn
County, among them Martin Funk, many years a citizen of
La Cygne. Ben F. Simpson was captain of Company C. Henry
M. Doud and his brother E. S. Doud of New Lancaster, after-
ward well known in Linn. Lee Mayfield at the age of seven-
teen, Oscar F. Dunlap was captain of Company H (and in
1870 built the present bridge at Trading Post), and in Metz's
own Company M there were Calvin T. Bell, Jere Johnson, and
Isaac A. Davis of Moneka, Francis Askens, Taylor W. Swaney,
C. M. Tompkins of Twin Springs, William M. Bell, Ambrose
Craft, John A. Craft, Alfred J. Pointer, James Arnett,
Emmual Arnold, William H. Ayres, Justin N. Ayres, Francis
Askens, A. B. Byram, Irvin R. Ball, Luther Bacon, Calvin
Barnard, James D. Critcher, Levi Dickinson, Andrew Gore,
John Hall, Phillip C. Hill, William Hendricks, David C. Hafford,
Thomas S. Inman, Ephraim James, John C. Keller, Jacob
Keitle, Eli Lamb, John T. Lindsay, John Morrison, Martin
Morris, Simon L. Morgan, James H. Martin, Alfred J. Pointer,
John C. Quinn, Samuel W. Rowcraft, Mathew Robinson,
Charles Reynolds, Temple Shockman, George A. Shadler,
William F. Shadler, James M. Symonds, John W. Symonds,
Samuel V. Sands, Caius M. Tompkins, and Joseph D. Tippie.
These were nearly all young men, many only boys of sixteen
to eighteen years old up to John C. Quinn who was forty-
five. These were the type of men in Company M who elected
Edward Boyd Metz to be their captain. After the war the
family lived in a "large two-story white house facing the main
road, with a lot of wild strawberries on the hill back of the
house", and later on at the "Woy" farm from where they
moved to Pleasanton—and of course that was at least after
1871. But here is where the wanderlust starts again. They
went to Colorado, where they visited Aunt Ruth Danford and
daughter Lily. On the way west they saw great herds of
buffalo and antelope. There were three of the Metz children
now—Alice born in 1863, Benjamin Blackford born 1865, and
Eva born 1868, all natives of Linn County. They lived in
Canon City two years and Eva died there. The old pioneer
spirit urged them on and they went to Southern Colorado and
New Mexico. They were well equipped and comfortable in
all weather, loitering along in the beautiful virgin country
till they got to Las Vegas, New Mexico, where they actually

"settled down" for two years, and then went back to the father's old home at Chambersburg, Illinois, and three years later went back to the "delectable mountains" of Colorado, and tried to get rich mining at Leadville and other camps. All this time the boy Benjamin Blackford Metz was growing into manhood and followed mining up to about 1907 when he married Jennie Marvin and they have four children, William B. nineteen years old, Alice L. fifteen, Charles Benjamin thirteen and Edward Henry nine, and now where do you think they are? Their home is on the north end of Chickagoff. Island in Southeastern Alaska, probably a hundred miles west of Juneau, the capital. From their home they look across Glacier Bay and have a beautiful view of Muir Glacier, with a magnificent background framed by the Fairweather Range of mountains.

Joel Moody was born near Fredericktown, New Brunswick, Canada, October 28, 1833. When he was a little less than a year old his parents moved to St. Charles, Illinois, and there young Moody received his elementary education. He afterward attended Oberlin College, graduating with high honors, and from there went to the University of Michigan, Ann Arbor, graduating in 1858. His parents died when he was but thirteen years of age and it was through his own efforts that he acquired his college education. He chose the law as his profession and was admitted to the bar in Columbus, Ohio. On January 1, 1859, he married Miss Elizabeth King and they came to Kansas, settling in Woodson county, but later made their home in Mound City. In July, 1862, Mr. Moody was commissioned a first lieutenant in the Second Indian regiment and on May 27, 1863, was advanced to captain, commanding Company H. Captain Moody repre-sented his district in the legislatures of 1865 and 1881 and was a member of the state senate sessions of 1889 and 1891. Sometime during the '80's Mrs. Moody died, leaving three sons, Robert, Ralph and Joel, and in 1891 Captain Moody married Mrs. Ella Choate Porter of Fort Scott. They moved to Abbeyville, Louisiana, where Captain Moody published a newspaper, but returned to Kansas in 1908, settling in Topeka, and here Captain Moody died February 18, 1914. He was the author of several books and contributed to magazines scientific and literary articles, as well as poems. Robert the eldest son married Susie Smith, daughter of Elwood Smith and they have four children Rebecca, Ruth, Robert, and June. Ralph married Loie Strong and their children are Henry S. and Catherine who married Dr. Carey. Another of the Moody boys named Joel died in New Mexico.

Elbert Hubbard (Fra Albertus) the popular writer and philosopher who went down with the Lusitania when that ship was torpedoed and sunk by a German submarine in the Irish sea, was a great admirer of Kansas. Shortly before his death the writer of this book met him at a dinner at the Coates House in Kansas City when he told me he had worked on a farm south of Osawatomie, but he was uncertain which county he was in. He particularly remembered his long days of plowing corn. He became a great writer and publisher, building a wonderful industrial plant at East Aurora, New York, where many things in art work as well as handsome books were produced. He wrote his praise in "Kansas in One Sentence" as follows:

"Kansas—A land of smiling sunshine, of winding streams, and waving corn and happy homes;

"Where you have but to tickle the soil to make it laugh a harvest;

"A land dotted with school houses and growing towns and villages that call themselves 'cities'—this by divine right, for they have the prophetic outlook, and tomorrow will be what they to-day think they are;

"A land of sensitive souls, where nothing is good enough, but must be better; where nothing is but all things are becoming;

"A land of pigs given to adipose, of sleek cattle, of strong horses, of handsome women, of bouncing babies, of homely, rugged men with individuality plus, who feel deeply and write vividly;

"A land where hens lay lavishly and cackle in proportion, where mules gambol on the green and are not ashamed of their pedigree;

"A land whose finest products are its superb physical health, their proud ambition, their high appreciation, their capacity for useful work and their right intent;

"A land where there is so much that is noble and pure and true and beautiful and good that if men in Kansas occasionally lapse, God in love and pity engages Gabriel in conversation, points to thePleiades, looks the other way, and forgets it—happy, prosperous, smiling Kansas."

This song of praise is now copied into all books on Kansas.

There are many curious developments in a study of American history wherever you begin. One particularly interesting thing is that the sons of Austin Wilbur Hall by Corolin Fisk his first wife are relatives not very remote of Senator Stephen A. Douglas who invited the American people to move into Kansas Territory and fight it out among themselves as to whether or not they should have slavery. Corolin Fisk was a remarkable woman who is affectionately remembered by the very few of her generation yet living. She came from a very old English family who had their homestead at the Manor of Stadhaugh, Parish of Laxfield in

County Suffolk, where Lord Lyman Fiske was lord of the manor from 1399 to 1422. They had fine old historic places, some still preserved to this day and a coat of arms to stimulate their pride. In 1637 scions of this family came to America and developed a wonderful progeny, as nearly every American Fisk is recorded in their family book. They have been wonderful pioneers, powerful preachers, and great doctors of medicine. They all took to higher education and many were graduates of Harvard. One of the Fisk women married a Scotchman of the rather proud name of Douglas, a name famous in the land of cakes. To her was born at the family home in Vermont a son who was named Stephen Arnold and he got into the United States Senate from Illinois and took a strenuous part in the public affairs of his time. He was of the same generation and only a little older than this remote cousin Corolin Fisk of Eden, Vermont, who became the wife of Austin W. Hall and made her home at Trading Post. I am unable to give the genealogy of Mr. Hall, whose American ancestry goes back beyond 1800, but they have left a monument to themselves in their sons, as follows:

Amos Homer Hall, born 1872 at Trading Post, married Miss Belle Hill of Nevada, and they have four children of rare accomplishments: Clark Homer, graduate of Kemper College, Missouri University, Jefferson Medical School of Philadelphia, interne at General Hospital in Kansas City, and now a child specialist at Oklahoma City; his wife was Susan Mary Roberts. Fern is a graduate of Cottey College and Pittsburg Normal, married Dr. Gerald C. Bates of Adrian, Missouri, now in practice at Independence, Kansas. John Austin graduated from William Jewell, Kansas University, Chicago Law School and now is in practice of law at Chicago. Beth A. was schooled in Cottey College, Lindenwood, Kansas University, Colorado University and now taking special work at University of California at Berkeley. The family home at Amsterdam is a model of good architecture with every modern convenience, having a private water system big enough for the village and electric lights and in a charming situation. Amos is now one of the leading property men of Bates county.

Carlton Fisk Hall, the second son, married Mellie Hicks, and they have a good home and general merchandise store at Amoret, Missouri. Their children are Thelma Corolin who graduated from Hardin College and the State Teachers College at Pittsburg, Kansas; Dorothy Corolin, a student at Hardin College; and Eugene Fisk, a boy at home.

John Austin Hall chose law as his profession taking collegiate courses at Kansas University and at Ann Arbor Law School, and settled down in the old home county where success has come to him very substantially. He is frequently called into public service, having recently served on a commission appointed by Governor Paulen to hold public hear-

ings over the state on the public roads question and is called
on for commencement addresses and had that difficult job
this year at the State School for the Deaf at Olathe. The
greatest compliment to him has been an invitation to serve
as a member of the American Law Institute which meets
at Washington for a lengthy session each year. There are
seven hundred members of this Institute, only five of whom
are from Kansas. It is sustained by an endowment by Laura
Spellman Rockefeller, and its purpose is by research and
study to obtain correct interpretation of all laws and to aid
in bringing about uniformity in the administration of justice
throughout the United States, and to aid our citizens in
foreign countries. John maintains a very good modern home
at Pleasanton presided over by Zella Cannon Hall, a charming
woman. They have a boy Carl Austin Hall.

By a second marriage to Edith Hill a fourth son was born
to Austin W. Hall who was named Clyde. This boy has found
his place in the world. He worked hard at his schooling,
taking the full course and special studies at the Rolla school
of Mines. He went into the employment of the United Clay
Products Company whom he represented several years in Old
Mexico. He is now at the main offices in Trenton, New Jersey.
He married Fannie Mitchell of Rolla and they have one child,
Marian Edith.

Among notable successes in life is that of Henry Nathaniel
Cary, popularly known as Harry Cary, whose father established the La Cygne Journal in association with John P.
Kenea in 1780. Along about 1878 Harry "graduated" from
the little country printing office and went to Milwaukee,
Wisconsin, where he was employed on a great daily newspaper owned by a relative. He began a career which achieved
real distinction. He was called to New York to manage the
Times Newspaper, later going to Chicago to be associated
with Joseph Medill in the making of the Chicago Tribune,
then back to New York on the New York World, and during
the Spanish American War was in charge of the news service
in the military and naval campaign about Cuba, having a
large number of reporters operating a fleet of dispatch boats
all over the area of operations. On his return home he was
called again to Chicago to become the agent of the association
of publishers there to represent them in everything pertaining
to ethical questions in their profession, and especially the
labor question, in which he showed rare strength of character
and the better qualities of a real diplomat. He died in Chicago,
where his widow and daughter Emile now live.

In my early boyhood days I knew one of the victims of
the border war. Though still in his early manhood he looked
aged. He was reticent, slow and careful of speech. Very few

became closely associated with him and none intimate. He patiently trudged along working out his own destiny. His family had belonged to the "other side" of the controversy and events cast an ominous shadow over his entire life. A few addressed him as "Julian" but nearly everybody spoke respectfully of him as "Mr. Scott." For at least fifteen years I knew him and felt a strange sympathy for this plodding taciturn man. Possibly in his loneliness he pictured the future of that fine farm as now described by Barney (B. J.) Sheridan in a recent number of the Western Spirit of Paola, as follows:

This is the original camping place of Julian Scott, now owned by Lee Scott, and occupied by Wilbur Lee Scott, his son. This spot is historical. Its original settlement was linked with the far back pioneer days. Within the last ten years oil development has added to the worth of it, and the splendid upland has been taken care of as years went by —clovered, soybeaned and manured. Wilbur Scott, whose wife was Miss Edna Hudson, formerly of La Cygne, farms the place on a modern system. The new dwelling is furnished with an up-to-date lighting system, with power pressure on the deep well that supplies the house. Hot and cold water runs in the kitchen and the bath. The cream separator is run by electricity. Cedar trees eighty years old surround the house and everything is attractive from the gate to the inside of the home, where three-year-old Marjorie Jane Scott is the central figure.

"We have about three hundred White Leghorns and the returns have been very good. The best feed I have found is made up of 40 bushels of corn ground and mixed with about 200 pounds of bran, along with 200 pounds of meat scraps. This is put in troughs about six feet long, five inches deep and ten inches wide. Bent over the top of each trough is a number 9 wire in circular form about two or three inches apart so that chickens cannot get their feet into the feed. Water is furnished from an automatic supply from a big barrel, and the birds are given a wide range. There are about 70 native sheep, with 50 promising lambs that will soon sell for about $8.00 a head. The wool clip this year was good and brought 40 cents a pound. Have made more off my sheep than anything else except the clover field, from which I sold $1,200 worth of seed last year."

Young Scott graduated from the La Cygne high school and from the early fall of 1917 until after the close of the World War was in the American Navy.

Along in the 80's a printer working on the La Cygne Journal was Mahlon Gore, whose brother, Rev. Albert Gore, had previously been editor of the paper. Mahlon was a remarkably bright man and we were curious that he should be working at a mechanical trade. It turned out he was a secret service agent who ferreted out a gang of counterfeiters operating around Trading Post.   Charlie Ovens was arrested and the operations were traced to Warrensburg, Missouri, where the bogus money was made.   Following this Mahlon Gore disappeared.   Years later we learned he was in Florida, where he was one of the founders of the town of Orlando, a very successful city in that beautiful country.   In 1892 Mahlon was the national committeeman of the Democratic party for Florida.   He wrote me that President Grover Cleveland had offered him the appointment of public printer at Washington.   Much as I wanted to be associated with him again I advised on a business basis against acceptance.   The loss of his only daughter took away all his ambition and he only survived her a little while.   It is interesting that at the time he lived here Newt Gaines and Charlie Ovens were both in old "Swayback" school district.   Newt became a state officer and now is an honored Democratic leader in Florida.   Charlie went to the federal pen.

Another notable success is that of Fred Trigg whose father William A. Trigg was probate judge from 1881 to 1885.   The family graduated from office to the newspaper business. Clarence Trigg, Fred's brother, became the owner and publisher of the Mound City Sentinel and postmaster of that town, while Fred and his father moved over to Garnett and published the Garnett Journal.   Fred had a likable nature which added to natural ability led him up to the top.   When George W. Martin established the Kansas City Kansan Fred was his principal lieutenant.   Martin became a candidate for governor and Fred managed his campaign.   All this brought him into intimate relations with Kansas at large.   As the years drifted along Nelson of the Kansas City Star picked him up and made him field representative of that great paper in all the state of Kansas, where he now has greater power than any other single person in the state, an influence he wisely uses.   Clarence and his family now live in Kansas City. His boy Otto served as a captain in the World War and is now in the Regular Army stationed at Fort Riley.   The daughter married Milton Luce, a successful business man of Kansas City.

J. Frank Smith has risen from a farm boy in Scott township to a place on the editorial staff of the Kansas City Journal after several years as manager of the Good Roads division of the Kansas City Chamber of Commerce in which he gave a much greater service with actual beneficial results than is accomplished by the average member of Congress.

Harry Caman "grew up" at La Cygne.   His mother died when he was an infant and the father and boy "kept house" alone. The father was the mainstay of the Presbyterian church as long at it kept its doors open. He bought the old "courthouse" on Market street when La Cygne lost the county seat in 1872, and conducted his wagon shop from it after moving the building across the street where it still exists. Harry had a love for music and qualified himself to be a leader in band and orchestra work, and several cities in turn had a "Caman Band" that was the pride of the community. Harry finally came from Beatrice, Nebraska, and took his father home with him.

Another boy that made good from that town was Thurman Harshman, who worked on the newspapers and then went out into the big cities as an advertising expert and kept on going up—somewhere, we have lost him.

Along about the time the town of La Cygne was started there lived among the Miami Indians in what is now Lincoln township a boy named Oliver Farrand, whose father was a Frenchman and the mother a Miami Indian woman. Oliver was an unusually bright boy and ambitious to be more than a tribesman. He received as a head-right the high mound three miles southeast of La Cygne known as Silver Mound because a man named J. H. Felter sank a shaft down through its center to determine the truth of an Indian legend that silver could be mined there. Oliver left that neighborhood and was next heard from in San Francisco, to which city he had gone overland on foot, sometimes falling in with emigrant trains that would give him a ride. Anyway, suffering many hardships, he arrived at the Golden Gate penniless and jobless. He went from door to door in the business district asking for employment till finally he was hired by a jeweler to sweep out his store and do odd jobs. His intelligence and good nature won friendships and after a while he began doing work in the manufacturing department making rings and trinkets for the miners. He became quite expert in recognizing precious stones and in classifying gems. The result was that he became a trusted and valuable member of the firm and a few years later he went across the continent to New York City and established himself at No. 1 Maiden Lane, a little street just off Broadway near Wall Street where all the diamond shops of that time were located. In 1885 I called on Oliver at the store and reminded him of old acquaintance and got a very cordial reception. He wanted to show me his business and opening a great safe he took out wooden receptacles which had in them about a quart each of high class diamonds. An exquisitely pretty woman came in at the street door whom he greeted cordially and left me with that mass of wealth—for each of those stones was worth a small fortune. When he saw I had backed away and was looking at them from a distance he laughed and said they would not bite me, and made another dive into the safe and brought out a great necklace which he placed about my neck telling how he had recently sold it, personally, to Emperor William of Germany, delivery to be made when he could match a missing stone. This good fortune had come to him by reason of his being a neighbor at his home in Newark to a brother-in-law of Senator Dan Voorhees of Indiana who had been appointed Ambassador to Germany by President Cleveland, and who presented this Linn County boy at the imperial court of Germany. Oliver took the La Cygne Journal to the day of his death and was always interested in Linn County people and the Silver Mound farm is still a part of his estate. There were a number of French people among the Miamis, one being Mrs. Howard, who read and spoke French fluently, a highly intelligent woman, whose pretty daughter Maggie married J. V. Donaldson, and they had a son Jay and a daughter Verne, and another daughter named Carrie. Mrs. Donaldson and her children now live in Seattle. I think. Had it been known I had been wearing the crown jewels of the Hohenzollerns no telling what might have happened to me in the World War.

A La Cygne boy who reached the top was Sam Spencer who became state oil inspector under Governor Hoch. His father was an old Mexican war veteran who lived down near the ford, a fine old fellow who just "wore out" in the hardships that came to him. Sam worked for the railway and lived at Fort Scott when the boss buster movement came along and the railway vote turned the trick and they lined up behind Sam for official honors.

George David Roy came to his present farm in Sheridan township near Prescott in 1868, with his wife, who was Ellen Adams, born September 21, 1847, in Park county, Indiana. Her parents were Kentuckians. They had five children, Ida May March, Daisy E. Winders of Kansas City, Della Harkness of Prescott, Robert L. and Perry E. Mr. Roy enlisted July 14, 1861, in the Union Army, serving in Company I, Twenty-first Indiana Volunteer Infantry, under Col. James W. McMullen, serving in the Army of the Potomac and later in Army of the Gulf. Mr. Roy's parents were both born in France, the father at Haut Sone October 10, 1813, and Appaline Brunst, the wife and mother, at Canton Douai, both their ancestors having served under Napoleon and Louis Phillippe. They were married in 1833 and located in what was then the village of Chicago and he was employed by the government in the Indian service. Later in 1844 they located in Vigo county, Indiana, twelve miles north of Terre Haute, and lived there until the Civil War, when George David Roy enlisted as stated above. One brother Joseph survives. The youngest brother William served under General Phil Sheridan and was killed in front of Richmond in 1863. Mr. Roy has won the esteem of his neighbors here and served them in various official ways, having been justice of the peace, township clerk, township trustee, constable and finally two terms as register of deeds. He is a member of the Baptist church, Grand Army of the Republic, the Odd Fellows and the Masons.

Linn County has had some notably successful farmers who accumulated fortunes as rewards for agricultural work. John Samuel Goodrich was a notable example of such success. He was of the heroic pioneer type, having gone when only twenty-two years old on an overland trip to Northern California and in four years saved up enough gold to astonish his parents and friends back in Hadley, Illinois, his return by ship and across Panama to New York giving him an enlarged outlook upon world affairs. On this trip he had his first car ride and his first taste of ice cream was in New York City. In 1858 he came to Kansas and located where the town bearing his name now is. He enlisted in Company E of the Sixth Kansas Cavalry and was in all the battles of that famous military unit, being at Cane Hill, Prairie Grove, Stone Farm Massacre, and in the constant bushwhacking carried on by the "hill billies" of Northern Arkansas, until he was discharged in January, 1865. January 1, 1871, he was married to Mrs. Frances M. Goode, who survives him, and also a daughter Mrs. Emma Thurman of Arma, Crawford county, and grandsons Carl L. Sabine of Parsons, Samuel D. Bearly who served in Company D of Three hundred and fifty-third Infantry in the World War, Glenn L. Bearly, Floyd A. Bearly of Machine Gun Company of the Thirty-seventh Infantry, and a sister named Mrs. Helen R. Cross of Topeka. He was a man of affairs being president of the La Cygne Exchange Bank for six years, postmaster at Goodrich, and for twenty years maintained a big herd of Galloway cattle. His farm had nearly thirteen hundred acres of the best land in the county. He was the main support of the Methodist church. He was born in Bainbridge, New York, October 9, 1831, and died at his home in Goodrich February 3, 1918, at the age of eighty-seven years, and will long be affectionately remembered as "Uncle Sammy."

William Gillenwater was a Tennesseean who moved to Schuyler county, Illinois, and married Henrietta Nall, a Kentucky woman. Their children were Fannie who married John Jackman, Charles married Stella Noland and Rolla married Laura Moore, daughter of Joseph Moore of Twin Springs. Henry is unmarried.

After a long lapse of time not much active interest is now felt, but at the time of the execution of Old John Brown all the intellectual world was aroused to a fever pitch. In every capital of Europe the outcome of the anti-slavery agitation in America was eagerly watched. Benjamin Disraeli, who was later prime minister to Queen Victoria, was enraptured with a speech by William M. Evarts in the United States Senate, reviewing events leading up to the tragedy at Harper's Ferry in which were cited these outrages in Kansas. Disraeli declared that speech finest oration in so many words ever delivered in the English language. In Paris Victor Hugo, then at the height of his fame, found in the story of Linn County—for then it was the whole Kansas story—a theme in harmony with his own great humanitarian programme. When Old John Brown was convicted and sentenced to death on the scaffold, Victor Hugo made this statement in a great public address:

John Brown—that's all; a serious-purposed man,
Hard-handed, tender-hearted; God's great plan
Through his gnarled, knotty nature pulsing ran.

"Fanatic!" hissed the mob, with loud acclaim:
They, unremembered; he, close-clasped by fame,
While fades away the gallows' dreadful shame.

Each cause its Christ, its sacrifice to might!
Scorn soon is done, and Freedom's piercing light
Dispels the mists 'round Calvary's awful height!
—W. H. Simpson.

Against this crime of crimes he fought and fell;
He freed a race and found a prison-cell;
In mid-air hung upon the gibbet's tree,
But lived and died, thank God, to make men free.

And dusky men the ages down will tell
For what he fought, and how he bravely fell;
And dim the jewels in each earthly crown,
Beside the luster of thy name, John Brown.
—J. G. Waters.

Had he been made of such poor clay as we,
Who, when we feel a little fire aglow
'Gainst wrong within us, dare not let it grow,
But crouch and hide it, lest the scorner see
And sneer, yet bask our self-complacency
In that faint warmth—had he been fashioned so,
The nation ne'er had come to that birth-throe
That gave the world a new humanity.
He was no vain professor of the word—
His life a mockery of the creed—he made
No discount on the Golden Rule, but heard
Above the senate's brawls and din of trade
Ever the clank of chains, until he stirred
The nation's heart on that immortal raid.
—William Herbert Carruth.

"The gaze of Europe is fixed at this moment on America. . . . . . The hangman of Brown—let us speak plainly—the hangman of Brown will be neither District Attorney Hunter, nor Judge Parker, nor Governor Wise, nor the little state of Virginia, but—you should shudder to think it and give it utterance—the whole great American Republic. It will open a latent fissure that will finally split the union asunder. The punishment of John Brown may consolidate slavery in Virginia, but it will certainly shatter the American democracy. You preserve your shame but you kill your glory."

On March 30, 1860, four months after the execution of Old John Brown, Victor Hugo wrote:

"Slavery in all its forms will disappear. What the South slew last December was not John Brown, but slavery. Henceforth, no matter what President Buchanan may say in his shameful message, the American Union must be considered

dissolved. Between the North and South stands the gallows
of John Brown. Union is no longer possible. Such a crime
cannot be shared."

In England, under a monarchical form of government the
American institution of slavery was looked upon with horror,
disdain, and derision. We were that far behind the en-
lightened progress of the world. Any black American bond
man who set foot on British soil was automatically a free
man with the British army and navy guaranteeing his liberty.
He had full rights in English courts, and in all the English
colonies, including Canada. Statutory enactments by Parliament as early as 1834 confirmed in the written laws what had
long been in force in principle. Every Englishman had his
gibe against the Declaration of Independence with its mockery
that all men were born free and equal and with inalienable
rights to life, liberty, and the pursuit of happiness.

This was the status of Old John Brown—and of Linn
County—in the eyes of the world in 1860!

Dr. A. H. Davis, the moving spirit in the founding of the
town of La Cygne, came of good Revolutionary stock. The
first ancestor we know of was William Hall, born Hopkinton,
Massachusetts, 1753; married Abigail Peace; their daughter
Lydia married Ebenezer Davis, son of Samuel and Deborah
Chapin Davis, to whom was born in Wardstown, Vermont,
a son named Alexander Hamilton Davis, who married Harriet
Hitchcock of Kantone, New York. The eldest son Orlando
served in the famous Third Wisconsin Battery. He married
Lucretia Boyd and came to La Cygne. Another son Francisco
Hamilton (our F. H.) married Cynthia Richardson in Busti,
New York. Their daughter Lena May grew up in La Cygne
and married Herman Smith, a very fine young man who
belonged to the Bucks county, Pennsylvania, group. Their
son Fred never married and now lives at Springfield, Missouri.
Edgar (Ned) married Edna Boyd of Baldwin and has a son
Boyd and daughter Lena Catherine. Catherine (Kate) married Robert Emmett Payne and now lives in Chicago. They
have a son Robert D. The Davis ancestors are very favorably
mentioned in the Massachusetts War Archives.

Linn County has always had a strong leadership in the
administration of affairs of Kansas. We have had a number of men in the state house, starting with state auditor
in 1861, attorney-general and state superintendent of public
instruction in 1892, and lieutenant governor in 1924. We
furnished a brigadier-general to the Union Army in the Civil
War and a great number of our boys served in the Spanish-
American and the Philippines wars. And now we have a
beloved son who wishes to and deserves to be governor as
this book goes to press. He has three initials that commonly

gives him the name of Dan Chase, but as a matter of fact
D. A. N. stands for his grandfather DeWayne Arthur Newton.
He was born in Vermont and was brought to Wichita county,
Kansas, when he was twelve years old, where he worked
on his father's claim, got a clerkship at Omaha, studied law,
and was admitted to the Nebraska bar by the supreme court
of that state.   He came to Pleasanton and carried on various
enterprises with good success, including a Ford agency and
a marble monument business, being in the mean time president of the First National Bank, and was active in all local
affairs.   He served in both branches of the state Legislature,
both as member and as presiding officer, now serving as lieu-
tenant-governor.   His wife was Miss Harriet A. Ayer of
Leavenworth, of Puritan New England family.   She has been
active in many of the women's organizations, a Daughter of
the American Revolution and of the P. E. O.   Their daughter
Donna Augusta married Charles N. McCarter, nephew of
Margaret Hill McCarter, and they have one child named Chase
McCarter.   Their son DeWayne Arthur Newton Chase, married Mary Ramsey of Osage City, a graduate of Washburn
College.   This family has been an asset to business and social
life, carrying on successfully several of the largest businesses
of the town.

The Pines were from Frederick county, Virginia, where
Joseph W. married Lydia Vincent.   They lived a time in
Iowa and came to Kansas and located in Allen county where
he built up a handsome farm property, and later came and
lived his last twenty years in Linn County.   Their children
were Alice who married Henry Knox, and had a son Charles
who married Grace Smith.   A son Warren V. Pine married
Nora Moore and had two children Raymond and Elsie; he
later married Myrtle Knox and had children Marsh, Lois,
Vincent and Vivia, this family now living at Willows,
California.   John W. Pine married Lizzie Cox, and had a
variety store in Pleasanton many years.   Ferne married R.
C. Cox.   Ethyle Pine married A. W. VanHercke of Trading
Post, where they have their home and three children, Betty,
Marjorie, and Jean.   Ethyle VanHercke has developed considerable ability as a writer and recently received one thousand
dollars as winner in the McFadden best letter contest, one
hundred dollars for the best essay in the Lehn and Fink peace
plan and fifty dollars in the Remington contest, in addition
to good money she receives as contributor to Modern Priscilla,
Midwest Merchant, Woman's page in Kansas City Star, and
many similar publications.

PROBATE JUDGES FROM THE BEGINNING

Ranson E. Elliott the first name appearing in the probate

journal as probate judge served from January 1856 to July 1857. The next instrument to be recorded in the Journal is dated March 8 1858 and is signed by D. W. Cannon, judge of probate, who appears to have acted until March 5 1860 when I. W. Babb signs as probate judge. During the remainder of the year 1860 D. W. Cannon again is in charge of the office.

J. R. Marr then served for an indefinite period from February 1861. No record can be found from December 1861 to 1866 when C. C. Thompkins was probate judge until 1867. From this time one the record is more clear and the names and the terms of their service are as follows:

Daniel Underhill from January, 1869, to October, 1869.
John C. Quinn from October, 1869, to January, 1873.
R. W. Blue from January, 1873, to January, 1877.
Theo. Botkin, 1877 to October, 1878.
J. H. Trego, from October, 1878, to January, 1879.
A. D. Hiatt, 1879.
W. A. Trigg, 1881.
R. W. Brann, 1885.
Enoch Estep, 1889.
N. W. Barnett, 1891.
Jacob Waymire, 1893.
D. C. Potter, 1897.
J. Q. Kennedy, 1901.
J. M. Iliff from June 1901 to January 1903.
W. E. McIntyre, 1903.

I. A. Davis, January 1907 to September 1908 when Jacob Waymire was appointed probate judge and served one month. Frank Davis was then appointed and served from September 29, 1908 to January, 1909.

G. Marion Moore. 1909.

H. W. Dingus, 1913 to March 1916 when he resigned and Ed. R. Smith was appointed and he served until January, 1917.

Warren W. Edeburn, 1917.

E. E. Thayer, 1921.

T. B. Nisely, 1925, and reelected for the term ending 1929, when his death created a vacancy filled by appointment of Arthur Rich.

CLERKS OF THE DISTRICT COURT

Asa Hairgrove, 1858.
Eli Babb, 1860.
Asa Hairgrove, 1861.
James C. Marshall, 1863.
J. R. Van Zandt, 1865.
Ira D. Bronson, 1867.
John T. Taylor, 1869.
Edwin R. Smith, 1871.
W. A. Ackerman, 1877.
W. A. Eaheart, 1889.

I. C. Ball, 1891.
C. R. Wheeler, 1895.
Frank J. Scott, 1897.
John O. Morse, 1901.
W. M. McDill, 1905.
B. E. Bradley, 1909.
E. D. Feemster, 1913.
C. H. Porter, 1917.
Owen E. Root, 1923.

LIST OF THE COUNTY CLERKS

Joseph E. Wilmot, 1856.   Joseph H. Barlow, 1857.
James A. Kennedy, 1856.   Harrison Crenshaw, 1857.
Jason H. Masterson, 1856.

From the above date to 1865 I do not find any record, but Col. Ed. R. Smith says that a man by the name of Chitwood was county clerk. There was an old settler by the name of Pleasant Chitwood. Barnett or "Barney" Mitchell, brother of Gen. R. B. Mitchell, is also said to have served as county clerk part of this time.

J. R. Vanzant, 1865.   John J. Hawkins, 1892.
J. W. Miller, 1868.   William H. Ward, 1896.
W. M. Nesbitt, 1872.   C. O. Hoag, 1898.
F. J. Weatherbie, 1874.   James A. Cady, 1900.
John W. Floria, 1876.   J. M. Wortman, 1905.
J. H. Martin, 1880.   Geo. W. Waymire, 1909.
J. H. Madden, 1882.   John A. Wood, 1913.
Thomas D. Cottle, 1886.   James P. Frisbie, 1917.
Henry A. Strong, 1890.   Oliver M. Gray, 1925.

ROSTER OF COUNTY SUPERINTENDENTS

H. L. Bailey, 1867.   O. B. Reddick, 1897.
G. W. Botkin, 1869.   O. M. West, 1899.
R. B. Bryan, 1875.   F. H. Harrin, 1903.
Geo. W. Jones, 1879.   A. S. Hiatt, 1907.
W. W. McCullough, 1885.   Lillian Potter, 1909.
R. F. Wilbur, 1887.   J. W. Hays, 1913.
S. J. Heaton, 1889.   Maud Hunts, 1917.
A. W. Leech, 1891.   M. Ellen Dingus, 1919.
J. C. Lowe, 1895.   Verna McClaughry, 1925.

ROSTER OF REGISTER OF DEEDS

I. H. Barlow, 1857.   G. D. Roy, 1892.
Jesse Brown, 1858.   W. H. Fleming, 1896.
A. A. Johns, 1860.   E. Clemans, 1898.
J. R. Van Zandt, 1864.   J. T. Holmes, 1900.
J. H. Marshall, 1866.   C. L. Martin, 1905.
J. H. Belding, 1870.   E. F. Campbell, 1909.
G. Marion Moore, 1874.   C. W. Kingsbury, 1913.
Will H. Ellis, 1876.   Ora Wortman, 1915.
Lovilo Swift, 1880.   Frances McDill Wuttke, 1919.
L. F. Williams, 1884.   Sadie B. Pollman, 1925.
J. E. Moore, 1888.

Dr. Lowe came here from Pennsylvania in 1866 and established himself on a farm northeast of Mound City. His son Crandall now lives at Prescott the only survivor of an interesting household. "Cran" is one of the fellows who had to be the architect of his own fortune and he built substantially and successfully. As a boy Cran farmed for himself, getting half the grain crop for his share. He raised forty bushels of wheat to the acre and fifty bushels of corn, selling the corn at fifty cents and the wheat at a dollar a bushel, so that he got three hundred dollars for his summer's work, with which he bought land three miles northwest of Prescott. He married Miss Kimsey whose father was a local preacher. Cran not only farmed but bought cattle and hogs and took them to market at Kansas City and prospered. One son Edward is a successful farmer in Sheridan township and the daughter married into the Holmes family. The oldest boy John was a school teacher and served a term about 1893 as county superintendent and now lives at Bristol Bay, Bellingham, Alaska, where he has his headquarters in the fur business, having seven stores at widely separated points, his fur purchases amounting to several hundred thousand dollars a year. Starting January 10 it took them three weeks to reach Seattle on a trip to Prescott this year.

John Scott Harrison, son of Colonel James F., who was well known about Linn County as a boy, is now in charge of government surveys at Helena, Montana. He married Mary Sophia Hill, and they have two boys perpetuating the family names as William Henry Harrison and Scott H. Harrison. "Will," the tall lanky boy who looks like his great grandfather the President, married Lura Adams and has two girls Alice and Virginia. Mary married John Walter Farrar and has a son Harrison and two girls Betty and Agnes. Will and Mary have their homes in Kansas City, Mo.

There was an excellent family who came here immediately following the Civil War and lived in the valley near Boicourt. He was William Parker and he had married Sarah Kennedy at Cleves, Ohio, in 1866, and came that year to Linn County. I am not sure but I think they were related to the family of Col. James F. Harrison. Their children were Rilla Alice who married William E. Eardley and had a daughter Rilla L. who married Grover H. Dean; Horace G. Parker married Mina Elizabeth Watkins and had a son Ernest W. who married Ethel Martha Nundt, now living at Helena, Montana; William Parker married Nellie Swift and they had a son Donald Craig; Edgar Parker is unmarried.

One of the biggest investments in Linn County land was the purchase by J. W. Parker of Atchison, Kansas, of sixteen quarter sections in Liberty township which he devoted exclusively to fruit growing, the tract being one immense apple orchard. A relative of Parker named Taft had charge of the property and planted the trees. When the Missouri,

Kansas and Texas Railway came through in 1888 a town was located in the orchard and given the name of Parker in honor of the fruit grower.

A beautiful thing in business life was the partnership in the newspaper business between John Phelps Kenea and Edwin Carlos Lane at La Cygne where they published the Journal. In 1893 they outgrew the town and moved to Clarinda, Iowa, where the firm continued till **Mr. Kenea's** death in 1926. Their influence here deserves a tribute more lasting than personal memory. The story of Mr. Lane is given in that of L. H. Lane of Prescott, his father. Mr. Kenea's family were of considerable note in American history. His paternal grandfather was John Jordan Kenea, a soldier in the Revolutionary war, and his maternal grandfather David Lee gave him the same heritage to be proud of. His mother Mabel Lee was blessed with a beautiful voice and was an artist in singing. From their home in Connecticut she was frequently invited to sing in old Trinity church in New York City, her every appearance being a real society event, and this back in the fifties prior to the Civil War. They were related to many of the best families of that period. Bronson D. Alcott was his uncle and Louisa M. Alcott his cousin was then at the height of her literary fame as author of "Little Men" and "Little Women" when he was here with us. Other cousins were Edward Eggleston, author of the "Hoosier Schoolmaster," and his sister Emile had married into the family of Alice and Phoebe Cary. His mother was a cousin to Old John Brown and they were firm believers in that staunch old patriot. Mr. Kenea's distinguishing trait was loyalty to relatives and friends. "Blood is thicker than water," and as they celebrated their fiftieth year of partnership they were looking up family history to supply the author of this book when it was disclosed that he and Mr. Lane were descended from the same ancestor of several generations ago back in Connecticut—Mabel Lee's grandfather. Mr. Kenea's wife was Carrie Gilson and to them was born at La Cygne a daughter Mabel, a remarkably capable bright woman who carries on the business since her father's death and the illness of Mr. Lane.

Henry Trinkle, numerously mentioned in the stories of early days here, was a keen bright man, highly prized as a friend by the author of this book. He married quite young to a Miami girl named Mary Bundy and she gave him two boys, William David and Joseph Lee. This mother died when her children only infants, and the boy Joe died in 1896. David is still living. By a subsequent marriage to Mary Ann Froman there were a number of children. Ella, the first married W. T. Gowing and had one child now Mrs. Edith Priser of La

Cygne. Metta Trinkle is not married. Clara married J. E. Shaw. Henry Oscar is now a successful lawyer at Garden City. Lucy is now Mrs. James Mendenhall. Emma married Dan Stainbrook. Charles F. is now our district judge by appointment from Governor Paulen to succeed the late Judge Gates; Charles married Miss Freda Schwaller of Hays, Kansas. Nora is now Mrs. W. P. Rose. Leona married Fred Irwin. Arthur, a farmer; and Cora at home. All of this family are living except Ella.

In 1869 a boy named Eben C. Mitchell arrived at La Cygne and got employment at the railway station helping the station agent who was also a mere boy, a nephew of Major Henning who was superintendent of the Gulf road. In September 1870 his mother, Mrs. Jemima A. Mitchell, arrived with her daughter Ardilla and two boys William A. and Eldridge H. Two years later the eldest son Charles and Sallie his wife arrived with two boys and a girl. This family was a part of the wreckage of the Civil War, at the beginning of which the head of the family was a railroad contractor at Gosport, Indiana, where they were neighbors of the Goss family so numerous in Linn County. Mrs. Mitchell was a heroic woman. Her father was an unusually propserous farmer named Charles Harriman adjoining the historic old town of Greenville, Ohio, where they had been very early settlers, one of Mrs. Mitchell's brothers being a Presbyterian preacher. The husband, Barton Warren Mitchell, was of an old Scotch family who in 1760 were neighbors to the parents of Daniel Boone at Exter, Pennsylvania, and went with that family with a party to establish a settlement on the Yadkin river about twenty miles west of the present town of Winston-Salem in North Carolina. They had just got settled comfortably when Daniel Boone returned and reported that he had found a better country in Kentucky, and persuaded the four Mitchell boys to go with him in the big party in which were the Lincolns and the Hanks families. Gavin the eldest was married and his wife carried John as a baby on horseback through the famed "Wilderness trail" by way of Cumberland Gap. This was the beginning of a great tribe of Mitchells in Kentucky, associated with the great pioneers of that period and showing up numerously in indexed histories of Abraham Lincoln. About the year 1800 John who came through as a baby moved over to Ohio where he located land in Preble county still in the family. It is interesting how history is influenced by minor incidents. These people were Presbyterians, very religious. About this time a serious embarrassment came to the pioneer preachers. The Presbyterians practiced "close communion." A staid old covenanter found in his congregation one day a backwoodsman hungry and thirsty for spiritual sustenance and in mercy invited him to partake of the Lord's Supper. He was bitterly criticized by the church authorities for this breach of church discipline and threatened with being unfrocked. It was the beginning of a breach that never healed, as this old preacher, Barton Warren Stone, withdrew and started the Disciples of Christ, now known as the Christian Church. In 1816 when the Mitchells had a son born to them they named him Barton Warren in compliment to their great pastor. But for this cleavage the Presbyterian church would have had a tremendously greater part in western history. Alexander Campbell, a younger man, came up from Kentucky and helped in the new church and was an intimate associate of both Mr. and Mrs. Mitchell in their youthful days. They went through all the pioneer experiences, settling where the town of Warren, Indiana, now is, and giving it this name, when there was only unbroken forests everywhere and this girl wife stayed two weeks alone in mid winter while the husband went back to Ohio with an ox team to get some needed supplies—no door, only a blanket hung at the opening, and a fire kept burning to keep the wolves out. In 1861 forty of Mr. Mitchell's employes went up to Camp Morton at Indianapolis and enlisted in a body, the son Charles then only eighteen being given a commission as first lieutenant by Governor Oliver Perry Morton. The father enlisted a few weeks later, then much beyond the age for active soldiery. He was an attractive public speaker and was in constant activity talking to the "boys." At Frederick, Maryland, on September 14, 1862, he found among some papers where an enemy tent had been the official papers of General D. H. Hill telling just what disposition was to be made of the Confederate army the next four days. He overtook his colonel, Silas Colegrove, and the two went at once to General George B. McClellan, the Union commander-in-chief, and within a half hour the skirmishing was on for the battle of South Mountain, followed by the battle of Antietam, described as "the bloodiest day in American history." Mr. Mitchell was severely wounded and of his company of forty-five that started in the battle at Antietam only five could walk after they crossed a ten-acre corn field. Abe Lincoln came that night to that battlefield and it was this experience that convinced him that the slaves must be emancipated as a military necessity, and he made there draft of the proclamation that was issued January 1, 1863. Mr. Mitchell received high commendation for this service. He died in January, 1868. The boy Eben was drowned at La Cygne in 1876. The grief stricken wife and mother lived to 1901. A daughter Mary was the wife of Henry Clay Hiner who was a descendant of Stephen Hopkins, a signer of the Declaration of Independence. They lived in La Cygne several years.

The romance of a little girl baby named Kate Davidson,

daughter of Thad Davidson of La Cygne in 1870, goes back
to the days of King Arthur and his Round Table, but she
became a celebrity in her own right. She grew up and married
a traveling salesman who worried a good deal about the
discomfort caused by his underwear, and the two of them
began devising a better garment for men. Then all such
garments were knit and fitted the body so closely that on
a hot day they caused torture, especially if it was a "two
piece" suit held together by a stout waist band. The garment
was finally worked out to perfection and a patent obtained
upon it, and it has for nearly a third of a century been sold
in every civilized country in the world as the "B. V. D." It
was the first such garment made out of "flat goods." The
father, Thad Davidson, was a wonderfully cultured man for
his time, having a special hobby for music, and it was through
his efforts that the La Cygne Band and Orchestra won the
first prize at a state contest in 1872. Thad was a Scotchman,
descended from the Wickwires who gave Lord de la Warre
to the world, who was one of the first crown representatives
in America, having come to Virginia in 1610. The state of
Deleware is so named in his honor. The family seat was at
what is now Manchester, England, an old Roman settlement
noted as the scene of the life of King Arthur. But this
Wickwire family developed at a much later date. Another
celebrity originating from that period is Miriam Burns Horn,
now women's national golf champion, who is a great granddaughter of the old Scotchman Beatty who lived on a farm
on the hill north of town. His daughter Lucy married Dan
Macomb and upon his death she married a Mr. Beery, and
her daughter married Mr. Burns in Kansas City, a very
prominent engineer, and Miriam of this marriage is now of
national prominence in the fourth generation. Miriam married
Robert Horn and has a son—now in the fifth generation from
that beginning at La Cygne. I mention these two in one
paragraph because after all these years they are now my
immediate neighbors in Kansas City.

There are many old timers who are lost to this record, to
my great regret. One was an old man named Pomeroy who
traced his ancestors back to William the Conqueror, and was
some old man himself. And I am not sure but there is a
lingering thought that the Wishart family of Scott township
were descendants of the old divine of that name who became
a celebrity as the assistant of John Knox in the Scottish
Reformation period. Gene Latimer of Pleasanton claims to
be a descendant of the Latimer who was burned at the stake
for daring to differ with the Pope on religion. There are a
host of old names—the Hafleys, Shinkles, Hessers, Lees, and
many others that can no longer be reached.

I hope that some of these days when I assemble Old John
Brown and Montgomery and Ed. R. Smith and Simon McGrew
and Temple Wayne and Gus Wattles and Hank McGlothlin
and Rufe Thorn and Tom Preston and possibly some of the
rest of you—when we get the gang all together and lead
them to the ramparts of Heaven and look down on Linn
County we will see something worth looking at.   There isn't
a more beautiful country on earth but man has taken away
much of its pristine glory by cutting roads and putting
fences across its smooth lawns.   Now let man do something
to replace the beauty he has destroyed.   Culture is such an
inexpensive thing and it pays tremendous dividends.   Why
not plant trees along our splendid system of highways?   Why
let the city dweller have a monopoly of flowers?   Why not
enjoy as we ride?   There are hundreds of native shrubs and
plants that will delight the eye and enrich the soul with
their beauty and their fragrance.   Pay dividends?   Why of
course they will.   Put a mile of wild prairie roses each side
of the Short Line and Kansas City people will eagerly drive
down to see it.   A mile of sumac on each side will be worth
coming to see in its fall dress of scarlet and brown.   A band
of wild verbenas will work two months for your pleasure.
Petunias year after year will return to do all the work of
delighting you.   These things can be so arranged their display
will be perpetual.   Put out snow-ball, weigelia, bridal wreath,
honeysuckle, mock orange.   Plant a row of zinnias a mile long
on each side—they will grow a finer display of color than
you ever saw in California.   Don't forget that the sunflower
not only furnishes us with beauty but attracts birds which
feed upon it.   Plant pecan trees on waste land and make it
valuable—it will produce actual money, pay interest on a
thousand dollars an acre.   Hickory will in an average life
time grow five hundred dollars worth of timber per acre.
Black walnut meats sell readily at a dollar a pound and should
furnish an industry for every indigent person in the county.
Will it pay?   Of course it will.   It is the age when people
travel and observe and want to buy what pleases them.
Lands should appreciate fifty dollars an acre in a county as
beautiful as Linn County should be.   Every farm owner should
have an increased value of from five to ten thousand dollars
put on his land.   This is not a joke.   It is what is happening
near all centers of congestion.   And mark your historic spots.
Make it so visitors will be enough interested to linger and
enjoy and learn.   Let all the globe-trotters know what we
have in a historical sense by readable tablets and flowers
testifying our affections.   Plant hollyhocks from Trading
Post to the Marais des Cygnes Massacre scene, to Fort Brown,
to Fort Montgomery, to Fort Defiance to Fort Lincoln.   Mark
all the spots that inquirers may see where valor won undying

fame. Do these things and I'll point them out to those old heroes and cheer their brave old hearts.

I had expected to have from the botanist at the state university complete instructions how to do these things—how to propagate shrubs and trees and graft nut trees and what flowers to plant that will freely reproduce. But it is too late to get it in this book but will be supplied in some other shape soon. Do these things—it will pay in culture—and in cold hard dollars!

This ancestry business is peculiarly interesting. You have two parents who each had two parents, which gives you four grandparents. This rate of increase very rapidly acquires for you a much greater ancestry than you can ever hope for in numbers of posterity. Along about the time of the Revolutionary War there were some two hundred and fifty-six persons who have since passed on down to you the blood strain that has had a positive influence on your life. These people were all imbued with the spirit and principles of their times; many of them associated with the greatest heroes in all history. In the next five generations backward you are carried to the period of the Religious Reformation (the days of the first ancestor of record of our local hero)—the days of Mary Stuart, of Count de Montgomery, of Martin Luther, of Catherine de Medici. This was the time of another crop of great ancestors and you had then sixty-five thousand people who passed on the blood mixture that has culminated in you, and beyond this the blood line spread out so widely that you might rightly claim to be a brother to every then living man, so far reaching is this thin blood line that goes back from you to the year 1575 and thereabouts, and to carry this out would give our citizens of greatest antiquity literally millions of ancestors at the time of the Crusades.

Some few of us can assume that we are the boiled-down essence of the best of all the ages—that in the process of refinement we have crystallized into "gems of purest ray serene" out of the "dark unfathomed caves" of antiquity—that we have sifted out the good and have discarded all the bad. But the fact is that the fathers and mothers of the Civil War period were the best and purest and bravest men and women that ever lived in anybody's time or country, and we who follow them are not the boiled-down essence of something good but rather the hard-boiled selfishness of the twentieth century failing in many ways to live up to the standards they set before us.

This disquisition on ancestry explains the motive for inquiring into the origin of the people of Linn County. They had come here from many widely separated states and communities. Had they been assembled by Divine Providence to do a definite work set out for them there could hardly have been a greater unanimity of thought and action among them. Prayerfully, and carefully estimating the probable consequences, they came here singly accompanied by the wife and children. They came into a new country as yet without laws, and under sinister circumstances which made every man a law unto himself. In the face of the most desperate resistance and intimidation they stayed here, lived their lives here, and have left a progeny that now constitutes a large community. They did valiant things and the record they made will for ages be studied and analyzed to understand the beginning and the end of it. Their place in the records of the human race entitles them to rank with the Spartans who are by common consent set apart and honored as the most notable example of fighters for human liberty of thought and action. The antecedents of these Linn County people are set out here as entirely respectable. In many individual cases they have had highly honorable part in the entire programme which has developed the great people speaking the English language.

But there are many whose remote origin can not be traced because the records are not available. You must remember that these people have the same number of ancestors as the most famous, and that back in the days when a great race was springing up out of the wrecks of older civilizations their forbears were leaders in the crusades for the betterment of mankind.

In contrast with this fine background of the free state settlers who made Linn County is the crowd of freebooters who came here from Georgia and South Carolina. When James Edward Oglethorpe conceived the idea of establishing a refuge in America for the scum of the English prison population it was a philanthropy, a charity for the lowest down and out class of the English people. Parliament appropriated a million dollars to pay the expense of getting rid of them. For a hundred years these moral derelicts propagated their kind and their true nature asserted itself when Kansas Territory was opened for settlement. They came here in hordes with murder in their hearts and with money and violent weapons of warfare to rob free Americans of their property and threaten their lives. Like begets like and we have the full story, from an authoritative source, of what these people were in their own country and under their own laws. Charity had established them in a fertile and beautiful country where they prospered—yet gratitude was not in their hearts nor was the quality of manliness or chivalry in their blood. The foul crime of treason festered in them and broke out into the open sore of rebellion. That they were originally narrow-minded is proven by their exclusion of Catholics from their colony. They were set up in a free country which excluded slavery yet in 1750 they altered their charter to establish black bondage. Their entire story is sordid, mean, nasty—very little good ever came out of this Nazareth. Read their story on page 217.

And the South Carolinians! Seeking a refuge from religious persecution they came to America in hordes under the name of Huguenots about the time of the infamous Massacre of St. Bartholomews which happened in 1572. They were hospitably received, nurtured, established, given a place in the world. They, too, prospered on what they had gotten as a gracious gift. Yet none were more bloodthirsty than they. It was they who furnished the Beauregards and such French ilk, to the treasonable crew. The magnificent patriotism of the John Rutledge of 1776 was dragged in bloody mire by the John Rutledge of 1861.

Enough is given in this book to establish the truth as to the character of the pioneer settlers of Linn County and to give them a place among the heroes of the world. The future belongs to their children and their children's children. I am closing this book with a patriotic sentiment written by our neighbor, Eugene F. Ware of Fort Scott, who tells in the last two lines what treason tried to do in four years of warfare:

There is something in a flag, and a little burnished eagle,
That is more than emblematic—it is glorious, it is regal.
You may never live to feel it, you may never be in danger,
You may never visit foreign lands and play the role of stranger;
You may never in an army check the march of an invader,
You may never on the ocean cheer the swarthy cannonader;
But if this should happen to you, then when age is on you pressing,
And your great big booby boy comes to ask your final blessing,
You will tell him: Son of mine, be your station proud or frugal,
When your Country calls her children, and you hear the blare of bugle,
Don't you stop to think of Kansas, or the quota of your county,
Don't you go to asking questions, don't you stop for pay or bounty,
But you volunteer at once; and you go where orders take you,
And obey them to the letter, if they make you or they break you;
Hunt that flag, and then stay with it, be you wealthy or plebean,
Let the women sing the dirges, scrape the lint, and chant the pean.

* * * * *

If that flag goes down to ruin, Time will then without a warning
Turn the dial back to midnight, and the world must wait till morning.

SHERIFFS

David Goss, 1866
Hiram Barrick, 1870
I. Croxton, 1872
D. R. Lamoreau, 1876
Wm. Goss, 1880
C. H. Chandler, 1884
Frank Gray, 1888
E. H. Warden, 1890
Lee Mayfield, 1894
C. M. Morrison, 1898
F. S. Preston, 1902
L. J. Higgins, 1906
J. C. Ireland, 1908
Geo. G. Davidson, 1912
D. Z. Engle, 1916
A. J. Ellington, 1920
D. Z. Engle 1924

TREASURERS

John T. Alexander, 1866
Harvey Smith (vacancy), 1867
John Hood, 1868
J. P. Way, 1870
A. G. Seaman, 1874
James P. Way, 1876
D. Underhill, 1878
G. W. Botkin, 1882
A. W. Burton, 1884
J. H. Madden, 1888
James Tyson, 1892
H. E. Burton, 1896
John M. Seright 1900
Henry F. Stowe, 1902
S. Dillon Moore, 1904
Elias F. Lee, 1908
W. G. Shinkle, 1912
J. T. Holt, 1914
W. H. Alexander, 1918
J. W. Hays, 1922
Geo. W. Wait, 1926

COUNTY SURVEYORS

Wm. B. Emerson, 1866
John P. Brown, 1872
James F. Harrison, 1874
W. H. Rose, 1876
L. Newell 1878
M. L. Bowman, 1882
W. C. Caldwell, 1884
J. F. Harrison, 1890
J. L. Gove, 1898
Frank Davis, 1902
James M. Mundell 1906

COUNTY ENGINEERS

(Appointed by commissioners)
Charles E. Clark, 1919
Chas. E. Kenney, 1920

COUNTY ATTORNEYS

J. F. Broadhead, 1866
A. F. Ely, 1868
W. R. Biddle, 1872
A. F. Ely, 1874
R. W. Blue, 1876
Selwyn Douglas, 1880
Daniel Rich, 1886
John C. Cannon, 1890
J. W. Poore, 1892
H. P. Clay, 1896
J. E. Wiley, 1898
H. O. Trinkle, 1900
John O. Morse, 1904
John A. Hall, 1908
B. J. Crosswhite, 1912
Harry W. Fisher, 1914
John O. Morse, 1920
W. W. Edeburn, 1922
H. D. Reeve, 1924

COUNTY COMMISSIONERS

J. H. Belding, I. N. Wright, Daniel Underhill, 1866.
J. C. Quinn, David Crocker, J. H. Jones, 1868.
Jefferson Fleming, D. A. Crocker, S. R. Hungerford, 1870.
Wm. Goss, Jeff. Fleming, J. W. Flora, 1872.
Wm. Shattuck, M. E. Woodford, W. Worden, 1874.
Morris Howard, D. Underhill, Wm. Worden, 1876.
Scott Shattuck, H. H. Woy, Jacob Rhoades, 1878.
M. E. Woodford, 1880.
H. Dellinger, N. A. Corbin, 1882.
George W. Creager, 1884.
O. E. Morse, James Goss, 1886.
Truman Ducett, 1887.
Thos. McGee, 1889.
J. W. Payne, 1890.
G. W. Nantz, 1891.
Thos. McGee, 1892.

J. Weickert, 1893.
Wash Nantz, 1894.
H. F. Stowe, 1895.
W. A. Gage, 1896.
S. Dillon Moore, 1897.
Wm. Brownrigg, 1899.
S. D. Moore, 1900.
D. F. VanBuskirk, 1901.
Wm. Brownrigg, 1902.
A. L. Humphrey, C. W. McClure, 1904.
H. L. Burnett, 1906.
Harry J. Clark, C. W. McClure, 1908.
H. L. Burnett, M. C. Robbins, 1910.
Wash Nantz, Harry Curry, 1912.
O. M. Priser, 1914.
Harry Curry, E. G. Perrine, 1916.
Clarence Allen, 1918.
Harry E. Ashley, John McGrew, 1920.
Theo. McIntyre, 1922.
E. E. Rees, Floyd Brown, 1924.

VOLUNTEERS IN TWENTIETH KANSAS REGIMENT

Volunteer enlistments from Linn County for service in the Philippines in the famous Twentieth Kansas under the noted Fred Funston in Company K were as follows:

John O. Morse, Mound City, served as private, corporal, sergeant; wounded at Caloocan.

Walter T. Smith, Mound City, corporal, sergeant.

Allen M. Hoover, La Cygne, Corporal.

Lorillard Wickham, Mound City, corporal.

Ernest R. Kincaid, Mound City, corporal, wounded at Rio Grande river.

Frank W. McQuaid, Mound City, corporal.

Courtland Fleming, Mound City, musician.

Edward M. Tucker, Pleasanton, musician.

Wilfred B. Helm, Mound City, musician.

Lee A. Limes, Mound City, cook.

Albert L. Baur, Mound City.

Ernest Baugh, Pleasanton.

Albert S. Bird, Pleasanton.

William Cline, La Cygne.

Walter L. Ellis, Pleasanton.

Edgar Fultz, Pleasanton.

Roy Hawkins, Mound City.

John F. Hopkins, La Cygne.

George H. Hudson, La Cygne.

Jacob Hartley, Pleasanton.

Leslie V. Kincaid, Pleasanton.

Ernest R. Kincaid. Mound City.

George Meyer, Pleasanton.

Isaiah Rusk, La Cygne.

Isaac L. Tulle, Pleasanton.

Donald Thorne, La Cygne.

Oscar G. Thorne, La Cygne, killed in action at Caloocan; brought home and buried at La Cygne.

Jacob Townsley, Pleasanton.

John A. White, Pleasanton.

Ernest Wagner, Pleasanton.

John H. Williamson, La Cygne.

Claude H. Helman of Pleasanton served as musician in Company I.

WORLD WAR SOLDIERS

Ten years after the greatest war fought in the history of all time, the great state of Kansas has not perfected its list of soldiers who took part in it. It is very complicated for the reason that many young men volunteered while the greater number were taken by the selective draft. The state has in its archives at Topeka ten thousand cards which have never been compiled for a permanent accessible record, a shameful situation. The government officials boxed up every memorandum of the Linn County Selective Draft board and sent them to Washington. Even a copy made for local use by James Frisbie as chairman of the board was seized and taken away.